2. 50

C000264073

THE TRAVELS OF
ROBERT LOUIS STEVENSON

2.50
PWS
ω

THE TRAVELS OF ROBERT LOUIS STEVENSON

◆

Robert Louis Stevenson

with an Introduction and Notes by
ROGER CARDINAL
University of Kent, Canterbury

WORDSWORTH CLASSICS

I

Readers who are interested in other titles from
Wordsworth Editions are invited to visit our website at
www.wordsworth-editions.com

For our latest list and a full mail-order service, contact
Bibliophile Books, 5 Datapoint, South Crescent, London E16 4TL
TEL: +44 (0)20 7474 2474 FAX: +44 (0)20 7474 8589
ORDERS: orders@bibliophilebooks.com
WEBSITE: www.bibliophilebooks.com

This edition first published in 2010 by
Wordsworth Editions Limited
8B East Street, Ware, Hertfordshire SG12 9HJ

ISBN 978 1 84022 633 1

Text © Wordsworth Editions Limited 2010
Introduction and Notes © Roger Cardinal 2010

Wordsworth® is a registered trademark of
Wordsworth Editions Limited

Typeset in Great Britain by Antony Gray
Printed and bound by Clays Ltd, St Ives plc

Contents

GENERAL INTRODUCTION

Wordsworth Classics are inexpensive editions designed to appeal to the general reader and students. We commissioned teachers and specialists to write wide-ranging, jargon-free Introductions and to provide Notes that would assist the understanding of our readers rather than interpret the stories for them. In the same spirit, because the pleasures of reading are inseparable from the surprises, secrets and revelations that all narratives contain, we strongly advise you to enjoy this book before turning to the Introduction.

General Adviser: KEITH CARABINE
Rutherford College, University of Kent

INTRODUCTION

Robert Louis Stevenson (1850–1894) is best known for his fiction and especially his adventure yarns set in wild places. Sometimes these are imaginary, as in *Treasure Island*, which is located in a deliberately vague West Indies, though they usually stick close to the real world, as in *Kidnapped*, which features a breathless chase across an inclement yet accurately described tract of the Scottish Highlands. If fantasy always tended to transport him to places associated with extravagant danger, Stevenson's life itself was not without its extremes of risk-taking and improvised jaunts into the unknown. A genius for quixotic challenges took him into the mountainous regions of France and California, and ultimately motivated him to settle on a Pacific island, the quintessential site of the Exotic and in many ways the antithesis of his native land. Aspiring to frank truthtelling as much as to verbal elegance, Stevenson learned his trade as a writer through writing up his peregrinations as first-person narratives. His travel books and essays anticipate the work of a whole stream of recent globetrotters and *raconteurs*, including Benedict Allen, Jan Morris, Dervla Murphy, Jonathan Raban, Paul Theroux, Colin Thubron and Kenneth White.

The present volume covers two of Stevenson's major excursions, namely: a solo trek on foot in southern France, related in the well-known *Travels with a Donkey in the Cevennes*; and a hair-raising journey across the Atlantic and on across the North American continent, told in *The Amateur Emigrant* and its sequel *Across the Plains*. *The Silverado Squatters* tells of a later sedentary sojourn in a ghost town in the Californian mountains. This is supplemented here by extracts from the original *Silverado Diary*, composed on the spot; while the selection is preceded by a sample of Stevenson's earliest travel writing, the essay 'Walking Tours'.

*　　*　　*

Born in Edinburgh, Robert Louis Stevenson grew up under the stern paternal eye of Thomas Stevenson, a successful civil engineer who specialised in lighthouse design. An only child, Stevenson was a sickly youngster, having inherited from his mother a weakness of the lungs which led to irregular schooling and affected him throughout his adult life in the form of grave respiratory difficulties and spectacular bouts of haemorrhaging. An early commitment to writing shaped Stevenson's developing self-image, and in his teens he began to compose in earnest, modelling himself on essayists like William Hazlitt, Charles Lamb and Michel de Montaigne. His first publication was a pamphlet about the bloody battles of the Scottish Covenanters. Once he became a student at the University of Edinburgh, he began to cut loose from parental control, cultivating the image of a liberal Bohemian who spurned respectability, changing his middle name from Lewis to Louis, smoking cigarettes, growing his hair long, and spending his allowance recklessly. Having acceded to his father's wishes by enrolling in the Faculty of Engineering, he later switched to Law; but although he was eventually admitted to the Scottish Bar, he never practised as a barrister. By now a confirmed atheist, he saw no reason to hide the fact from his parents, to the enduring despair of his father. Stevenson disdained the latter's strict Presbyterianism and adherence to doctrinal and social proprieties. These attitudes were of a piece with his vision of what it takes to be a freelance writer and a freethinker.

In 1873, severe health problems led Stevenson to seek out the climate of the French Riviera, and he was soon making regular trips to France, adding the role of adept francophile to his growing repertoire. Two of these journeys gave rise to books: *An Inland Voyage* (1878) and *Travels with a Donkey in the Cevennes* (1879). In these narratives, Belgian waterways or rough mountain tracks serve as the background for the elaboration of a literary persona, that of the accomplished 'coper' and vigilant observer, rarely judgemental and always eager to communicate his sightings of exotic persons and places. Stevenson's earlier essays on travel, such as 'Roads' (1873), 'Ordered South' (1874) and 'Walking Tours' (1876), had been accepted by the literary magazines of London; he was also making a name for himself with literary pieces on the likes of Victor Hugo, Edgar Allan Poe and Jules Verne, as well as whimsical pirouettes on such topics as 'An Apology for Idlers' (1877) or 'On Falling in Love' (1877). By the age of thirty, he was a regular contributor to the *Cornhill Magazine*, and fully launched on his chosen career. Friendships ensued with such literati as Edmund Gosse, Leslie Stephen and W. E. Henley, while Sidney Colvin became his adviser and literary executor.[1]

In 1876, while staying in the picturesque French village of Grez in the Forest of Fontainebleau, Stevenson met and fell in love with Fanny Osbourne, an American woman who had separated from her husband. She was mourning the recent death of a son, Hervey, and was with her grown-up daughter Belle and her eight-year-old son Lloyd Osbourne. Stevenson's parents were outraged when they learned of their son's Gallic-style liaison with a married woman ten years his senior, and were relieved when news came of Fanny's return to California in August 1878. Her departure seems to have provoked the solo jaunt described in *Travels with a Donkey*, though she is never directly mentioned in the text. A whole year passed, and then a telegram came from Fanny which propelled Stevenson into action. Without informing his parents, he took ship from Glasgow, and, having crossed the Atlantic to New York, carried on by train to the West Coast. When he turned up in Monterey to meet Fanny, he impressed the young Lloyd Osbourne by his cavalier manner and vagabond garb. Still married, Fanny was in an equivocal mood, and, having little money, Stevenson set off on horseback into the Carmel hills, camping alone in the open. The episode proved to be an entirely negative rerun of *Travels with a Donkey*, for, still weak after his stressful journey, he lost his bearings and almost died before being rescued. He spent three months recuperating in Monterey. When at last Fanny obtained her divorce, the couple were married in San Francisco in May 1880. Unpredictable as ever, Stevenson came up with the idea of spending their honeymoon roughing it in an abandoned silver-mine, the subject of *The Silverado Squatters* (1883). A full reconciliation with his parents was to follow, along with assurance of their financial support.

Stevenson spent the following years seeking respite in places such as the Swiss health-spa of Davos, where the diagnosis of his condition wavered between consumption (tuberculosis) and erosion of the lungs. At Hyères, by the Mediterranean, he wrote *Treasure Island* (1883), inspired by an imaginary map drawn by his stepson. Visits to Edinburgh had cruelly exposed the weakness of his lungs, and a lengthy stay in Bournemouth on the south coast of England proved no more restorative. Nevertheless, Stevenson was producing some of his best fiction at this time, including the adventure yarn *Kidnapped* (1886) and the uncanny urban shocker *The Strange Case of Dr Jekyll and Mr Hyde* (1886). After being present at Thomas Stevenson's death in Edinburgh in July 1887, Stevenson crossed the Atlantic once again, together with Fanny and Lloyd. His reputation in America was now at its peak, and he had begun to command substantial fees for his work. However, ill-health still forced him to seek a more congenial climate.

The final chapters of his life were to unfold in an entirely fresh environment, for in June 1888 Stevenson chartered a luxury schooner in San Francisco and, with wife and stepson, embarked on a pleasure trip around the Pacific Ocean, largely funded by advances from American magazines. At last he had found a realm where he could breathe freely. Over the following months, his wanderings took him to the Marquesas Islands, to Tahiti, and to Hawaii, where he visited a leper colony. His onshore stays allowed him to complete *The Master of Ballantrae* (1889), a novel set, like *Kidnapped*, in a Scotland he would never see again. Descriptions of ports of call and observations of native culture are retailed in his most ambitious travel book, *In the South Seas* (published by Colvin in 1896, after Stevenson's death). Having navigated for months in strange waters, Stevenson eventually chose to settle on the island of Upolu in Western Samoa, where he built a mansion he called Villa Vailima. For four more years, he enjoyed an idyllic exile, surrounded by native servants and his family, including his widowed mother. His health having dramatically improved, Stevenson was now at his happiest, albeit regretful that old friends never stopped by. He worked intermittently on *The Weir of Hermiston* (1896), arguably the best of his Scottish fictions, which he never finished. One evening in early December 1894, a massive cerebral haemorrhage brought an abrupt end to his short life. He was forty-four.[2]

*   *   *

One of Stevenson's earliest essays, 'Walking Tours' (1876), evokes the delights of carefree rambling, an activity best conducted alone and at one's own congenial pace, 'open to all impressions' and in no hurry to get to anywhere. 'A walking tour should be gone upon alone, because freedom is of the essence,' he asserts. The writing is imbued with a young man's puffy hyperbole, as he extols the virtues of 'an equable stride' and a blithely unfocused mind. The reader is lulled into supposing that the summit of pleasure can be reached at the price of a day's march through bluff country and a drowsy pipe smoked under the stars. A literary debt is declared to William Hazlitt, whose 1822 essay 'On Going a Journey' is praised for its meshing of literary digression and gently effortful travel experience.[3] Thus does Stevenson enter the field of travel writing, already defining the nature of a genre within and through which he would develop his distinctive voice.

As a literary activity, travel writing dates back at least to the *Odyssey*, which offers the model structure of a purposeful journey slowed down by intriguing digressions, not to mention passages where travellers sit down to expound their tall stories. Stevenson is aware of the two strands of reading or hearing about travel, and of travel proper, and his early essays lay down precepts and prescriptions designed to thrill the stay-at-home reader, while encouraging him or her to get out their walking shoes. In his first published travel essay 'Roads' (1873), he speaks rapturously of the challenge of the road winding ahead, and in 'On the Enjoyment of Unpleasant Places' (1874) gives instructions as to how to enhance even an unpromising stretch of countryside. 'Ordered South' (1874) examines the predicament of the invalid who pictures the healthy and restful destination which is always so hard to reach. One feels the briskness of these essays pressing the author himself toward the brink of real departure: his next step must be to practise what he preaches and literally to step forth into unknown territory. Stevenson's first travel book was *An Inland Voyage*, in which he and a friend explore the canals of the Belgian–French borderlands in sailing-skiffs. But his first fully recorded ramble *on foot* was the one taken in 1878, when he sets out accompanied only by a donkey and motivated, so he claims, by the simple fact of needing to move: 'For my part, I travel not to go anywhere, but to go. I travel for travel's sake.'[4]

One by one, the text of *Travels with a Donkey in the Cevennes* ticks off the requirements of authenticity. A basic chronology enframes the writing, with Stevenson often citing the date in the morning and ending the day's report with details of his sleeping arrangements, now under a roof, now under the stars. No corroborative map was provided in the original edition of the book, though subsequent publishers have catered to popular demand by furnishing one. Indeed, a number of recent books set out Stevenson's full itinerary, along with instructions as to how best to replicate it and even recommendations as to where to spend the night and how to hire a donkey.[5] Stevenson is clearly adhering to one of the tacit rules of travel writing, namely: that one should not only conjure up exotic scenes, but substantiate them by quoting verifiable place-names and landmarks. As readers stepping vicariously into another's remembered footsteps, we need reassurance that he is telling the truth. Stevenson supplies a rich fund of what the French Romantics called *couleur locale*, including references to almost anything that can be called 'typically French' or 'strikingly foreign', such as the way people dress, eat and speak, their religious beliefs, the lie of the land, its vegetation and cultivation. However, once confident of his reader's attention, the writer can afford to take risks. He is at liberty to bend the facts, change an emphasis, digress, invent or interpolate almost at will. Whereas the traveller is obliged to tackle an uncertain and often intractable landscape, the travel writer enjoys absolute dominion over the narrative terrain.

To understand the pleasures of the best travel writing, we should consider our posture as armchair travellers. When someone's real journey is submitted as a retrospective report, we may begin by feeling critical and distant; yet, if the writing is attractive, we are likely to slip into a posture of passive participation, enjoying the fantasy of moving along in the company of a reliable and likeable companion. Our guide's manner – sometimes beguiling and poetic, sometimes bluff and envigorating – is of course deliberately designed to win our allegiance. We tend to succumb to its tacit demands, which could be interpreted as: 'you must listen to me, watch me, admire me, and become my friend'. Stevenson was hardly the first travel writer to exploit his personal charm, creating a circle of *aficionados* equivalent to a doting fan-club. His special gift was to achieve this without archness, without phoneyness. On the whole, we are lulled into ignoring certain excesses, and into accepting the literary persona he is constructing. We tend to judge him a successful traveller, for he has learnt the ultimate dodge of travel writing: to appear not only brave, doughty, committed and competent, but also to make a few strategic admissions of his shortcomings. For we love best the hero who is exactly as panicky as we would be ourselves, the adroit coper who nevertheless confesses his humiliation or depression. A special note is struck – a nonchalant boldness tempered by wonderment – when Stevenson speaks of waking in the open air after the third night of his march.

> I have been after an adventure all my life, a pure dispassionate adventure, such as befell early and heroic voyagers; and thus to be found by morning in a random woodside nook in Gévaudan – not knowing north from south, as strange to my surroundings as the first man upon the earth, an inland castaway – was to find a fraction of my daydreams realised.   [p. 40]

Adventure here becomes indistinguishable from a rapturous embrace of freedom, an escape from one's conditioning, a fresh beginning, a rebirth. Stevenson seems never to have renounced this youthful idealism, an expectancy immune to cynicism.

The abstract spirit of adventure is, I suspect, the true theme of *Travels with a Donkey*, although its author does take the trouble to provide a documentary basis for his narrative enterprise. The temporal progress of the text is confirmed by regular reference to dates, from 22 September to 4 October 1878, and occasional mentions of keeping a diary. However, no great emphasis is laid on the distances covered, so that the stay-at-home reader may not entirely realise how far Stevenson actually trudged: he covered some 230 kilometres in 12 days, at an average height of 1,000 metres above sea level. His north-south itinerary from Le Monastier to Saint-Jean-du-Gard often zigzags west and east, passing through four different *départements*, and across highlands whence flow four major rivers – the Loire and the Allier toward the north-east, the Lot and the Tarn to the west. Even now, this southernmost range of the Massif Central remains a harsh and largely desolate area. Latterday writers who have trekked in his footsteps, such as Richard Holmes and Christopher Rush, testify to Stevenson's prowess as a hiker who was in effect an adventurous explorer afoot in genuinely wild territory.[6]

As befits a true travel writer, Stevenson cannot adhere to stark narrative outlines and a rigid schedule. The genre in which he is working is as stretchable as his floppy sleeping-bag, and accommodates a good many sub-genres, including those of the historical retrospect, the topographical survey, the landscape description and the reported conversation. While preparing for his walk, Stevenson had spent three or four weeks in the small town of

Le Monastier-sur-Gazeille in the Haute Loire, and his book opens with a rehearsal of more or less sober facts. With its outlook across rough uplands towards the Loire river, into which tumbles the Gazeille stream, its steep access road 'where the wolves sometimes pursue the diligence in winter' (pause for effect), its narrow main street, its occasional livestock market, its communal fountain, its noisy hostelry, its political quarrelling and its tradition of lacemaking, Le Monastier turns out to be a credible, if relatively humdrum, place to start out from. Stevenson takes the trouble to befriend various locals, including an old granny of whom he does a pencil portrait and who teases him with a Scottish twinkle in her eye. Already we may see an authorial ploy, for it is a telltale feature of almost all Stevenson's travel memoirs that he should compare a foreign place with Scotland. He persuades himself that the landscape around Le Monastier is very Scottish ('although not so noble as the best in Scotland'), and even claims that the local *patois* is the exact equivalent of the Lowland Scots dialect. 'The population is, in its way, as Scottish as the country,' he concludes happily.

Before setting forth on an ambitious jaunt, the travel-writer often spends time on an inventory of necessities to be taken along: here is, as it were, the man of experience acting as solicitous mentor to a reader who may in practice never need these hot tips, but who is grateful for information that establishes veracity and indeed complicity. You really shouldn't bother with a tent, Stevenson implies, when you can be just as cosy in a sleeping-bag: especially if it's two yards square and lined in blue wool, big enough for one but allowing room for two 'at a pinch'. (Who is the nocturnal companion imagined here?) The rest of the camper's gear includes a spirit-lamp, a pan, a whisk for making egg-nog, a lantern with candles, a flask, a rug, clothes, a few books, a notebook, a knife and a handgun. In the spirit of making his trip sound enviable, the writer even lists such victuals as chocolate, tins of Italian sausage, bread, wine and milk. Despite the droll detail of the egg-whisk, the mundane list hints at the arduous journey ahead, for the armchair traveller thrills to the implication that a carefully monitored minimum is vital when one confronts the Great Unknown.

A little comedy ensues, as Stevenson confides one of his material difficulties, which is getting the affectionately named Modestine to carry all this gear. The loading and goading of the obdurate beast of burden give rise to much slapstick, with lengthy extemporisations on the theme of an inarticulate creature's resistance to human will, not to mention the baggage's resistance to being properly tied on. When the whole load slides to the ground in Ussel, a small crowd of onlookers gathers to smirk. Here Stevenson anticipates the burlesque world of early Hollywood cinema, or the literary one of a Jerome K. Jerome, whose *Three Men in a Boat (Not Forgetting the Dog)* (1889) perfected the comic topos of the perverse rebelliousness of mute objects.

Stevenson's landscape descriptions are carefully weighted to present a region in both negative and positive terms. At times, his winding open road becomes an unfriendly maze of misleading by-roads, some of which seem to 'lead everywhere at the same time', while hamlets bear names easily confused, like Fouzilhic and Fouzilhac. There are grotty inns where grunting pigs rub against your legs while you are trying to swallow your plain repast, whereas other places are welcoming and even cosy. From time to time, the trudging hiker pauses to study his whereabouts, as when he reaches the edge of a plateau near Bouchet St Nicolas and paints for us a Ruisdael-like verbal landscape of sad and windswept peaks and of fields drowned in shadow, marked by the white spots of farmhouses and the meandering lines of watercourses. The foggy gloom of the Gévaudan hills prompts a digression about the mythic Beast of Gévaudan, which terrorised the peasant population in the eighteenth century. Stevenson doesn't tell us why he is carrying a revolver, but its presence in the baggage seems a natural precaution in a territory saturated with such past horrors. As readers, we are being reminded that this is genuine travel and real adventure, an authentic confrontation with all those things that 'this feather-bed of civilisation' fails to equip us to confront. We are being asked to agree that our author is truly in the blackest thick of things, and we naturally sympathise when, on his second night in the open air, he is kept awake by innumerable tiny sounds – ants, mosquitoes, bats and rats. In short, he confesses to an urban dweller's panic, and we feel a little *Schadenfreude* at the same time as we shiver and bless him for not insisting on our literal company. For travel *reading* is always far less demanding than the real thing.

Stevenson's rather obvious (yet welcome) trick is to use a framework of exotic strangeness (tinted with a little Gothick horror) as a foil to those moments when the Cévennes hills are transfigured and conduce to wonderment and felicity. As our traveller heads downhill at speed to reach Pont de Montvert, he is startled and charmed to hear a boy yodelling to him from across the wide valley. One night, the ludicrous sleeping-bag turns into a warm, protective nest and when Stevenson stirs to sip some water, he sits up and smokes a cigarette, gazing up at the Milky Way and hearing no sound save that of the grazing Modestine. Each time he raises the cigarette to his lips, the silver ring on his finger catches the light, while the tobacco glow illuminates the inside of his hand. The miniaturism of these tender observations summons up an epiphany of contentment as the author savours a perfect sense of belonging in the world, while adding: 'I have not often enjoyed a more serene possession of myself' (p. 62). It's perhaps the highpoint of the journey, with sleeping-bag, stars, cigarette and glinting ring forming a felicitous cameo, replete with libidinal connotations.

On other occasions, Stevenson deploys his considerable descriptive skills, naming rocks and trees and evoking heather-covered slopes and misted crags, the panoramic view from the windswept Pic de Finiels, the waterfalls splashing down to the Tarn gorge. One passage is devoted to an encomium on the chestnut trees which abound in the Tarn valley, yet are more 'a herd of stalwart individuals' than an undifferentiated woodland mass. They prove impossible to sketch, our guide informs us, since each tree is different, partaking of the characteristics of other trees while yet embodying individuality. The chestnut, we infer, symbolises the traveller's ideal of distinctiveness and self-reliance.

Stevenson's narrative is repeatedly enlivened by encounters with strangers, and he becomes an adept of the spontaneous verbal portrait. Some peasants pay him the compliment of simply ignoring him, as if he truly belonged; others cruelly send the bemused wayfarer in the wrong direction; yet others are inquisitive, and prove to be cordial and even generous, if only in their conversation. It can be lonely on the road, and a brief chat always lifts the spirits. The reader senses Stevenson raising his play whenever he greets someone, fishing for attention by trying out various personae: the bumbling foreigner, the eccentric gypsy, the sturdy coper, the maverick to be reckoned with. When a lordly gent sneers at his camping arrangements and tries to interrogate him, he is secretly pleased that the man should notice the revolver peeping out of the sleeping-bag. An ancient shepherd hobbling on sticks mistakes him for a pedlar, while a merchant cannot get over his pluck in spending the night out in the open. Although someone looming up on a misty path can seem capable of aggression, an unmistakeable expression of solicitude is the customary outcome; almost invariably, the thirty-six-year-old wanderer falls in with grizzled old-timers eager for contact. One man helps him re-load his spilled luggage, while a former muleteer advises him to divide the load into two even parts. In the monastery of Our Lady of the Snows, he enjoys unstinting hospitality, and chats happily with several Trappist monks, even sparring with a pair of Catholic zealots eager to convert him.

In these successive encounters Stevenson seems to be adumbrating his own version of a knightly ethos. His avowed vulnerability is of a piece with a strong sense of decency. He faces each successive stranger, anticipating their confused look. As he puts it in a later text, 'There is no foreign land. It is the traveller only that is foreign' (p. 230). Moving through terrain historically marked by extremes of religious feeling, he comes across another old chap, a member of the Plymouth Brethren, who keeps shaking his hand. When challenged about his atheism, our traveller placates the man with a display of quasi-theological eloquence, and the two become firm friends. Despite differences of belief, Stevenson concludes, one should always strive for human concord; moreover, a few white lies about one's religious commitment are a justifiable diplomacy. Later, in the Catholic hamlet of St Germain de Calberte, he dines with two locals, one of whom pronounces on someone's marital loyalty in converting to the religion of his wife by saying, 'It's a bad idea for a man to change' (p. 85). The phrase sticks in Stevenson's mind and he assesses its wisdom, deciding that to switch (Christian) creeds can hardly make any difference in the eyes of God. But if the reader reflects on the phrase in the wider context of Stevenson's existential quest, it is possible to envisage another application, for our author is himself poised for the radical change involved in pursuing a woman, Fanny Osbourne, who has entered his life from far beyond his familiar orbit.

In many respects, Stevenson is no innocent or 'inland castaway'. On top of his camping necessities, he is transporting plenty of cultural baggage. One reason why he is drawn to the Cévennes, that 'confused and shaggy country', as he calls it, is that it was the setting for the legendary Camisard rebellion. Stevenson is responding to a perceived parallel between the Camisard freedom-fighters and the Scottish Covenanters, about whom he had written in his teenage years.[7]

The Protestant Covenanters of 1638 had sworn to resist the imposition of the English *Book of Common Prayer* and were persecuted by Government troops in continual raids. In 1666, an insurrection originating in south-west Scotland was crushed by a superior military force near the Pentland Hills close to Edinburgh. In 1678, a horde of Highlanders recruited by the Government swept through the Lowlands, pillaging and killing. Stevenson's Scottish-Protestant (Presbyterian) background led him to sympathise with the oppressed Lowland Covenanters, and this is what fuels his sympathy for the beleaguered Camisards of the Cévennes highlands. These too were Protestants, this time rebelling against the Catholicism imposed by King Louis XIV, who revoked the tolerant Edict of Nantes in 1685 and persecuted all dissenters. While the Protestant (Huguenot) population largely fled from France, the Camisards stayed in their native mountains and rose against the royalist army in the early 1700s, fighting legendary battles and bloodthirsty guerrilla skirmishes until a peace settlement was finally agreed in 1715. Stevenson relates rollicking tales of heroes such as Jean Cavalier, Spirit Séguier and Salomon Couderc, men of initiative, wit and bravado, and, drawing the parallel with the outlawed Covenanters, celebrates the equation of rugged resistance and rugged terrain, mythologising a landscape that nurtures trenchant nonconformity. Stevenson's exuberance is tempered at the last when, conversing in Florac with a group of Protestants and Catholics alike, he comes to accept their wise tolerance of differing beliefs, even though the consensus is that no man ought to betray the religion into which he is born. Brought up within Scottish Presbyterianism, he seems embarrassed to find that he feels closer to the Protestants than to the Catholics; this emotional kinship sits a little awkwardly beside his professed atheism.

We may notice that, in all this time, the stoic hiker has never once referred to his poor health, which could hardly have improved in the highland weather conditions. The other thing lacking in his travel memoir is the name of the woman he is evidently pining for. Fanny Osbourne hardly exists in the text, although the biographer Richard Holmes, in a brilliant chapter in *Footsteps*, sees her as an unspoken ghost, hovering as it were in the text's unconscious. Holmes cites one passage where the load-bearing Modestine reminds Stevenson of a lady 'who formerly loaded me with kindness' (p. 25). When, on a late march to St German de Calberte, Stevenson knocks back some Volnay wine in homage to the moon, the shadows of the two companions mingle on the road in a moment of incongruous togetherness that could be taken as a further oblique reminder of what Stevenson is missing. Holmes picks out another resonant remark: 'And to live out of doors with the woman a man loves is of all lives the most complete and free' (p. 62).

*   *   *

Close to the end of his Cévennes trek, Stevenson seeks out a quiet terrace and tries to sketch the chestnut trees, enjoying a well-earned rest. The relaxed context gives rise to the strongest textual allusion to Fanny. All that he lets slip is the remark 'perhaps someone was thinking of me in a far country', yet this is enough for us to understand what state he is in. All the same, Stevenson did nothing more than return north to Scotland, where he worked up his diary for publication as *Travels with a Donkey*.[8] Fully a year would pass before Fanny sent him a telegram out of the blue. Its contents have never been made public, but evidently provoked a swift reflex, for Stevenson immediately rushed to take ship to North America. Embarking at Greenock, after descending the Clyde from Glasgow, he boards a vessel chock-a-block with anxious emigrants, who look like criminals desperate to flee Europe. The crossing will take ten days.

Stevenson had deliberately not bought a first-class ticket. Was this due to some fantasy of doing penance, or a desire to demonstrate resilience and thus confirm his status as a fully qualified travel writer? He makes the claim that he was 'anxious to see the worst in the emigrant life', as though he now sees himself as conducting an undercover journalistic or sociological enquiry. However, true to his knack of turning things to his advantage, he enjoys the relative comfort of the Second Cabin, where he can sleep on a floor cooled by a pleasant draught, or spend time with his notes at a writing-table, which he persists in doing, despite the teasing of the ship's officers. From here he can infiltrate the nearby Steerage, where tickets cost six guineas, two less than his, and find out about the travails of those who have abandoned their former life. In fact, he himself remains only an 'amateur emigrant', an uncommitted experimenter, a person of consequence slumming it among the poorest voyagers. Stevenson's sensitivity to the issue of class now becomes a dominant in the narrative.

A sea-journey could hardly give rise to the same order of observation that characterises his mountain hike. Despite the size of the vessel, Stevenson is confined to a narrow space, and must practise his observational skills on his immediate surroundings. We learn that the coffee and tea served on board are indistinguishable. We are given lists of the foodstuffs consumed and told that it is inadvisable to descend into Steerage on an empty stomach because of the rancid smell. As readers, we glean no information about the ship's progress, and we hardly glimpse the vast Atlantic. Stevenson spends the day chatting, his usual hobby, and crowds his text with the noteworthy characters he dubs 'Steerage Types'. Many of these are great gasbags. We meet a chronic panicker who, at the slightest swell, assumes the vessel is foundering; an Irish-American man dressed in tatters; an artisan on the run from a drunken wife; an alcoholic Scotsman; a nihilistic Russian; an antiquated Scotswoman on her way to Kansas who keeps her watch set to Glasgow time; an argumentative pessimist who exhibits a shocking aimlessness in his life; a fun-lover named Barney; a shrewd stowaway named Alick; a Welsh blacksmith who touts a patent medicine called Golden Oil and shares Stevenson's passion for people-watching. All imaginable types are here: the questors on the Ship of Fools are endlessly diverse, though Stevenson sees them as united in their ignorance of what emigration actually entails.

The veteran of umpteen chats with French old-timers boasts of his unhesitating comradeship with the Steerage Types and is delighted to discover how easy it is to pass as one himself. His aim seems to be to obliterate the class barrier. Yet it is, he argues, not really a matter of money or class, for 'to be a gentleman is to be one all the world over, and in every relation and grade of society' (p. 138). I think Stevenson's implication is that the perfect traveller should always comport himself with tact and tolerance. He despises the rich couple who stray into Steerage one day and peer around in mute disdain, and whom he imagines returning to their first-class quarters to giggle over the 'tatters and incongruities' of the underclass.

Some of Stevenson's general reflections qualify his rosy picture of the proletarian masses. We hear of the instantaneous clan formed by all the children dashing merrily about, but Steerage adults consent to comradeliness only when they join in a sing-song. For all his pretentions to solidarity, Stevenson cannot but deplore their shameless idleness, and the grumpy thoughtlessness they exhibit when blurting out that a violent revolution is the only cure for social ills. He decides that emigration is nothing other than an avowal of hopelessness, for his companions are far less likely to be young men of ambition than defeated older ones. Our reporter reveals his political sympathies in a moving passage about the collapse of British labour, the strikes and closures, the joblessness and homelessness. 'We were a shipful of failures, the broken men of England,' he concludes. His portrayal of the European emigrant as a jittery refugee contrasts violently with the conventional image of the confident and enterprising pioneer who throws off the shackles of poverty and class in order to seek a new life in a progressive and welcoming democracy.[9] Small wonder that his father found the book intolerable and sought to block its publication.[10]

The ship docks at Sandy Hook below Staten Island and when Stevenson sets foot in New York, it looks no different from Liverpool. Sustained none the less by his fantasy of a 'promised land', he sets out on the city streets, 'spying for things foreign' (p. 147). Having found a French restaurant where he can at last order a decent cup of coffee, he drifts back to his sleazy hotel and steels himself for an early start next day on the emigrant train.

After the discomforts of shipboard and the first night ashore, *Across the Plains* continues the travel narrative in no less distressing terms. Four ships have arrived from Europe almost simultaneously, and the onward trajectory by train makes for a veritable Babel of emigrants, each damp, weary and heartily disillusioned. Stevenson has managed to purchase a six-volume history of the United States as a token of individual resolve, but is propelled across the Hudson to a railtrack in Jersey in a mass stampede that threatens his autonomy. This is not how our writer likes to travel. The train clatters away at last, but it is not till it halts next morning in the middle of nowhere that he can look out at the world in the sunlight and start to retune his jangled sensibility. The journey can now proceed on Stevensonian terms. He gallantly attends to a talkative Dutch widow and her children, and has his first encounter with a black man, a waiter who behaves so naturally that Stevenson is able to tip him with no sense of patronising.

Crossing a continent by rail proves to be a monotonous succession of days and nights, of cities and vistas, of encounters and occasional changes of berth. As on shipboard, there is no latitude for capricious meandering: the journey is purely sedentary and undeviating. We are told how to make one's toilet in an overcrowded carriage, and how to get rid of a garrulous German. The feeble globetrotter records his weariness, his hunger, his comatose sleeps. At sea, Stevenson had said little about feeling poorly, but now confides how, as he sprawled on the carriage floor, a lowly newsboy took pity and slipped him a juicy pear and a few free newspapers.[11] Landscapes continue to matter to him, yet the views are invariably dull, vast and empty. The plains of Nebraska are splendidly featureless, a void that is at first exhilarating, then depressing. The Black Hills of Wyoming and the Rockies shunt by similarly, endlessly repetitive and drearily unpeopled. We may guess that Stevenson has scanned his history books, but can find no information to fill this 'spacious vacancy', for nothing has ever happened here. He is out of his depth in the middle of the Uttermost

Unknown: it is not a bit like Scotland. (And, we may wonder, has nature's impassive expression anything to do with Fanny?) He spots a few antelopes and the odd creek, but cannot latch on to the numbing immensity of the continent. A single moment of insight comes when he notices a woman selling milk at a halt. He is shown her house, a wooden shack, newly built. The place seems ghastly, artificial, unreal. And yet the woman exudes such utter contentment with her lot that Stevenson's cameo turns into a sort of admonition to himself to bear up and make the most of his circumstances. The social lesson of travel is repeated: the visitor must not condescend or belittle the inhabitant, but honour the alien Other as an equal.

The last pages of *Across the Plains* deal with the bewildering diversity of the nationalities of his fellow passengers. Stevenson realises there are dozens of Chinese emigrants, segregated in a separate carriage. The text culminates in reflections on the deplorable racism of many of his white fellows, and with remarks on the degradation of the Native American people, of which he gets a few glimpses. 'I was ashamed for the thing we call civilisation,' he writes (p. 178).

Arrival at the golden city of San Francisco concludes this least satisfactory of his trajectories. An interval in the textual continuum now ensues. Stevenson made his way down to Monterey to contact Fanny, yet found her stand-offish and ambivalent. Some impulse of bravado prompted him to leave at once for the wilderness south of the city, this time accompanied by a horse. It was to be his most extravagant bid for 'pure dispassionate adventure' in the New World, and it's noteworthy that the professed travel writer never wrote it up after-wards. In *Travels with a Donkey*, he had vowed 'to come down off this feather-bed of civilisation' (p. 43), but in the Carmel Valley he roughed it to the very limits of his frail being. After wandering lost for three days in a delirium, he was rescued in the nick of time by the owners of an angora-goat ranch, who nursed him back to health. All bravado extinguished, Stevenson settled in a Monterey hotel, doing a little paid journalism for the local paper and preparing his evocative essays on *The Old and New Pacific Capitals*.[12] He later moved up to San Francisco to join Fanny, who had at last filed for divorce. The couple were married in May 1880 by a Scots Presbyterian minister. Immediately, Stevenson perked up and declared that their honeymoon must take the form of an adventure in the wilds. Young Lloyd would come too.

The Silverado Squatters tells of the couple's two-month sojourn in an old mining camp some seventy miles north of San Francisco. Silverado was an abandoned silver-mine, and Stevenson wanted to prospect its primitive beauty as well as benefit from its clean air. He was thrilled by the loftiness of the site and its outlook across to Mount St Helena, a peak which, at 1,324 metres, outstrips the highest crests of the Cévennes. Stevenson's text begins with technical details about the mighty summit and summarises the journey from San Francisco, which involves ferryboats, a rail trip and an ascent by horse-drawn carriage. An unpleasant overnight stay in the flea-bitten Frisby House hotel is converted by the writer into a *tour de force* of hyperbolic seediness worthy of a George Orwell. The rail trip up the Napa Valley to Calistoga gives rise to comments about local geysers, while Stevenson cannot resist a digression in praise of Californian viniculture, complete with an inventory of the vintages he has tasted. A stagecoach carries the three adventurers to the Toll House Hotel, after which they toil on foot up the steep track to Silverado, where they take over the deserted mining mill and establish their quarters. Like an excited schoolboy, Stevenson runs off to explore, and finds a tunnel into the cliff; adult wisdom prevails and he returns to help Fanny prepare their beds. Stevenson does his documentary duty by giving a half-factual, half-lyrical account of the mine's dramatic rise and fall. Despite finding next to no trace of any past transactions, he has no difficulty in imagining the racket of the mill-engine and the ore-carts trundling downhill. Now steeped in purely natural sounds, such as that of buffeting breezes, the place is ideal for resting and meditating. By now inured (or even addicted) to a modicum of discomfort, the writer can relax with his diary, gazing out from time to time at the panorama. As usual, the starry night sky can be relied on to enliven his spirits.

At one point in the stay, he is obliged to accompany Fanny and Lloyd down to Calistoga, where the two recuperate from a mild bout of diphtheria. However, he doesn't enlarge on this interlude, which is extraneous to his main Silverado themes. Predictably, verbal portraits of local characters begin to pepper his account. We are introduced to the Russian-Jewish entrepreneur Mr Kelmar, who seems to hold every local household in his debt; Rufe Hanson, a kind of noble savage who has become a practised layabout; or the swaggering Chinese bandit who curses while knocking back his drink at the Toll House ('one of life's crossing-places' [p. 253]) and thrills the future author of *Treasure Island* as the piratical type supreme, a man who walks with Death at his elbow. As is his wont, Stevenson especially enjoys bumping into Scotsmen, and confesses that a fellow-countryman whom he would utterly ignore in Scotland itself becomes a cherished clansman when encountered in foreign parts. Such sentimental patriotism is typical of a writer whose cosmopolitanism is always tinged with an ancestral allegiance. We may smile to observe that, whereas his genuine memories of Edinburgh are largely those of grey downpours, freezing winds and dreary church-bells, he can bring himself to make the unabashed claim that 'there are no stars so lovely as Edinburgh street-lamps' (p. 216). There is a willed self-delusion here that some readers may not forgive.

The *Silverado* writings are dominated by topography. As so often, it is the setting that inspires the stylist, and despite the grind of a difficult daily routine Stevenson is keen to develop the myth of an ethereal idyll, the source of a revelation beyond the earthly mundane. As he'd done in the French mountains, Stevenson aspires to a Neo-Romantic merging with the natural world. The highpoint of *The Silverado Squatters* is one of his classic epiphanies, the description of a sea-fog which, billowing up from the valley, levels out below the mill platform to form an uncanny ocean. Exulting in the 'breathless, crystal stillness' (p. 247), he accedes to a state of unalloyed quietude. The traveller's unhesitating response is paramount, and can be taken to imply an ultimate acceptance of the American landscape, sublime in its boundlessness. As readers, we become aware that Stevenson's ardent (and sometimes effortful) prose, with its tendency to poeticise even shabby and awkward situations, is central to his whole project as a writer and as a man.

*   *   *

Whether squatting in a decrepit mining-camp up a Californian mountain, or camping out in the desolate highlands of the Cévennes, Stevenson prospects his surroundings with a constant eye for the gleam of the Poetic, the treasure trove of beauty or intensity inhering in some lonely corner. As many travel narrators would admit, it is remoteness and the thrill of the unknown which conduce to those extreme states of being which force the nomadic writer to get to grips with his own latent capacities, while grappling with actual foreign sites and actual foreign people. In his texts of travel, Stevenson clutches at himself, or at least at those images of himself that make for good reading: the boisterous wayfarer, the connoisseur of discomfort, the doughty trekker who *just about* reaches his goal, the sickly aesthete intent on union with his fellows, and with the wider universe.

ROGER CARDINAL

1 All these were powerful figures on the London literary scene. Edmund Gosse (1849–1928) wrote the famous memoir *Father and Son* (1907). The critic Leslie Stephen (1832–1904) was editor of the *Dictionary of National Biography*, and father of Virginia Woolf. William Ernest Henley (1849–1903) was a critic and patriotic poet who co-authored some plays with Stevenson. Sidney Colvin (1845–1927) was Keeper of the National Collection of Prints and Drawings at the British Museum and wrote on both art and literature. He edited several volumes of Stevenson's letters after his death, as well as the Edinburgh Edition of his collected works (1894–97).

2 For further information on the author, see *The Robert Louis Stevenson Website* at http://www.robert-louis-stevenson.org.

3 The journalist and essayist William Hazlitt (1778–1830) also wrote *Notes of a Journey through France and Italy* (1826).

4 D. H. Lawrence echoes the spirit of this watchword in the opening lines of *Sea and Sardinia* (1923) and, as late as 1969, Laurie Lee's *As I Walked Out One Midsummer Morning* keeps alive the Romantic trope of the blissful departure. In his essay 'The Road to the Isles' (1974), Bruce Chatwin judges Stevenson to be a fey mythmaker and dismisses *Travels* as 'the prototype of the incompetent undergraduate voyage'. However, as Philip Callow points out in his Stevenson biography, Chatwin's own career was marked by a similar theatricality.

5 Stevenson's trail is nowadays honoured with the name *Le Chemin Stevenson*, and appears as 'GR70' on hikers' maps. For information about Stevenson's route, see the website: http:// www.gr70-stevenson.com.

6 In fact, Stevenson found a pretext to terminate his walk at Saint-Jean-du-Gard. Modestine was worn out, and he decided to sell her and take the stagecoach to his original destination of Alès (he calls it Alais), where he could pick up his post and rest before taking a train northwards via Lyon.

7 The sixteen-year-old's pamphlet on the Covenanters' uprising of 1666, *The Pentland Rising. A Page of History* (1866), was privately published and financed by his father.

8 The diary kept on the journey in a schoolboy's exercise-book carries 26 pencil drawings, nearly all landscapes, among the daily entries. This original draft remained unpublished for a century before appearing as *The Cévennes Journal. Notes of a Journey through the French Highlands* (1978). It is surprisingly close to the published

version, proving that *Travels with a Donkey* was indeed largely composed *en route*, in writing sessions in the evening or early morning. The fresh material added later deals mainly with the Camisard rebellion and the Beast of Gévaudan, and was derived from researches pursued in the Advocates' Library in Edinburgh, to which Stevenson's legal qualifications allowed convenient access.

9 A well-known text that helped nourish the myth of an open-armed, egalitarian America is *Letters from an American Farmer* (1782) by J. Hector St John Crèvecoeur (1735–1813).

10 Sidney Colvin, Stevenson's literary agent, was shocked by the counter-myth of emigration implied in the first part of *The Amateur Emigrant* and was able to curtail distribution of the book. Thomas Stevenson manifested his own disapproval, and was probably appalled by the revelation of his son's socialising with the lower classes. The sequel *Across the Plains* would appear as a magazine essay in 1883, and, with other essays, as a volume in 1892. But the two main instalments of *The Amateur Emigrant* were only brought together in 1895, some months after Stevenson's death.

11 Although Stevenson's writings contain occasional allusions to his poor health, only the essay 'Ordered South' (1874) focuses fully on the sad lot of the lifelong invalid. Even then he avoids spelling out the truth about his symptoms or the opinions of his doctors.

12 'Monterey' first came out in a magazine in 1880; 'San Francisco' likewise, in 1883. The two essays were brought together by Sidney Colvin as supplements to *The Amateur Emigrant*, in the 1895 Edinburgh Edition of Stevenson's *Works*.

FURTHER READING

The most recent publication of the complete works is in paperback: *The Complete Works of Robert Louis Stevenson*, 35 volumes, edited by Barry Menikoff, Newcastle, Cambridge Scholars Publishing, 2009.

1   STEVENSON'S TRAVEL WRITINGS

Travel Books

Edinburgh. Picturesque Notes, 1878

An Inland Voyage, 1878

Travels with a Donkey in the Cevennes, 1879

The Silverado Squatters, 1883

Across the Plains with other Memories and Essays, 1892

The Amateur Emigrant, 1894

Vailima Letters, 1895

In the South Seas, 1896

Travels in Hawaii, 1973

Selected Travel Essays

'Roads' (1873), 'Ordered South' (1874), 'On the Enjoyment of Unpleasant Places' (1874) & 'Walking Tours' (1876), in *Virginibus Puerisque and Other Essays in Belles Lettres*, 1881; reprinted 2010

'The Foreigner at Home' (1882) & 'Memoirs of an Islet' (1887), in *Memories and Portraits*, 1887; reprinted 2009

'Forest Notes' (1875–6), 'Fontainebleau' (1882), 'Beggars' (1888) & 'Epilogue to *An Inland Voyage*' (1888), in *Across the Plains with Other Memories and Essays*, 1892

'Roads' (1873), 'On the Enjoyment of Unpleasant Places' (1874), 'A Winter's Walk in Carrick and Galloway' (1876), 'A Mountain Town in France' (1879), 'Davos in Winter' (1881) & 'The Stimulation of the Alps' (1881), in *Essays of Travel*, 1905; reprinted 1996

'Forest Notes' (1875–6), 'Three Walking Tours' (1876), 'Alpine Diversions' (1881) & 'The Coast of Fife' (1888), in *Further Memories*, 1924; reprinted 2009

Edited Versions of the Travel Books

An Inland Voyage, with a Travel Guide to the Route by Andrew Sanger,
   Heathfield, Cockbird, 1991

An Inland Voyage / Travels with a Donkey, ed. James Cloyd Bowman,
   Boston, Allyn & Bacon, 1918

The Cévennes Journal. Notes of a Journey through the French Highlands,
   ed. Gordon Golding, Edinburgh, Mainstream Publishing, 1978

Travels with a Donkey / The Amateur Emigrant, ed. Christopher
   MacLachlan, London, Penguin Books, 2004

Travels with a Donkey / An Inland Voyage / The Silverado Squatters,
   ed. Trevor Royle, London, J. M. Dent, 1993

*From the Clyde to California: Robert Louis Stevenson's Emigrant
   Journey*, ed. Andrew Noble, Aberdeen, Aberdeen University
   Press, 1985

The Amateur Emigrant with Some First Impressions of America, ed. Roger
   G. Swearingen, 2 vols, Ashland, Oregon, Osborne, 1976–7

Island Landfalls. Reflections from the South Seas, ed. Jenni Calder,
   Edinburgh, Canongate, 1987

In the South Seas, ed. Jeremy Treglown, London, Hogarth Press,
   1987

In the South Seas, ed. Neil Rennie, London, Penguin Books, 1998

*Dreams of Elsewhere: The Selected Travel Writings of Robert Louis
   Stevenson*, ed. June Skinner Sawyers, Glasgow, Neil Wilson
   Publishing, 2002

2   CRITICAL WRITINGS ON STEVENSON'S WORK

Ambrosini, Richard, ' "Painting and Words": Landscape-Writing in
   R. L. Stevenson's Literary Apprenticeship and Early Essays',
   Merope, Vol. XIV, Nos 35–36, 2002

Bevan, Bryan, 'The Versatility of Robert Louis Stevenson',
   Contemporary Review, Vol. 264, No. 1541, June 1994

Chareyre-Méjan, Alain, 'La vie est un paysage. Stevenson, ou
   l'esthétique de la vie au grand air', in *R. L. Stevenson & A.
   Conan Doyle. Aventures de la Fiction*, Gilles Menegaldo & Jean-
   Pierre Naugrette (eds), Rennes, Terre de Brume, 2003

Chatwin, Bruce, 'The Road to the Isles' (1974), in *Anatomy of Restlessness. Uncollected Writings*, Jan Borm & Matthew Graves (eds), London, Picador, 1997

Clunas, Alex, ' "Out of my country and myself I go": Identity and Writing in Stevenson's Early Travel Books', in *Nineteenth-Century Prose*, 22 March 1996

Colley, Ann C., *Robert Louis Stevenson and the Colonial Image*, Aldershot, Ashgate, 2004

Daws, Gavan, 'Robert Louis Stevenson', in *A Dream of Islands. Voyages of Self-Discovery in the South Seas*, New York & London, Norton, 1980

Gray, William, *Robert Louis Stevenson: A Literary Life*, Basingstoke, Palgrave, 2004

Hillier, Robert Irwin, *The South Seas Fictions of Robert Louis Stevenson*, Peter Lang, New York, 1989

Jolly, Roslyn, *Robert Louis Stevenson in the Pacific: Travel, Empire and the Author's Profession*, Farnham, Surrey, Ashgate, 2009

Kiely, Robert, *Robert Louis Stevenson and the Fiction of Adventure*, Cambridge, Harvard University Press, 1965

Menikoff, Barry, *Narrating Scotland: The Imagination of Robert Louis Stevenson*, Columbia, University of South Carolina Press, 2005

Menikoff, Barry, ' "These Problematic Shores": Robert Louis Stevenson in the South Seas', in *English Literature and the Wider World. Vol. IV: The Ends of the Earth: 1876–1918*, Simon Gatrell (ed.), London, Ashfield, 1992

Noble, Andrew (ed.), *Robert Louis Stevenson*, London, Vision, 1983

Norquay, Glenda, *Robert Louis Stevenson and Theories of Reading*, Manchester, Manchester University Press, 2007

Swearingen, Roger G., *The Prose Writings of Robert Louis Stevenson: A Guide*, Hamden CT, Archon, 1980

Zlosnik, Sue, ' "Home is the sailor, home from the sea": Robert Louis Stevenson and the End of Wandering', in *Yearbook of English Studies*, January 2004

3 BIOGRAPHIES OF STEVENSON AND OTHER PUBLICATIONS OF INTEREST

Balfour, Graham, *The Life of Robert Louis Stevenson*, London, Methuen, 1901

Bell, Gavin, *In Search of Tusitala: Travels in the Pacific after Robert Louis Stevenson*, London, Picador, 1994

Bell, Ian, *Robert Louis Stevenson: Dreams of Exile*, Edinburgh, Mainstream Publishing, 1992

Botton, Alain de, *The Art of Travel*, London, Hamish Hamilton, 2002

Calder, Jenni, *R L S: A Life Study*, Glasgow, Richard Drew Publishing, 1990

Callow, Philip, *Louis. A Life of Robert Louis Stevenson*, London, Constable, 2001

Castle, Alan, *The Robert Louis Stevenson Trail. The GR70 from Le Puy to St-Jean-du-Gard*, Milnthorpe, Cumbria, Cicerone, 2007

Cooper, Bruce C., *Riding the Transcontinental Rails: Overland Travel on the Pacific Railroad 1865–1881*, Philadelphia, Polyglot Press, 2005

Davies, Hunter, *The Teller of Tales. In Search of Robert Louis Stevenson*, London, Sinclair-Stevenson, 1994

Deering, Susan, *Silverado Canyon*, San Francisco, Arcadia Publishing, 2008

Duddles, David, ed., *Silverado Squatters in Pictures*, Orlando, Blue Pylon Creative, 2008

Furnas, J. C., *Voyage to Windward: The Life of Robert Louis Stevenson*, London, Faber & Faber, 1952

Hammerton, J. A., *In the Track of R. L. S. and Elsewhere in Old France*, New York, E. P. Dutton, 1903

Hazlitt, William, 'On Going a Journey', in *Table Talk*, 1822

Hodgson, Geoffrey M., 'Stevenson's Ghost. Travels without a Donkey in the Cévennes', http:// www.gr70-stevenson.com/ en/hodgson.htm

Holmes, Lowell D., *Treasured Islands: Cruising the South Seas with Robert Louis Stevenson*, London, A. & C. Black, 2002

Holmes, Richard, *Footsteps. Adventures of a Romantic Biographer*, London, Hodder & Stoughton, 1985

Islam, Syed Manzurul, *The Ethics of Travel: From Marco Polo to Kafka*, Manchester & New York, Manchester University Press, 1996

Issler, Anne Roller, *Our Mountain Hermitage: Silverado and Robert Louis Stevenson*, Stanford, Stanford University Press, 1950

McLynn, Frank, *Robert Louis Stevenson. A Biography*, London, Hutchinson, 1993

Pomeroy, Earl, *In Search of the Golden West. The Tourist in Western America* (1957), 2nd edition, Lincoln, Nebraska University Press, 1990

Pope-Hennessy, James, *Robert Louis Stevenson*, London, Jonathan Cape, 1974

Rush, Christopher, *To Travel Hopefully. Journal of a Death Foretold*, London, Profile Books, 2005

Smith, Janet Adam, *Robert Louis Stevenson*, London, Duckworth, 1937

Speake, Jennifer (ed.), *Literature of Travel and Exploration. An Encyclopedia*, 3 vols, New York & London, Fitzroy Dearborn, 2000

White, Kenneth, *Le Chemin des crêtes. Avec Robert Louis Stevenson à travers les Cévennes*, Bez-et-Esparon, Études & Communication Éditions, 1999

Walking Tours

It must not be imagined that a walking tour, as some would have us fancy, is merely a better or worse way of seeing the country. There are many ways of seeing landscape quite as good; and none more vivid, in spite of canting dilettantes, than from a railway train. But landscape on a walking tour is quite accessory. He who is indeed of the brotherhood does not voyage in quest of the picturesque, but of certain jolly humours – of the hope and spirit with which the march begins at morning, and the peace and spiritual repletion of the evening's rest. He cannot tell whether he puts his knapsack on, or takes it off, with more delight. The excitement of the departure puts him in key for that of the arrival. Whatever he does is not only a reward in itself, but will be further rewarded in the sequel; and so pleasure leads on to pleasure in an endless chain. It is this that so few can understand; they will either be always lounging or always at five miles an hour; they do not play off the one against the other, prepare all day for the evening, and all evening for the next day. And, above all, it is here that your over-walker fails of comprehension. His heart rises against those who drink their curaçao in liqueur glasses, when he himself can swill it in a brown john. He will not believe that the flavour is more delicate in the smaller dose. He will not believe that to walk this unconscionable distance is merely to stupefy and brutalise himself, and come to his inn, at night, with a sort of frost on his five wits, and a starless night of darkness in his spirit. Not for him the mild luminous evening of the temperate walker! He has nothing left of man but a physical need for bedtime and a double nightcap; and even his pipe, if he be a smoker, will be savourless and disenchanted. It is the fate of such a one to take twice as much trouble as is needed to obtain happiness, and miss the happiness in the end; he is the man of the proverb, in short, who goes further and fares worse.

Now, to be properly enjoyed, a walking tour should be gone upon alone. If you go in a company, or even in pairs, it is no longer a walking tour in anything but name; it is something else and more in the nature of a picnic. A walking tour should be gone upon alone, because freedom is of the essence; because you should be able to stop and go on, and follow this way or that, as the freak takes you; and because you must have your own pace, and neither trot alongside a champion walker, nor mince in time with a girl. And then you must be open to all impressions and let your thoughts take colour from what you see. You should be as a pipe for any wind to play upon. 'I cannot see the wit,' says Hazlitt,[1] 'of walking and talking at the same time. When I am in the country I wish to vegetate like the country' – which is the gist of all that can be said upon the matter. There should be no cackle of voices at your elbow, to jar on the meditative silence of the morning. And so long as a man is reasoning he cannot surrender himself to that fine intoxication that comes of much motion in the open air, that begins in a sort of dazzle and sluggishness of the brain, and ends in a peace that passes comprehension.

During the first day or so of any tour there are moments of bitterness, when the traveller feels more than coldly towards his knapsack, when he is half in a mind to throw it bodily over the hedge and, like Christian on a similar occasion, 'give three leaps and go on singing'. And yet it soon acquires a property of easiness. It becomes magnetic; the spirit of the journey enters into it. And no sooner have you passed the straps over your shoulder than the lees of sleep are cleared from you, you pull yourself together with a shake, and fall at once into your stride. And surely, of all possible moods, this, in which a man takes the road, is the best. Of course, if he *will* keep thinking of his anxieties, if he *will* open the merchant Abudah's chest and walk arm in arm with the hag – why, wherever he is, and whether he walk fast or slow, the chances are that he will not be happy. And so much the more shame to himself! There are perhaps thirty men setting forth at that same hour, and I would lay a large wager there is not another dull face among the thirty. It would be a fine thing to follow, in a coat of darkness, one after another of these wayfarers, some summer morning, for the first few miles upon the road. This one, who walks fast, with a keen look in his eyes, is all concentrated in his own mind; he is up at his loom, weaving and weaving, to set the landscape to words. This one peers about, as he goes, among the grasses; he waits by the canal to watch the dragonflies; he leans on the gate of the pasture, and cannot look enough upon the complacent kine. And here comes another, talking, laughing, and gesticulating to himself. His face changes from time to time, as indignation flashes from his eyes or anger clouds his forehead. He is composing articles, delivering orations, and conducting the most impassioned interviews, by the way. A little farther on, and it is as like as not he will begin to sing. And well for him, supposing him to be no great master in that art, if he stumble across no stolid peasant at a corner; for on such an occasion, I scarcely know which is the more troubled, or whether it is worse to suffer the confusion of your troubadour, or the unfeigned alarm of your clown. A sedentary population, accustomed, besides, to the strange mechanical bearing of the common tramp, can in no wise explain to itself the gaiety of these passers-by. I knew one man who was arrested as a runaway lunatic, because, although a full-grown person with a red beard, he skipped as he went like a child. And you would be astonished if I were to tell you all the grave and learned heads who have confessed to me that, when on walking tours, they sang – and sang very ill – and had a pair of red ears when, as described above, the inauspicious peasant plumped into their arms from round a corner. And here, lest you should think I am exaggerating, is Hazlitt's own confession, from his essay 'On Going a Journey', which is so good that there should be a tax levied on all who have not read it:

> Give me the clear blue sky over my head [says he] and the green turf beneath my feet, a winding road before me, and a three hours' march to dinner – and then to thinking! It is hard if I cannot start some game on these lone heaths. I laugh, I run, I leap, I sing for joy.

Bravo! After that adventure of my friend with the policeman, you would not have cared, would you, to publish that in the first person? But we have no bravery nowadays, and, even in books, must all pretend to be as dull and foolish as our neighbours. It was not so with Hazlitt. And notice how learned he is (as, indeed, throughout the essay) in the theory of walking tours. He is none of your athletic men in purple stockings, who walk their fifty miles a day: three hours' march is his ideal. And then he must have a winding road, the epicure!

Yet there is one thing I object to in these words of his, one thing in the great master's practice that seems to me not wholly wise. I do not approve of that leaping and running. Both of these hurry the respiration; they both shake up the brain out of its glorious open-air confusion; and they both break the pace. Uneven walking is not so agreeable to the body, and it distracts and irritates the mind. Whereas, when once you have fallen into an equable stride, it requires no conscious thought from you to keep it up, and yet it prevents you from thinking earnestly of anything else. Like knitting, like the work of a copying clerk, it gradually neutralises and sets to sleep the serious activity of the mind. We can think of this or that, lightly and laughingly, as a child thinks, or as we think in a morning dose; we can make puns or puzzle out acrostics, and trifle in a thousand ways with words and rhymes; but when it comes to honest work, when we come to gather ourselves together for an effort, we may sound the trumpet as loud and long as we please; the great barons of the mind will not rally to the standard, but sit, each one, at home, warming his hands over his own fire and brooding on his own private thought!

In the course of a day's walk, you see, there is much variance in the mood. From the exhilaration of the start, to the happy phlegm of the arrival, the change is certainly great. As the day goes on, the traveller moves from the one extreme towards the other. He becomes more and more incorporated with the material landscape, and the open-air drunkenness grows upon him with great strides, until he posts along the road, and sees everything about him, as in a cheerful dream. The first is certainly brighter, but the second stage is the more peaceful. A man does not make so many articles towards the end, nor does he laugh aloud; but the purely animal pleasures, the sense of physical wellbeing, the delight of every inhalation, of every time the muscles tighten down the thigh, console him for the absence of the others, and bring him to his destination still content.

Nor must I forget to say a word on bivouacs. You come to a milestone on a hill, or some place where deep ways meet under trees; and off goes the knapsack, and down you sit to smoke a pipe in the shade. You sink into yourself, and the birds come round and look at you; and your smoke dissipates upon the afternoon under the blue dome of heaven; and the sun lies warm upon your feet, and the cool air visits your neck and turns aside your open shirt. If you are not happy, you must have an evil conscience. You may dally as long as you like by the roadside. It is almost as if the millennium were arrived, when we shall throw our clocks and watches over the house top, and remember time and seasons no more. Not to keep hours for a lifetime is, I was going to say, to live for ever. You have no idea, unless you have tried it, how endlessly long is a summer's day, that you measure out only by hunger, and bring to an end only when you are drowsy. I know a village where there are hardly any clocks, where no one knows more of the days of the week than by a sort of instinct for the fête on Sundays, and where only one person can tell you the day of the month, and she is generally wrong; and if people were aware how slow Time journeyed in that village, and what armfuls of spare hours he gives, over and above the bargain, to its wise inhabitants, I believe there would be a stampede out of London, Liverpool, Paris, and a variety of large towns, where the clocks lose their heads, and shake the hours out each one faster than the other, as though they were all in a wager. And all these foolish pilgrims would each bring his own misery along with him, in a watch-pocket! It is to be noticed, there were no clocks and watches in the much-vaunted days before the flood. It follows, of course, there were no appointments, and punctuality was not yet thought upon. 'Though ye take from a covetous man all his treasure,' says Milton, 'he has yet one jewel left; ye cannot deprive him of his covetousness.' And so I would say of a modern man of business, you may do what you will for him, put him in Eden, give him the elixir of life – he has still a flaw at heart, he still has his business habits. Now, there is no time when business habits are more mitigated than on a walking tour. And so during these halts, as I say, you will feel almost free.

But it is at night, and after dinner, that the best hour comes. There are no such pipes to be smoked as those that follow a good day's march; the flavour of the tobacco is a thing to be remembered, it is so dry and aromatic, so full and so fine. If you wind up the evening with grog, you will own there was never such grog; at every sip a jocund tranquillity spreads about your limbs, and sits easily in your heart. If you read a book – and you will never do so save by fits and starts – you find the language strangely racy and harmonious; words take a new meaning; single sentences possess the ear for half an hour together; and the writer endears himself to you, at every page, by the nicest coincidence of sentiment. It seems as if it were a book you had written yourself in a dream. To all we have read on such occasions we look back with special favour. 'It was on the 10th of April, 1798,' says Hazlitt, with amorous precision, 'that I sat down to a volume of the new *Héloïse*, at the Inn at Llangollen, over a bottle of sherry and a cold chicken.' I should wish to quote more, for though we are mighty fine fellows nowadays, we cannot write like Hazlitt. And, talking of that, a volume of Hazlitt's essays would be a capital pocketbook on such a journey; so would a volume of Heine's songs; and for *Tristram Shandy* I can pledge a fair experience.

If the evening be fine and warm, there is nothing better in life than to lounge before the inn door in the sunset, or lean over the parapet of the bridge, to watch the weeds and the quick fishes. It is then, if ever, that you taste joviality to the full significance of that audacious word. Your muscles are so agreeably slack, you feel so clean and so strong and so idle, that whether you move or sit still, whatever you do is done with pride and a kingly sort of pleasure. You fall in talk with anyone, wise or foolish, drunk or sober. And it seems as if a hot walk purged you, more than of anything else, of all narrowness and pride, and left curiosity to play its part freely, as in a child or a man of science. You lay aside all your own hobbies, to watch provincial humours develop themselves before you, now as a laughable farce, and now grave and beautiful like an old tale.

Or perhaps you are left to your own company for the night, and surly weather imprisons you by the fire. You may remember how Burns, numbering past pleasures, dwells upon the hours when he has been 'happy thinking'. It is a phrase that may well perplex a poor modern, girt about on every side by clocks and chimes, and haunted, even at night, by flaming dial-plates. For we are all so busy, and have so many far-off projects to realise, and castles in the fire to turn into solid habitable mansions on a gravel soil, that we can find no time for pleasure trips into the Land of Thought and among the Hills of Vanity. Changed times, indeed, when we must sit all night, beside the fire, with folded hands; and a changed world for most of us, when we find we can pass the hours without discontent and be happy thinking. We are in such haste to be doing, to be writing, to be gathering gear, to make our voice audible a moment in the derisive silence of eternity, that we forget that one thing, of which these are but the parts – namely, to live. We fall in love, we drink hard, we run to and fro upon the earth like frightened sheep. And now you are to ask yourself if, when all is done, you would not have been better to sit by the fire at home, and be happy thinking. To sit still and contemplate – to remember the faces of women without desire, to be pleased by the great deeds of men without envy, to be everything and everywhere in sympathy, and yet content to remain where and what you are – is not this to know both wisdom and virtue, and to dwell with happiness? After all, it is not they who carry flags, but they who look upon it from a private chamber, who have the fun of the procession. And once you are at that, you are in the very humour of all social heresy. It is no time for shuffling or for big, empty words. If you ask yourself what you mean by fame, riches or learning, the answer is far to seek; and you go back into that kingdom of light imaginations, which seem so vain in the eyes of Philistines perspiring after wealth, and so momentous to those who are stricken with the disproportions of the world, and, in the face of the gigantic stars, cannot stop to split differences between two degrees of the infinitesimally small, such as a tobacco pipe or the Roman Empire, a million of money or a fiddlestick's end.

You lean from the window, your last pipe reeking whitely into the darkness, your body full of delicious pains, your mind enthroned in the seventh circle of content; when suddenly the mood changes, the weathercock goes about, and you ask yourself one question more: whether, for the interval, you have been the wisest philosopher or the most egregious of donkeys? Human experience is not yet able to reply; but at least you have had a fine moment, and looked down upon all the kingdoms of the earth. And whether it was wise or foolish, tomorrow's travel will carry you, body and mind, into some different parish of the infinite.

A map
of the towns
and rivers of the
CÉVENNES
which shows the
route taken by
the author
in *1878*

Le Puy ○
Cayres ●
Lac du Bouchet
Costaros
Le Bouchet-St-Nicolas
Ussel
Montagnac
Goudet
St-Martin-de-Fugères
Le Monastier
St Victor
R. Gazeille
Landos
Les Uffernets
Pradelles
R. Loire
R. Allier
Lac de Naussac
Langogne
St Flour de Mercoire
Fouzillac
Fouzillic
Cheylard-l'Évêque
Les Pradels
Luc
Forêt de Mercoire
La Bastide-Puylaurent
Our Lady of the Snows
R. Chassezac
Montagne du Goulet
R. Lot
Chasseradès
Le Bleymard
Mont Lozère
Pic de Finiels
Le Pont-de-Montvert
R. Tarn
Florac
Montagne du Bougès
R. Mimente
Cassagnas
Mont Mars
St-Germain-de-Calberte
St Étienne Vallée Française
Col de St Pierre
St-Jean-du-Gard
Alès

N

Paris
Bordeaux
Lyon
Cévennes
Marseille

Stevenson's Itinerary

September 22	Le Monastier
September 23	Langogne
September 24	Cheylard-l'Évêque
September 25	Luc
September 25	La Bastide-Puylaurent
September 27	Chasseradès, Le Bleymard
September 29	Le Pont-de-Montvert
September 30	Florac
October 2	St-Germain-de-Calberte
	St Étienne Vallée Française
October 3	St-Jean-du-Gard

0 MILES	6	12
0 KILOMETRES	10	20

Travels with a Donkey in the Cevennes

My dear Sidney Colvin,

The journey which this little book is to describe was very agreeable and fortunate for me. After an uncouth beginning, I had the best of luck to the end. But we are all travellers in what John Bunyan[2] calls the wilderness of this world – all, too, travellers with a donkey: and the best that we find in our travels is an honest friend. He is a fortunate voyager who finds many. We travel, indeed, to find them. They are the end and the reward of life. They keep us worthy of ourselves; and when we are alone, we are only nearer to the absent.

Every book is, in an intimate sense, a circular letter to the friends of him who writes it. They alone take his meaning; they find private messages, assurances of love and expressions of gratitude dropped for them in every corner. The public is but a generous patron who defrays the postage. Yet though the letter is directed to all, we have an old and kindly custom of addressing it on the outside to one. Of what shall a man be proud, if he is not proud of his friends? And so, my dear Sidney Colvin, it is with pride that I sign myself affectionately yours,

R. L. S.

A Mountain Town in France [3]

Le Monastier [4] is the chief place of a hilly canton in Haute Loire, the ancient Velay. As the name betokens, the town is of monastic origin; and it still contains a towered bulk of monastery and a church of some architectural pretensions, the seat of an arch-priest and several vicars. It stands on the side of a hill above the River Gazeille, about fifteen miles from Le Puy, up a steep road where the wolves sometimes pursue [5] the diligence in winter. The road, which is bound for Vivarais, passes through the town from end to end in a single narrow street; there you may see the fountain where women fill their pitchers; there also some old houses with carved doors and pediments and ornamental work in iron. For Monastier, like Maybole in Ayrshire, was a sort of country capital, where the local aristocracy had their town mansions for the winter; and there is a certain baron still alive and, I am told, extremely penitent, who found means to ruin himself by high living in this village on the hills. He certainly has claims to be considered the most remarkable spendthrift on record. How he set about it, in a place where there are no luxuries for sale, and where the board at the best inn comes to little more than a shilling a day, is a problem for the wise. His son, ruined as the family was, went as far as Paris to sow his wild oats; and so the cases of father and son mark an epoch in the history of centralisation in France. Not until the latter had got into the train was the work of Richelieu complete.

It is a people of lace-makers. The women sit in the streets by groups of five or six; and the noise of the bobbins is audible from one group to another. Now and then you will hear one woman clattering off prayers for the edification of the others at their work. They wear gaudy shawls, white caps with a gay ribbon about the head, and sometimes a black felt brigand hat above the cap; and so they give the street colour and brightness and a foreign air. A while ago, when England largely supplied herself from this district with the lace called *torchon*, it was not unusual to earn five francs a day; and five francs in Monastier is worth a pound in London. Now, from a change in the market, it takes a clever and industrious workwoman to earn from three to four in the week, or less than an eighth of what she made easily a few years ago. The tide of prosperity came and went, as with our northern pitmen, and left nobody the richer. The women bravely squandered their gains, kept the men in idleness and gave themselves up, as I was told, to sweethearting and a merry life. From week's end to week's end it was one continuous gala in Monastier; people spent the day in the wine-shops, and the drum or the bagpipes led on the *bourrées* up to ten at night. Now these dancing days are over. '*Il n'y a plus de jeunesse*,' said Victor the garçon. I hear of no great advance in what are thought the essentials of morality; but the *bourrée*, with its rambling, sweet, interminable music, and alert and rustic figures, has fallen into disuse, and is mostly remembered as a custom of the past. Only on the occasion of the fair shall you hear a drum discreetly in a wine-shop or perhaps one of the company singing the measure while the others dance. I am sorry at the change, and marvel once more at the complicated scheme of things upon this earth, and how a turn of fashion in England can silence so much mountain merriment in France. The lace-makers themselves have not entirely forgiven our countrywomen; and I think they take a special pleasure in the legend of the northern quarter of the town, called L'Anglade, because there the English freelances were arrested and driven back by the potency of a little Virgin Mary on the wall.

From time to time a market is held, and the town has a season of revival: cattle and pigs are stabled in the streets; and pickpockets have been known to come all the way from Lyons for the occasion. Every Sunday the country folk throng in with daylight to buy apples, to attend mass, and to visit one of the wine-shops, of which there are no fewer than fifty in this little town. Sunday wear for the men is a green tailcoat of some coarse sort of drugget, and usually a complete suit to match. I have never set eyes on such degrading raiment. Here it clings, there bulges; and the human body, with its agreeable and lively lines, is turned into a mockery and laughing-stock. Another piece of Sunday business with the peasants is to take their ailments to the chemist for advice. It is as much a matter for Sunday as churchgoing. I have seen a woman who had been unable to speak since the Monday before, wheezing, catching her breath, endlessly and painfully coughing; and yet she had waited upwards of a hundred hours before coming to seek help, and had the week been twice as long, she would have waited still. There was a canonical day for consultation; such was the ancestral habit, to which a respectable lady must study to conform.

Two conveyances go daily to Le Puy, but they rival each other in polite concessions rather than in speed. Each will wait an hour or two hours cheerfully while an old lady does her marketing or a gentleman finishes the papers in a café. The Courrier (such is the

name of one) should leave Le Puy by two in the afternoon on the
return voyage, and arrive at Monastier in good time for a six-o'clock
dinner. But the driver dares not disoblige his customers. He will
postpone his departure again and again, hour after hour; and I have
known the sun to go down on his delay. These purely personal
favours, this consideration of men's fancies, rather than the hands of
a mechanical clock, as marking the advance of the abstraction, time,
makes a more humorous business of stagecoaching than we are used
to see it.

As far as the eye can reach, one swelling line of hilltop rises and
falls behind another; and if you climb an eminence, it is only to see
new and farther ranges behind these. Many little rivers run from all
sides in cliffy valleys; and one of them, a few miles from Monastier,
bears the great name of Loire. The mean level of the country is a
little more than three thousand feet above the sea, which makes the
atmosphere proportionally brisk and wholesome. There is little
timber except pines, and the greater part of the country lies in
moorland pasture. The country is wild and tumbled rather than
commanding; an upland rather than a mountain district; and the
most striking as well as the most agreeable scenery lies low beside
the rivers. There, indeed, you will find many corners that take the
fancy; such as made the English noble choose his grave by a Swiss
streamlet, where nature is at her freshest, and looks as young as on
the seventh morning. Such a place is the course of the Gazeille,
where it waters the common of Monastier and thence downwards till
it joins the Loire; a place to hear birds singing; a place for lovers to
frequent. The name of the river was perhaps suggested by the sound
of its passage over the stones; for it is a great warbler, and at night,
after I was in bed at Monastier, I could hear it go singing down the
valley till I fell asleep.

On the whole, this is a Scottish landscape, although not so noble as
the best in Scotland; and by an odd coincidence, the population is, in
its way, as Scottish as the country. They have abrupt, uncouth,
Fifeshire manners, and accost you, as if you were trespassing, with an
'Où'st-ce que vous allez?' only translatable into the Lowland 'Whaur
ye gaun?' They keep the Scottish Sabbath. There is no labour done
on that day but to drive in and out the various pigs and sheep and
cattle that make so pleasant a tinkling in the meadows. The lace-
makers have disappeared from the street. Not to attend mass would
involve social degradation; and you may find people reading Sunday
books, in particular a sort of Catholic *Monthly Visitor* on the doings

of Our Lady of Lourdes. I remember one Sunday, when I was walking in the country, that I fell on a hamlet and found all the inhabitants, from the patriarch to the baby, gathered in the shadow of a gable at prayer. One strapping lass stood with her back to the wall and did the solo part, the rest chiming in devoutly. Not far off, a lad lay flat on his face asleep among some straw, to represent the worldly element.

Again, this people is eager to proselytise; and the postmaster's daughter used to argue with me by the half-hour about my heresy, until she grew quite flushed. I have heard the reverse process going on between a Scotswoman and a French girl; and the arguments in the two cases were identical. Each apostle based her claim on the superior virtue and attainments of her clergy, and clenched the business with a threat of hell-fire. 'Pas bong prêtres ici,' said the Presbyterian, 'bong prêtres en Ecosse.' And the postmaster's daughter, taking up the same weapon, plied me, so to speak, with the butt of it instead of the bayonet. We are a hopeful race, it seems, and easily persuaded for our good. One cheerful circumstance I note in these guerrilla missions, that each side relies on hell, and Protestant and Catholic alike address themselves to a supposed misgiving in their adversary's heart. And I call it cheerful, for faith is a more supporting quality than imagination.

Here, as in Scotland, many peasant families boast a son in holy orders. And here, also, the young men have a tendency to emigrate. It is certainly not poverty that drives them to the great cities or across the seas, for many peasant families, I was told, have a fortune of at least forty thousand francs. The lads go forth pricked with the spirit of adventure and the desire to rise in life, and leave their homespun elders grumbling and wondering over the event. Once, at a village called Laussonne, I met one of these disappointed parents: a drake who had fathered a wild swan and seen it take wing and disappear. The wild swan in question was now an apothecary in Brazil. He had flown by way of Bordeaux, and first landed in America, bareheaded and barefoot, and with a single halfpenny in his pocket. And now he was an apothecary! Such a wonderful thing is an adventurous life! I thought he might as well have stayed at home; but you never can tell wherein a man's life consists, nor in what he sets his pleasure: one to drink, another to marry, a third to write scurrilous articles and be repeatedly caned in public, and now this fourth, perhaps, to be an apothecary in Brazil. As for his old father, he could conceive no reason for the lad's behaviour. 'I had always bread for him,' he said; 'he ran away to annoy me. He loved to annoy me. He had no gratitude.' But at heart he was swelling with pride over his travelled offspring, and he produced a letter out of his pocket, where, as he said, it was rotting, a mere lump of paper rags, and waved it gloriously in the air. 'This comes from America,' he cried, 'six thousand leagues away!' And the wine-shop audience looked upon it with a certain thrill.

I soon became a popular figure, and was known for miles in the country. *Où'st-ce que vous allez?* was changed for me into *Quoi, vous rentrez au Monastier ce soir?* and in the town itself every urchin seemed to know my name, although no living creature could pronounce it. There was one particular group of lace-makers who brought out a chair for me whenever I went by, and detained me from my walk to gossip. They were filled with curiosity about England, its language, its religion, the dress of the women, and were never weary of seeing the Queen's head on English postage-stamps, or seeking for French words in English journals. The language, in particular, filled them with surprise.

'Do they speak *patois*[6] in England?' I was once asked; and when I told them not, 'Ah, then, French?' said they.

'No, no,' I said, 'not French.'

'Then,' they concluded, 'they speak *patois*.'

You must obviously either speak French or *patios*. Talk of the force of logic – here it was in all its weakness. I gave up the point, but proceeding to give illustrations of my native jargon, I was met with a new mortification. Of all *patios* they declared that mine was the most preposterous and the most jocose in sound. At each new word there was a new explosion of laughter, and some of the younger ones were glad to rise from their chairs and stamp about the street in ecstasy; and I looked on upon their mirth in a faint and slightly disagreeable bewilderment. 'Bread', which sounds a commonplace, plain-sailing monosyllable in England, was the word that most delighted these good ladies of Monastier; it seemed to them frolicsome and racy, like a page of Pickwick; and they all got it carefully by heart, as a stand-by, I presume, for winter evenings. I have tried it since then with every sort of accent and inflection, but I seem to lack the sense of humour.

They were of all ages: children at their first web of lace, a stripling girl with a bashful but encouraging play of eyes, solid married women and grandmothers, some on the top of their age and some falling towards decrepitude. One and all were pleasant and natural, ready to laugh and ready with a certain quiet solemnity when that was called for by the subject of our talk. Life, since the fall in wages, had begun to appear to them with a more serious air. The stripling girl would sometimes laugh at me in a provocative and not unadmiring manner, if I judge aright; and one of the grandmothers, who was my great friend of the party, gave me many a sharp word of judgement on my sketches, my heresy or even my arguments, and gave them with a wry mouth and a humorous twinkle in her eye that were eminently Scottish. But the rest used me with a certain reverence, as something come from afar and not entirely human. Nothing would put them at their ease but the irresistible gaiety of my native tongue. Between the old lady and myself I think there was a real attachment. She was never weary of sitting to me for her portrait, in her best cap and brigand hat, and with all her wrinkles tidily composed, and though she never failed to repudiate the result, she would always insist upon another trial. It was as good as a play to see her sitting in judgement over the last. 'No, no,' she would say, 'that is not it. I am old, to be sure, but I am better-looking than that. We must try again.' When I was about to leave she bade me goodbye for this life in a somewhat touching manner. We should not meet again, she said; it was a long farewell, and she was sorry. But life is so full of crooks, old lady, that who knows? I have said goodbye to people for greater distances and times, and, please God, I mean to see them yet again.

One thing was notable about these women, from the youngest to the oldest, and with hardly an exception. In spite of their piety, they could twang off an oath with Sir Toby Belch[7] in person. There was nothing so high or so low, in heaven or earth or in the human body, but a woman of this neighbourhood would whip out the name of it, fair and square, by way of conversational adornment. My landlady, who was pretty and young, dressed like a lady and avoided *patois* like a weakness, commonly addressed her child in the language of a drunken bully. And of all the swearers that I ever heard, commend me to an old lady in Gondet, a village of the Loire. I was making a sketch, and her curse was not yet ended when I had finished it and took my departure. It is true she had a right to be angry; for here was her son, a hulking fellow, visibly the worse for drink before the day was well begun. But it was strange to hear her unwearying flow of oaths and obscenities, endless like a river, and now and then rising to a passionate shrillness, in the clear and silent air of the morning. In city slums, the thing might have passed unnoticed; but in a country valley, and from a plain and honest countrywoman, this beastliness of speech surprised the ear.

The Conductor, as he is called, of Roads and Bridges was my principal companion. He was generally intelligent, and could have spoken more or less falsetto on any of the trite topics; but it was his speciality to have a generous taste in eating. This was what was most indigenous in the man; it was here he was an artist; and I found in his company what I had long suspected, that enthusiasm and special knowledge are the great social qualities, and what they are about, whether white sauce or Shakespeare's plays, an altogether secondary question.

I used to accompany the Conductor on his professional rounds, and grew to believe myself an expert in the business. I thought I could make an entry in a stone-breaker's time-book, or order manure off the wayside with any living engineer in France. Gondet was one of the places we visited together; and Laussonne, where I met the apothecary's father, was another. There, at Laussonne, George Sand spent a day while she was gathering material for the *Marquis de Villemer*;[8] and I have spoken with an old man, who was then a child running about the inn kitchen, and who still remembers her with a sort of reverence. It appears that he spoke French imperfectly; for this reason George Sand chose him for companion, and whenever he let slip a broad and picturesque phrase in *patois*, she would make him repeat it again and again till it was graven in her memory. The word for a frog particularly pleased her fancy; and it would be curious to know if she afterwards employed it in her works. The peasants, who knew nothing of letters and had never so much as heard of local colour, could not explain her chattering with this backward child; and to them she seemed a very homely lady and far from beautiful: the most famous man-killer of the age appealed so little to Velaisian swineherds!

On my first engineering excursion, which lay up by Crouzials towards Mount Mézenc and the borders of Ardèche, I began an improving acquaintance with the foreman road-mender. He was in great glee at having me with him, passed me off among his subalterns as the supervising engineer, and insisted on what he called 'the gallantry' of paying for my breakfast in a roadside wine-shop. On the whole, he was a man of great weather-wisdom, some spirits, and a social temper. But I am afraid he was superstitious. When he was nine years old, he had seen one night a company of *bourgeois et dames qui faisaient la manège avec des chaises*, and concluded that he was in the presence of a witches' Sabbath. I suppose, but venture with timidity on the suggestion, that this may have been a romantic and nocturnal picnic party. Again, coming from Pradelles with his brother, they saw a great empty cart drawn by six enormous horses before them on the road. The driver cried aloud and filled the mountains with the cracking of his whip. He never seemed to go faster than a walk, yet it was impossible to overtake him; and at length, at the corner of a hill, the whole equipage disappeared bodily into the night. At the time, people said it was the devil *qui s'amusait à faire ça*.[9]

I suggested there was nothing more likely, as he must have some amusement.

The foreman said it was odd, but there was less of that sort of thing than formerly. '*C'est difficile*,' he added, '*à expliquer*.'

When we were well up on the moors and the Conductor was trying some road-metal with the gauge – 'Hark!' said the foreman, 'do you hear nothing?'

We listened, and the wind, which was blowing chilly out of the east, brought a faint, tangled jangling to our ears.

'It is the flocks of Vivarais,' said he.

For every summer, the flocks out of all Ardèche[10] are brought up to pasture on these grassy plateaux.

Here and there a little private flock was being tended by a girl, one spinning with a distaff, another seated on a wall and intently making lace. This last, when we addressed her, leaped up in a panic and put out her arms, like a person swimming, to keep us at a distance, and it was some seconds before we could persuade her of the honesty of our intentions.

The Conductor told me of another herdswoman from whom he had once asked his road while he was yet new to the country, and who fled from him, driving her beasts before her, until he had given up the information in despair. A tale of old lawlessness may yet be read in these uncouth timidities.

The winter in these uplands is a dangerous and melancholy time. Houses are snowed up, and wayfarers lost in a flurry within hail of their own fireside. No man ventures abroad without meat and a bottle of wine, which he replenishes at every wine-shop; and even thus equipped he takes the road with terror. All day the family sits about the fire in a foul and airless hovel, and equally without work or diversion. The father may carve a rude piece of furniture, but that is all that will be done until the spring sets in again, and along with it the labours of the field. It is not for nothing that you find a clock in the meanest of these mountain habitations. A clock and an almanac, you would fancy, were indispensable in such a life . . .

Velay

Many are the mighty things, and nought is more mighty than man. . . . He masters by his devices the tenant of the fields.

Sophocles

Who hath loosed the bands of the wild ass?   *Job* [11]

The Donkey, the Pack and the Pack Saddle

In a little place called Le Monastier, in a pleasant highland valley fifteen miles from Le Puy, I spent about a month of fine days. Monastier is notable for the making of lace, for drunkenness, for freedom of language, and for unparalleled political dissension. There are adherents of each of the four French parties – Legitimists, Orleanists, Imperialists and Republicans – in this little mountain-town; and they all hate, loathe, decry and calumniate each other. Except for business purposes, or to give each other the lie in a tavern brawl, they have laid aside even the civility of speech. 'Tis a mere mountain Poland. In the midst of this Babylon I found myself a rallying-point; everyone was anxious to be kind and helpful to the stranger. This was not merely from the natural hospitality of mountain people, nor even from the surprise with which I was regarded as a man living of his own free will in Le Monastier, when he might just as well have lived anywhere else in this big world; it arose a good deal from my projected excursion southward through the Cévennes. A traveller of my sort was a thing hitherto unheard of in that district. I was looked upon with contempt, like a man who should project a journey to the moon, but yet with a respectful interest, like one setting forth for the inclement Pole. All were ready to help in my preparations; a crowd of sympathisers supported me at the critical moment of a bargain; not a step was taken but was heralded by glasses round and celebrated by a dinner or a breakfast.

It was already hard upon October before I was ready to set forth, and at the high altitudes over which my road lay there was no Indian summer to be looked for. I was determined, if not to camp out, at least to have the means of camping out in my possession; for there is nothing more harassing to an easy mind than the necessity of reaching shelter by dusk, and the hospitality of a village inn is not always to be reckoned sure by those who trudge on foot. A tent, above all for a solitary traveller, is troublesome to pitch, and troublesome to strike again; and even on the march it forms a conspicuous feature in your baggage. A sleeping-sack, on the other hand, is always ready – you have only to get into it; it serves a double purpose – a bed by night, a portmanteau by day; and it does not advertise your intention of camping out to every curious passer-by. This is a huge point. If a camp is not secret, it is but a troubled resting-place; you become a public character; the convivial rustic visits your bedside after an early supper; and you must sleep with one eye open, and be up before the day. I decided on a sleeping-sack; and after repeated visits to Le Puy, and a deal of high living for myself and my advisers, a sleeping-sack was designed, constructed and triumphantly brought home.

This child of my invention was nearly six feet square, exclusive of two triangular flaps to serve as a pillow by night and as the top and bottom of the sack by day. I call it 'the sack', but it was never a sack by more than courtesy: only a sort of long roll or sausage, green waterproof cart-cloth without and blue sheep's fur within. It was commodious as a valise, warm and dry for a bed. There was luxurious turning room for one; and at a pinch the thing might serve for two. I could bury myself in it up to the neck; for my head I trusted to a fur cap, with a hood to fold down over my ears and a band to pass under my nose like a respirator; and in case of heavy rain I proposed to make myself a little tent, or tentlet, with my waterproof coat, three stones, and a bent branch.

It will readily be conceived that I could not carry this huge package on my own, merely human, shoulders. It remained to choose a beast of burden. Now, a horse is a fine lady among animals, flighty, timid, delicate in eating, of tender health; he is too valuable and too restive to be left alone, so that you are chained to your brute as to a fellow galley-slave; a dangerous road puts him out of his wits; in short, he's an uncertain and exacting ally, and adds thirty-fold to the troubles of the voyager. What I required was something cheap and small and hardy, and of a stolid and peaceful temper; and all these requisites pointed to a donkey.

There dwelt an old man in Monastier, of rather unsound intellect according to some, much followed by street-boys, and known to fame as Father Adam. Father Adam had a cart, and to draw the cart a diminutive she-ass, not much bigger than a dog, the colour of a mouse, with a kindly eye and a determined under-jaw. There was something neat and high-bred, a quakerish elegance, about the rogue that hit my fancy on the spot. Our first interview was in Monastier marketplace. To prove her good temper, one child after another was set upon her back to ride, and one after another went head over heels into the air; until a want of confidence began to reign in youthful bosoms, and the experiment was discontinued from a dearth of subjects. I was already backed by a deputation of my friends; but as if this were not enough, all the buyers and sellers came round and helped me in the bargain; and the ass and I and Father Adam were the centre of a hubbub for near half an hour. At length she passed into my service for the consideration of sixty-five francs and a glass of brandy. The sack had already cost eighty francs and two glasses of beer; so that Modestine, as I instantly baptised her, was upon all accounts the cheaper article. Indeed, that was as it should be; for she was only an appurtenance of my mattress, or self-acting bedstead on four castors.

I had a last interview with Father Adam in a billiard-room at the witching hour of dawn, when I administered the brandy. He professed himself greatly touched by the separation, and declared he had often bought white bread for the donkey when he had been content with black bread for himself; but this, according to the best authorities, must have been a flight of fancy. He had a name in the village for brutally misusing the ass; yet it is certain that he shed a tear, and the tear made a clean mark down one cheek.

By the advice of a fallacious local saddler, a leather pad was made for me with rings to fasten on my bundle; and I thoughtfully completed my kit and arranged my toilette. By way of armoury and utensils, I took a revolver, a little spirit-lamp and pan, a lantern and some halfpenny candles, a jack-knife and a large leather flask. The main cargo consisted of two entire changes of warm clothing – besides my travelling wear of country velveteen, pilot-coat, and knitted spencer – some books, and my railway-rug, which, being also in the form of a bag, made me a double castle for cold nights. The permanent larder was represented by cakes of chocolate and tins of Bologna sausage. All this, except what I carried about my person, was easily stowed into the sheepskin bag; and by good fortune I threw in my empty knapsack, rather for convenience of carriage than from any thought that I should want it on my journey. For more immediate needs I took a leg of cold mutton, a bottle of Beaujolais, an empty bottle to carry milk, an egg-beater, and a considerable quantity of black bread and white, like Father Adam, for myself and donkey, only in my scheme of things the destinations were reversed.

Monastrians, of all shades of thought in politics, had agreed in threatening me with many ludicrous misadventures, and with sudden death in many surprising forms. Cold, wolves, robbers, above all the nocturnal practical joker, were daily and eloquently forced on my attention. Yet in these vaticinations, the true, patent danger was left out. Like Christian,[12] it was from my pack I suffered by the way. Before telling my own mishaps, let me in two words relate the lesson of my experience. If the pack is well strapped at the ends, and hung at full length – not doubled, for your life – across the pack-saddle, the traveller is safe. The saddle will certainly not fit, such is the imperfection of our transitory life; it will assuredly topple and tend to over set; but there are stones on every roadside, and a man soon learns the art of correcting any tendency to overbalance with a well-adjusted stone.

On the day of my departure I was up a little after five; by six, we began to load the donkey; and ten minutes after, my hopes were in the dust. The pad would not stay on Modestine's back for half a moment. I returned it to its maker, with whom I had so contumelious a passage that the street outside was crowded from wall to wall with gossips looking on and listening. The pad changed hands with much vivacity; perhaps it would be more descriptive to say that we threw it at each other's heads; and, at any rate, we were very warm and unfriendly, and spoke with a deal of freedom.

I had a common donkey pack-saddle – a *barde*, as they call it – fitted upon Modestine; and once more loaded her with my effects. The doubled sack, my pilot-coat (for it was warm, and I was to walk in my waistcoat), a great bar of black bread, and an open basket containing the white bread, the mutton, and the bottles, were all corded together in a very elaborate system of knots, and I looked on the result with fatuous content. In such a monstrous deck-cargo, all poised above the donkey's shoulders, with nothing below to balance, on a brand-new pack-saddle that had not yet been worn to fit the animal, and fastened with brand-new girths that might be expected to stretch and slacken by the way, even a very careless traveller should have seen disaster brewing. That elaborate system of knots, again, was the work of too many sympathisers to be very artfully designed. It is true they tightened the cords with a will; as many as three at a time would have a foot against Modestine's quarters, and be hauling with clenched teeth; but I learned afterwards that one thoughtful person, without any exercise of force, can make a more solid job than half a dozen heated and enthusiastic grooms. I was then but a novice; even after the misadventure of the pad nothing could disturb my security, and I went forth from the stable door as an ox goeth to the slaughter.[13]

The Green Donkey-Driver

The bell of Monastier was just striking nine as I got quit of these preliminary troubles and descended the hill through the common. As long as I was within sight of the windows, a secret shame and the fear of some laughable defeat withheld me from tampering with Modestine. She tripped along upon her four small hoofs with a sober daintiness of gait; from time to time she shook her ears or her tail; and she looked so small under the bundle that my mind misgave me. We got across the ford without difficulty – there was no doubt about the matter, she was docility itself – and once on the other bank, where the road begins to mount through pine-woods, I took in my right hand the unhallowed staff, and with a quaking spirit applied it to the donkey. Modestine brisked up her pace for perhaps three steps, and then relapsed into her former minuet. Another application had the same effect, and so with the third. I am worthy the name of an Englishman, and it goes against my conscience to lay my hand rudely on a female. I desisted, and looked her all over from head to foot; the poor brute's knees were trembling and her breathing was distressed; it was plain that she could go no faster on a hill. God forbid, thought I, that I should brutalise this innocent creature; let her go at her own pace, and let me patiently follow.

What that pace was, there is no word mean enough to describe; it was something as much slower than a walk as a walk is slower than a run; it kept me hanging on each foot for an incredible length of time; in five minutes it exhausted the spirit and set up a fever in all the muscles of the leg. And yet I had to keep close at hand and measure my advance exactly upon hers; for if I dropped a few yards into the rear, or went on a few yards ahead, Modestine came instantly to a halt and began to browse. The thought that this was to last from here to Alais nearly broke my heart. Of all conceivable journeys, this promised to be the most tedious. I tried to tell myself it was a lovely day; I tried to charm my foreboding spirit with tobacco; but I had a vision ever present to me of the long, long roads, up hill and down dale, and a pair of figures ever infinitesimally moving, foot by foot, a yard to the minute, and, like things enchanted in a nightmare, approaching no nearer to the goal.

In the meantime there came up behind us a tall peasant, perhaps forty years of age, of an ironical snuffy countenance, and arrayed in the green tail-coat of the country. He overtook us hand over hand, and stopped to consider our pitiful advance.

'Your donkey,' says he, 'is very old?'

I told him, I believed not.

Then, he supposed, we had come far.

I told him, we had but newly left Monastier.

'*Et vous marchez comme ça!*'[14] cried he; and, throwing back his head, he laughed long and heartily. I watched him, half prepared to feel offended, until he had satisfied his mirth; and then, 'You must have no pity on these animals,' said he; and, plucking a switch out of a thicket, he began to lace Modestine about the stern-works, uttering a cry. The rogue pricked up her ears and broke into a good round pace, which she kept up without flagging, and without exhibiting the least symptom of distress, as long as the peasant kept beside us. Her former panting and shaking had been, I regret to say, a piece of comedy.

My *deus ex machina*, before he left me, supplied some excellent, if inhumane, advice; presented me with the switch, which he declared she would feel more tenderly than my cane; and finally taught me the true cry or masonic word of donkey-drivers, 'Proot!' All the time, he regarded me with a comical, incredulous air, which was embarrassing to confront; and smiled over my donkey-driving, as I might have smiled over his orthography, or his green tail-coat. But it was not my turn for the moment.

I was proud of my new lore, and thought I had learned the art to perfection. And certainly Modestine did wonders for the rest of the forenoon, and I had a breathing space to look about me. It was Sabbath; the mountain-fields were all vacant in the sunshine; and as we came down through St Martin de Frugères, the church was crowded to the door, there were people kneeling without upon the steps, and the sound of the priest's chanting came forth out of the dim interior. It gave me a home feeling on the spot; for I am a countryman of the Sabbath, so to speak, and all Sabbath observances, like a Scottish accent, strike in me mixed feelings, grateful and the reverse. It is only a traveller, hurrying by like a person from another planet, who can rightly enjoy the peace and beauty of the great ascetic feast. The sight of the resting country does his spirit good.

There is something better than music in the wide unusual silence; and it disposes him to amiable thoughts, like the sound of a little river or the warmth of sunlight.

In this pleasant humour I came down the hill to where Goudet stands in a green end of a valley, with Château Beaufort opposite upon a rocky steep, and the stream, as clear as crystal, lying in a deep pool between them. Above and below, you may hear it wimpling over the stones, an amiable stripling of a river, which it seems absurd to call the Loire.[15] On all sides, Goudet is shut in by mountains; rocky footpaths, practicable at best for donkeys, join it to the outer world of France; and the men and women drink and swear, in their green corner, or look up at the snow-clad peaks in winter from the threshold of their homes, in an isolation, you would think, like that of Homer's Cyclops. But it is not so; the postman reaches Goudet with the letter-bag; the aspiring youth of Goudet are within a day's walk of the railway at Le Puy; and here in the inn you may find an engraved portrait of the host's nephew, Régis Senac, 'Professor of Fencing and Champion of the two Americas', a distinction gained by him, along with the sum of five hundred dollars, at Tammany Hall, New York, on the 10th April 1876.

I hurried over my midday meal, and was early forth again. But, alas, as we climbed the interminable hill upon the other side, 'Proot!' seemed to have lost its virtue. I prooted like a lion, I prooted mellifluously like a sucking-dove; but Modestine would be neither softened nor intimidated. She held doggedly to her pace; nothing but a blow would move her, and that only for a second. I must follow at her heels, incessantly belabouring. A moment's pause in this ignoble toil, and she relapsed into her own private gait. I think I never heard of anyone in as mean a situation. I must reach the lake of Bouchet, where I meant to camp, before sundown, and, to have even a hope of this, I must instantly maltreat this uncomplaining animal. The sound of my own blows sickened me. Once, when I looked at her, she had a faint resemblance to a lady of my acquaintance who formerly loaded me with kindness; and this increased my horror of my cruelty.

To make matters worse, we encountered another donkey, ranging at will upon the roadside; and this other donkey chanced to be a gentleman. He and Modestine met nickering for joy, and I had to separate the pair and beat down their young romance with a renewed and feverish bastinado. If the other donkey had had the heart of a male under his hide, he would have fallen upon me tooth and hoof;

and this was a kind of consolation – he was plainly unworthy of Modestine's affection. But the incident saddened me, as did everything that spoke of my donkey's sex.

It was blazing hot up the valley, windless, with vehement sun upon my shoulders; and I had to labour so consistently with my stick that the sweat ran into my eyes. Every five minutes, too, the pack, the basket, and the pilot-coat would take an ugly slew to one side or the other; and I had to stop Modestine, just when I had got her to a tolerable pace of about two miles an hour, to tug, push, shoulder, and readjust the load. And at last, in the village of Ussel, saddle and all, the whole hypothec turned round and grovelled in the dust below the donkey's belly. She, none better pleased, incontinently drew up and seemed to smile; and a party of one man, two women, and two children came up, and, standing round me in a half-circle, encouraged her by their example.

I had the devil's own trouble to get the thing righted; and the instant I had done so, without hesitation, it toppled and fell down upon the other side. Judge if I was hot! And yet not a hand was offered to assist me. The man, indeed, told me I ought to have a package of a different shape. I suggested, if he knew nothing better to the point in my predicament, he might hold his tongue. And the good-natured dog agreed with me smilingly. It was the most despicable fix. I must plainly content myself with the pack for Modestine, and take the following items for my own share of the portage: a cane, a quart-flask, a pilot-jacket heavily weighted in the pockets, two pounds of black bread, and an open basket full of meats and bottles. I believe I may say I am not devoid of greatness of soul, for I did not recoil from this infamous burden. I disposed it, heaven knows how, so as to be mildly portable, and then proceeded to steer Modestine through the village. She tried, as was indeed her invariable habit, to enter every house and every courtyard in the whole length; and, encumbered as I was, without a hand to help myself, no words can render an idea of my difficulties. A priest, with six or seven others, was examining a church in process of repair, and he and his acolytes laughed loudly as they saw my plight.

I remembered having laughed myself when I had seen good men struggling with adversity in the person of a jackass, and the recollection filled me with penitence. That was in my old light days, before this trouble came upon me. God knows at least that I shall never laugh again, thought I. But oh, what a cruel thing is a farce to those engaged in it!

A little out of the village, Modestine, filled with the demon, set her heart upon a by-road, and positively refused to leave it. I dropped all my bundles, and, I am ashamed to say, struck the poor sinner twice across the face. It was pitiful to see her lift her head with shut eyes, as if waiting for another blow. I came very near crying; but I did a wiser thing than that, and sat squarely down by the roadside to consider my situation under the cheerful influence of tobacco and a nip of brandy. Modestine, in the meanwhile, munched some black bread with a contrite hypocritical air. It was plain that I must make a sacrifice to the gods of shipwreck. I threw away the empty bottle destined to carry milk; I threw away my own white bread, and, disdaining to act by general average, kept the black bread for Modestine; lastly, I threw away the cold leg of mutton and the egg-whisk, although this last was dear to my heart. Thus I found room for everything in the basket, and even stowed the boating-coat on the top. By means of an end of cord I slung it under one arm; and although the cord cut my shoulder, and the jacket hung almost to the ground, it was with a heart greatly lightened that I set forth again.

I had now an arm free to thrash Modestine, and cruelly I chastised her. If I were to reach the lakeside before dark, she must bestir her little shanks to some tune. Already the sun had gone down into a windy-looking mist; and although there were still a few streaks of gold far off to the east on the hills and the black fir-woods, all was cold and grey about our onward path. An infinity of little country by-roads led hither and thither among the fields. It was the most pointless labyrinth. I could see my destination overhead, or rather the peak that dominates it; but choose as I pleased, the roads always ended by turning away from it, and sneaking back towards the valley, or northward along the margin of the hills. The failing light, the waning colour, the naked, unhomely, stony country through which I was travelling, threw me into some despondency. I promise you, the stick was not idle; I think every decent step that Modestine took must have cost me at least two emphatic blows. There was not another sound in the neighbourhood but that of my unwearying bastinado.

Suddenly, in the midst of my toils, the load once more bit the dust, and, as by enchantment, all the cords were simultaneously loosened, and the road scattered with my dear possessions. The packing was to begin again from the beginning; and as I had to invent a new and better system, I do not doubt but I lost half an hour. It began to be dusk in earnest as I reached a wilderness of turf and stones. It had the air of being a road which should lead everywhere at the same time; and I was falling into something not unlike despair when I saw two figures stalking towards me over the stones. They walked one behind the other like tramps, but their pace was remarkable. The son led the way, a tall, ill-made, sombre, Scottish-looking man; the mother followed, all in her Sunday's best, with an elegantly embroidered ribbon to her cap, and a new felt hat atop, and proffering, as she strode along with kilted petticoats, a string of obscene and blasphemous oaths.

I hailed the son, and asked him my direction. He pointed loosely west and north-west, muttered an inaudible comment, and, without slackening his pace for an instant, stalked on, as he was going, right athwart my path. The mother followed without so much as raising her head. I shouted and shouted after them, but they continued to scale the hillside, and turned a deaf ear to my outcries. At last, leaving Modestine by herself, I was constrained to run after them, hailing the while. They stopped as I drew near, the mother still cursing; and I could see she was a handsome, motherly, respectable-looking woman. The son once more answered me roughly and inaudibly, and was for setting out again. But this time I simply collared the mother, who was nearest me, and, apologising for my violence, declared that I could not let them go until they had put me on my road. They were neither of them offended – rather mollified than otherwise; told me I had only to follow them; and then the mother asked me what I wanted by the lake at such an hour. I replied, in the Scottish manner, by enquiring if she had far to go herself. She told me, with another oath, that she had an hour and a half's road before her. And then, without salutation, the pair strode forward again up the hillside in the gathering dusk.

I returned for Modestine, pushed her briskly forward, and, after a sharp ascent of twenty minutes, reached the edge of a plateau. The view, looking back on my day's journey, was both wild and sad. Mount Mézenc and the peaks beyond St Julien stood out in trenchant gloom against a cold glitter in the east; and the intervening field of hills had fallen together into one broad wash of shadow, except here and there the outline of a wooded sugar-loaf in black, here and there a white irregular patch to represent a cultivated farm, and here and there a blot where the Loire, the Gazeille, or the Laussonne wandered in a gorge.

Soon we were on a high-road, and surprise seized on my mind as I

beheld a village of some magnitude close at hand; for I had been told
that the neighbourhood of the lake was uninhabited except by trout.
The road smoked in the twilight with children driving home cattle
from the fields; and a pair of mounted stride-legged women, hat and
cap and all, dashed past me at a hammering trot from the canton
where they had been to church and market. I asked one of the children
where I was. At Bouchet St Nicolas, he told me. Thither, about a
mile south of my destination, and on the other side of a respectable
summit, had these confused roads and treacherous peasantry conducted me. My shoulder was cut, so that it hurt sharply; my arm
ached like toothache from perpetual beating; I gave up the lake and
my design to camp, and asked for the auberge.

I Have a Goad

The auberge of Bouchet St Nicolas was among the least pretentious
I have ever visited; but I saw many more of the like upon my journey.
Indeed, it was typical of these French highlands. Imagine a cottage
of two storeys, with a bench before the door; the stable and kitchen
in a suite, so that Modestine and I could hear each other dining;
furniture of the plainest, earthen floors, a single bedchamber for
travellers, and that without any convenience but beds. In the kitchen
cooking and eating go forward side by side, and the family sleep at
night. Anyone who has a fancy to wash must do so in public at the
common table. The food is sometimes spare; hard fish and omelette
have been my portion more than once; the wine is of the smallest,
the brandy abominable to man; and the visit of a fat sow, grouting
under the table and rubbing against your legs, is no impossible
accompaniment to dinner.

But the people of the inn, in nine cases out of ten, show themselves
friendly and considerate. As soon as you cross the doors you cease to
be a stranger; and although these peasantry are rude and forbidding
on the highway, they show a tincture of kind breeding when you
share their hearth. At Bouchet, for instance, I uncorked my bottle of
Beaujolais, and asked the host to join me. He would take but little.

'I am an amateur of such wine, do you see?' he said, 'and I am
capable of leaving you not enough.'

In these hedge-inns[16] the traveller is expected to eat with his own
knife; unless he ask, no other will be supplied: with a glass, a whang
of bread, and an iron fork, the table is completely laid. My knife was
cordially admired by the landlord of Bouchet, and the spring filled
him with wonder.

'I should never have guessed that,' he said. 'I would bet,' he added, weighing it in his hand, 'that this cost you not less than five francs.'

When I told him it had cost me twenty, his jaw dropped.

He was a mild, handsome, sensible, friendly old man, astonishingly ignorant. His wife, who was not so pleasant in her manners, knew how to read, although I do not suppose she ever did so. She had a share of brains and spoke with a cutting emphasis, like one who ruled the roost.

'My man knows nothing,' she said, with an angry nod; 'he is like the beasts.'

And the old gentleman signified acquiescence with his head. There was no contempt on her part, and no shame on his; the facts were accepted loyally, and no more about the matter.

I was tightly cross-examined about my journey; and the lady understood in a moment, and sketched out what I should put into my book when I got home. 'Whether people harvest or not in such or such a place; if there were forests; studies of manners; what, for example, I and the master of the house say to you; the beauties of nature, and all that.' And she interrogated me with a look.

'It is just that,' said I.

'You see,' she added to her husband, 'I understood that.'

They were both much interested by the story of my misadventures.

'In the morning,' said the husband, 'I will make you something better than your cane. Such a beast as that feels nothing; it is in the proverb – *dur comme un âne*; you might beat her insensible with a cudgel, and yet you would arrive nowhere.'

Something better! I little knew what he was offering.

The sleeping-room was furnished with two beds. I had one; and I will own I was a little abashed to find a young man and his wife and child in the act of mounting into the other. This was my first experience of the sort; and if I am always to feel equally silly and extraneous, I pray God it be my last as well. I kept my eyes to myself, and know nothing of the woman except that she had beautiful arms, and seemed no whit embarrassed by my appearance. As a matter of fact, the situation was more trying to me than to the pair. A pair keep each other in countenance; it is the single gentleman who has to blush. But I could not help attributing my sentiments to the husband, and sought to conciliate his tolerance with a cup of brandy from my flask. He told me that he was a cooper of Alais travelling to St Etienne in search of work, and that in his spare moments he followed the fatal calling of a maker of matches. Me he readily enough divined to be a brandy merchant.

I was up first in the morning (Monday, September 23rd), and hastened my toilette guiltily, so as to leave a clear field for madam, the cooper's wife. I drank a bowl of milk, and set off to explore the neighbourhood of Bouchet. It was perishing cold, a grey, windy, wintry morning; misty clouds flew fast and low; the wind piped over the naked platform; and the only speck of colour was away behind Mount Mézenc and the eastern hills, where the sky still wore the orange of the dawn.

It was five in the morning, and four thousand feet above the sea; and I had to bury my hands in my pockets and trot. People were trooping out to the labours of the field by twos and threes, and all turned round to stare upon the stranger. I had seen them coming back last night, I saw them going afield again; and there was the life of Bouchet in a nutshell.

When I came back to the inn for a bit of breakfast, the landlady was in the kitchen combing out her daughter's hair; and I made her my compliments upon its beauty.

'Oh no,' said the mother; 'it is not so beautiful as it ought to be. Look, it is too fine.'

Thus does a wise peasantry console itself under adverse physical circumstances, and, by a startling democratic process, the defects of the majority decide the type of beauty.

'And where,' said I, 'is monsieur?'

'The master of the house is upstairs,' she answered, 'making you a goad.'

Blessed be the man who invented goads! Blessed the innkeeper of Bouchet St Nicolas, who introduced me to their use! This plain wand, with an eighth of an inch of pin, was indeed a sceptre when he put it in my hands. Thenceforward Modestine was my slave. A prick, and she passed the most inviting stable door. A prick, and she broke forth into a gallant little trotlet that devoured the miles. It was not a remarkable speed, when all was said; and we took four hours to cover ten miles at the best of it. But what a heavenly change since yesterday! No more wielding of the ugly cudgel; no more flailing with an aching arm; no more broadsword exercise, but a discreet and gentlemanly fence. And what if now and then a drop of blood should appear on Modestine's mouse-coloured wedge-like rump? I should have preferred it otherwise, indeed; but yesterday's exploits had purged my heart of all humanity. The perverse little devil, since she would not be taken with kindness, must even go with pricking.

It was bleak and bitter cold, and, except a cavalcade of stride-legged ladies and a pair of post-runners, the road was dead solitary all the way to Pradelles. I scarce remember an incident but one. A handsome foal with a bell about his neck came charging up to us upon a stretch of common, sniffed the air martially as one about to do great deeds, and suddenly thinking otherwise in his green young heart, put about and galloped off as he had come, the bell tinkling in the wind. For a long while afterwards I saw his noble attitude as he drew up, and heard the note of his bell; and when I struck the high-road, the song of the telegraph-wires seemed to continue the same music.

Pradelles stands on a hillside, high above the Allier,[17] surrounded by rich meadows. They were cutting aftermath on all sides, which gave the neighbourhood, this gusty autumn morning, an untimely smell of hay. On the opposite bank of the Allier the land kept mounting for miles to the horizon: a tanned and sallow autumn landscape, with black blots of fir-wood and white roads wandering through the hills. Over all this the clouds shed a uniform and purplish shadow, sad and somewhat menacing, exaggerating height and distance, and throwing into still higher relief the twisted ribbons of the highway. It was a cheerless prospect, but one stimulating to a traveller. For I was now upon the limit of Velay, and all that I beheld lay in another county – wild Gévaudan,[18] mountainous, uncultivated, and but recently disforested from terror of the wolves.

Wolves, alas, like bandits, seem to flee the traveller's advance; and you may trudge through all our comfortable Europe, and not meet with an adventure worth the name. But here, if anywhere, a man was on the frontiers of hope. For this was the land of the ever-memorable 'Beast', the Napoleon Bonaparte of wolves. What a career was his! He lived ten months at free quarters in Gévaudan and Vivarais; he ate women and children and 'shepherdesses celebrated for their beauty'; he pursued armed horsemen; he had been seen at broad noonday chasing a post-chaise and outrider along the king's high-road, chaise and outrider fleeing before him at the gallop. He was placarded like a political offender, and ten thousand francs were offered for his head. And yet, when he was shot and sent to Versailles, behold! a common wolf, and even small for that. 'Though I could reach from pole to pole,' sang Alexander Pope; the Little Corporal shook Europe; and if all wolves had been as this wolf, they would have changed the history of man. M. Élie Berthet has made him the hero of a novel, which I have read, and do not wish to read again.

I hurried over my lunch, and was proof against the landlady's desire that I should visit our Lady of Pradelles, 'who performed many miracles, although she was of wood'; and before three-quarters of an hour I was goading Modestine down the steep descent that leads to Langogne on the Allier. On both sides of the road, in big dusty fields, farmers were preparing for next spring. Every fifty yards a yoke of great-necked stolid oxen were patiently haling at the plough. I saw one of these mild formidable servants of the glebe, who took a sudden interest in Modestine and me. The furrow down which he was journeying lay at an angle to the road, and his head was solidly fixed to the yoke like those of caryatides below a ponderous cornice; but he screwed round his big honest eyes and followed us with a ruminating look, until his master bade him turn the plough and proceed to reascend the field. From all these furrowing ploughshares, from the feet of oxen, from a labourer here and there who was breaking the dry clods with a hoe, the wind carried away a thin dust like so much smoke. It was a fine, busy, breathing, rustic landscape; and as I continued to descend, the highlands of Gévaudan kept mounting in front of me against the sky.

I had crossed the Loire the day before; now I was to cross the Allier; so near are these two confluents in their youth. Just at the bridge of Langogne, as the long-promised rain was beginning to fall, a lassie of some seven or eight addressed me in the sacramental phrase, '*D'où'st-ce-que vous venez?*'[19] She did it with so high an air that she set me laughing; and this cut her to the quick. She was evidently one who reckoned on respect, and stood looking after me in silent dudgeon, as I crossed the bridge and entered the county of Gévaudan.

Upper Gévaudan

> The way also here was very wearisome through dirt and
> slabbiness; nor was there on all this ground so much as one
> inn or victualling-house wherein to refresh the feebler sort.
>
> *The Pilgrim's Progress*[20]

A Camp in the Dark

The next day (Tuesday, September 24th), it was two o'clock in the
afternoon before I got my journal[21] written up and my knapsack
repaired, for I was determined to carry my knapsack in the future
and have no more ado with baskets; and half an hour afterwards I set
out for Le Cheylard l'Évêque, a place on the borders of the forest of
Mercoire. A man, I was told, should walk there in an hour and a
half; and I thought it scarce too ambitious to suppose that a man
encumbered with a donkey might cover the same distance in four
hours.

All the way up the long hill from Langogne it rained and hailed
alternately; the wind kept freshening steadily, although slowly;
plentiful hurrying clouds – some dragging veils of straight rain-
shower, others massed and luminous as though promising snow –
careered out of the north and followed me along my way. I was soon
out of the cultivated basin of the Allier, and away from the ploughing
oxen, and suchlike sights of the country. Moor, heathery marsh,
tracts of rock and pines, woods of birch all jewelled with the autumn
yellow, here and there a few naked cottages and bleak fields – these
were the characters of the country. Hill and valley followed valley
and hill; the little green and stony cattle-tracks wandered in and out
of one another, split into three or four, died away in marshy hollows,
and began again sporadically on hillsides or at the borders of a
wood.

There was no direct road to Cheylard, and it was no easy affair to
make a passage in this uneven country and through this intermittent
labyrinth of tracks. It must have been about four when I struck
Sagnerousse, and went on my way rejoicing in a sure point of
departure. Two hours afterwards, the dusk rapidly falling, in a lull of
the wind, I issued from a fir wood where I had long been wandering,
and found, not the looked-for village, but another marish bottom

among rough-and-tumble hills. For some time past I had heard the ringing of cattle-bells ahead; and now, as I came out of the skirts of the wood, I saw near upon a dozen cows and perhaps as many more black figures, which I conjectured to be children, although the mist had almost unrecognisably exaggerated their forms. These were all silently following each other round and round in a circle, now taking hands, now breaking up with chains and reverences. A dance of children appeals to very innocent and lively thoughts; but, at nightfall on the marshes, the thing was eerie and fantastic to behold. Even I, who am well enough read in Herbert Spencer,[22] felt a sort of silence fall for an instant on my mind. The next, I was pricking Modestine forward, and guiding her like an unruly ship through the open. In a path, she went doggedly ahead of her own accord, as before a fair wind; but once on the turf or among heather, and the brute became demented. The tendency of lost travellers to go round in a circle was developed in her to the degree of passion, and it took all the steering I had in me to keep even a decently straight course through a single field.

While I was thus desperately tacking through the bog, children and cattle began to disperse, until only a pair of girls remained behind. From these I sought direction on my path. The peasantry in general were but little disposed to counsel a wayfarer. One old devil simply retired into his house, and barricaded the door on my approach; and I might beat and shout myself hoarse, he turned a deaf ear. Another, having given me a direction which, as I found afterwards, I had misunderstood, complacently watched me going wrong without adding a sign. He did not care a stalk of parsley if I wandered all night upon the hills! As for these two girls, they were a pair of impudent sly sluts, with not a thought but mischief. One put out her tongue at me, the other bade me follow the cows; and they both giggled and jogged each other's elbows. The Beast of Gévaudan ate about a hundred children of this district; I began to think of him with sympathy.

Leaving the girls, I pushed on through the bog, and got into another wood and upon a well-marked road. It grew darker and darker. Modestine, suddenly beginning to smell mischief, bettered the pace of her own accord, and from that time forward gave me no trouble. It was the first sign of intelligence I had occasion to remark in her. At the same time, the wind freshened into half a gale, and another heavy discharge of rain came flying up out of the north. At the other side of the wood I sighted some red windows in the dusk.

This was the hamlet of Fouzilhic; three houses on a hillside, near a wood of birches. Here I found a delightful old man, who came a little way with me in the rain to put me safely on the road for Cheylard. He would hear of no reward; but shook his hands above his head almost as if in menace, and refused volubly and shrilly, in unmitigated *patois*.

All seemed right at last. My thoughts began to turn upon dinner and a fireside, and my heart was agreeably softened in my bosom. Alas, and I was on the brink of new and greater miseries! Suddenly, at a single swoop, the night fell. I have been abroad in many a black night, but never in a blacker. A glimmer of rocks, a glimmer of the track where it was well beaten, a certain fleecy density, or night within night, for a tree – this was all that I could discriminate. The sky was simply darkness overhead; even the flying clouds pursued their way invisibly to human eyesight. I could not distinguish my hand at arm's-length from the track, nor my goad, at the same distance, from the meadows or the sky.

Soon the road that I was following split, after the fashion of the country, into three or four in a piece of rocky meadow. Since Modestine had shown such a fancy for beaten roads, I tried her instinct in this predicament. But the instinct of an ass is what might be expected from the name; in half a minute she was clambering round and round among some boulders, as lost a donkey as you would wish to see. I should have camped long before had I been properly provided; but as this was to be so short a stage, I had brought no wine, no bread for myself, and little over a pound for my lady friend. Add to this, that I and Modestine were both handsomely wetted by the showers. But now, if I could have found some water, I should have camped at once in spite of all. Water, however, being entirely absent, except in the form of rain, I determined to return to Fouzilhic, and ask a guide a little farther on my way – 'a little farther lend thy guiding hand'.

The thing was easy to decide, hard to accomplish. In this sensible roaring blackness I was sure of nothing but the direction of the wind. To this I set my face; the road had disappeared, and I went across country, now in marshy opens, now baffled by walls unscalable to Modestine, until I came once more in sight of some red windows. This time they were differently disposed. It was not Fouzilhic, but Fouzilhac,[23] a hamlet little distant from the other in space, but worlds away in the spirit of its inhabitants. I tied Modestine to a gate, and groped forward, stumbling among rocks, plunging mid-leg in bog, until I gained the entrance of the village. In the first lighted house there was a woman who would not open to me. She could do nothing, she cried to me through the door, being alone and lame; but if I would apply at the next house, there was a man who could help me if he had a mind.

They came to the next door in force, a man, two women, and a girl, and brought a pair of lanterns to examine the wayfarer. The man was not ill-looking, but had a shifty smile. He leaned against the doorpost, and heard me state my case. All I asked was a guide as far as Cheylard.

'*C'est que, voyez-vous, il fait noir*,'[24] said he.

I told him that was just my reason for requiring help.

'I understand that,' said he, looking uncomfortable; '*mais – c'est – de la peine*.'

I was willing to pay, I said. He shook his head. I rose as high as ten francs; but he continued to shake his head. 'Name your own price, then,' said I.

'*Ce n'est pas ça*,' he said at length, and with evident difficulty; 'but I am not going to cross the door – mais je ne sortirai pas de la porte.'

I grew a little warm, and asked him what he proposed that I should do.

'Where are you going beyond Cheylard?' he asked by way of answer.

'That is no affair of yours,' I returned, for I was not going to indulge his bestial curiosity; 'it changes nothing in my present predicament.'

'*C'est vrai, ça*,' he acknowledged, with a laugh; '*oui, c'est vrai. Et d'où venez-vous?*'

A better man than I might have felt nettled.

'Oh,' said I, 'I am not going to answer any of your questions, so you may spare yourself the trouble of putting them. I am late enough already; I want help. If you will not guide me yourself, at least help me to find someone else who will.'

'Hold on,' he cried suddenly. 'Was it not you who passed in the meadow while it was still day?'

'Yes, yes,' said the girl, whom I had not hitherto recognised; 'it was monsieur; I told him to follow the cow.'

'As for you, mademoiselle,' said I, 'you are a *farceuse*.'

'And,' added the man, 'what the devil have you done to be still here?'

What the devil, indeed! But there I was.

'The great thing,' said I, 'is to make an end of it'; and once more proposed that he should help me to find a guide.

'*C'est que*,' he said again, '*c'est que – il fait noir.*'

'Very well,' said I; 'take one of your lanterns.'

'No,' he cried, drawing a thought backward, and again entrenching himself behind one of his former phrases; 'I will not cross the door.'

I looked at him. I saw unaffected terror struggling on his face with unaffected shame; he was smiling pitifully and wetting his lip with his tongue, like a detected schoolboy. I drew a brief picture of my state, and asked him what I was to do.

'I don't know,' he said; 'I will not cross the door.'

Here was the Beast of Gévaudan, and no mistake.

'Sir,' said I, with my most commanding manners, 'you are a coward.'

And with that I turned my back upon the family party, who hastened to retire within their fortifications; and the famous door was closed again, but not till I had overheard the sound of laughter. *Filia barbara pater barbarior.*[25] Let me say it in the plural: the Beasts of Gévaudan.

The lanterns had somewhat dazzled me, and I ploughed distressfully among stones and rubbish-heaps. All the other houses in the village were both dark and silent; and though I knocked at here and there a door, my knocking was unanswered. It was a bad business; I gave up Fouzilhac with my curses. The rain had stopped, and the wind, which still kept rising, began to dry my coat and trousers. 'Very well,' thought I, 'water or no water, I must camp.' But the first thing was to return to Modestine. I am pretty sure I was twenty minutes groping for my lady in the dark; and if it had not been for the unkindly services of the bog, into which I once more stumbled, I might have still been groping for her at the dawn. My next business was to gain the shelter of a wood, for the wind was cold as well as boisterous. How, in this well-wooded district, I should have been so long in finding one, is another of the insoluble mysteries of this day's adventures; but I will take my oath that I put near an hour to the discovery.

At last black trees began to show upon my left, and, suddenly crossing the road, made a cave of unmitigated blackness right in front. I call it a cave without exaggeration; to pass below that arch of leaves was like entering a dungeon. I felt about until my hand encountered a stout branch, and to this I tied Modestine, a haggard, drenched, desponding donkey. Then I lowered my pack, laid it along the wall on the margin of the road, and unbuckled the straps. I knew well enough where the lantern was; but where were the candles? I groped and groped among the tumbled articles, and, while I was thus groping, suddenly I touched the spirit-lamp. Salvation! This would serve my turn as well. The wind roared unwearyingly among the trees; I could hear the boughs tossing and the leaves churning through half a mile of forest; yet the scene of my encampment was not only as black as the pit, but admirably sheltered. At the second match the wick caught flame. The light was both livid and shifting; but it cut me off from the universe, and doubled the darkness of the surrounding night.

I tied Modestine more conveniently for herself, and broke up half the black bread for her supper, reserving the other half against the morning. Then I gathered what I should want within reach, took off my wet boots and gaiters, which I wrapped in my waterproof, arranged my knapsack for a pillow under the flap of my sleeping-bag, insinuated my limbs into the interior, and buckled myself in like a bambino. I opened a tin of Bologna sausage and broke a cake of chocolate, and that was all I had to eat. It may sound offensive, but I ate them together, bite by bite, by way of bread and meat. All I had to wash down this revolting mixture was neat brandy: a revolting beverage in itself. But I was rare and hungry; ate well, and smoked one of the best cigarettes in my experience. Then I put a stone in my straw hat, pulled the flap of my fur cap over my neck and eyes, put my revolver ready to my hand, and snuggled well down among the sheepskins.

I questioned at first if I were sleepy, for I felt my heart beating faster than usual, as if with an agreeable excitement to which my mind remained a stranger. But as soon as my eyelids touched, that subtle glue leaped between them, and they would no more come separate. The wind among the trees was my lullaby. Sometimes it sounded for minutes together with a steady, even rush, not rising nor abating; and again it would swell and burst like a great crashing breaker, and the trees would patter me all over with big drops from the rain of the afternoon. Night after night, in my own bedroom in the country, I have given ear to this perturbing concert of the wind among the woods; but whether it was a difference in the trees, or the lie of the ground, or because I was myself outside and in the midst of it, the fact remains that the wind sang to a different tune among these woods of Gévaudan. I hearkened and hearkened; and meanwhile sleep took gradual possession of my body and subdued my thoughts and senses; but still my last waking effort was to listen and distinguish, and my last conscious state was one of wonder at the foreign clamour in my ears.

Twice in the course of the dark hours – once when a stone galled me underneath the sack, and again when the poor patient Modestine, growing angry, pawed and stamped upon the road – I was recalled for a brief while to consciousness, and saw a star or two overhead, and the lace-like edge of the foliage against the sky. When I awoke for the third time (Wednesday, September 25th), the world was flooded with a blue light, the mother of the dawn. I saw the leaves labouring in the wind and the ribbon of the road; and, on turning my head, there was Modestine tied to a beech, and standing half across the path in an attitude of inimitable patience. I closed my eyes again, and set to thinking over the experience of the night. I was surprised to find how easy and pleasant it had been, even in this tempestuous weather. The stone which annoyed me would not have been there, had I not been forced to camp blindfold in the opaque night; and I had felt no other inconvenience, except when my feet encountered the lantern or the second volume of Peyrat's[26] Pastors of the Desert among the mixed contents of my sleeping-bag; nay, more, I had felt not a touch of cold, and awakened with unusually lightsome and clear sensations.

With that, I shook myself, got once more into my boots and gaiters, and, breaking up the rest of the bread for Modestine, strolled about to see in what part of the world I had awakened. Ulysses, left on Ithaca,[27] and with a mind unsettled by the goddess, was not more pleasantly astray. I have been after an adventure all my life, a pure dispassionate adventure, such as befell early and heroic voyagers; and thus to be found by morning in a random woodside nook in Gévaudan – not knowing north from south, as strange to my surroundings as the first man upon the earth, an inland castaway – was to find a fraction of my daydreams realised. I was on the skirts of a little wood of birch, sprinkled with a few beeches; behind, it adjoined another wood of fir; and in front, it broke up and went down in open order into a shallow and meadowy dale. All around there were bare hilltops, some near, some far away, as the perspective closed or opened, but none apparently much higher than the rest. The wind huddled the trees. The golden specks of autumn in the birches tossed shiveringly. Overhead the sky was full of strings and shreds of vapour, flying, vanishing, reappearing, and turning about an axis like tumblers, as the wind hounded them through heaven. It was wild weather and famishing cold. I ate some chocolate, swallowed a mouthful of brandy, and smoked a cigarette before the cold should have time to disable my fingers. And by the time I had got all this done, and had made my pack and bound it on the pack-saddle, the day was tiptoe on the threshold of the east. We had not gone many steps along the lane, before the sun, still invisible to me, sent a glow of gold over some cloud mountains that lay ranged along the eastern sky.

The wind had us on the stern, and hurried us bitingly forward. I buttoned myself into my coat, and walked on in a pleasant frame of mind with all men, when suddenly, at a corner, there was Fouzilhic once more in front of me. Nor only that, but there was the old gentleman who had escorted me so far the night before, running out of his house at sight of me, with hands upraised in horror.

'My poor boy!' he cried, 'what does this mean?'

I told him what had happened. He beat his old hands like clappers in a mill, to think how lightly he had let me go; but when he heard of the man of Fouzilhac, anger and depression seized upon his mind.

'This time, at least,' said he, 'there shall be no mistake.'

And he limped along, for he was very rheumatic, for about half a mile, and until I was almost within sight of Cheylard, the destination I had hunted for so long.

Cheylard and Luc

Candidly, it seemed little worthy of all this searching. A few broken ends of village, with no particular street, but a succession of open places heaped with logs and fagots; a couple of tilted crosses, a shrine to Our Lady of all Graces on the summit of a little hill; and all this, upon a rattling highland river, in the corner of a naked valley. What went ye out for to see? thought I to myself. But the place had a life of its own. I found a board, commemorating the liberalities of Cheylard for the past year, hung up, like a banner, in the diminutive and tottering church. In 1877, it appeared, the inhabitants subscribed forty-eight francs ten centimes for the 'Work of the Propagation of the Faith'. Some of this, I could not help hoping, would be applied to my native land. Cheylard scrapes together halfpence for the darkened souls in Edinburgh; while Balquhidder and Dunrossness bemoan the ignorance of Rome. Thus, to the high entertainment of the angels, do we pelt each other with evangelists, like schoolboys bickering in the snow.

The inn was again singularly unpretentious. The whole furniture of a not ill-to-do family was in the kitchen: the beds, the cradle, the clothes, the plate-rack, the meal-chest, and the photograph of the parish priest. There were five children, one of whom was set to its morning prayers at the stair-foot soon after my arrival, and a sixth would ere long be forthcoming. I was kindly received by these good folk. They were much interested in my misadventure. The wood in which I had slept belonged to them; the man of Fouzilhac they thought a monster of iniquity, and counselled me warmly to summon him at law – 'because I might have died'. The good wife was horror-stricken to see me drink over a pint of uncreamed milk.

'You will do yourself an evil,' she said. 'Permit me to boil it for you.'

After I had begun the morning on this delightful liquor, she having an infinity of things to arrange, I was permitted, nay requested, to make a bowl of chocolate for myself. My boots and gaiters were hung up to dry, and, seeing me trying to write my journal on my knee, the eldest daughter let down a hinged table in the chimney-corner for my convenience. Here I wrote, drank my chocolate, and finally ate an omelette before I left. The table was thick with dust; for, as they explained, it was not used except in winter weather. I had a clear look up the vent, through brown agglomerations of soot and blue vapour, to the sky; and whenever a handful of twigs was thrown on to the fire, my legs were scorched by the blaze.

The husband had begun life as a muleteer, and when I came to charge Modestine showed himself full of the prudence of his art. 'You will have to change this package,' said he; 'it ought to be in two parts, and then you might have double the weight.'

I explained that I wanted no more weight; and for no donkey hitherto created would I cut my sleeping-bag in two.

'It fatigues her, however,' said the innkeeper; 'it fatigues her greatly on the march. Look.'

Alas, there were her two forelegs no better than raw beef on the inside, and blood was running from under her tail. They told me when I started, and I was ready to believe it, that before a few days I should come to love Modestine like a dog. Three days had passed, we had shared some misadventures, and my heart was still as cold as a potato towards my beast of burden. She was pretty enough to look at; but then she had given proof of dead stupidity, redeemed indeed by patience, but aggravated by flashes of sorry and ill-judged light-heartedness. And I own this new discovery seemed another point against her. What the devil was the good of a she-ass if she could not carry a sleeping-bag and a few necessaries? I saw the end of the fable rapidly approaching, when I should have to carry Modestine. Aesop was the man to know the world! I assure you I set out with heavy thoughts upon my short day's march.

It was not only heavy thoughts about Modestine that weighted me upon the way; it was a leaden business altogether. For first, the wind blew so rudely that I had to hold on the pack with one hand from Cheylard to Luc; and second, my road lay through one of the most beggarly countries in the world. It was like the worst of the Scottish Highlands, only worse; cold, naked, and ignoble, scant of wood, scant of heather, scant of life. A road and some fences broke the unvarying waste, and the line of the road was marked by upright pillars, to serve in time of snow.

Why anyone should desire to visit either Luc or Cheylard is more than my much-inventing spirit can suppose. For my part, I travel not to go anywhere, but to go. I travel for travel's sake. The great affair is to move; to feel the needs and hitches of our life more nearly; to come down off this feather-bed of civilisation, and find the globe granite underfoot and strewn with cutting flints. Alas, as we get up in life, and are more preoccupied with our affairs, even a holiday is a thing that must be worked for. To hold a pack upon a pack-saddle against a gale out of the freezing north is no high industry, but it is one that serves to occupy and compose the mind. And when the present is so exacting, who can annoy himself about the future?

I came out at length above the Allier. A more unsightly prospect at this season of the year it would be hard to fancy. Shelving hills rose round it on all sides, here dabbled with wood and fields, there rising to peaks alternately naked and hairy with pines. The colour throughout was black or ashen, and came to a point in the ruins of the castle of Luc, which pricked up impudently from below my feet, carrying on a pinnacle a tall white statue of Our Lady, which, I heard with interest, weighed fifty quintals, and was to be dedicated on the 6th of October. Through this sorry landscape trickled the Allier and a tributary of nearly equal size, which came down to join it through a broad nude valley in Vivarais. The weather had somewhat lightened, and the clouds massed in squadron; but the fierce wind still hunted them through heaven, and cast great ungainly splashes of shadow and sunlight over the scene.

Luc itself was a straggling double file of houses wedged between hill and river. It had no beauty, nor was there any notable feature, save the old castle overhead with its fifty quintals of brand-new Madonna. But the inn was clean and large. The kitchen, with its two box-beds hung with clean check curtains, with its wide stone chimney, its chimney-shelf four yards long and garnished with lanterns and religious statuettes, its array of chests and pair of ticking clocks, was the very model of what a kitchen ought to be – a melodrama kitchen, suitable for bandits or noblemen in disguise. Nor was the scene disgraced by the landlady, a handsome, silent, dark old woman, clothed and hooded in black like a nun. Even the public bedroom had a character of its own, with the long deal tables and benches, where fifty might have dined, set out as for a harvest-home, and the three box-beds along the wall. In one of these, lying on straw and covered with a pair of table-napkins, did I do penance all night long in goose-flesh and chattering teeth, and sigh, from time to time as I awakened, for my sheepskin sack and the lee of some great wood.

Our Lady of the Snows

I behold
The House, the Brotherhood austere –
And what am I, that I am here?

Matthew Arnold[28]

Father Apollinaris

Next morning (Thursday, 26th September) I took the road in a new order. The sack was no longer doubled, but hung at full length across the saddle, a green sausage six feet long with a tuft of blue wool hanging out of either end. It was more picturesque, it spared the donkey, and, as I began to see, it would ensure stability, blow high, blow low. But it was not without a pang that I had so decided. For although I had purchased a new cord, and made all as fast as I was able, I was yet jealously uneasy lest the flaps should tumble out and scatter my effects along the line of march.

My way lay up the bald valley of the river, along the march of Vivarais and Gévaudan. The hills of Gévaudan on the right were a little more naked, if anything, than those of Vivarais upon the left, and the former had a monopoly of a low dotty underwood that grew thickly in the gorges and died out in solitary burrs upon the shoulders and the summits. Black bricks of fir wood were plastered here and there upon both sides, and here and there were cultivated fields. A railway ran beside the river, the only bit of railway in Gévaudan, although there are many proposals afoot and surveys being made, and even, as they tell me, a station standing ready built in Mende.[29] A year or two hence and this may be another world. The desert is beleaguered. Now may some Languedocian Wordsworth turn the sonnet into *patois*: 'Mountains and vales and floods, heard YE that whistle?'[30]

At a place called La Bastide I was directed to leave the river, and follow a road that mounted on the left among the hills of Vivarais, the modern Ardèche; for I was now come within a little way of my strange destination, the Trappist monastery of Our Lady of the Snows. The sun came out as I left the shelter of a pine wood, and I beheld suddenly a fine wild landscape to the south. High rocky hills, as blue as sapphire, closed the view, and between these lay ridge upon ridge, heathery, craggy, the sun glittering on veins of rock, the underwood clambering in the hollows, as rude as God made them[31] at the first. There was not a sign of man's hand in all the prospect; and indeed not a trace of his passage, save where generation after generation had walked in twisted footpaths, in and out among the beeches, and up and down upon the channelled slopes. The mists, which had hitherto beset me, were now broken into clouds, and fled swiftly and shone brightly in the sun. I drew a long breath. It was grateful to come, after so long, upon a scene of some attraction for the human heart. I own I like definite form in what my eyes are to rest upon; and if landscapes were sold, like the sheets of characters of my boyhood, one penny plain and twopence coloured, I should go the length of twopence every day of my life.

But if things had grown better to the south, it was still desolate and inclement near at hand. A spidery cross on every hilltop marked the neighbourhood of a religious house; and a quarter of a mile beyond, the outlook southward opening out and growing bolder with every step, a white statue of the Virgin at the corner of a young plantation directed the traveller to Our Lady of the Snows.[32] Here, then, I struck leftward, and pursued my way, driving my secular donkey before me, and creaking in my secular boots and gaiters, towards the asylum of silence.

I had not gone very far ere the wind brought to me the clanging of a bell, and somehow, I can scarce tell why, my heart sank within me at the sound. I have rarely approached anything with more unaffected terror than the monastery of Our Lady of the Snows. This it is to have had a Protestant education. And suddenly, on turning a corner, fear took hold on me from head to foot – slavish, superstitious fear; and though I did not stop in my advance, yet I went on slowly, like a man who should have passed a bourne unnoticed, and strayed into the country of the dead. For there, upon the narrow new-made road, between the stripling pines, was a medieval friar, fighting with a barrowful of turfs. Every Sunday of my childhood I used to study the Hermits of Marco Sadeler[33] – enchanting prints, full of wood and field and medieval landscapes, as large as a county, for the imagination to go a-travelling in; and here, sure enough, was one of Marco Sadeler's heroes. He was robed in white like any spectre, and the hood falling back, in the instancy of his contention with the barrow, disclosed a pate as bald and yellow as a skull. He might have been buried any time these thousand years, and all the lively parts of him resolved into earth and broken up with the farmer's harrow.

I was troubled besides in my mind as to etiquette. Durst I address a person who was under a vow of silence? Clearly not. But drawing near, I doffed my cap to him with a faraway superstitious reverence. He nodded back, and cheerfully addressed me. Was I going to the monastery? Who was I? An Englishman? Ah, an Irishman, then?

'No,' I said, 'a Scotsman.'

A Scotsman? Ah, he had never seen a Scotsman before. And he looked me all over, his good, honest, brawny countenance shining with interest, as a boy might look upon a lion or an alligator. From him I learned with disgust that I could not be received at Our Lady of the Snows; I might get a meal, perhaps, but that was all. And then, as our talk ran on, and it turned out that I was not a pedlar, but a literary man, who drew landscapes[34] and was going to write a book, he changed his manner of thinking as to my reception (for I fear they respect persons even in a Trappist monastery), and told me I must be sure to ask for the Father Prior, and state my case to him in full. On second thoughts he determined to go down with me himself; he thought he could manage for me better. Might he say that I was a geographer?

No; I thought, in the interests of truth, he positively might not.

'Very well, then' (with disappointment), 'an author.'

It appeared he had been in a seminary with six young Irishmen, all priests long since, who had received newspapers and kept him informed of the state of ecclesiastical affairs in England. And he asked me eagerly after Dr Pusey, for whose conversion the good man had continued ever since to pray night and morning.

'I thought he was very near the truth,' he said; 'and he will reach it yet; there is so much virtue in prayer.'

He must be a stiff, ungodly Protestant who can take anything but pleasure in this kind and hopeful story. While he was thus near the subject, the good father asked me if I were a Christian; and when he found I was not, or not after his way, he glossed it over with great goodwill.

The road which we were following, and which this stalwart father had made with his own two hands within the space of a year, came to a corner, and showed us some white buildings a little farther on beyond the wood. At the same time, the bell once more sounded abroad. We were hard upon the monastery. Father Apollinaris (for that was my companion's name) stopped me.

'I must not speak to you down there,' he said. 'Ask for the Brother Porter, and all will be well. But try to see me as you go out again through the wood, where I may speak to you. I am charmed to have made your acquaintance.'

And then suddenly raising his arms, flapping his fingers, and crying out twice, 'I must not speak, I must not speak!' he ran away in front of me, and disappeared into the monastery door.

I own this somewhat ghastly eccentricity went a good way to revive my terrors. But where one was so good and simple, why should not all be alike? I took heart of grace, and went forward to the gate as fast as Modestine, who seemed to have a disaffection for monasteries, would permit. It was the first door, in my acquaintance of her, which she had not shown an indecent haste to enter. I summoned the place in form, though with a quaking heart. Father Michael, the Father Hospitaller, and a pair of brown-robed brothers came to the gate and spoke with me a while. I think my sack was the great attraction; it had already beguiled the heart of poor Apollinaris, who had charged me on my life to show it to the Father Prior. But whether it was my address, or the sack, or the idea speedily published among that part of the brotherhood who attend on strangers that I was not a pedlar after all, I found no difficulty as to my reception. Modestine was led away by a layman to the stables, and I and my pack were received into Our Lady of the Snows.

The Monks

Father Michael, a pleasant, fresh-faced, smiling man, perhaps of thirty-five, took me to the pantry, and gave me a glass of liqueur to stay me until dinner. We had some talk, or rather I should say he listened to my prattle indulgently enough, but with an abstracted air, like a spirit with a thing of clay. And truly, when I remember that I descanted principally on my appetite, and that it must have been by that time more than eighteen hours since Father Michael had so much as broken bread, I can well understand that he would find an earthly savour in my conversation. But his manner, though superior, was exquisitely gracious; and I find I have a lurking curiosity as to Father Michael's past.

The whet administered, I was left alone for a little in the monastery garden. This is no more than the main court, laid out in sandy paths and beds of parti-coloured dahlias, and with a fountain and a black statue of the Virgin in the centre. The buildings stand around it foursquare, bleak, as yet unseasoned by the years and weather, and with no other features than a belfry and a pair of slated gables. Brothers in white, brothers in brown, passed silently along the sanded alleys; and when I first came out, three hooded monks were kneeling on the terrace at their prayers. A naked hill commands the monastery upon one side, and the wood commands it on the other. It lies exposed to wind; the snow falls off and on from October to May, and sometimes lies six weeks on end; but if they stood in Eden, with a climate like heaven's, the buildings themselves would offer the same wintry and cheerless aspect; and for my part, on this wild September day, before I was called to dinner, I felt chilly in and out.

When I had eaten well and heartily, Brother Ambrose, a hearty conversible Frenchman (for all those who wait on strangers have the liberty to speak), led me to a little room in that part of the building which is set apart for *messieurs les retraitants*. It was clean and whitewashed, and furnished with strict necessaries, a crucifix, a bust of the late Pope, the *Imitation*[35] in French, a book of religious meditations, and the *Life of Elizabeth Seton*, evangelist, it would appear, of North America and of New England in particular. As far as my experience goes, there is a fair field for some more evangelisation in these quarters; but think of Cotton Mather![36] I should like to give him a reading of this little work in heaven, where I hope he dwells; but perhaps he knows all that already, and much more; and perhaps he and Mrs Seton are the dearest friends, and gladly unite their voices in the everlasting psalm. Over the table, to conclude the inventory of the room, hung a set of regulations for *messieurs les retraitants*: what services they should attend, when they were to tell their beads or meditate, and when they were to rise and go to rest. At the foot was a notable NB: *Le temps libre est employé à l'examen de conscience, à la confession, à faire de bonnes résolutions, etc.*[37] To make good resolutions, indeed! You might talk as fruitfully of making the hair grow on your head.

I had scarce explored my niche when Brother Ambrose returned. An English boarder, it appeared, would like to speak with me. I professed my willingness, and the friar ushered in a fresh, young, little Irishman of fifty, a deacon of the Church, arrayed in strict canonicals, and wearing on his head what, in default of knowledge, I can only call the ecclesiastical shako. He had lived seven years in retreat at a convent of nuns in Belgium, and now five at Our Lady of the Snows; he never saw an English newspaper; he spoke French imperfectly, and had he spoken it like a native, there was not much chance of conversation where he dwelt. With this, he was a man eminently sociable, greedy of news, and simple-minded like a child.

If I was pleased to have a guide about the monastery, he was no less delighted to see an English face and hear an English tongue.

He showed me his own room, where he passed his time among breviaries, Hebrew Bibles and the Waverley Novels.[38] Thence he led me to the cloisters, into the chapter-house, through the vestry, where the brothers' gowns and broad straw hats were hanging up, each with his religious name upon a board – names full of legendary suavity and interest, such as Basil, Hilarion, Raphael or Pacifique; into the library, where were all the works of Veuillot and Chateaubriand, and the *Odes et Ballades*,[39] if you please, and even Molière, to say nothing of innumerable fathers and a great variety of local and general historians. Thence my good Irishman took me round the workshops, where brothers bake bread, and make cartwheels, and take photographs; where one superintends a collection of curiosities, and another a gallery of rabbits. For in a Trappist monastery each monk has an occupation of his own choice, apart from his religious duties and the general labours of the house. Each must sing in the choir, if he has a voice and ear, and join in the haymaking if he has a hand to stir; but in his private hours, although he must be occupied, he may be occupied on what he likes. Thus I was told that one brother was engaged with literature; while Father Apollinaris busies himself in making roads, and the Abbot employs himself in binding books. It is not so long since this Abbot was consecrated, by the way; and on that occasion, by a special grace, his mother was permitted to enter the chapel and witness the ceremony of consecration. A proud day for her to have a son a mitred abbot; it makes you glad to think they let her in.

In all these journeyings to and fro, many silent fathers and brethren fell in our way. Usually they paid no more regard to our passage than if we had been a cloud; but sometimes the good deacon had a permission to ask of them, and it was granted by a peculiar movement of the hands, almost like that of a dog's paws in swimming, or refused by the usual negative signs, and in either case with lowered eyelids and a certain air of contrition, as of a man who was steering very close to evil.

The monks, by special grace of their Abbot, were still taking two meals a day; but it was already time for their grand fast, which begins somewhere in September and lasts till Easter, and during which they eat but once in the twenty-four hours, and that at two in the afternoon, twelve hours after they have begun the toil and vigil of the day. Their meals are scanty, but even of these they eat sparingly; and though each is allowed a small carafe of wine, many refrain from this indulgence. Without doubt, the most of mankind grossly overeat themselves; our meals serve not only for support, but as a hearty and natural diversion from the labour of life. Yet, though excess may be hurtful, I should have thought this Trappist regimen defective. And I am astonished, as I look back, at the freshness of face and cheerfulness of manner of all whom I beheld. A happier nor a healthier company I should scarce suppose that I have ever seen. As a matter of fact, on this bleak upland, and with the incessant occupation of the monks, life is of an uncertain tenure, and death no infrequent visitor, at Our Lady of the Snows. This, at least, was what was told me. But if they die easily, they must live healthily in the meantime, for they seemed all firm of flesh and high in colour; and the only morbid sign that I could observe, an unusual brilliancy of eye, was one that served rather to increase the general impression of vivacity and strength.

Those with whom I spoke were singularly sweet-tempered, with what I can only call a holy cheerfulness in air and conversation. There is a note, in the direction to visitors, telling them not to be offended at the curt speech of those who wait upon them, since it is proper to monks to speak little. The note might have been spared; to a man the hospitallers were all brimming with innocent talk, and, in my experience of the monastery, it was easier to begin than to break off a conversation. With the exception of Father Michael, who was a man of the world, they showed themselves full of kind and healthy interest in all sorts of subjects – in politics, in voyages, in my sleeping-sack – and not without a certain pleasure in the sound of their own voices.

As for those who are restricted to silence, I can only wonder how they bear their solemn and cheerless isolation. And yet, apart from any view of mortification, I can see a certain policy, not only in the exclusion of women, but in this vow of silence. I have had some experience of lay phalansteries, of an artistic, not to say a bacchanalian character; and seen more than one association easily formed and yet more easily dispersed. With a Cistercian rule, perhaps they might have lasted longer. In the neighbourhood of women it is but a touch-and-go association that can be formed among defenceless men; the stronger electricity is sure to triumph; the dreams of boyhood, the schemes of youth, are abandoned after an interview of ten minutes, and the arts and sciences, and professional male jollity, deserted at once for two sweet eyes and a caressing accent. And next after this, the tongue is the great divider.

I am almost ashamed to pursue this worldly criticism of a religious rule; but there is yet another point in which the Trappist order appeals to me as a model of wisdom. By two in the morning the clapper goes upon the bell, and so on, hour by hour, and sometimes quarter by quarter, till eight, the hour of rest; so infinitesimally is the day divided among different occupations. The man who keeps rabbits, for example, hurries from his hutches to the chapel, the chapter-room, or the refectory, all day long: every hour he has an office to sing, a duty to perform; from two, when he rises in the dark, till eight, when he returns to receive the comfortable gift of sleep, he is upon his feet and occupied with manifold and changing business. I know many persons, worth several thousands in the year, who are not so fortunate in the disposal of their lives. Into how many houses would not the note of the monastery bell, dividing the day into manageable portions, bring peace of mind and healthful activity of body! We speak of hardships, but the true hardship is to be a dull fool, and permitted to mismanage life in our own dull and foolish manner.

From this point of view, we may perhaps better understand the monk's existence. A long novitiate and every proof of constancy of mind and strength of body is required before admission to the order; but I could not find that many were discouraged. In the photo-grapher's studio, which figures so strangely among the outbuildings, my eye was attracted by the portrait of a young fellow in the uniform of a private of foot. This was one of the novices, who came of the age for service, and marched and drilled and mounted guard for the proper time among the garrison of Algiers. Here was a man who had surely seen both sides of life before deciding; yet as soon as he was set free from service he returned to finish his novitiate.

This austere rule entitles a man to heaven as by right. When the Trappist sickens, he quits not his habit; he lies in the bed of death as he has prayed and laboured in his frugal and silent existence; and when the Liberator comes, at the very moment, even before they have carried him in his robe to lie his little last in the chapel among continual chantings, joy-bells break forth, as if for a marriage, from the slated belfry, and proclaim throughout the neighbourhood that another soul has gone to God.

At night, under the conduct of my kind Irishman, I took my place in the gallery to hear compline and Salve Regina,[40] with which the Cistercians bring every day to a conclusion. There were none of those circumstances which strike the Protestant as childish or as tawdry in the public offices of Rome. A stern simplicity, heightened by the romance of the surroundings, spoke directly to the heart. I recall the whitewashed chapel, the hooded figures in the choir, the lights alternately occluded and revealed, the strong manly singing, the silence that ensued, the sight of cowled heads bowed in prayer, and then the clear trenchant beating of the bell, breaking in to show that the last office was over and the hour of sleep had come; and when I remember, I am not surprised that I made my escape into the court with somewhat whirling fancies, and stood like a man bewildered in the windy starry night.

But I was weary; and when I had quieted my spirits with Elizabeth Seton's[41] memoirs – a dull work – the cold and the raving of the wind among the pines (for my room was on that side of the monastery which adjoins the woods) disposed me readily to slumber. I was wakened at black midnight, as it seemed, though it was really two in the morning, by the first stroke upon the bell. All the brothers were then hurrying to the chapel; the dead in life, at this untimely hour, were already beginning the uncomforted labours of their day. The dead in life – there was a chill reflection. And the words of a French song came back into my memory, telling of the best of our mixed existence:

> Que t'as de belles filles,
> Giroflé!
> Girofla!
> Que t'as de belles filles,
> L'amour les comptera![42]

And I blessed God that I was free to wander, free to hope, and free to love.

The Boarders

But there was another side to my residence at Our Lady of the Snows. At this late season there were not many boarders; and yet I was not alone in the public part of the monastery. This itself is hard by the gate, with a small dining-room on the ground-floor and a whole corridor of cells similar to mine upstairs. I have stupidly forgotten the board for a regular *retraitant*; but it was somewhere between three and five francs a day, and I think most probably the first. Chance visitors like myself might give what they chose as a free-will offering, but nothing was demanded. I may mention that when I was going away, Father Michael refused twenty francs as excessive. I explained the reasoning which led me to offer him so much; but even then, from a curious point of honour, he would not accept it with his own hand. 'I have no right to refuse for the monastery,' he explained, 'but I should prefer if you would give it to one of the brothers.'

I had dined alone, because I arrived late; but at supper I found two other guests. One was a country parish priest, who had walked over that morning from the seat of his cure near Mende to enjoy four days of solitude and prayer. He was a grenadier in person, with the hale colour and circular wrinkles of a peasant; and as he complained much of how he had been impeded by his skirts upon the march, I have a vivid fancy portrait of him, striding along, upright, big-boned, with kilted cassock, through the bleak hills of Gévaudan. The other was a short, grizzling, thick-set man, from forty-five to fifty, dressed in tweed with a knitted spencer, and the red ribbon of a decoration in his button-hole. This last was a hard person to classify. He was an old soldier, who had seen service and risen to the rank of commandant; and he retained some of the brisk decisive manners of the camp. On the other hand, as soon as his resignation was accepted, he had come to Our Lady of the Snows as a boarder, and, after a brief experience of its ways, had decided to remain as a novice. Already the new life was beginning to modify his appearance; already he had acquired somewhat of the quiet and smiling air of the brethren; and he was as yet neither an officer nor a Trappist, but partook of the character of each. And certainly here was a man in an interesting nick of life. Out of the noise of cannon and trumpets, he was in the act of passing into this still country bordering on the grave, where men sleep nightly in their grave-clothes, and, like phantoms, communicate by signs.

At supper we talked politics. I make it my business, when I am in France, to preach political goodwill and moderation, and to dwell on the example of Poland, much as some alarmists in England dwell on the example of Carthage. The priest and the commandant assured me of their sympathy with all I said, and made a heavy sighing over the bitterness of contemporary feeling.

'Why, you cannot say anything to a man with which he does not absolutely agree,' said I, 'but he flies up at you in a temper.'

They both declared that such a state of things was antichristian.

While we were thus agreeing, what should my tongue stumble upon but a word in praise of Gambetta's[43] moderation. The old soldier's countenance was instantly suffused with blood; with the palms of his hands he beat the table like a naughty child.

'*Comment, monsieur?*' he shouted. '*Comment?* Gambetta moderate? Will you dare to justify these words?'

But the priest had not forgotten the tenor of our talk. And suddenly, in the height of his fury, the old soldier found a warning look directed on his face; the absurdity of his behaviour was brought home to him in a flash; and the storm came to an abrupt end, without another word.

It was only in the morning, over our coffee (Friday, September 27th), that this couple found out I was a heretic. I suppose I had misled them by some admiring expressions as to the monastic life around us; and it was only by a point-blank question that the truth came out. I had been tolerantly used both by simple Father Apollinaris and astute Father Michael; and the good Irish deacon, when he heard of my religious weakness, had only patted me upon the shoulder and said, 'You must be a Catholic and come to heaven.' But I was now among a different sect of orthodox. These two men were bitter and upright and narrow, like the worst of Scotsmen, and indeed, upon my heart, I fancy they were worse. The priest snorted aloud like a battle-horse.

'*Et vous prétendez mourir dans cette espèce de croyance?*'[44] he demanded; and there is no type used by mortal printers large enough to qualify his accent.

I humbly indicated that I had no design of changing.

But he could not away with such a monstrous attitude. 'No, no,' he cried; 'you must change. You have come here, God has led you here, and you must embrace the opportunity.'

I made a slip in policy; I appealed to the family affections, though I was speaking to a priest and a soldier, two classes of men circumstantially divorced from the kind and homely ties of life.

'Your father and mother?' cried the priest. 'Very well; you will convert them in their turn when you go home.'

I think I see my father's face! I would rather tackle the Gaetulian lion in his den than embark on such an enterprise against the family theologian.

But now the hunt was up; priest and soldier were in full cry for my conversion; and the Work of the Propagation of the Faith, for which the people of Cheylard subscribed forty-eight francs ten centimes during 1877, was being gallantly pursued against myself. It was an odd but most effective proselytising. They never sought to convince me in argument, where I might have attempted some defence; but took it for granted that I was both ashamed and terrified at my position, and urged me solely on the point of time. Now, they said, when God had led me to Our Lady of the Snows, now was the appointed hour.

'Do not be withheld by false shame,' observed the priest, for my encouragement.

For one who feels very similarly to all sects of religion, and who has never been able, even for a moment, to weigh seriously the merit of this or that creed on the eternal side of things, however much he may see to praise or blame upon the secular and temporal side, the situation thus created was both unfair and painful. I committed my second fault in tact, and tried to plead that it was all the same thing in the end, and we were all drawing near by different sides to the same kind and undiscriminating Friend and Father. That, as it seems to lay spirits, would be the only gospel worthy of the name. But different men think differently; and this revolutionary aspiration brought down the priest with all the terrors of the law. He launched into harrowing details of hell. The damned, he said – on the authority of a little book which he had read not a week before, and which, to add conviction to conviction, he had fully intended to bring along with him in his pocket – were to occupy the same attitude through all eternity in the midst of dismal tortures. And as he thus expatiated, he grew in nobility of aspect with his enthusiasm.

As a result the pair concluded that I should seek out the Prior, since the Abbot was from home, and lay my case immediately before him.

'*C'est mon conseil comme ancien militaire,*' observed the commandant; 'et celui de monsieur comme prêtre.'

'*Oui,*' added the curé, sententiously nodding; '*comme ancien militaire – et comme prêtre.*'

At this moment, whilst I was somewhat embarrassed how to answer, in came one of the monks, a little brown fellow, as lively as a grig, and with an Italian accent, who threw himself at once into the contention, but in a milder and more persuasive vein, as befitted one of these pleasant brethren. Look at him, he said. The rule was very hard; he would have dearly liked to stay in his own country, Italy – it was well known how beautiful it was, the beautiful Italy; but then there were no Trappists in Italy; and he had a soul to save; and here he was.

I am afraid I must be, at bottom, what a cheerful Indian critic has dubbed me, 'a faddling hedonist', for this description of the brother's motives gave me somewhat of a shock. I should have preferred to think he had chosen the life for its own sake, and not for ulterior purposes; and this shows how profoundly I was out of sympathy with these good Trappists, even when I was doing my best to sympathise. But to the curé the argument seemed decisive.

'Hear that!' he cried. 'And I have seen a marquis here, a marquis, a marquis' – he repeated the holy word three times over – 'and other persons high in society; and generals. And here, at your side, is this gentleman, who has been so many years in armies – decorated, an old warrior. And here he is, ready to dedicate himself to God.'

I was by this time so thoroughly embarrassed that I pleaded cold feet, and made my escape from the apartment. It was a furious windy morning, with a sky much cleared, and long and potent intervals of sunshine; and I wandered until dinner in the wild country towards the east, sorely staggered and beaten upon by the gale, but rewarded with some striking views.

At dinner the Work of the Propagation of the Faith was re-commenced, and on this occasion still more distastefully to me. The priest asked me many questions as to the contemptible faith of my fathers, and received my replies with a kind of ecclesiastical titter.

'Your sect,' he said once; 'for I think you will admit it would be doing it too much honour to call it a religion.'

'As you please, monsieur,' said I. '*La parole est à vous.*'

At length I grew annoyed beyond endurance; and although he was on his own ground and, what is more to the purpose, an old man, and so holding a claim upon my toleration, I could not avoid a protest against this uncivil usage. He was sadly discountenanced.

'I assure you,' he said, 'I have no inclination to laugh in my heart. I have no other feeling but interest in your soul.'

And there ended my conversion. Honest man! he was no dangerous deceiver; but a country parson, full of zeal and faith. Long may he tread Gévaudan with his kilted skirts – a man strong to walk and strong to comfort his parishioners in death! I dare say he would beat bravely through a snowstorm where his duty called him; and it is not always the most faithful believer who makes the cunningest apostle.

Upper Gévaudan (continued)

The bed was made, the room was fit,
By punctual eve the stars were lit;
The air was still, the water ran;
No need there was for maid or man,
When we put up, my ass and I,
At God's green caravanserai.[45]

Across the Goulet

The wind fell during dinner, and the sky remained clear; so it was under better auspices that I loaded Modestine before the monastery gate. My Irish friend accompanied me so far on the way. As we came through the wood, there was Père Apollinaire hauling his barrow; and he too quitted his labours to go with me for perhaps a hundred yards, holding my hand between both of his in front of him. I parted first from one and then from the other with unfeigned regret, but yet with the glee of the traveller who shakes off the dust of one stage before hurrying forth upon another. Then Modestine and I mounted the course of the Allier, which here led us back into Gévaudan towards its sources in the forest of Mercoire. It was but an inconsiderable burn before we left its guidance. Thence, over a hill, our way lay through a naked plateau, until we reached Chasseradès at sundown.

The company in the inn kitchen that night were all men employed in survey for one of the projected railways. They were intelligent and conversible, and we decided the future of France over hot wine, until the state of the clock frightened us to rest. There were four beds in the little upstairs room; and we slept six. But I had a bed to myself, and persuaded them to leave the window open.

'Hé, bourgeois; il est cinq heures!'[46] was the cry that wakened me in the morning (Saturday, September 28th). The room was full of a transparent darkness, which dimly showed me the other three beds and the five different nightcaps on the pillows. But out of the window the dawn was growing ruddy in a long belt over the hilltops, and day was about to flood the plateau. The hour was inspiriting; and there seemed a promise of calm weather, which was perfectly fulfilled. I was soon under way with Modestine. The road lay for a while over the plateau, and then descended through a precipitous village into the valley of the Chassezac.[47] This stream ran among green meadows, well hidden from the world by its steep banks; the broom was in flower, and here and there was a hamlet sending up its smoke.

At last the path crossed the Chassezac upon a bridge, and, forsaking this deep hollow, set itself to cross the mountain of La Goulet. It wound up through Lestampes by upland fields and woods of beech and birch, and with every corner brought me into an acquaintance with some new interest. Even in the gully of the Chassezac my ear had been struck by a noise like that of a great bass bell ringing at the distance of many miles; but this, as I continued to mount and draw nearer to it, seemed to change in character, and I found at length that it came from someone leading flocks afield to the note of a rural horn. The narrow street of Lestampes stood full of sheep, from wall to wall – black sheep and white, bleating with one accord like the birds in spring, and each one accompanying himself upon the sheep-bell round his neck. It made a pathetic concert, all in treble. A little higher, and I passed a pair of men in a tree with pruning-hooks, and one of them was singing the music of a *bourrée*. Still farther, and when I was already threading the birches, the crowing of cocks came cheerfully up to my ears, and along with that the voice of a flute discoursing a deliberate and plaintive air from one of the upland villages. I pictured to myself some grizzled, apple-cheeked, country schoolmaster fluting in his bit of a garden in the clear autumn sunshine. All these beautiful and interesting sounds filled my heart with an unwonted expectation; and it appeared to me that, once past this range which I was mounting, I should descend into the garden of the world. Nor was I deceived, for I was now done with rains and winds and a bleak country. The first part of my journey ended here; and this was like an induction of sweet sounds into the other and more beautiful.

There are other degrees of feyness, as of punishment, besides the capital; and I was now led by my good spirits into an adventure which I relate in the interest of future donkey-drivers. The road zigzagged so widely on the hillside, that I chose a short cut by map and compass, and struck through the dwarf woods to catch the road again upon a higher level. It was my one serious conflict with Modestine. She would none of my short cut; she turned in my face; she backed, she reared; she, whom I had hitherto imagined to be dumb, actually brayed with a loud hoarse flourish, like a cock crowing for the dawn. I plied the goad with one hand; with the other, so steep was the ascent, I had to hold on the pack-saddle. Half a dozen times she was nearly over backwards on the top of me; half a dozen times, from sheer weariness of spirit, I was nearly giving it up, and leading her down again to follow the road. But I took the thing as a wager, and fought it through. I was surprised, as I went on my way again, by what appeared to be chill raindrops falling on my hand, and more than once looked up in wonder at the cloudless sky. But it was only sweat which came dropping from my brow.

Over the summit of the Goulet there was no marked road – only upright stones[48] posted from space to space to guide the drovers. The turf underfoot was springy and well scented. I had no company but a lark or two, and met but one bullock-cart between Lestampes and Bleymard. In front of me I saw a shallow valley, and beyond that the range of the Lozère, sparsely wooded and well enough modelled in the flanks, but straight and dull in outline. There was scarce a sign of culture; only about Bleymard, the white high-road from Villefort to Mende traversed a range of meadows, set with spiry poplars, and sounding from side to side with the bells of flocks and herds.

A Night among the Pines

From Bleymard after dinner, although it was already late, I set out to scale a portion of the Lozère. An ill-marked stony drove-road guided me forward; and I met nearly half a dozen bullock-carts descending from the woods, each laden with a whole pine tree for the winter's firing. At the top of the woods, which do not climb very high upon this cold ridge, I struck leftward by a path among the pines, until I hit on a dell of green turf, where a streamlet made a little spout over some stones to serve me for a water-tap. 'In a more sacred or sequestered bower . . . nor nymph nor faunus haunted.'[49] The trees were not old, but they grew thickly round the glade: there was no outlook, except north-eastward upon distant hilltops, or straight upward to the sky; and the encampment felt secure and private like a room. By the time I had made my arrangements and fed Modestine, the day was already beginning to decline. I buckled myself to the knees into my sack and made a hearty meal; and as soon as the sun went down, I pulled my cap over my eyes and fell asleep.

Night is a dead, monotonous period under a roof; but in the open world it passes lightly, with its stars and dews and perfumes, and the hours are marked by changes in the face of nature. What seems a kind of temporal death to people choked between walls and curtains is only a light and living slumber to the man who sleeps afield. All night long he can hear nature breathing deeply and freely; even as she takes her rest, she turns and smiles; and there is one stirring hour unknown to those who dwell in houses, when a wakeful influence goes abroad over the sleeping hemisphere, and all the outdoor world are on their feet. It is then that the cock first crows, not this time to announce the dawn, but like a cheerful watchman speeding the course of night. Cattle awake on the meadows; sheep break their fast on dewy hillsides, and change to a new lair among the ferns; and houseless men, who have lain down with the fowls, open their dim eyes and behold the beauty of the night.

At what inaudible summons, at what gentle touch of nature, are all these sleepers thus recalled in the same hour to life? Do the stars rain down an influence, or do we share some thrill of mother earth below our resting bodies? Even shepherds and old country-folk, who are the deepest read in these arcana, have not a guess as to the means or purpose of this nightly resurrection. Towards two in the morning they declare the thing takes place; and neither know nor enquire further. And at least it is a pleasant incident. We are disturbed in our slumber only, like the luxurious Montaigne,[50] 'that we may the better and more sensibly relish it'. We have a moment to look upon the stars. And there is a special pleasure for some minds in the reflection that we share the impulse with all outdoor creatures in our neighbourhood, that we have escaped out of the Bastille of civilisation, and are become, for the time being, a mere kindly animal and a sheep of nature's flock.

When that hour came to me among the pines, I wakened thirsty. My tin was standing by me half full of water. I emptied it at a draught; and feeling broad awake after this internal cold aspersion, sat upright to make a cigarette. The stars were clear, coloured and jewel-like, but not frosty. A faint silvery vapour stood for the Milky Way. All around me the black fir-points stood upright and stock-still. By the whiteness of the pack-saddle, I could see Modestine walking round and round at the length of her tether; I could hear her steadily munching at the sward; but there was not another sound, save the indescribable quiet talk of the runnel over the stones. I lay lazily smoking and studying the colour of the sky, as we call the void of space, from where it showed a reddish grey behind the pines to where it showed a glossy blue-black between the stars. As if to be more like a pedlar, I wear a silver ring. This I could see faintly shining as I raised or lowered the cigarette; and at each whiff the inside of my hand was illuminated, and became for a second the highest light in the landscape.

A faint wind, more like a moving coolness than a stream of air, passed down the glade from time to time; so that even in my great chamber the air was being renewed all night long. I thought with horror of the inn at Chasseradès and the congregated nightcaps; with horror of the nocturnal prowesses of clerks and students, of hot theatres and pass-keys and close rooms. I have not often enjoyed a more serene possession of myself, nor felt more independent of material aids. The outer world, from which we cower into our houses, seemed after all a gentle habitable place; and night after night a man's bed, it seemed, was laid and waiting for him in the fields, where God keeps an open house. I thought I had rediscovered one of those truths which are revealed to savages and hid from political economists: at the least, I had discovered a new pleasure for myself. And yet even while I was exulting in my solitude I became aware of a strange lack. I wished a companion to lie near me in the starlight, silent and not moving, but ever within touch. For there is a fellowship more quiet even than solitude, and which, rightly understood, is solitude made perfect. And to live out of doors with the woman a man loves is of all lives the most complete and free.

As I thus lay, between content and longing, a faint noise stole towards me through the pines. I thought, at first, it was the crowing of cocks or the barking of dogs at some very distant farm; but steadily and gradually it took articulate shape in my ears, until I became aware that a passenger was going by upon the high-road in the valley, and singing loudly as he went. There was more of goodwill than grace in his performance; but he trolled with ample lungs; and the sound of his voice took hold upon the hillside and set the air shaking in the leafy glens. I have heard people passing by night in sleeping cities; some of them sang; one, I remember, played loudly on the bagpipes. I have heard the rattle of a cart or carriage spring up suddenly after hours of stillness, and pass, for some minutes, within the range of my hearing as I lay abed. There is a romance about all who are abroad in the black hours, and with something of a thrill we try to guess their business. But here the romance was double: first, this glad passenger, lit internally with wine, who sent up his voice in music through the night; and then I, on the other hand, buckled into my sack, and smoking alone in the pine woods between four and five thousand feet towards the stars.

When I awoke again (Sunday, 29th September), many of the stars had disappeared; only the stronger companions of the night still burned visibly overhead; and away towards the east I saw a faint haze of light upon the horizon, such as had been the Milky Way when I was last awake. Day was at hand. I lit my lantern, and by its glowworm light put on my boots and gaiters; then I broke up some bread for Modestine, filled my can at the water-tap, and lit my spirit-lamp to boil myself some chocolate. The blue darkness lay long in the glade where I had so sweetly slumbered; but soon there was a broad streak of orange melting into gold along the mountain-tops of Vivarais. A solemn glee possessed my mind at this gradual and lovely coming in of day. I heard the runnel with delight; I looked round me for something beautiful and unexpected; but the still black pine trees, the hollow glade, the munching ass, remained unchanged in figure. Nothing had altered but the light, and that, indeed, shed over all a spirit of life and of breathing peace, and moved me to a strange exhilaration.

I drank my water-chocolate, which was hot if it was not rich, and strolled here and there, and up and down about the glade. While I was thus delaying, a gush of steady wind, as long as a heavy sigh, poured direct out of the quarter of the morning. It was cold, and set me sneezing. The trees near at hand tossed their black plumes in its passage; and I could see the thin distant spires of pine along the edge of the hill rock slightly to and fro against the golden east. Ten minutes after, the sunlight spread at a gallop along the hillside, scattering shadows and sparkles, and the day had come completely.

I hastened to prepare my pack, and tackle the steep ascent that lay before me; but I had something on my mind. It was only a fancy; yet a fancy will sometimes be importunate. I had been most hospitably received and punctually served in my green caravanserai. The room was airy, the water excellent, and the dawn had called me to a moment. I say nothing of the tapestries or the inimitable ceiling, nor yet of the view which I commanded from the windows; but I felt I was in someone's debt for all this liberal entertainment. And so it pleased me, in a half-laughing way, to leave pieces of money on the turf as I went along, until I had left enough for my night's lodging. I trust they did not fall to some rich and churlish drover.

The Country of the Camisards

We travelled in the print of olden wars;
      Yet all the land was green;
      And love we found, and peace,
      Where fire and war had been.
They pass and smile, the children of the sword –
      No more the sword they wield;
      And O, how deep the corn
      Along the battlefield!

                       W. P. Bannatyne[51]

Across the Lozère

The track that I had followed in the evening soon died out, and I continued to follow over a bald turf ascent a row of stone pillars, such as had conducted me across the Goulet. It was already warm. I tied my jacket on the pack, and walked in my knitted waistcoat. Modestine herself was in high spirits, and broke of her own accord, for the first time in my experience, into a jolting trot that set the oats swashing in the pocket of my coat. The view, back upon the northern Gévaudan, extended with every step; scarce a tree, scarce a house, appeared upon the fields of wild hill that ran north, east and west, all blue and gold in the haze and sunlight of the morning. A multitude of little birds kept sweeping and twittering about my path; they perched on the stone pillars, they pecked and strutted on the turf, and I saw them circle in volleys in the blue air, and show, from time to time, translucent flickering wings between the sun and me.

Almost from the first moment of my march, a faint large noise, like a distant surf, had filled my ears. Sometimes I was tempted to think it the voice of a neighbouring waterfall, and sometimes a subjective result of the utter stillness of the hill. But as I continued to advance, the noise increased, and became like the hissing of an enormous tea-urn, and at the same time breaths of cool air began to reach me from the direction of the summit. At length I understood. It was blowing stiffly from the south upon the other slope of the Lozère, and every step that I took I was drawing nearer to the wind.

Although it had been long desired, it was quite unexpectedly at last that my eyes rose above the summit. A step that seemed no way more decisive than many other steps that had preceded it – and, 'like stout Cortez[52] when, with eagle eyes, he stared on the Pacific', I took possession, in my own name, of a new quarter of the world. For behold, instead of the gross turf rampart I had been mounting for so long, a view into the hazy air of heaven, and a land of intricate blue hills below my feet.

The Lozère lies nearly east and west, cutting Gévaudan into two unequal parts; its highest point, this Pic de Finiels,[53] on which I was then standing, rises upwards of five thousand six hundred feet above the sea, and in clear weather commands a view over all lower Languedoc to the Mediterranean Sea. I have spoken with people who either pretended or believed that they had seen, from the Pic de Finiels, white ships sailing by Montpellier and Cette. Behind was the upland northern country through which my way had lain, peopled by a dull race, without wood, without much grandeur of hill-form, and famous in the past for little beside wolves. But in front of me, half veiled in sunny haze, lay a new Gévaudan, rich, picturesque, illustrious for stirring events. Speaking largely, I was in the Cévennes at Monastier, and during all my journey; but there is a strict and local sense in which only this confused and shaggy country at my feet has any title to the name, and in this sense the peasantry employ the word. These are the Cévennes with an emphasis: the Cévennes of the Cévennes. In that undecipherable labyrinth of hills, a war of bandits, a war of wild beasts, raged for two years between the Grand Monarch with all his troops and marshals on the one hand, and a few thousand Protestant mountaineers upon the other. A hundred and eighty years ago, the Camisards held a station even on the Lozère, where I stood; they had an organisation, arsenals, a military and religious hierarchy; their affairs were 'the discourse of every coffee-house' in London; England sent fleets in their support; their leaders prophesied and murdered; with colours and drums, and the singing of old French psalms, their bands sometimes affronted daylight, marched before walled cities, and dispersed the generals of the king; and sometimes at night, or in masquerade, possessed themselves of strong castles, and avenged treachery upon their allies and cruelty upon their foes. There, a hundred and eighty years ago, was the chivalrous Roland, 'Count and Lord Roland, generalissimo of the Protestants in France', grave, silent, imperious, pock-marked ex-dragoon, whom a lady followed in his wanderings out of love. There was Cavalier, a baker's apprentice with a genius for war, elected brigadier of Camisards at seventeen, to die at fifty-five the English governor of Jersey. There again was Castanet, a partisan leader in a voluminous peruke and with a taste for controversial divinity. Strange generals, who moved apart to take counsel with the God of Hosts, and fled or offered battle, set sentinels or slept in an unguarded camp, as the Spirit whispered to their hearts! And there, to follow these and other leaders, was the rank and file of prophets and disciples, bold, patient, indefatigable, hardy to run upon the mountains, cheering their rough life with psalms, eager to fight, eager to pray, listening devoutly to the oracles of brain-sick children, and mystically putting a grain of wheat among the pewter balls with which they charged their muskets.

I had travelled hitherto through a dull district, and in the track of nothing more notable than the child-eating beast of Gévaudan, the Napoleon Bonaparte of wolves. But now I was to go down into the scene of a romantic chapter – or, better, a romantic footnote in the history of the world. What was left of all this bygone dust and heroism? I was told that Protestantism still survived in this head seat of Protestant resistance; so much the priest himself had told me in the monastery parlour. But I had yet to learn if it were a bare survival, or a lively and generous tradition. Again, if in the northern Cévennes the people are narrow in religious judgements, and more filled with zeal than charity, what was I to look for in this land of persecution and reprisal – in a land where the tyranny of the Church produced the Camisard rebellion, and the terror of the Camisards threw the Catholic peasantry into legalised revolt upon the other side, so that Camisard and Florentin skulked for each other's lives among the mountains?

Just on the brow of the hill, where I paused to look before me, the series of stone pillars came abruptly to an end; and only a little below, a sort of track appeared and began to go down a breakneck slope, turning like a corkscrew as it went. It led into a valley between falling hills, stubbly with rocks like a reaped field of corn, and floored farther down with green meadows. I followed the track with precipitation; the steepness of the slope, the continual agile turning of the line of the descent, and the old unwearied hope of finding something new in a new country, all conspired to lend me wings. Yet a little lower and a stream began, collecting itself together out of many fountains, and soon making a glad noise among the hills. Sometimes it would cross the track in a bit of waterfall, with a pool, in which Modestine refreshed her feet.

The whole descent is like a dream to me, so rapidly was it

accomplished. I had scarcely left the summit ere the valley had closed round my path, and the sun beat upon me, walking in a stagnant lowland atmosphere. The track became a road, and went up and down in easy undulations. I passed cabin after cabin, but all seemed deserted; and I saw not a human creature, nor heard any sound except that of the stream. I was, however, in a different country from the day before. The stony skeleton of the world was here vigorously displayed to sun and air. The slopes were steep and changeful. Oak trees clung along the hills, well grown, wealthy in leaf, and touched by the autumn with strong and luminous colours. Here and there another stream would fall in, from the right or the left, down a gorge of snow-white and tumultuary boulders. The river in the bottom (for it was rapidly growing a river, collecting on all hands as it trotted on its way) here foamed a while in desperate rapids, and there lay in pools of the most enchanting sea-green shot with watery browns. As far as I have gone, I have never seen a river of so changeful and delicate a hue; crystal was not more clear, the meadows were not by half so green; and at every pool I saw I felt a thrill of longing to be out of these hot, dusty and material garments and bathe my naked body in the mountain air and water. All the time as I went on I never forgot it was the Sabbath: the stillness was a perpetual reminder; and I heard in spirit the church-bells clamouring all over Europe, and the psalms of a thousand churches.

At length a human sound struck upon my ear – a cry strangely modulated between pathos and derision; and looking across the valley, I saw a little urchin sitting in a meadow, with his hands about his knees, and dwarfed to almost comical smallness by the distance. But the rogue had picked me out as I went down the road, from oak wood on to oak wood, driving Modestine; and he made me the compliments of the new country in this tremulous high-pitched salutation. And as all noises are lovely and natural at a sufficient distance, this also, coming through so much clean hill air and crossing all the green valley, sounded pleasant to my ear, and seemed a thing rustic, like the oaks or the river.

A little after, the stream that I was following fell into the Tarn at Pont de Montvert of bloody memory.

Pont de Montvert

One of the first things I encountered in Pont de Montvert was, if I remember rightly, the Protestant temple; but this was but the type of other novelties. A subtle atmosphere distinguishes a town in England from a town in France, or even in Scotland. At Carlisle you can see you are in the one country; at Dumfries, thirty miles away, you are as sure that you are in the other. I should find it difficult to tell in what particulars Pont de Montvert differed from Monastier or Langogne, or even Bleymard; but the difference existed, and spoke eloquently to the eyes. The place, with its houses, its lanes, its glaring riverbed, wore an indescribable air of the South.

All was Sunday bustle in the streets and in the public-house, as all had been Sabbath peace among the mountains. There must have been near a score of us at dinner by eleven before noon; and after I had eaten and drunken, and sat writing up my journal, I suppose as many more came dropping in one after another, or by twos and threes. In crossing the Lozère I had not only come among new natural features, but moved into the territory of a different race. These people, as they hurriedly despatched their viands in an intricate sword-play of knives, questioned and answered me with a degree of intelligence which excelled all that I had met, except among the railway folk at Chasseradès. They had open, telling faces, and were lively both in speech and manner. They not only entered thoroughly into the spirit of my little trip, but more than one declared, if he were rich enough, he would like to set forth on such another.

Even physically there was a pleasant change. I had not seen a pretty woman since I left Monastier, and there but one. Now of the three who sat down with me to dinner, one was certainly not beautiful – a poor timid thing of forty, quite troubled at this roaring *table d'hôte*, whom I squired and helped to wine, and pledged and tried generally to encourage, with quite a contrary effect; but the other two, both married, were both more handsome than the average of women. And Clarisse? What shall I say of Clarisse? She waited the table with a heavy placable nonchalance, like a performing cow; her great grey eyes were steeped in amorous languor; her features, although fleshy, were of an original and accurate design; her mouth had a curl; her nostril spoke of dainty pride; her cheek fell into strange and interesting lines. It was a face capable of strong emotion, and, with training, it offered the promise of delicate sentiment. It seemed pitiful to see so good a model left to country admirers and a country way of thought. Beauty should at least have touched society; then, in a moment, it throws off a weight that lay upon it, it becomes conscious of itself, it puts on an elegance, learns a gait and a carriage of the head, and, in a moment, *patet dea*.[54] Before I left I assured Clarisse of my hearty admiration. She took it like milk, without embarrassment or wonder, merely looking at me steadily with her great eyes; and I own the result upon myself was some confusion. If Clarisse could read English, I should not dare to add that her figure was unworthy of her face. Hers was a case for stays; but that may perhaps grow better as she gets up in years.

Pont de Montvert, or Greenhill Bridge, as we might say at home, is a place memorable in the story of the Camisards. It was here that the war broke out; here that those southern Covenanters[55] slew their Archbishop Sharp. The persecution on the one hand, the febrile enthusiasm on the other, are almost equally difficult to understand in these quiet modern days, and with our easy modern beliefs and disbeliefs. The Protestants were one and all beside their right minds with zeal and sorrow. They were all prophets and prophetesses. Children at the breast would exhort their parents to good works. 'A child of fifteen months at Quissac spoke from its mother's arms, agitated and sobbing, distinctly and with a loud voice.' Marshal Villars has seen a town where all the women 'seemed possessed by the devil', and had trembling fits, and uttered prophecies publicly upon the streets. A prophetess of Vivarais was hanged at Montpellier because blood flowed from her eyes and nose, and she declared that she was weeping tears of blood for the misfortunes of the Protestants. And it was not only women and children. Stalwart dangerous fellows, used to swing the sickle or to wield the forest axe, were likewise shaken with strange paroxysms, and spoke oracles with sobs and streaming tears. A persecution unsurpassed in violence had lasted near a score of years, and this was the result upon the persecuted; hanging, burning, breaking on the wheel, had been in vain; the dragoons had left their hoof-marks over all the countryside; there were men rowing in the galleys, and women pining in the prisons of the Church; and not a thought was changed in the heart of any upright Protestant.

Now the head and forefront of the persecution – after Lamoignon de Bâvile – François de Langlade Du Chayla (pronounce Chéila), Archpriest of the Cévennes and Inspector of Missions in the same country, had a house in which he sometimes dwelt in the town of Pont de Montvert. He was a conscientious person, who seems to have been intended by nature for a pirate, and now fifty-five, an age by which a man has learned all the moderation of which he is capable. A missionary in his youth in China, he there suffered martyrdom, was left for dead, and only succoured and brought back to life by the charity of a pariah. We must suppose the pariah devoid of second-sight, and not purposely malicious in this act. Such an experience, it might be thought, would have cured a man of the desire to persecute; but the human spirit is a thing strangely put together; and, having been a Christian martyr, Du Chayla became a Christian persecutor. The Work of the Propagation of the Faith went roundly forward in his hands. His house in Pont de Montvert served him as a prison. There he closed the hands of his prisoners upon live coal, and plucked out the hairs of their beards, to convince them that they were deceived in their opinions. And yet had not he himself tried and proved the inefficacy of these carnal arguments among the Buddhists in China?

Not only was life made intolerable in Languedoc, but flight was rigidly forbidden. One Massip, a muleteer, and well acquainted with the mountain-paths, had already guided several troops of fugitives in safety to Geneva; and on him, with another convoy, consisting mostly of women dressed as men, Du Chayla, in an evil hour for himself, laid his hands. The Sunday following, there was a conventicle of Protestants in the woods of Altefage, upon Mount Bougès, where there stood up one Séguier – Spirit Séguier, as his companions called him – a wool-carder, tall, black-faced and toothless, but a man full of prophecy. He declared, in the name of God, that the time for submission had gone by, and they must betake themselves to arms for the deliverance of their brethren and the destruction of the priests.

The next night, 24th July 1702, a sound disturbed the Inspector of Missions as he sat in his prison-house at Pont de Montvert: the voices of many men upraised in psalmody drew nearer and nearer through the town. It was ten at night; he had his court about him, priests, soldiers and servants, to the number of twelve or fifteen; and now dreading the insolence of a conventicle below his very windows, he ordered forth his soldiers to report. But the psalm-singers were already at his door, fifty strong, led by the inspired Séguier and breathing death. To their summons, the archpriest made answer like a stout old persecutor, and bade his garrison fire upon the mob. One Camisard (for, according to some, it was in this night's work that they came by the name) fell at this discharge: his comrades burst in the door with hatchets and a beam of wood, overran the lower storey of the house, set free the prisoners, and finding one of them in the vine, a sort of Scavenger's Daughter of the place and period, redoubled in fury against Du Chayla, and sought by repeated assaults to carry the upper floors. But he, on his side, had given absolution to his men, and they bravely held the staircase.

'Children of God,' cried the prophet, 'hold your hands. Let us burn the house, with the priest and the satellites of Baal.'

The fire caught readily. Out of an upper window Du Chayla and his men lowered themselves into the garden by means of knotted sheets; some escaped across the river under the bullets of the insurgents; but the archpriest himself fell, broke his thigh, and could only crawl into the hedge. What were his reflections as this second martyrdom drew near? A poor, brave, besotted, hateful man, who had done his duty resolutely according to his light, both in the Cévennes and China. He found at least one telling word to say in his defence; for when the roof fell in and the up-bursting flames discovered his retreat, and they came and dragged him to the public place of the town, raging and calling him damned – 'If I be damned,' said he, 'why should you also damn yourselves?'

Here was a good reason for the last; but in the course of his inspectorship he had given many stronger which all told in a contrary direction; and these he was now to hear. One by one, Séguier first, the Camisards drew near and stabbed him. 'This,' they said, 'is for my father broken on the wheel. This for my brother in the galleys. That for my mother or my sister imprisoned in your cursed convents.' Each gave his blow and his reason; and then all kneeled and sang psalms around the body till the dawn. With the dawn, still singing, they defiled away towards Frugères, farther up the Tarn, to pursue the work of vengeance, leaving Du Chayla's prison-house in ruins, and his body pierced with two-and-fifty wounds upon the public place.

'Tis a wild night's work, with its accompaniment of psalms; and it seems as if a psalm must always have a sound of threatening in that town upon the Tarn. But the story does not end, even so far as concerns Pont de Montvert, with the departure of the Camisards. The career of Séguier was brief and bloody. Two more priests and a whole family at Ladevèze, from the father to the servants, fell by his hand or by his orders; and yet he was but a day or two at large, and restrained all the time by the presence of the soldiery. Taken at length by a famous soldier of fortune, Captain Poul, he appeared unmoved before his judges.

'Your name?' they asked.

'Pierre Séguier.'

'Why are you called Spirit?'

'Because the Spirit of the Lord is with me.'

'Your domicile?'

'Lately in the desert, and soon in heaven.'

'Have you no remorse for your crimes?'

'I have committed none. *My soul is like a garden full of shelter and of fountains.*'[56]

At Pont de Montvert, on the 12th of August, he had his right hand stricken from his body, and was burned alive. And his soul was like a garden? So perhaps was the soul of Du Chayla, the Christian martyr. And perhaps if you could read in my soul, or I could read in yours, our own composure might seem little less surprising.

Du Chayla's house still stands, with a new roof, beside one of the bridges of the town; and if you are curious you may see the terrace-garden into which he dropped.

In the Valley of the Tarn

A new road leads from Pont de Montvert to Florac by the valley of the Tarn; a smooth sandy ledge, it runs about halfway between the summit of the cliffs and the river in the bottom of the valley; and I went in and out, as I followed it, from bays of shadow into promontories of afternoon sun. This was a pass like that of Killiecrankie,[57] a deep turning gully in the hills, with the Tarn making a wonderful hoarse uproar far below, and craggy summits standing in the sunshine high above. A thin fringe of ash trees ran about the hilltops, like ivy on a ruin; but on the lower slopes, and far up every glen, the Spanish chestnut trees stood each foursquare to heaven under its tented foliage. Some were planted, each on its own terrace no larger than a bed; some, trusting in their roots, found strength to grow and prosper and be straight and large upon the rapid slopes of the valley; others, where there was a margin to the river, stood marshalled in a line and mighty like cedars of Lebanon. Yet even where they grew most thickly they were not to be thought of as a wood, but as a herd of stalwart individuals; and the dome of each tree stood forth separate and large, and as it were a little hill, from among the domes of its companions. They gave forth a faint sweet perfume which pervaded the air of the afternoon; autumn had put tints of gold and tarnish in the green; and the sun so shone through and kindled the broad foliage, that each chestnut was relieved against another, not in shadow, but in light. A humble sketcher here laid down his pencil in despair.

I wish I could convey a notion of the growth of these noble trees; of how they strike out boughs like the oak, and trail sprays of drooping foliage like the willow; of how they stand on upright fluted columns like the pillars of a church; or like the olive, from the most shattered bole can put out smooth and youthful shoots, and begin a new life upon the ruins of the old. Thus they partake of the nature of many different trees; and even their prickly top-knots, seen near at hand against the sky, have a certain palm-like air that impresses the imagination. But their individuality, although compounded of so many elements, is but the richer and the more original. And to look down upon a level filled with these knolls of foliage, or to see a clan of old unconquerable chestnuts cluster 'like herded elephants'[58] upon the spur of a mountain, is to rise to higher thoughts of the powers that are in nature.

Between Modestine's laggard humour and the beauty of the scene, we made little progress all that afternoon; and at last finding the sun, although still far from setting, was already beginning to desert the narrow valley of the Tarn, I began to cast about for a place to camp in. This was not easy to find; the terraces were too narrow, and the ground, where it was unterraced, was usually too steep for a man to lie upon. I should have slipped all night, and awakened towards morning with my feet or my head in the river.

After perhaps a mile, I saw, some sixty feet above the road, a little plateau large enough to hold my sack, and securely parapeted by the trunk of an aged and enormous chestnut. Thither, with infinite trouble, I goaded and kicked the reluctant Modestine, and there I hastened to unload her. There was only room for myself upon the plateau, and I had to go nearly as high again before I found so much as standing-room for the ass. It was on a heap of rolling stones, on an artificial terrace, certainly not five feet square in all. Here I tied her to a chestnut, and having given her corn and bread and made a pile of chestnut-leaves, of which I found her greedy, I descended once more to my own encampment.

The position was unpleasantly exposed. One or two carts went by upon the road; and as long as daylight lasted I concealed myself, for all the world like a hunted Camisard, behind my fortification of vast chestnut trunk; for I was passionately afraid of discovery and the visit of jocular persons in the night. Moreover, I saw that I must be early awake; for these chestnut gardens had been the scene of industry no further gone than on the day before. The slope was strewn with lopped branches, and here and there a great package of leaves was propped against a trunk; for even the leaves are serviceable, and the peasants use them in winter by way of fodder for their animals. I picked a meal in fear and trembling, half lying down to hide myself from the road; and I dare say I was as much concerned as if I had been a scout from Joani's band above upon the Lozère, or from Salomon's across the Tarn, in the old times of psalm-singing and blood. Or, indeed, perhaps more; for the Camisards had a remarkable confidence in God; and a tale comes back into my memory of how the Count of Gévaudan, riding with a party of dragoons and a notary at his saddlebow to enforce the oath of fidelity in all the country hamlets, entered a valley in the woods, and found Cavalier and his men at dinner, gaily seated on the grass, and their hats crowned with box-tree garlands, while fifteen women washed their linen in the stream. Such was a field festival in 1703; at that date Antony Watteau[59] would be painting similar subjects.

This was a very different camp from that of the night before in the cool and silent pine-woods. It was warm and even stifling in the valley. The shrill song of frogs, like the tremolo note of a whistle with a pea in it, rang up from the riverside before the sun was down. In the growing dusk, faint rustlings began to run to and fro among the fallen leaves; from time to time a faint chirping or cheeping noise would fall upon my ear; and from time to time I thought I could see the movement of something swift and indistinct between the chestnuts. A profusion of large ants swarmed upon the ground; bats whisked by and mosquitoes droned overhead. The long boughs with their bunches of leaves hung against the sky like garlands; and those immediately above and around me had some-what the air of a trellis which should have been wrecked and half overthrown in a gale of wind.

Sleep for a long time fled my eyelids; and just as I was beginning to feel quiet stealing over my limbs, and settling densely on my mind, a noise at my head startled me broad awake again, and, I will frankly confess it, brought my heart into my mouth.

It was such a noise as a person would make scratching loudly with a fingernail; it came from under the knapsack which served me for a pillow, and it was thrice repeated before I had time to sit up and turn about. Nothing was to be seen, nothing more was to be heard, but a few of these mysterious rustlings far and near, and the ceaseless accompaniment of the river and the frogs. I learned next day that the chestnut gardens are infested by rats; rustling, chirping and scraping were probably all due to these; but the puzzle, for the moment, was insoluble, and I had to compose myself for sleep, as best I could, in wondering uncertainty about my neighbours.

I was wakened in the grey of the morning (Monday, 30th September) by the sound of footsteps not far off upon the stones, and opening

my eyes, I beheld a peasant going by among the chestnuts by a
footpath that I had not hitherto observed. He turned his head neither
to the right nor to the left, and disappeared in a few strides among
the foliage. Here was an escape! But it was plainly more than time to
be moving. The peasantry were abroad; scarce less terrible to me in
my nondescript position than the soldiers of Captain Poul to an
undaunted Camisard. I fed Modestine with what haste I could; but as
I was returning to my sack, I saw a man and a boy come down the
hillside in a direction crossing mine. They unintelligibly hailed me,
and I replied with inarticulate but cheerful sounds, and hurried
forward to get into my gaiters.

The pair, who seemed to be father and son, came slowly up to the
plateau, and stood close beside me for some time in silence. The bed
was open, and I saw with regret my revolver lying patently disclosed
on the blue wool.

At last, after they had looked me all over, and the silence had
grown laughably embarrassing, the man demanded in what seemed
unfriendly tones: 'You have slept here?'

'Yes,' said I. 'As you see.'

'Why?' he asked.

'My faith,' I answered lightly, 'I was tired.'

He next enquired where I was going and what I had had for dinner;
and then, without the least transition, '*C'est bien*,' he added, 'come
along.' And he and his son, without another word, turned off to the
next chestnut tree but one, which they set to pruning. The thing had
passed of more simply than I hoped. He was a grave, respectable
man; and his unfriendly voice did not imply that he thought he was
speaking to a criminal, but merely to an inferior.

I was soon on the road, nibbling a cake of chocolate and seriously
occupied with a case of conscience. Was I to pay for my night's
lodging? I had slept ill, the bed was full of fleas in the shape of ants,
there was no water in the room, the very dawn had neglected to call
me in the morning. I might have missed a train, had there been any
in the neighbourhood to catch. Clearly, I was dissatisfied with my
entertainment; and I decided I should not pay unless I met a beggar.

The valley looked even lovelier by morning; and soon the road
descended to the level of the river. Here, in a place where many
straight and prosperous chestnuts stood together, making an aisle
upon a swarded terrace, I made my morning toilette in the water of
the Tarn. It was marvellously clear, thrillingly cool; the soapsuds
disappeared as if by magic in the swift current, and the white boulders

gave one a model for cleanliness. To wash in one of God's rivers in the open air seems to me a sort of cheerful solemnity or semi-pagan act of worship. To dabble among dishes in a bedroom may perhaps make clean the body; but the imagination takes no share in such a cleansing. I went on with a light and peaceful heart, and sang psalms to the spiritual ear as I advanced.

Suddenly up came an old woman, who point-blank demanded alms. 'Good,' thought I; 'here comes the waiter with the bill.'

And I paid for my night's lodging on the spot. Take it how you please, but this was the first and the last beggar[60] that I met with during all my tour.

A step or two farther I was overtaken by an old man in a brown nightcap, clear-eyed, weather-beaten, with a faint, excited smile. A little girl followed him, driving two sheep and a goat; but she kept in our wake, while the old man walked beside me and talked about the morning and the valley. It was not much past six; and for healthy people who have slept enough, that is an hour of expansion and of open and trustful talk.

'*Connaissez-vous le Seigneur?*'[61] he said at length.

I asked him what Seigneur he meant; but he only repeated the question with more emphasis and a look in his eyes denoting hope and interest.

'Ah,' said I, pointing upwards, 'I understand you now. Yes, I know Him; He is the best of acquaintances.'

The old man said he was delighted. 'Hold,' he added, striking his bosom; 'it makes me happy here.' There were a few who knew the Lord in these valleys, he went on to tell me; not many, but a few. 'Many are called,' he quoted, 'and few chosen.'

'My father,' said I, 'it is not easy to say who know the Lord; and it is none of our business. Protestants and Catholics, and even those who worship stones, may know Him and be known by Him; for He has made all.'

I did not know I was so good a preacher.

The old man assured me he thought as I did, and repeated his expressions of pleasure at meeting me. 'We are so few,' he said. 'They call us Moravians here; but down in the Department of Gard, where there are also a good number, they are called Derbists, after an English pastor.'[62]

I began to understand that I was figuring, in questionable taste, as a member of some sect to me unknown; but I was more pleased with the pleasure of my companion than embarrassed by my own equivocal position. Indeed, I can see no dishonesty in not avowing a difference; and especially in these high matters, where we have all a sufficient assurance that, whoever may be in the wrong, we ourselves are not completely in the right. The truth is much talked about; but this old man in a brown nightcap showed himself so simple, sweet, and friendly, that I am not unwilling to profess myself his convert. He was, as a matter of fact, a Plymouth Brother.[63] Of what that involves in the way of doctrine I have no idea nor the time to inform myself; but I know right well that we are all embarked upon a troublesome world, the children of one Father, striving in many essential points to do and to become the same. And although it was somewhat in a mistake that he shook hands with me so often and showed himself so ready to receive my words, that was a mistake of the truth-finding sort. For charity begins blindfold; and only through a series of similar misapprehensions rises at length into a settled principle of love and patience, and a firm belief in all our fellow-men. If I deceived this good old man, in the like manner I would willingly go on to deceive others. And if ever at length, out of our separate and sad ways, we should all come together into one common house, I have a hope, to which I cling dearly, that my mountain Plymouth Brother will hasten to shake hands with me again.

Thus, talking like Christian and Faithful by the way, he and I came down upon a hamlet by the Tarn. It was but a humble place, called La Vernède, with less than a dozen houses, and a Protestant chapel on a knoll. Here he dwelt; and here, at the inn, I ordered my breakfast. The inn was kept by an agreeable young man, a stone-breaker on the road, and his sister, a pretty and engaging girl. The village school-master dropped in to speak with the stranger. And these were all Protestants – a fact which pleased me more than I should have expected; and, what pleased me still more, they seemed all upright and simple people. The Plymouth Brother hung round me with a sort of yearning interest, and returned at least thrice to make sure I was enjoying my meal. His behaviour touched me deeply at the time, and even now moves me in recollection. He feared to intrude, but he would not willingly forgo one moment of my society; and he seemed never weary of shaking me by the hand.

When all the rest had drifted off to their day's work, I sat for near half an hour with the young mistress of the house, who talked pleasantly over her seam of the chestnut harvest, and the beauties of the Tarn, and old family affections, broken up when young folk go from home, yet still subsisting. Hers, I am sure, was a sweet nature, with a country plainness and much delicacy underneath; and he who takes her to his heart will doubtless be a fortunate young man.

The valley below La Vernède pleased me more and more as I went forward. Now the hills approached from either hand, naked and crumbling, and walled in the river between cliffs; and now the valley widened and became green. The road led me past the old castle of Miral on a steep; past a battlemented monastery, long since broken up and turned into a church and parsonage; and past a cluster of black roofs, the village of Cocurès, sitting among vineyards, and meadows, and orchards thick with red apples, and where, along the highway, they were knocking down walnuts from the roadside trees, and gathering them in sacks and baskets. The hills, however much the vale might open, were still tall and bare, with cliffy battlements and here and there a pointed summit; and the Tarn still rattled through the stones with a mountain noise. I had been led, by bagmen of a picturesque turn of mind, to expect a horrific country after the heart of Byron; but to my Scottish eyes it seemed smiling and plentiful, as the weather still gave an impression of high summer to my Scottish body; although the chestnuts were already picked out by the autumn, and the poplars, that here began to mingle with them, had turned into pale gold against the approach of winter.

There was something in this landscape, smiling although wild, that explained to me the spirit of the Southern Covenanters. Those who took to the hills for conscience' sake in Scotland had all gloomy and bedevilled thoughts; for once that they received God's comfort they would be twice engaged with Satan; but the Camisards had only bright and supporting visions. They dealt much more in blood, both given and taken; yet I find no obsession of the Evil One in their records. With a light conscience, they pursued their life in these rough times and circumstances. The soul of Séguier, let us not forget, was like a garden. They knew they were on God's side, with a knowledge that has no parallel among the Scots; for the Scots, although they might be certain of the cause, could never rest confident of the person.

'We flew,' says one old Camisard, 'when we heard the sound of psalm-singing, we flew as if with wings. We felt within us an animating ardour, a transporting desire. The feeling cannot be expressed in words. It is a thing that must have been experienced to be understood. However weary we might be, we thought no more of our weariness, and grew light so soon as the psalms fell upon our ears.'

The valley of the Tarn and the people whom I met at La Vernède not only explain to me this passage, but the twenty years of suffering which those, who were so stiff and so bloody when once they betook themselves to war, endured with the meekness of children and the constancy of saints and peasants.

Florac[64]

On a branch of the Tarn stands Florac, the seat of a sub-prefecture, with an old castle, an alley of planes, many quaint street corners, and a live fountain welling from the hill. It is notable, besides, for handsome women, and as one of the two capitals, Alais being the other, of the country of the Camisards.

The landlord of the inn took me, after I had eaten, to an adjoining café, where I, or rather my journey, became the topic of the afternoon. Everyone had some suggestion for my guidance; and the sub-prefectorial map was fetched from the sub-prefecture itself, and much thumbed among coffee-cups and glasses of liqueur. Most of these kind advisers were Protestant, though I observed that Protestant and Catholic intermingled in a very easy manner; and it surprised me to see what a lively memory still subsisted of the religious war. Among the hills of the south-west, by Mauchline, Cumnock or Carsphairn, in isolated farms or in the manse, serious Presbyterian people still recall the days of the great persecution, and the graves of local martyrs are still piously regarded. But in towns and among the so-called better classes, I fear that these old doings have become an idle tale. If you met a mixed company in the King's Arms at Wigton, it is not likely that the talk would run on Covenanters. Nay, at Muirkirk of Glenluce, I found the beadle's wife had not so much as heard of Prophet Peden.[65] But these Cévenols were proud of their ancestors in quite another sense; the war was their chosen topic; its exploits were their own patent of nobility; and where a man or a race has had but one adventure, and that heroic, we must expect and pardon some prolixity of reference. They told me the country was still full of legends hitherto uncollected; I heard from them about Cavalier's descendants – not direct descendants, be it understood, but only cousins or nephews – who were still prosperous people in the scene of the boy-general's exploits; and one farmer had seen the bones of old combatants dug up into the air of an afternoon in the nineteenth century, in a field where the ancestors had fought, and the great-grandchildren were peaceably ditching.

Later in the day one of the Protestant pastors was so good as to visit me: a young man, intelligent and polite, with whom I passed an hour or two in talk. Florac, he told me, is part Protestant, part Catholic; and the difference in religion is usually doubled by a difference in politics. You may judge of my surprise, coming as I did from such a babbling purgatorial Poland of a place as Monastier, when I learned that the population lived together on very quiet terms; and there was even an exchange of hospitalities between households thus doubly separated. Black Camisard and White Camisard, militiaman and Miquelet and dragoon, Protestant prophet and Catholic cadet of the White Cross, they had all been sabring and shooting, burning, pillaging and murdering, their hearts hot with indignant passion; and here, after a hundred and seventy years, Protestant is still Protestant, Catholic still Catholic, in mutual toleration and mild amity of life. But the race of man, like that indomitable nature whence it sprang, has medicating virtues of its own; the years and seasons bring various harvests; the sun returns after the rain; and mankind outlives secular animosities, as a single man awakens from the passions of a day. We judge our ancestors from a more divine position; and the dust being a little laid with several centuries, we can see both sides adorned with human virtues and fighting with a show of right.

. I have never thought it easy to be just, and find it daily even harder than I thought. I own I met these Protestants with a delight and a sense of coming home. I was accustomed to speak their language, in another and deeper sense of the word than that which distinguishes between French and English; for the true Babel is a divergence upon morals. And hence I could hold more free communication with the Protestants, and judge them more justly, than the Catholics. Father Apollinaris may pair off with my mountain Plymouth Brother as two guileless and devout old men; yet I ask myself if I had as ready a feeling for the virtues of the Trappist; or, had I been a Catholic, if I should have felt so warmly to the dissenter of La Vernède. With the first I was on terms of mere forbearance; but with the other, although only on a misunderstanding and by keeping on selected points, it was still possible to hold converse and exchange some honest thoughts. In this world of imperfection we gladly welcome even partial intimacies. And if we find but one to whom we can speak out of our heart freely, with whom we can walk in love and simplicity without dissimulation, we have no ground of quarrel with the world or God.

In the Valley of the Mimente

On Tuesday, 1st October, we left Florac late in the afternoon, a tired donkey and tired donkey-driver. A little way up the Tarnon, a covered bridge of wood introduced us into the valley of the Mimente. Steep rocky red mountains overhung the stream; great oaks and chestnuts grew upon the slopes or in stony terraces; here and there was a red field of millet or a few apple trees studded with red apples; and the road passed hard by two black hamlets, one with an old castle atop to please the heart of the tourist.

It was difficult here again to find a spot fit for my encampment. Even under the oaks and chestnuts the ground had not only a very rapid slope, but was heaped with loose stones; and where there was no timber the hills descended to the stream in a red precipice tufted with heather. The sun had left the highest peak in front of me, and the valley was full of the lowing sound of herdsmen's horns as they recalled the flocks into the stable, when I spied a bight of meadow some way below the roadway in an angle of the river. Thither I descended, and, tying Modestine provisionally to a tree, proceeded to investigate the neighbourhood. A grey pearly evening shadow filled the glen; objects at a little distance grew indistinct and melted bafflingly into each other; and the darkness was rising steadily like an exhalation. I approached a great oak which grew in the meadow, hard by the river's brink; when to my disgust the voices of children fell upon my ear, and I beheld a house round the angle on the other bank. I had half a mind to pack and be gone again, but the growing darkness moved me to remain. I had only to make no noise until the night was fairly come, and trust to the dawn to call me early in the morning. But it was hard to be annoyed by neighbours in such a great hotel.

A hollow underneath the oak was my bed. Before I had fed Modestine and arranged my sack, three stars were already brightly shining, and the others were beginning dimly to appear. I slipped down to the river, which looked very black among its rocks, to fill my can; and dined with a good appetite in the dark, for I scrupled to light a lantern while so near a house. The moon, which I had seen a pallid crescent all afternoon, faintly illuminated the summit of the hills, but not a ray fell into the bottom of the glen where I was lying. The oak rose before me like a pillar of darkness; and overhead the heartsome stars were set in the face of the night. No one knows the stars who has not slept, as the French happily put it, *à la belle étoile*.[66]

He may know all their names and distances and magnitudes, and yet be ignorant of what alone concerns mankind – their serene and gladsome influence on the mind. The greater part of poetry is about the stars; and very justly, for they are themselves the most classical of poets. These same faraway worlds, sprinkled like tapers or shaken together like a diamond dust upon the sky, had looked not otherwise to Roland or Cavalier, when, in the words of the latter, they had 'no other tent but the sky, and no other bed than my mother earth'.

All night a strong wind blew up the valley, and the acorns fell pattering over me from the oak. Yet, on this first night of October, the air was as mild as May, and I slept with the fur thrown back.

I was much disturbed by the barking of a dog, an animal that I fear more than any wolf. A dog is vastly braver, and is besides supported by the sense of duty. If you kill a wolf, you meet with encouragement and praise; but if you kill a dog, the sacred rights of property and the domestic affections come clamouring round you for redress. At the end of a fagging day, the sharp cruel note of a dog's bark is in itself a keen annoyance; and to a tramp like myself, he represents the sedentary and respectable world in its most hostile form. There is something of the clergyman or the lawyer about this engaging animal; and if he were not amenable to stones, the boldest man would shrink from travelling afoot. I respect dogs much in the domestic circle; but on the highway, or sleeping afield, I both detest and fear them.

I was wakened next morning (Wednesday, October 2nd) by the same dog – for I knew his bark – making a charge down the bank, and then, seeing me sit up, retreating again with great alacrity. The stars were not yet quite extinguished. The heaven was of that enchanting mild grey-blue of the early morn. A still clear light began to fall, and the trees on the hillside were outlined sharply against the sky. The wind had veered more to the north, and no longer reached me in the glen; but as I was going on with my preparations, it drove a white cloud very swiftly over the hilltop; and looking up, I was surprised to see the cloud dyed with gold. In these high regions of the air, the sun was already shining as at noon. If only the clouds travelled high enough, we should see the same thing all night long. For it is always daylight in the fields of space.

As I began to go up the valley, a draught of wind came down it out of the seat of the sunrise, although the clouds continued to run overhead in an almost contrary direction. A few steps farther, and I saw a whole hillside gilded with the sun; and still a little beyond, between two peaks, a centre of dazzling brilliancy appeared floating in the sky, and I was once more face to face with the big bonfire that occupies the kernel of our system.

I met but one human being that forenoon, a dark military-looking wayfarer, who carried a game-bag on a baldric; but he made a remark that seems worthy of record. For when I asked him if he were Protestant or Catholic – 'Oh,' said he, 'I make no shame of my religion. I am a Catholic.'

He made no shame of it! The phrase is a piece of natural statistics; for it is the language of one in a minority. I thought with a smile of Bavile and his dragoons, and how you may ride rough-shod over a religion for a century, and leave it only the more lively for the friction. Ireland is still Catholic; the Cévennes still Protestant. It is not a basketful of law-papers, nor the hoofs and pistol-butts of a regiment of horse, that can change one tittle of a ploughman's thoughts. Outdoor rustic people have not many ideas, but such as they have are hardy plants, and thrive flourishingly in persecution. One who has grown a long while in the sweat of laborious noons, and under the stars at night, a frequenter of hills and forests, an old honest countryman, has, in the end, a sense of communion with the powers of the universe, and amicable relations towards his God. Like my mountain Plymouth Brother, he knows the Lord. His religion does not repose upon a choice of logic; it is the poetry of the man's experience, the philosophy of the history of his life. God, like a great power, like a great shining sun, has appeared to this simple fellow in the course of years, and become the ground and essence of his least reflections; and you may change creeds and dogmas by authority, or proclaim a new religion with the sound of trumpets, if you will; but here is a man who has his own thoughts, and will stubbornly adhere to them in good and evil. He is a Catholic, a Protestant, or a Plymouth Brother, in the same indefeasible sense that a man is not a woman, or a woman not a man. For he could not vary from his faith, unless he could eradicate all memory of the past, and, in a strict and not a conventional meaning, change his mind.

The Heart of the Country

I was now drawing near to Cassagnas, a cluster of black roofs upon the hillside, in this wild valley, among chestnut gardens, and looked upon in the clear air by many rocky peaks. The road along the Mimente is yet new, nor have the mountaineers recovered their surprise when the first cart arrived at Cassagnas. But although it lay thus apart from the current of men's business, this hamlet had already made a figure in the history of France. Hard by, in caverns of the mountain, was one of the five arsenals of the Camisards; where they laid up clothes and corn and arms against necessity, forged bayonets and sabres, and made themselves gunpowder with willow charcoal and saltpetre boiled in kettles. To the same caves, amid this multi-farious industry, the sick and wounded were brought up to heal; and there they were visited by the two surgeons, Chabrier and Tavan, and secretly nursed by women of the neighbourhood.

Of the five legions into which the Camisards were divided, it was the oldest and the most obscure that had its magazines by Cassagnas. This was the band of Spirit Séguier; men who had joined their voices with his in the 68th Psalm as they marched down by night on the archpriest of the Cévennes. Séguier, promoted to heaven, was succeeded by Salomon Couderc, whom Cavalier treats in his memoirs as chaplain-general to the whole army of the Camisards. He was a prophet; a great reader of the heart, who admitted people to the sacrament, or refused them, by 'intensively viewing every man' between the eyes; and had the most of the Scriptures off by rote. And this was surely happy; since in a surprise in August 1703, he lost his mule, his portfolios and his Bible. It is only strange that they were not surprised more often and more effectually; for this legion of Cassagnas was truly patriarchal in its theory of war, and camped without sentries, leaving that duty to the angels of the God for whom they fought. This is a token, not only of their faith, but of the trackless country where they harboured. M. de Caladon, taking a stroll one fine day, walked without warning into their midst, as he might have walked into 'a flock of sheep in a plain', and found some asleep and some awake and psalm-singing. A traitor had need of no recommendation to insinuate himself among their ranks, beyond 'his faculty of singing psalms'; and even the prophet Salomon 'took him into a particular friendship'. Thus, among their intricate hills, the rustic troop sub-sisted; and history can attribute few exploits to them but sacraments and ecstasies.

People of this tough and simple stock will not, as I have just been saying, prove variable in religion; nor will they get nearer to apostasy than a mere external conformity like that of Naaman in the house of Rimmon. When Louis XVI, in the words of the edict, 'convinced by the uselessness of a century of persecutions, and rather from necessity than sympathy', granted at last a royal grace of toleration, Cassagnas was still Protestant; and to a man, it is so to this day. There is, indeed, one family that is not Protestant, but neither is it Catholic. It is that of a Catholic curé in revolt, who has taken to his bosom a schoolmistress. And his conduct, it is worth noting, is disapproved by the Protestant villagers.

'It is a bad idea for a man,' said one, 'to go back from his engagements.'

The villagers whom I saw seemed intelligent after a countrified fashion, and were all plain and dignified in manner. As a Protestant myself, I was well looked upon, and my acquaintance with history gained me further respect. For we had something not unlike a religious controversy at table, a gendarme and a merchant with whom I dined being both strangers to the place, and Catholics. The young men of the house stood round and supported me; and the whole discussion was tolerantly conducted, and surprised a man brought up among the infinitesimal and contentious differences of Scotland. The merchant, indeed, grew a little warm, and was far less pleased than some others with my historical acquirements. But the gendarme was mighty easy over it all.

'It's a bad idea for a man to change,' said he; and the remark was generally applauded.

That was not the opinion of the priest and soldier at Our Lady of the Snows. But this is a different race; and perhaps the same great-heartedness that upheld them to resist, now enables them to differ in a kind spirit. For courage respects courage; but where a faith has been trodden out, we may look for a mean and narrow population. The true work of Bruce and Wallace[67] was the union of the nations; not that they should stand apart a while longer, skirmishing upon their borders; but that, when the time came, they might unite with self-respect.

The merchant was much interested in my journey, and thought it dangerous to sleep afield.

'There are the wolves,' said he; 'and then it is known you are an Englishman. The English have always long purses, and it might very well enter into someone's head to deal you an ill blow some night.'

I told him I was not much afraid of such accidents; and at any rate judged it unwise to dwell upon alarms or consider small perils in the arrangement of life. Life itself, I submitted, was a far too risky business as a whole to make each additional particular of danger worth regard. 'Something,' said I, 'might burst in your inside any day of the week, and there would be an end of you, if you were locked into your room with three turns of the key.'

'*Cependant*,' said he, '*coucher dehors!*'[68]

'God,' said I, 'is everywhere.'

'*Cependant, coucher dehors!*' he repeated, and his voice was eloquent of terror.

He was the only person, in all my voyage, who saw anything hardy in so simple a proceeding; although many considered it superfluous. Only one, on the other hand, professed much delight in the idea; and that was my Plymouth Brother, who cried out, when I told him I sometimes preferred sleeping under the stars to a close and noisy alehouse, 'Now I see that you know the Lord!'

The merchant asked me for one of my cards as I was leaving, for he said I should be something to talk of in the future, and desired me to make a note of his request and reason; a desire with which I have thus complied.

A little after two I struck across the Mimente, and took a rugged path southward up a hillside covered with loose stones and tufts of heather. At the top, as is the habit of the country, the path disappeared; and I left my she-ass munching heather, and went forward alone to seek a road.

I was now on the separation of two vast watersheds: behind me all the streams were bound for the Garonne and the Western Ocean; before me was the basin of the Rhone. Hence, as from the Lozère, you can see in clear weather the shining of the Gulf of Lyons; and perhaps from here the soldiers of Salomon may have watched for the topsails of Sir Cloudesley Shovel, and the long-promised aid from England. You may take this ridge as lying in the heart of the country of the Camisards; four of the five legions camped all round it and almost within view – Salomon and Joani to the north, Castanet and Roland to the south; and when Julien had finished his famous work, the devastation of the High Cévennes, which lasted all through October and November 1703, and during which four hundred and sixty villages and hamlets were, with fire and pickaxe, utterly subverted, a man standing on this eminence would have looked forth upon a silent, smokeless and dispeopled land. Time and man's activity have now repaired these ruins; Cassagnas is once more roofed and sending up domestic smoke; and in the chestnut gardens, in low and leafy corners, many a prosperous farmer returns, when the day's work is done, to his children and bright hearth. And still it was perhaps the wildest view of all my journey. Peak upon peak, chain upon chain of hills ran surging southward, channelled and sculptured by the winter streams, feathered from head to foot with chestnuts, and here and there breaking out into a coronal of cliffs. The sun, which was still far from setting, sent a drift of misty gold across the hilltops, but the valleys were already plunged in a profound and quiet shadow.

A very old shepherd, hobbling on a pair of sticks, and wearing a black cap of liberty, as if in honour of his nearness to the grave, directed me to the road for St Germain de Calberte. There was something solemn in the isolation of this infirm and ancient creature. Where he dwelt, how he got upon this high ridge, or how he proposed to get down again, were more than I could fancy. Not far off upon my right was the famous Plan de Font Morte, where Poul with his Armenian sabre slashed down the Camisards of Séguier. This, methought, might be some Rip van Winkle[69] of the war, who had lost his comrades, fleeing before Poul, and wandered ever since upon the mountains. It might be news to him that Cavalier had surrendered, or Roland had fallen fighting with his back against an olive. And while I was thus working on my fancy, I heard him hailing in broken tones, and saw him waving me to come back with one of his two sticks. I had already got some way past him; but, leaving Modestine once more, retraced my steps.

Alas, it was a very commonplace affair. The old gentleman had forgot to ask the pedlar what he sold, and wished to remedy this neglect.

I told him sternly, 'Nothing.'

'Nothing?' cried he.

I repeated 'Nothing,' and made off.

It's odd to think of, but perhaps I thus became as inexplicable to the old man as he had been to me.

The road lay under chestnuts, and though I saw a hamlet or two below me in the vale, and many lone houses of the chestnut farmers, it was a very solitary march all afternoon; and the evening began early underneath the trees. But I heard the voice of a woman singing some sad, old, endless ballad not far off. It seemed to be about love and a *bel amoureux*, her handsome sweetheart; and I wished I could have taken up the strain and answered her, as I went on upon my invisible woodland way, weaving, like Pippa[70] in the poem, my own thoughts with hers. What could I have told her? Little enough; and yet all the heart requires. How the world gives and takes away, and brings sweethearts near only to separate them again into distant and strange lands; but to love is the great amulet which makes the world a garden; and 'hope, which comes to all', outwears the accidents of life, and reaches with tremulous hand beyond the grave and death. Easy to say: yea, but also, by God's mercy, both easy and grateful to believe!

We struck at last into a wide white high-road carpeted with noiseless dust. The night had come; the moon had been shining for a long while upon the opposite mountain, when on turning a corner my donkey and I issued ourselves into her light. I had emptied out my brandy at Florac, for I could bear the stuff no longer, and replaced it with some generous and scented Volnay;[71] and now I drank to the moon's sacred majesty upon the road. It was but a couple of mouthfuls; yet I became thenceforth unconscious of my limbs, and my blood flowed with luxury. Even Modestine was inspired by this purified nocturnal sunshine, and bestirred her little hoofs as to a livelier measure. The road wound and descended swiftly among masses of chestnuts. Hot dust rose from our feet and flowed away. Our two shadows[72] – mine deformed with the knapsack, hers comically bestridden by the pack – now lay before us clearly outlined on the road, and now, as we turned a corner, went off into the ghostly distance, and sailed along the mountain like clouds. From time to time a warm wind rustled down the valley, and set all the chestnuts dangling their bunches of foliage and fruit; the ear was filled with whispering music, and the shadows danced in tune. And next moment the breeze had gone by, and in all the valley nothing moved except our travelling feet. On the opposite slope, the monstrous ribs and gullies of the mountain were faintly designed in the moonshine; and high overhead, in some lone house, there burned one lighted window, one square spark of red in the huge field of sad nocturnal colouring.

At a certain point, as I went downward, turning many acute angles, the moon disappeared behind the hill; and I pursued my way in great darkness, until another turning shot me without preparation into St Germain de Calberte. The place was asleep and silent, and buried in opaque night. Only from a single open door, some lamplight escaped upon the road to show me that I was come among men's habitations. The two last gossips of the evening, still talking by a garden wall, directed me to the inn. The landlady was getting her chicks to bed; the fire was already out, and had, not without grumbling, to be rekindled; half an hour later, and I must have gone supperless to roost.

The Last Day

When I awoke (Thursday, 2nd October), and, hearing a great flourishing of cocks and chuckling of contented hens, betook me to the window of the clean and comfortable room where I had slept the night, I looked forth on a sunshiny morning in a deep vale of chestnut gardens. It was still early, and the cockcrows, and the slanting lights, and the long shadows encouraged me to be out and look round me.

St Germain de Calberte is a great parish nine leagues round about. At the period of the wars, and immediately before the devastation, it was inhabited by two hundred and seventy-five families, of which only nine were Catholic; and it took the curé seventeen September days to go from house to house on horseback for a census. But the place itself, although capital of a canton, is scarce larger than a hamlet. It lies terraced across a steep slope in the midst of mighty chestnuts. The Protestant chapel stands below upon a shoulder; in the midst of the town is the quaint old Catholic church.

It was here that poor Du Chayla, the Christian martyr, kept his library and held a court of missionaries; here he had built his tomb, thinking to lie among a grateful population whom he had redeemed from error; and hither on the morrow of his death they brought the body, pierced with two-and-fifty wounds, to be interred. Clad in his priestly robes, he was laid out in state in the church. The curé, taking his text from Second Samuel, twentieth chapter and twelfth verse, 'And Amasa wallowed in his blood in the highway,' preached a rousing sermon, and exhorted his brethren to die each at his post, like their unhappy and illustrious superior. In the midst of this eloquence there came a breeze that Spirit Séguier was near at hand; and behold! all the assembly took to their horses' heels, some east, some west, and the curé himself as far as Alais.

Strange was the position of this little Catholic metropolis, a thimbleful of Rome, in such a wild and contrary neighbourhood. On the one hand, the legion of Salomon overlooked it from Cassagnas; on the other, it was cut off from assistance by the legion of Roland at Mialet. The curé, Louvrelenil, although he took a panic at the arch-priest's funeral, and so hurriedly decamped to Alais, stood well by his isolated pulpit, and thence uttered fulminations against the crimes of the Protestants. Salomon besieged the village for an hour and a half, but was beaten back. The militiamen, on guard before the curé's door, could be heard, in the black hours, singing Protestant psalms and holding friendly talk with the insurgents. And in the morning, although not a shot had been fired, there would not be a round of powder in their flasks. Where was it gone? All handed over to the Camisards for a consideration. Untrusty guardians for an isolated priest!

That these continual stirs were once busy in St Germain de Calberte, the imagination with difficulty receives; all is now so quiet, the pulse of human life now beats so low and still in this hamlet of the mountains. Boys followed me a great way off, like a timid sort of lion-hunters; and people turned round to have a second look, or came out of their houses, as I went by. My passage was the first event, you would have fancied, since the Camisards. There was nothing rude or forward in this observation; it was but a pleased and wondering scrutiny, like that of oxen or the human infant; yet it wearied my spirits, and soon drove me from the street.

I took refuge on the terraces, which are here greenly carpeted with sward, and tried to imitate with a pencil the inimitable attitudes of the chestnuts as they bear up their canopy of leaves. Ever and again a little wind went by, and the nuts dropped all around me, with a light and dull sound, upon the sward. The noise was as of a thin fall of great hailstones; but there went with it a cheerful human sentiment of an approaching harvest and farmers rejoicing in their gains. Looking up, I could see the brown nut peering through the husk, which was already gaping; and between the stems the eye embraced an amphitheatre of hill, sunlit and green with leaves.

I have not often enjoyed a place more deeply. I moved in an atmosphere of pleasure, and felt light and quiet and content. But perhaps it was not the place alone that so disposed my spirit. Perhaps someone was thinking of me in another country; or perhaps some thought of my own had come and gone unnoticed, and yet done me good. For some thoughts, which sure would be the most beautiful, vanish before we can rightly scan their features; as though a god, travelling by our green highways, should but ope the door, give one smiling look into the house, and go again for ever. Was it Apollo, or Mercury, or Love with folded wings? Who shall say? But we go the lighter about our business, and feel peace and pleasure in our hearts.

I dined with a pair of Catholics. They agreed in the condemnation of a young man, a Catholic, who had married a Protestant girl and gone over to the religion of his wife. A Protestant born they could understand and respect; indeed, they seemed to be of the mind of an old Catholic woman, who told me that same day there was no difference between the two sects, save that 'wrong was more wrong for the Catholic', who had more light and guidance; but this of a man's desertion filled them with contempt.

'It is a bad idea for a man to change,' said one.

It may have been accidental, but you see how this phrase pursued me; and for myself, I believe it is the current philosophy in these parts. I have some difficulty in imagining a better. It's not only a great flight of confidence for a man to change his creed and go out of his family for heaven's sake; but the odds are – nay, and the hope is – that, with all this great transition in the eyes of man, he has not changed himself a hairbreadth to the eyes of God. Honour to those who do so, for the wrench is sore. But it argues something narrow, whether of strength or weakness, whether of the prophet or the fool, in those who can take a sufficient interest in such infinitesimal and human operations, or who can quit a friendship for a doubtful process of the mind. And I think I should not leave my old creed for another, changing only words for other words; but by some brave reading, embrace it in spirit and truth, and find wrong as wrong for me as for the best of other communions.

The phylloxera[73] was in the neighbourhood; and instead of wine we drank at dinner a more economical juice of the grape – La Parisienne, they call it. It is made by putting the fruit whole into a cask with water; one by one the berries ferment and burst; what is drunk during the day is supplied at night in water: so, with ever another pitcher from the well, and ever another grape exploding and giving out its strength, one cask of Parisienne may last a family till spring. It is, as the reader will anticipate, a feeble beverage, but very pleasant to the taste.

What with dinner and coffee, it was long past three before I left St Germain de Calberte. I went down beside the Gardon of Mialet, a great glaring watercourse devoid of water, and through St Etienne de Vallée Française, or Val Francesque, as they used to call it; and towards evening began to ascend the hill of St Pierre. It was a long and steep ascent. Behind me an empty carriage returning to St Jean du Gard kept hard upon my tracks, and near the summit overtook me. The driver, like the rest of the world, was sure I was a pedlar; but, unlike others, he was sure of what I had to sell. He had noticed the blue wool which hung out of my pack at either end; and from this he had decided, beyond my power to alter his decision, that I dealt in blue-wool collars, such as decorate the neck of the French draught-horse.

I had hurried to the topmost powers of Modestine, for I dearly desired to see the view upon the other side before the day had faded. But it was night when I reached the summit; the moon was riding high and clear, and only a few grey streaks of twilight lingered in the west. A yawning valley, gulfed in blackness, lay like a hole in created nature at my feet; but the outline of the hills was sharp against the sky. There was Mount Aigoal, the stronghold of Castanet. And Castanet, not only as an active undertaking leader, deserves some mention among Camisards; for there is a spray of rose among his laurel; and he showed how, even in a public tragedy, love will have its way. In the high tide of war he married, in his mountain citadel, a young and pretty lass called Mariette. There were great rejoicings; and the bridegroom released five-and-twenty prisoners in honour of the glad event. Seven months afterwards, Mariette, the Princess of the Cévennes, as they called her in derision, fell into the hands of the authorities, where it was like to have gone hard with her. But Castanet was a man of execution, and loved his wife. He fell on Valleraugue, and got a lady there for a hostage; and for the first and last time in that war there was an exchange of prisoners. Their daughter, pledge of some starry night upon Mount Aigoal, has left descendants to this day.

Modestine and I – it was our last meal together – had a snack upon the top of St Pierre, I on a heap of stones, she standing by me in the moonlight and decorously eating bread out of my hand. The poor brute would eat more heartily in this manner; for she had a sort of affection for me, which I was soon to betray.

It was a long descent upon St Jean du Gard, and we met no one but a carter, visible afar off by the glint of the moon on his extinguished lantern.

Before ten o'clock we had got in and were at supper; fifteen miles and a stiff hill in little beyond six hours!

Farewell, Modestine!

On examination, on the morning of October 3rd, Modestine was pronounced unfit for travel. She would need at least two days' repose, according to the ostler; but I was now eager to reach Alais for my letters; and, being in a civilised country of stagecoaches, I determined to sell my lady friend and be off by the diligence that afternoon. Our yesterday's march, with the testimony of the driver who had pursued us up the long hill of St Pierre, spread a favourable notion of my donkey's capabilities. Intending purchasers were aware of an unrivalled opportunity. Before ten I had an offer of twenty-five francs; and before noon, after a desperate engagement, I sold her, saddle and all, for five-and-thirty. The pecuniary gain is not obvious, but I had bought freedom into the bargain.

St Jean du Gard is a large place, and largely Protestant. The maire, a Protestant, asked me to help him in a small matter which is itself characteristic of the country. The young women of the Cévennes profit by the common religion and the difference of the language to go largely as governesses into England; and here was one, a native of Mialet, struggling with English circulars from two different agencies in London. I gave what help I could; and volunteered some advice, which struck me as being excellent.

One thing more I note. The phylloxera had ravaged the vineyards in this neighbourhood; and in the early morning, under some chestnuts by the river, I found a party of men working with a cider-press. I could not at first make out what they were after, and asked one fellow to explain.

'Making cider,' he said. *'Oui, c'est comme ça. Comme dans le nord!'*

There was a ring of sarcasm in his voice: the country was going to the devil.

It was not until I was fairly seated by the driver, and rattling through a rocky valley with dwarf olives, that I became aware of my bereavement. I had lost Modestine. Up to that moment I had thought I hated her; but now she was gone,

And oh!
The difference to me![74]

For twelve days we had been fast companions; we had travelled upwards of a hundred and twenty miles, crossed several respectable ridges, and jogged along with our six legs by many a rocky and many a boggy by-road. After the first day, although sometimes I was hurt and distant in manner, I still kept my patience; and as for her, poor soul! she had come to regard me as a god. She loved to eat out of my hand. She was patient, elegant in form, the colour of an ideal mouse, and inimitably small. Her faults were those of her race and sex; her virtues were her own. Farewell, and if for ever – [75]

Father Adam wept when he sold her to me; after I had sold her in my turn, I was tempted to follow his example; and being alone with a stage-driver and four or five agreeable young men, I did not hesitate to yield to my emotion.

The Amateur Emigrant

From the Clyde to Sandy Hook

The Second Cabin

I first encountered my fellow-passengers on the Broomielaw[76] in Glasgow. Thence we descended the Clyde in no familiar spirit, but looking askance on each other as on possible enemies. A few Scandinavians, who had already grown acquainted on the North Sea, were friendly and voluble over their long pipes; but among English speakers distance and suspicion reigned supreme. The sun was soon overclouded, the wind freshened and grew sharp as we continued to descend the widening estuary; and with the falling temperature the gloom among the passengers increased. Two of the women wept. Anyone who had come aboard might have supposed we were all absconding from the law. There was scarce a word interchanged, and no common sentiment but that of cold united us, until at length, having touched at Greenock,[77] a pointing arm and a rush to the starboard now announced that our ocean steamer[78] was in sight. There she lay in mid-river, at the Tail of the Bank, her sea-signal flying: a wall of bulwark, a street of white deck-houses, an aspiring forest of spars, larger than a church, and soon to be as populous as many an incorporated town in the land to which she was to bear us.

I was not, in truth, a steerage passenger. Although anxious to see the worst of emigrant life, I had some work to finish on the voyage, and was advised to go by the second cabin, where at least I should have a table at command. The advice was excellent; but to understand the choice, and what I gained, some outline of the internal disposition of the ship will first be necessary. In her very nose is Steerage No. 1, down two pair of stairs. A little abaft, another companion, labelled Steerage Nos 2 and 3, gives admission to three galleries, two running forward towards Steerage No. 1, and the third aft towards the engines.

The starboard forward gallery is the second cabin. Away abaft the engines and below the officers' cabins, to complete our survey of the vessel, there is yet a third nest of steerages, labelled 4 and 5. The second cabin, to return, is thus a modified oasis in the very heart of the steerages. Through the thin partition you can hear the steerage passengers being sick, the rattle of tin dishes as they sit at meals, the varied accents in which they converse, the crying of their children terrified by this new experience, or the clean flat smack of the parental hand in chastisement.

There are, however, many advantages for the inhabitant of this strip. He does not require to bring his own bedding or dishes, but finds berths and a table completely if somewhat roughly furnished. He enjoys a distinct superiority in diet; but this, strange to say, differs not only on different ships, but on the same ship according as her head is to the east or west. In my own experience, the principal difference between our table and that of the true steerage passenger was the table itself, and the crockery plates from which we ate. But lest I should show myself ungrateful, let me recapitulate every advantage. At breakfast we had a choice between tea and coffee for beverage; a choice not easy to make, the two were so surprisingly alike. I found that I could sleep after the coffee and lay awake after the tea, which is proof conclusive of some chemical disparity; and even by the palate I could distinguish a smack of snuff in the former from a flavour of boiling and dishcloths in the second. As a matter of fact, I have seen passengers, after many sips, still doubting which had been supplied them. In the way of eatables at the same meal we were gloriously favoured; for in addition to porridge, which was common to all, we had Irish stew, sometimes a bit of fish, and sometimes rissoles. The dinner of soup, roast fresh beef, boiled salt junk, and potatoes, was, I believe, exactly common to the steerage and the second cabin; only I have heard it rumoured that our potatoes were of a superior brand; and twice a week, on pudding-days, instead of duff, we had a saddle-bag filled with currants under the name of a plum-pudding. At tea we were served with some broken meat from the saloon; sometimes in the comparatively elegant form of spare patties or rissoles; but as a general thing mere chicken-bones and flakes of fish, neither hot nor cold. If these were not the scrapings of plates their looks belied them sorely; yet we were all too hungry to be proud, and fell to these leavings greedily. These, the bread, which was excellent, and the soup and porridge which were both good, formed my whole diet throughout the voyage; so that except for the broken meat and the convenience of a table I might as well have been in the steerage outright. Had they given me porridge again in the evening, I should have been perfectly contented with the fare. As it was, with a few biscuits and some whisky and water before turning in, I kept my body going and my spirits up to the mark.

The last particular in which the second-cabin passenger remarkably stands ahead of his brother of the steerage is one altogether of sentiment. In the steerage there are males and females; in the second cabin, ladies and gentlemen. For some time after I came aboard I thought I was only a male; but in the course of a voyage of discovery between decks, I came on a brass plate, and learned that I was still a gentleman. Nobody knew it, of course. I was lost in the crowd of males and females, and rigorously confined to the same quarter of the deck. Who could tell whether I housed on the port or starboard side of steerage Nos 2 and 3? And it was only there that my superiority became practical; everywhere else I was incognito, moving among my inferiors with simplicity, not so much as a swagger to indicate that I was a gentleman after all, and had broken meat to tea. Still, I was like one with a patent of nobility in a drawer at home; and when I felt out of spirits I could go down and refresh myself with a look of that brass plate.

For all these advantages I paid but two guineas. Six guineas is the steerage fare; eight that by the second cabin; and when you remember that the steerage passenger must supply bedding and dishes, and, in five cases out of ten, either brings some dainties with him, or privately pays the steward for extra rations, the difference in price becomes almost nominal. Air comparatively fit to breathe, food comparatively varied, and the satisfaction of being still privately a gentleman, may thus be had almost for the asking. Two of my fellow-passengers in the second cabin had already made the passage by the cheaper fare, and declared it was an experiment not to be repeated. As I go on to tell about my steerage friends, the reader will perceive that they were not alone in their opinion. Out of ten with whom I was more or less intimate, I am sure not fewer than five vowed, if they returned, to travel second cabin; and all who had left their wives behind them assured me they would go without the comfort of their presence until they could afford to bring them by saloon.

Our party in the second cabin was not perhaps the most interesting on board. Perhaps even in the saloon there was as much goodwill and character. Yet it had some elements of curiosity. There was a mixed group of Swedes, Danes and Norsemen, one of whom, generally known by the name of 'Johnny', in spite of his own protests, greatly diverted us by his clever, cross-country efforts to speak English, and became on the strength of that a universal favourite – it takes so little in this world of shipboard to create a popularity. There was, besides, a Scots mason, known from his favourite dish as 'Irish Stew', three or four nondescript Scots, a fine young Irishman, O'Reilly, and a pair of young men who deserve a special word of condemnation. One of them was Scots; the other claimed to be American, admitted, after some fencing, that he was born in England, and ultimately proved to be an Irishman born and nurtured, but ashamed to own his country. He had a sister on board, whom he faithfully neglected throughout the voyage, though she was not only sick, but much his senior, and had nursed and cared for him in childhood. In appearance he was like an imbecile Henry III of France. The Scotsman, though perhaps as big an ass, was not so dead of heart; and I have only bracketed them together because they were fast friends, and disgraced themselves equally by their conduct at the table.

Next, to turn to topics more agreeable, we had a newly-married couple, devoted to each other, with a pleasant story of how they had first seen each other years ago at a preparatory school, and that very afternoon he had carried her books home for her. I do not know if this story will be plain to southern readers; but to me it recalls many a school idyll, with wrathful swains of eight and nine confronting each other stride-legs, flushed with jealousy; for to carry home a young lady's books was both a delicate attention and a privilege.

Then there was an old lady, or indeed I am not sure that she was as much old as antiquated and strangely out of place, who had left her husband, and was travelling all the way to Kansas by herself. We had to take her own word that she was married; for it was sorely contradicted by the testimony of her appearance. Nature seemed to have sanctified her for the single state; even the colour of her hair was incompatible with matrimony, and her husband, I thought, should be a man of saintly spirit and phantasmal bodily presence. She was ill, poor thing; her soul turned from the viands; the dirty tablecloth shocked her like an impropriety; and the whole strength of her endeavour was bent upon keeping her watch true to Glasgow time till she should reach New York. They had heard reports, her husband and she, of some unwarrantable disparity of hours between these two cities; and with a spirit commendably scientific, she had seized on this occasion to put them to the proof. It was a good thing for the old lady; for she passed much leisure time in studying the watch. Once, when prostrated by sickness, she let it run down. It was inscribed on her harmless mind in letters of adamant that the hands of a watch must never be turned backwards; and so it behoved her to lie in wait for the exact moment ere she started it again. When she imagined this was about due, she sought out one of the young second-cabin Scotsmen, who was embarked on the same experiment as herself and had hitherto been less neglectful. She was in quest of two o'clock; and when she learned it was already seven on the shores of Clyde, she lifted up her voice and cried 'Gravy!' I had not heard this innocent expletive since I was a young child; and I suppose it must have been the same with the other Scotsmen present, for we all laughed our fill.

Last but not least, I come to my excellent friend Mr Jones. It would be difficult to say whether I was his right-hand man, or he mine, during the voyage. Thus at table I carved, while he only scooped gravy; but at our concerts, of which more anon, he was the president who called up performers to sing and I but his messenger who ran his errands and pleaded privately with the over-modest. I knew I liked Mr Jones from the moment I saw him. I thought him by his face to be Scottish; nor could his accent undeceive me. For as there is a *lingua franca* of many tongues on the moles and in the feluccas of the Mediterranean, so there is a free or common accent among English-speaking men who follow the sea. They catch a twang in a New England Port; from a cockney skipper, even a Scotsman sometimes learns to drop an h; a word of a dialect is picked up from another band in the forecastle; until often the result is undecipherable, and you have to ask for the man's place of birth. So it was with Mr Jones. I thought him a Scotsman who had been long to sea; and yet he was from Wales, and had been most of his life a blacksmith at an inland forge; a few years in America and half a score of ocean voyages having sufficed to modify his speech into the common pattern. By his own account he was both strong and skilful in his trade. A few years back, he had been married and after a fashion a rich man; now the wife was dead and the money gone. But his was the nature that looks forward, and goes on from one year to another and through all the extremities of fortune undismayed; and if the sky were to fall tomorrow, I should look to see Jones, the day following, perched on a stepladder and getting things to rights. He was always hovering round inventions like a bee over a flower, and lived in a dream of patents. He had with him a patent medicine, for instance, the composition of which he had bought years ago for five dollars from an American pedlar, and sold the other day for a hundred pounds

(I think it was) to an English apothecary. It was called Golden Oil,
cured all maladies without exception; and I am bound to say that I
partook of it myself with good results. It is a character of the man
that he was not only perpetually dosing himself with Golden Oil, but
wherever there was a head aching or a finger cut, there would be
Jones with his bottle.

If he had one taste more strongly than another, it was to study
character. Many an hour have we two walked upon the deck dissecting
our neighbours in a spirit that was too purely scientific to be called
unkind; whenever a quaint or human trait slipped out in conversation,
you might have seen Jones and me exchanging glances; and we could
hardly go to bed in comfort till we had exchanged notes and discussed
the day's experience. We were then like a couple of anglers comparing
a day's kill. But the fish we angled for were of a metaphysical species,
and we angled as often as not in one another's baskets. Once, in the
midst of a serious talk, each found there was a scrutinising eye upon
himself; I own I paused in embarrassment at this double detection;
but Jones, with a better civility, broke into a peal of unaffected
laughter, and declared, what was the truth, that there was a pair of us
indeed.

Early Impressions

We steamed out of the Clyde on Thursday night, and early on the
Friday forenoon we took in our last batch of emigrants at Lough
Foyle, in Ireland, and said farewell to Europe. The company was
now complete, and began to draw together, by inscrutable
magnetisms, upon the decks. There were Scots and Irish in plenty, a
few English, a few Americans, a good handful of Scandinavians, a
German or two, and one Russian; all now belonging for ten days to
one small iron country on the deep.

As I walked the deck and looked round upon my fellow-passengers,
thus curiously assorted from all northern Europe, I began for the
first time to understand the nature of emigration. Day by day throughout the passage, and thenceforward across all the States, and on to
the shores of the Pacific, this knowledge grew more clear and
melancholy. Emigration, from a word of the most cheerful import,
came to sound most dismally in my ear. There is nothing more
agreeable to picture and nothing more pathetic to behold. The
abstract idea, as conceived at home, is hopeful and adventurous. A
young man, you fancy, scorning restraints and helpers, issues forth
into life, that great battle, to fight for his own hand. The most

pleasant stories of ambition, of difficulties overcome, and of ultimate success, are but as episodes to this great epic of self-help. The epic is composed of individual heroisms; it stands to them as the victorious war which subdued an empire stands to the personal act of bravery which spiked a single cannon and was adequately rewarded with a medal. For in emigration the young men enter direct and by the shipload on their heritage of work; empty continents swarm, as at the bosun's whistle, with industrious hands, and whole new empires are domesticated to the service of man.

This is the closet picture, and is found, on trial, to consist mostly of embellishments. The more I saw of my fellow-passengers, the less I was tempted to the lyric note. Comparatively few of the men were below thirty; many were married, and encumbered with families; not a few were already up in years; and this itself was out of tune with my imaginations, for the ideal emigrant should certainly be young. Again, I thought he should offer to the eye some bold type of humanity, with bluff or hawk-like features, and the stamp of an eager and pushing disposition. Now those around me were for the most part quiet, orderly, obedient citizens, family men broken by adversity, elderly youths who had failed to place themselves in life, and people who had seen better days. Mildness was the prevailing character; mild mirth and mild endurance. In a word, I was not taking part in an impetuous and conquering sally, such as swept over Mexico or Siberia, but found myself, like Marmion, 'in the lost battle, borne down by the flying'.[79]

Labouring mankind had in the last years, and throughout Great Britain, sustained a prolonged and crushing series of defeats. I had heard vaguely of these reverses; of whole streets of houses standing deserted by the Tyne, the cellar-doors broken and removed for firewood; of homeless men loitering at the street corners of Glasgow with their chests beside them; of closed factories, useless strikes, and starving girls. But I had never taken them home to me or represented these distresses livingly to my imagination.

A turn of the market may be a calamity as disastrous as the French retreat from Moscow; but it hardly lends itself to lively treatment, and makes a trifling figure in the morning papers. We may struggle as we please, we are not born economists. The individual is more affecting than the mass. It is by the scenic accidents, and the appeal to the carnal eye, that for the most part we grasp the significance of tragedies. Thus it was only now, when I found myself involved in the rout, that I began to appreciate how sharp had been the battle. We were a company of the rejected; the drunken, the incompetent, the weak, the prodigal, all who had been unable to prevail against circumstances in the one land, were now fleeing pitifully to another; and though one or two might still succeed, all had already failed. We were a shipful of failures, the broken men of England. Yet it must not be supposed that these people exhibited depression. The scene, on the contrary, was cheerful. Not a tear was shed on board the vessel. All were full of hope for the future, and showed an inclination to innocent gaiety. Some were heard to sing, and all began to scrape acquaintance with small jests and ready laughter.

The children found each other out like dogs, and ran about the decks scraping acquaintance after their fashion also. 'What do you call your mither?' I heard one ask. 'Mawmaw,' was the reply, indicating, I fancy, a shade of difference in the social scale. When people pass each other on the high seas of life at so early an age, the contact is but slight, and the relation more like what we may imagine to be the friendship of flies than that of men; it is so quickly joined, so easily dissolved, so open in its communications and so devoid of deeper human qualities. The children, I observed, were all in a band, and as thick as thieves at a fair, while their elders were still ceremoniously manoeuvring on the outskirts of acquaintance. The sea, the ship, and the seamen were soon as familiar as home to these half-conscious little ones. It was odd to hear them, throughout the voyage, employ shore words to designate portions of the vessel. 'Go 'way doon to yon dyke,' I heard one say, probably meaning the bulwark. I often had my heart in my mouth, watching them climb into the shrouds or on the rails, while the ship went swinging through the waves; and I admired and envied the courage of their mothers, who sat by in the sun and looked on with composure at these perilous feats. 'He'll maybe be a sailor,' I heard one remark; 'now's the time to learn.' I had been on the point of running forward to interfere, but stood back at that, reproved. Very few in the more delicate classes have the nerve to look upon the peril of one dear to them; but the life of poorer folk, where necessity is so much more immediate and imperious, braces even a mother to this extreme of endurance. And perhaps, after all, it is better that the lad should break his neck than that you should break his spirit.

And since I am here on the chapter of the children, I must mention one little fellow, whose family belonged to Steerage Nos 4 and 5, and who, wherever he went, was like a strain of music round the ship. He was an ugly, merry, unbreeched child of three, his lintwhite hair in a tangle, his face smeared with suet and treacle; but he ran to and fro with so natural a step, and fell and picked himself up again with such grace and good-humour, that he might fairly be called beautiful when he was in motion. To meet him, crowing with laughter and beating an accompaniment to his own mirth with a tin spoon upon a tin cup, was to meet a little triumph of the human species. Even when his mother and the rest of his family lay sick and prostrate around him, he sat upright in their midst and sang aloud in the pleasant heartlessness of infancy.

Throughout the Friday, intimacy among us men made but a few advances. We discussed the probable duration of the voyage, we exchanged pieces of information, naming our trades, what we hoped to find in the new world, or what we were fleeing from in the old; and, above all, we condoled together over the food and the vileness of the steerage. One or two had been so near famine that you may say they had run into the ship with the devil at their heels; and to these all seemed for the best in the best of possible steamers. But the majority were hugely contented. Coming as they did from a country in so low a state as Great Britain, many of them from Glasgow, which commercially speaking was as good as dead, and many having long been out of work, I was surprised to find them so dainty in their notions. I myself lived almost exclusively on bread, porridge and soup, precisely as it was supplied to them, and found it, if not luxurious, at least sufficient. But these working men were loud in their outcries. It was not 'food for human beings', it was 'only fit for pigs', it was 'a disgrace'. Many of them lived almost entirely upon biscuit, others on their own private supplies, and some paid extra for better rations from the ship. This marvellously changed my notion of the degree of luxury habitual to the artisan. I was prepared to hear him grumble, for grumbling is the traveller's pastime; but I was not prepared to find him turn away from a diet which was palatable to myself. Words I should have disregarded, or taken with a liberal allowance; but when a man prefers dry biscuit there can be no question of the sincerity of his disgust.

With one of their complaints I could most heartily sympathise. A single night of the steerage had filled them with horror. I had myself suffered, even in my decent second-cabin berth, from the lack of air; and as the night promised to be fine and quiet, I determined to sleep on deck, and advised all who complained of their quarters to follow my example. I dare say a dozen of the others agreed to do so, and I thought we should have been quite a party. Yet, when I brought up my rug about seven bells, there was no one to be seen but the watch. That chimerical terror of good night-air, which makes men close their windows, list their doors, and seal themselves up with their own poisonous exhalations, had sent all these healthy workmen down below. One would think we had been brought up in a fever country; yet in England the most malarious districts are in the bedchambers.

I felt saddened at this defection, and yet half-pleased to have the night so quietly to myself. The wind had hauled a little ahead on the starboard bow, and was dry but chilly. I found a shelter near the fire-hole, and made myself snug for the night.

The ship moved over the uneven sea with a gentle and cradling movement. The ponderous, organic labours of the engine in her bowels occupied the mind, and prepared it for slumber. From time to time a heavier lurch would disturb me as I lay, and recall me to the obscure borders of consciousness; or I heard, as it were through a veil, the clear note of the clapper on the brass and the beautiful sea-cry, 'All's well!' I know nothing, whether for poetry or music, that can surpass the effect of these two syllables in the darkness of a night at sea.

The day dawned fairly enough, and during the early part we had some pleasant hours to improve acquaintance in the open air; but towards nightfall the wind freshened, the rain began to fall, and the sea rose so high that it was difficult to keep one's footing on the deck. I have spoken of our concerts. We were indeed a musical ship's company, and cheered our way into exile with the fiddle, the accordion and the songs of all nations. Good, bad or indifferent – Scottish, English, Irish, Russian, German or Norse – the songs were received with generous applause. Once or twice, a recitation, very spiritedly rendered in a powerful Scottish accent, varied the proceedings; and once we sought in vain to dance a quadrille, eight men of us together, to the music of the violin. The performers were all humorous, frisky fellows, who loved to cut capers in private life; but as soon as they were arranged for the dance, they conducted themselves like so many mutes at a funeral. I have never seen decorum pushed so far; and as this was not expected, the quadrille was soon whistled down, and the dancers departed under a cloud. Eight Frenchmen, even eight Englishmen from another rank of society, would have dared to make some fun for themselves and the spectators; but the working man, when sober, takes an extreme and even melancholy view of personal deportment. A fifth-form schoolboy is not more careful of dignity. He dares not be comical; his fun must escape from him unprepared, and above all, it must be unaccompanied by any physical demonstration. I like his society under most circumstances, but let me never again join with him in public gambols.

But the impulse to sing was strong, and triumphed over modesty and even the inclemencies of sea and sky. On this rough Saturday night, we got together by the main deck-house, in a place sheltered from the wind and rain. Some clinging to a ladder which led to the hurricane deck, and the rest knitting arms or taking hands, we made a ring to support the women in the violent lurching of the ship; and when we were thus disposed, sang to our hearts' content. Some of the songs were appropriate to the scene; others strikingly the reverse. Bastard doggerel of the music-hall, such as, 'Around her splendid form, I weaved the magic circle,' sounded bald, bleak, and pitifully silly. 'We don't want to fight, but, by Jingo, if we do,' was in some measure saved by the vigour and unanimity with which the chorus was thrown forth into the night. I observed a Platt-Deutsch mason, entirely innocent of English, adding heartily to the general effect. And perhaps the German mason is but a fair example of the sincerity with which the song was rendered; for nearly all with whom I conversed upon the subject were bitterly opposed to war, and attributed their own misfortunes, and frequently their own taste for whisky, to the campaigns in Zululand and Afghanistan.

Every now and again, however, some song that touched the pathos of our situation was given forth; and you could hear by the voices that took up the burden how the sentiment came home to each, 'The Anchor's Weighed' was true for us. We were indeed 'Rocked on the bosom of the stormy deep'. How many of us could say with the singer, 'I'm lonely tonight, love, without you,' or, 'Go, someone, and tell them from me, to write me a letter from home'! And when was there a more appropriate moment for 'Auld Lang Syne' than now, when the land, the friends, and the affections of that mingled but beloved time were fading and fleeing behind us in the vessel's wake? It pointed forward to the hour when these labours should be overpast, to the return voyage, and to many a meeting in the sanded inn, when those who had parted in the spring of youth should again drink a cup of kindness in their age. Had not Burns contemplated emigration, I scarce believe he would have found that note.

All Sunday the weather remained wild and cloudy; many were prostrated by sickness; only five sat down to tea in the second cabin, and two of these departed abruptly ere the meal was at an end. The Sabbath was observed strictly by the majority of the emigrants. I heard an old woman express her surprise that 'the ship didna gae doon', as she saw someone pass her with a chessboard on the holy day. Some sang Scottish psalms. Many went to service, and in true Scottish fashion came back ill pleased with their divine. 'I didna think he was an experienced preacher,' said one girl to me.

Is was a bleak, uncomfortable day; but at night, by six bells, although the wind had not yet moderated, the clouds were all wrecked and blown away behind the rim of the horizon, and the stars came out thickly overhead. I saw Venus burning as steadily and sweetly across this hurly-burly of the winds and waters as ever at home upon the summer woods. The engine pounded, the screw tossed out of the water with a roar, and shook the ship from end to end; the bows battled with loud reports against the billows: and as I stood in the lee-scuppers and looked up to where the funnel leaned out, over my head, vomiting smoke, and the black and monstrous topsails blotted, at each lurch, a different crop of stars, it seemed as if all this trouble were a thing of small account, and that just above the mast reigned peace unbroken and eternal.

Steerage Scenes

Our companion (Steerage Nos 2 and 3) was a favourite resort. Down one flight of stairs there was a comparatively large open space, the centre occupied by a hatchway, which made a convenient seat for about twenty persons, while barrels, coils of rope, and the carpenter's bench afforded perches for perhaps as many more. The canteen, or steerage bar, was on one side of the stair; on the other, a no less attractive spot, the cabin of the indefatigable interpreter. I have seen people packed into this space like herrings in a barrel, and many merry evenings prolonged there until five bells, when the lights were ruthlessly extinguished and all must go to roost.

It had been rumoured since Friday that there was a fiddler aboard, who lay sick and unmelodious in Steerage No. 1; and on the Monday forenoon, as I came down the companion, I was saluted by something in Strathspey time. A white-faced Orpheus was cheerily playing to an audience of white-faced women. It was as much as he could do to play, and some of his hearers were scarce able to sit; yet they had crawled from their bunks at the first experimental flourish, and found better than medicine in the music. Some of the heaviest heads began to nod in time, and a degree of animation looked from some of the palest eyes. Humanly speaking, it is a more important matter to play the fiddle, even badly, than to write huge works upon recondite subjects. What could Mr Darwin have done for these sick women? But this fellow scraped away; and the world was positively a better place for all who heard him. We have yet to understand the economical value of these mere accomplishments. I told the fiddler he was a happy man, carrying happiness about with him in his fiddle-case, and he seemed alive to the fact.

'It is a privilege,' I said. He thought a while upon the word, turning it over in his Scots head, and then answered with conviction, 'Yes, a privilege.'

That night I was summoned by 'Merrily danced the Quake's wife' into the companion of Steerage Nos 4 and 5. This was, properly speaking, but a strip across a deck-house, lit by a sickly lantern which swung to and fro with the motion of the ship. Through the open slide-door we had a glimpse of a grey night sea, with patches of phosphorescent foam flying, swift as birds, into the wake, and the horizon rising and falling as the vessel rolled to the wind. In the centre the companion ladder plunged down sheerly like an open pit. Below, on the first landing, and lighted by another lamp, lads and lasses danced, not more than three at a time for lack of space, in jigs and reels and hornpipes. Above, on either side, there was a recess railed with iron, perhaps two feet wide and four long, which stood for orchestra and seats of honour. In the one balcony, five slatternly Irish lasses sat woven in a comely group. In the other was posted Orpheus, his body, which was convulsively in motion, forming an odd contrast to his somnolent, imperturbable Scots face. His brother, a dark man with a vehement, interested countenance, who made a god of the fiddler, sat by with open mouth, drinking in the general admiration and throwing out remarks to kindle it.

'That's a bonny hornpipe now,' he would say, 'it's a great favourite with performers; they dance the sand dance to it.' And he expounded the sand dance. Then, suddenly, it would be a long, 'Hush!' with uplifted finger and glowing, supplicating eyes, 'he's going to play 'Auld Robin Grey' on one string!' And throughout this excruciating movement – 'On one string, that's on one string!' he kept crying. I would have given something myself that it had been on none; but the hearers were much awed. I called for a tune or two, and thus introduced myself to the notice of the brother, who directed his talk to me for some little while, keeping, I need hardly mention, true to his topic, like the seamen to the star. 'He's grand of it,' he said confidentially. 'His master was a music-hall man.' Indeed the music-hall man had left his mark, for our fiddler was ignorant of many of our best old airs; 'Logie o' Buchan', for instance, he only knew as a quick, jigging figure in a set of quadrilles, and had never heard it called by name. Perhaps, after all, the brother was the more interesting performer of the two. I have spoken with him afterwards repeatedly, and found him always the same quick, fiery bit of a man, not without brains; but he never showed to such advantage as when he was thus squiring the fiddler into public note. There is nothing more becoming than a genuine admiration; and it shares this with love, that it does not become contemptible although misplaced.

The dancing was but feebly carried on. The space was almost impracticably small; and the Irish wenches combined the extreme of bashfulness about this innocent display with a surprising impudence and roughness of address. Most often, either the fiddle lifted up its voice unheeded, or only a couple of lads would be footing it and snapping fingers on the landing. And such was the eagerness of the brother to display all the acquirements of his idol, and such the sleepy indifference of the performer, that the tune would as often as not be changed, and the hornpipe expire into a ballad, before the dancers had cut half a dozen shuffles.

In the meantime, however, the audience had been growing more and more numerous every moment; there was hardly standing-room round the top of the companion; and the strange instinct of the race moved some of the newcomers to close both the doors, so that the atmosphere grew insupportable. It was a good place, as the saying is, to leave.

The wind hauled ahead with a head sea. By ten at night heavy sprays were flying and drumming over the forecastle; the companion of Steerage No. 1 had to be closed, and the door of communication through the second cabin thrown open. Either from the convenience of the opportunity, or because we had already a number of acquaintances in that part of the ship, Mr Jones and I paid it a late visit. Steerage No. 1 is shaped like an isosceles triangle, the sides opposite the equal angles bulging outward with the contour of the ship. It is lined with eight pens of sixteen bunks apiece, four bunks below and four above on either side. At night the place is lit with two lanterns, one to each table. As the steamer beat on her way among the rough billows, the light passed through violent phases of change, and was thrown to and fro and up and down with startling swiftness. You were tempted to wonder, as you looked, how so thin a glimmer could control and disperse such solid blackness. When Jones and I entered we found a little company of our acquaintances seated together at the triangular foremost table. A more forlorn party, in more dismal circumstances, it would be hard to imagine. The motion here in the ship's nose was very violent; the uproar of the sea often overpoweringly loud. The yellow flicker of the lantern spun round and round and tossed the shadows in masses. The air was hot, but it struck a chill from its foetor.

From all round in the dark bunks, the scarcely human noises of the sick joined into a kind of farmyard chorus. In the midst, these five friends of mine were keeping up what heart they could in company. Singing was their refuge from discomfortable thoughts and sensations. One piped, in feeble tones, 'Oh, why left I my hame?' which seemed a pertinent question in the circumstances. Another, from the invisible horrors of a pen where he lay dog-sick upon the upper-shelf, found courage, in a blink of his sufferings, to give us several verses of the 'Death of Nelson'; and it was odd and eerie to hear the chorus breathe feebly from all sorts of dark corners, and 'this day has done his dooty' rise and fall and be taken up again in this dim inferno, to an accompaniment of plunging, hollow-sounding bows and the rattling spray-showers overhead.

All seemed unfit for conversation; a certain dizziness had interrupted the activity of their minds; and except to sing they were tongue-tied. There was present, however, one tall, powerful fellow of doubtful nationality, being neither quite Scotsman nor altogether Irish, but of surprising clearness of conviction on the highest problems. He had gone nearly beside himself on the Sunday, because of a general backwardness to endorse his definition of mind as 'a living, thinking substance which cannot be felt, heard, or seen' – nor, I presume, although he failed to mention it, smelt. Now he came forward in a pause with another contribution to our culture.

'Just by way of change,' said he, 'I'll ask you a Scripture riddle. There's profit in them too,' he added ungrammatically.

This was the riddle –

> C and P
> Did agree
> To cut down C;
> But C and P
> Could not agree
> Without the leave of G;
> All the people cried to see
> The crueltie
> Of C and P.

Harsh are the words of Mercury after the songs of Apollo! We were a long while over the problem, shaking our heads and gloomily wondering how a man could be such a fool; but at length he put us out of suspense and divulged the fact that C and P stood for Caiaphas and Pontius Pilate.

I think it must have been the riddle that settled us; but the motion and the close air likewise hurried our departure. We had not been gone long, we heard next morning, ere two or even three out of the five fell sick. We thought it little wonder on the whole, for the sea kept contrary all night. I now made my bed upon the second cabin floor, where, although I ran the risk of being stepped upon, I had a free current of air, more or less vitiated indeed, and running only from steerage to steerage, but at least not stagnant; and from this couch, as well as the usual sounds of a rough night at sea, the hateful coughing and retching of the sick and the sobs of children, I heard a man run wild with terror beseeching his friend for encouragement. 'The ship's going down!' he cried with a thrill of agony. 'The ship's going down!' he repeated, now in a blank whisper, now with his voice rising towards a sob; and his friend might reassure him, reason with him, joke at him – all was in vain, and the old cry came back, 'The ship's going down!' There was something panicky and catching in the emotion of his tones; and I saw in a clear flash what an involved and hideous tragedy was a disaster to an emigrant ship. If this whole parishful of people came no more to land, into how many houses would the newspaper carry woe, and what a great part of the web of our corporate human life would be rent across for ever!

The next morning when I came on deck I found a new world indeed. The wind was fair; the sun mounted into a cloudless heaven; through great dark blue seas the ship cut a swath of curded foam. The horizon was dotted all day with companionable sails, and the sun shone pleasantly on the long, heaving deck.

We had many fine-weather diversions to beguile the time. There was a single chessboard and a single pack of cards. Sometimes as many as twenty of us would be playing dominoes for love. Feats of dexterity, puzzles for the intelligence, some arithmetical, some of the same order as the old problem of the fox and goose and cabbage, were always welcome; and the latter, I observed, more popular as well as more conspicuously well done than the former. We had a regular daily competition to guess the vessel's progress; and twelve o'clock, when the result was published in the wheelhouse, came to be a moment of considerable interest. But the interest was unmixed.

Not a bet was laid upon our guesses. From the Clyde to Sandy Hook I never heard a wager offered or taken. We had, besides, romps in plenty. Puss in the Corner, which we had rebaptised, in more manly style, Devil and four Corners, was my own favourite game; but there were many who preferred another, the humour of which was to box a person's ears until he found out who had cuffed him.

This Tuesday morning we were all delighted with the change of weather, and in the highest possible spirits. We got in a cluster like bees, sitting between each other's feet under lee of the deck-houses. Stories and laughter went around. The children climbed about the shrouds. White faces appeared for the first time, and began to take on colour from the wind. I was kept hard at work making cigarettes for one amateur after another, and my less than moderate skill was heartily admired. Lastly, down sat the fiddler in our midst and began to discourse his reels, and jigs, and ballads, with now and then a voice or two to take up the air and throw in the interest of human speech.

Through this merry and good-hearted scene there came three cabin passengers, a gentleman and two young ladies, picking their way with little gracious titters of indulgence, and a Lady-Bountiful air about nothing, which galled me to the quick. I have little of the radical in social questions, and have always nourished an idea that one person was as good as another. But I began to be troubled by this episode. It was astonishing what insults these people managed to convey by their presence. They seemed to throw their clothes in our faces. Their eyes searched us all over for tatters and incongruities. A laugh was ready at their lips; but they were too well-mannered to indulge it in our hearing. Wait a bit, till they were all back in the saloon, and then hear how wittily they would depict the manners of the steerage. We were in truth very innocently, cheerfully and sensibly engaged, and there was no shadow of excuse for the swaying elegant superiority with which these damsels passed among us, or for the stiff and waggish glances of their squire. Not a word was said; only when they were gone Mackay sullenly damned their impudence under his breath; but we were all conscious of an icy influence and a dead break in the course of our enjoyment.

Steerage Types

We had a fellow on board, an Irish-American, for all the world like a beggar in a print by Callot:[80] one-eyed, with great, splay crow's-feet round the sockets; a knotty squab nose coming down over his moustache; a miraculous hat; a shirt that had been white, ay, ages long ago; an alpaca coat in its last sleeves; and, without hyperbole, no buttons to his trousers. Even in these rags and tatters, the man twinkled all over with impudence like a piece of sham jewellery; and I have heard him offer a situation to one of his fellow-passengers with the air of a lord. Nothing could overlie such a fellow; a kind of base success was written on his brow. He was then in his ill days; but I can imagine him in Congress with his mouth full of bombast and sawder. As we moved in the same circle, I was brought necessarily into his society. I do not think I ever heard him say anything that was true, kind or interesting; but there was entertainment in the man's demeanour. You might call him a half-educated Irish Tigg.

Our Russian made a remarkable contrast to this impossible fellow. Rumours and legends were current in the steerages about his antecedents. Some said he was a Nihilist escaping; others set him down for a harmless spendthrift, who had squandered fifty thousand roubles, and whose father had now despatched him to America by way of penance. Either tale might flourish in security; there was no contradiction to be feared, for the hero spoke not one word of English. I got on with him lumberingly enough in broken German, and learned from his own lips that he had been an apothecary. He carried the photograph of his betrothed in a pocketbook, and remarked that it did not do her justice. The cut of his head stood out from among the passengers with an air of startling strangeness. The first natural instinct was to take him for a desperado; but although the features, to our Western eyes, had a barbaric and unhomely cast, the eye both reassured and touched. It was large and very dark and soft, with an expression of dumb endurance, as if it had often looked on desperate circumstances and never looked on them without resolution.

He cried out when I used the word. 'No, no,' he said, 'not resolution.'

'The resolution to endure,' I explained.

And then he shrugged his shoulders, and said, 'Ach, ja,' with gusto, like a man who has been flattered in his favourite pretensions. Indeed, he was always hinting at some secret sorrow; and his life, he said, had been one of unusual trouble and anxiety; so the legends of the steerage may have represented at least some shadow of the truth. Once, and once only, he sang a song at our concerts; standing forth without embarrassment, his great stature somewhat humped, his long arms frequently extended, his Kalmuck head thrown backward. It was a suitable piece of music, as deep as a cow's bellow and wild like the

White Sea. He was struck and charmed by the freedom and sociality
of our manners. At home, he said, no one on a journey would speak
to him, but those with whom he would not care to speak; thus
unconsciously involving himself in the condemnation of his countrymen. But Russia was soon to be changed; the ice of the Neva was
softening under the sun of civilisation; the new ideas, '*wie eine feine
Violine*', were audible among the big empty drum notes of Imperial
diplomacy; and he looked to see a great revival, though with a
somewhat indistinct and childish hope.

We had a father and son who made a pair of Jacks-of-all-trades. It
was the son who sang the 'Death of Nelson' under such contrarious
circumstances. He was by trade a shearer of ship plates; but he could
touch the organ, and led two choirs, and played the flute and piccolo
in a professional string band. His repertory of songs was, besides,
inexhaustible, and ranged impartially from the very best to the very
worst within his reach. Nor did he seem to make the least distinction
between these extremes, but would cheerily follow up 'Tom Bowling'
with 'Around her splendid form'.

The father, an old, cheery, small piece of manhood, could do
everything connected with tin work from one end of the process to
the other, use almost every carpenter's tool, and make picture frames
to boot. 'I sat down with silver plate every Sunday,' said he, 'and
pictures on the wall. I have made enough money to be rolling in my
carriage. But, sir,' looking at me unsteadily with his bright rheumy
eyes, 'I was troubled with a drunken wife.' He took a hostile view of
matrimony in consequence. 'It's an old saying,' he remarked: 'God
made 'em, and the devil he mixed 'em.'

I think he was justified by his experience. It was a dreary story. He
would bring home three pounds on Saturday, and on Monday all
the clothes would be in pawn. Sick of the useless struggle, he gave
up a paying contract, and contented himself with small and ill-paid
jobs. 'A bad job was as good as a good job for me,' he said; 'it all
went the same way.' Once the wife showed signs of amendment; she
kept steady for weeks on end; it was again worth while to labour and
to do one's best. The husband found a good situation some distance
from home, and, to make a little upon every hand, started the wife
in a cook-shop; the children were here and there, busy as mice;
savings began to grow together in the bank, and the golden age of
hope had returned again to that unhappy family. But one week my
old acquaintance, getting earlier through with his work, came home
on the Friday instead of the Saturday, and there was his wife to

receive him reeling drunk. He 'took and gave her a pair o' black eyes', for which I pardon him, nailed up the cook-shop door, gave up his situation, and resigned himself to a life of poverty, with the workhouse at the end. As the children came to their full age they fled the house, and established themselves in other countries; some did well, some not so well; but the father remained at home alone with his drunken wife, all his sound-hearted pluck and varied accomplishments depressed and negatived.

Was she dead now? or, after all these years, had he broken the chain, and run from home like a schoolboy? I could not discover which; but here at least he was out on the adventure, and still one of the bravest and most youthful men on board.

'Now, I suppose, I must put my old bones to work again,' said he; 'but I can do a turn yet.'

And the son to whom he was going, I asked, was he not able to support him?

'Oh yes,' he replied. 'But I'm never happy without a job on hand. And I'm stout; I can eat a'most anything. You see no craze about me.'

This tale of a drunken wife was paralleled on board by another of a drunken father. He was a capable man, with a good chance in life; but he had drunk up two thriving businesses like a bottle of sherry, and involved his sons along with him in ruin. Now they were on board with us, fleeing his disastrous neighbourhood.

Total abstinence, like all ascetical conclusions, is unfriendly to the most generous, cheerful and human parts of man; but it could have adduced many instances and arguments from among our ship's company. I was, one day conversing with a kind and happy Scotsman, running to fat and perspiration in the physical, but with a taste for poetry and a genial sense of fun. I had asked him his hopes in emigrating. They were like those of so many others, vague and unfounded; times were bad at home; they were said to have a turn for the better in the States; a man could get on anywhere, he thought. That was precisely the weak point of his position; for if he could get on in America, why could he not do the same in Scotland? But I never had the courage to use that argument, though it was often on the tip of my tongue, and instead I agreed with him heartily, adding, with reckless originality, 'If the man stuck to his work, and kept away from drink.'

'Ah!' said he slowly, 'the drink! You see, that's just my trouble.'

He spoke with a simplicity that was touching, looking at me at the same time with something strange and timid in his eye, half-ashamed, half-sorry, like a good child who knows he should be beaten. You would have said he recognised a destiny to which he was born, and accepted the consequences mildly. Like the merchant Abudah, he was at the same time fleeing from his destiny and carrying it along with him, the whole at an expense of six guineas.

As far as I saw, drink, idleness and incompetency were the three great causes of emigration, and for all of them, and drink first and foremost, this trick of getting transported overseas appears to me the silliest means of cure. You cannot run away from a weakness; you must sometime fight it out or perish; and if that be so, why not now, and where you stand? *Coelum non animam.*[81] Change Glenlivet for Bourbon, and it is still whisky, only not so good. A sea-voyage will not give a man the nerve to put aside cheap pleasure; emigration has to be done before we climb the vessel; an aim in life is the only fortune worth the finding; and it is not to be found in foreign lands, but in the heart itself.

Speaking generally, there is no vice of this kind more contemptible than another; for each is but a result and outward sign of a soul tragically shipwrecked. In the majority of cases, cheap pleasure is resorted to by way of anodyne. The pleasure-seeker sets forth upon life with high and difficult ambitions: he meant to be nobly good and nobly happy, though at as little pains as possible to himself; and it is because all has failed in his celestial enterprise that you now behold him rolling in the garbage. Hence the comparative success of the teetotal pledge; because to a man who had nothing it sets at least a negative aim in life. Somewhat as prisoners beguile their days by taming a spider, the reformed drunkard makes an interest out of abstaining from intoxicating drinks, and may live for that negation. There is something, at least, *not to be done* each day; and a cold triumph awaits him every evening.

We had one on board with us, whom I have already referred to under the name Mackay, who seemed to me not only a good instance of this failure in life of which we have been speaking, but a good type of the intelligence which here surrounded me. Physically he was a small Scotsman, standing a little back as though he were already carrying the elements of a corporation, and his looks somewhat marred by the smallness of his eyes. Mentally, he was endowed above the average. There were but few subjects on which he could not converse with understanding and a dash of wit; delivering himself slowly and with gusto like a man who enjoyed his own sententiousness. He was a dry, quick, pertinent debater, speaking with a small voice, and swinging on his heels to launch and emphasise an argument. When he began a discussion, he could not bear to leave it off, but would pick the subject to the bone, without once relinquishing a point. An engineer by trade, Mackay believed in the unlimited perfectibility of all machines except the human machine. The latter he gave up with ridicule for a compound of carrion and perverse gases. He had an appetite for disconnected facts which I can only compare to the savage taste for beads. What is called information was indeed a passion with the man, and he not only delighted to receive it, but could pay you back in kind.

With all these capabilities, here was Mackay, already no longer young, on his way to a new country, with no prospects, no money, and but little hope. He was almost tedious in the cynical disclosures of his despair. 'The ship may go down for me,' he would say, 'now or tomorrow. I have nothing to lose and nothing to hope.' And again: 'I am sick of the whole damned performance.' He was, like the kind little man already quoted, another so-called victim of the bottle. But Mackay was miles from publishing his weakness to the world; laid the blame of his failure on corrupt masters and a corrupt state policy; and after he had been one night overtaken and had played the buffoon in his cups, sternly, though not without tact, suppressed all reference to his escapade. It was a treat to see him manage this: the various jesters withered under his gaze, and you were forced to recognise in him a certain steely force, and a gift of command which might have ruled a senate.

In truth it was not whisky that had ruined him; he was ruined long before for all good human purposes but conversation. His eyes were sealed by a cheap, schoolbook materialism. He could see nothing in the world but money and steam-engines. He did not know what you meant by the word happiness. He had forgotten the simple emotions of childhood, and perhaps never encountered the delights of youth. He believed in production, that useful figment of economy, as if it had been real like laughter; and production, without prejudice to liquor, was his god and guide. One day he took me to task – novel cry to me – upon the over-payment of literature. Literary men, he said, were more highly paid than artisans; yet the artisan made threshing-machines and butter-churns, and the man of letters, except in the way of a few useful handbooks, made nothing worth the while. He produced a mere fancy article. Mackay's notion of a book was Hoppus's *Measurer*.[82] Now in my time I have possessed and even studied that work; but if I were to be left tomorrow on

Juan Fernandez, Hoppus's is not the book that I should choose for my companion volume.

I tried to fight the point with Mackay. I made him own that he had taken pleasure in reading books otherwise, to his view, insignificant; but he was too wary to advance a step beyond the admission. It was in vain for me to argue that here was pleasure ready-made and running from the spring, whereas his ploughs and butter-churns were but means and mechanisms to give men the necessary food and leisure before they start upon the search for pleasure; he jibbed and ran away from such conclusions. The thing was different, he declared, and nothing was serviceable but what had to do with food. 'Eat, eat, eat!' he cried; 'that's the bottom and the top.' By an odd irony of circumstance, he grew so much interested in this discussion that he let the hour slip by unnoticed and had to go without his tea. He had enough sense and humour, indeed he had no lack of either, to have chuckled over this himself in private; and even to me he referred to it with the shadow of a smile.

Mackay was a hot bigot. He would not hear of religion. I have seen him waste hours of time in argument with all sorts of poor human creatures who understood neither him nor themselves, and he had had the boyishness to dissect and criticise even so small a matter as the riddler's definition of mind. He snorted aloud with zealotry and the lust for intellectual battle. Anything, whatever it was, that seemed to him likely to discourage the continued passionate production of corn and steam-engines he resented like a conspiracy against the people. Thus, when I put in the plea for literature, that it was only in good books, or in the society of the good, that a man could get help in his conduct, he declared I was in a different world from him. 'Damn my conduct!' said he. 'I have given it up for a bad job. My question is, "Can I drive a nail?"' And he plainly looked upon me as one who was insidiously seeking to reduce the people's annual bellyful of corn and steam-engines.

It may be argued that these opinions spring from the defect of culture; that a narrow and pinching way of life not only exaggerates to a man the importance of material conditions, but indirectly, by denying him the necessary books and leisure, keeps his mind ignorant of larger thoughts; and that hence springs this overwhelming concern about diet, and hence the bald view of existence professed by Mackay. Had this been an English peasant the conclusion would be tenable. But Mackay had most of the elements of a liberal education. He had skirted metaphysical and mathematical studies. He had a thoughtful hold of what he knew, which would be exceptional among bankers. He had been brought up in the midst of hot-house piety, and told, with incongruous pride, the story of his own brother's deathbed ecstasies. Yet he had somehow failed to fulfil himself, and was adrift like a dead thing among external circumstances, without hope or lively preference or shaping aim. And further, there seemed a tendency among many of his fellows to fall into the same blank and unlovely opinions. One thing, indeed, is not to be learned in Scotland, and that is the way to be happy. Yet that is the whole of culture, and perhaps two-thirds of morality. Can it be that the Puritan school, by divorcing a man from nature, by thinning out his instincts, and setting a stamp of its disapproval on whole fields of human activity and interest, leads at last directly to material greed?

Nature is a good guide through life, and the love of simple pleasures next, if not superior, to virtue; and we had on board an Irishman who based his claim to the widest and most affectionate popularity precisely upon these two qualities, that he was natural and happy. He boasted a fresh colour, a tight little figure, unquenchable gaiety and in-defatigable goodwill. His clothes puzzled the diagnostic mind, until you heard he had been once a private coachman, when they became eloquent and seemed a part of his biography. His face contained the rest, and, I fear, a prophecy of the future: the hawk's nose above accorded so ill with the pink baby's mouth below. His spirit and his pride belonged, you might say, to the nose; while it was the general shiftlessness expressed by the other that had thrown him from situation to situation, and at length on board the emigrant ship. Barney ate, so to speak, nothing from the galley; his own tea, butter, and eggs supported him throughout the voyage; and about mealtime you might often find him up to the elbows in amateur cookery. His was the first voice heard singing among all the passengers; he was the first who fell to dancing. From Loch Foyle to Sandy Hook, there was not a piece of fun undertaken but there was Barney in the midst.

You ought to have seen him when he stood up to sing at our concerts – his tight little figure stepping to and fro, and his feet shuffling to the air, his eyes seeking and bestowing encouragement – and to have enjoyed the bow, so nicely calculated between jest and earnest, between grace and clumsiness, with which he brought each song to a conclusion. He was not only a great favourite among ourselves, but his songs attracted the lords of the saloon, who often leaned to hear him over the rails of the hurricane-deck. He was somewhat pleased, but not at all abashed, by this attention; and one night, in the midst of his famous performance of 'Billy Keogh', I saw him spin half round in a pirouette and throw an audacious wink to an old gentleman above.

This was the more characteristic, as, for all his daffing, he was a modest and very polite little fellow among ourselves.

He would not have hurt the feelings of a fly, nor throughout the passage did he give a shadow of offence; yet he was always, by his innocent freedoms and love of fun, brought upon that narrow margin where politeness must be natural to walk without a fall. He was once seriously angry, and that in a grave, quiet manner, because they supplied no fish on Friday; for Barney was a conscientious Catholic. He had likewise strict notions of refinement; and when, late one evening, after the women had retired, a young Scotsman struck up an indecent song, Barney's drab clothes were immediately missing from the group. His taste was for the society of gentlemen, of whom, with the reader's permission, there was no lack in our five steerages and second cabin; and he avoided the rough and positive with a girlish shrinking. Mackay, partly from his superior powers of mind, which rendered him incomprehensible, partly from his extreme opinions, was especially distasteful to the Irishman. I have seen him slink off with backward looks of terror and offended delicacy, while the other, in his witty, ugly way, had been professing hostility to God, and an extreme theatrical readiness to be shipwrecked on the spot. These utterances hurt the little coachman's modesty like a bad word.

The Sick Man

One night Jones, the young O'Reilly and myself were walking arm in arm and briskly up and down the deck. Six bells had rung; a head wind blew chill and fitful, the fog was closing in with a sprinkle of rain, and the fog-whistle had been turned on, and now divided time with its unwelcome outcries, loud like a bull, thrilling and intense like a mosquito. Even the watch lay somewhere snugly out of sight.

For some time we observed something lying black and huddled in the scuppers, which at last heaved a little and moaned aloud. We ran to the rails. An elderly man, but whether passenger or seaman it was impossible in the darkness to determine, lay grovelling on his belly in the wet scuppers, and kicking feebly with his outspread toes. We asked him what was amiss, and he replied incoherently, with a strange accent and in a voice unmanned by terror, that he had cramp in the stomach, that he had been ailing all day, had seen the doctor twice, and had walked the deck against fatigue till he was overmastered and had fallen where we found him.

Jones remained by his side, while O'Reilly and I hurried off to seek the doctor. We knocked in vain at the doctor's cabin; there came no reply; nor could we find anyone to guide us. It was no time for delicacy; so we ran once more forward; and I, whipping up a ladder and touching my hat to the officer of the watch, addressed him as politely as I could: 'I beg your pardon, sir; but there is a man lying bad with cramp in the lee scuppers; and I can't find the doctor.'

He looked at me peeringly in the darkness; and then, somewhat harshly, 'Well, *I* can't leave the bridge, my man,' said he.

'No, sir; but you can tell me what to do,' I returned.

'Is it one of the crew?' he asked.

'I believe him to be a fireman,' I replied.

I dare say officers are much annoyed by complaints and alarmist information from their freight of human creatures; but certainly, whether it was the idea that the sick man was one of the crew, or from something conciliatory in my address, the officer in question was immediately relieved and mollified; and, speaking in a voice much freer from constraint, advised me to find a steward and despatch him in quest of the doctor, who would now be in the smoking-room over his pipe.

One of the stewards was often enough to be found about this hour down our companion, Steerage Nos 2 and 3; that was his smoking-room of a night. Let me call him Blackwood. O'Reilly and I rattled down the companion, breathing hurry; and in his shirt-sleeves and perched across the carpenter's bench upon one thigh, found Blackwood: a neat, bright, dapper, Glasgow-looking man, with a bead of an eye and a rank twang in his speech. I forget who was with him, but the pair were enjoying a deliberate talk over their pipes. I dare say he was tired with his day's work, and eminently comfortable at that moment; and the truth is, I did not stop to consider his feelings, but told my story in a breath.

'Steward,' said I, 'there's a man lying bad with cramp, and I can't find the doctor.'

He turned upon me as pert as a sparrow, but with a black look that is the prerogative of man; and taking his pipe out of his mouth, 'That's none of my business,' said he. 'I don't care.'

I could have strangled the little ruffian where he sat. The thought of his cabin civility and cabin tips filled me with indignation. I glanced at O'Reilly; he was pale and quivering, and looked like assault and battery, every inch of him. But we had a better card than violence.

'You will have to make it your business,' said I, 'for I am sent to you by the officer on the bridge.'

Blackwood was fairly tripped. He made no answer, but put out his pipe, gave me one murderous look, and set off upon his errand, strolling. From that day forward, I should say, he improved to me in courtesy, as though he had repented his evil speech and were anxious to leave a better impression.

When we got on deck again, Jones was still beside the sick man; and two or three late stragglers had gathered round, and were offering suggestions. One proposed to give the patient water, which was promptly negatived. Another bade us hold him up; he himself prayed to be let lie; but as it was at least as well to keep him off the streaming decks, O'Reilly and I supported him between us. It was only by main force that we did so, and neither an easy nor an agreeable duty; for he fought in his paroxysms like a frightened child, and moaned miserably when he resigned himself to our control.

'Oh, let me lie!' he pleaded. 'I'll no' get better anyway.' And then, with a moan that went to my heart, 'Oh, why did I come upon this miserable journey?'

I was reminded of the song which I had heard a little while before in the close, tossing steerage: 'Oh, why left I my hame?'

Meantime Jones, relieved of his immediate charge, had gone off to the galley, where we could see a light. There he found a belated cook scouring pans by the radiance of two lanterns, and one of these he sought to borrow. The scullion was backward. 'Was it one of the crew?' he asked. And when Jones, smitten with my theory, had assured him that it was a fireman, he reluctantly left his scouring and came towards us at an easy pace, with one of the lanterns swinging from his finger. The light, as it reached the spot, showed us an elderly man, thick-set, and grizzled with years; but the shifting and coarse shadows concealed from us the expression and even the design of his face.

So soon as the cook set eyes on him he gave a sort of whistle.

'*It's only a passenger!*' said he; and turning about, made, lantern and all, for the galley.

'He's a man anyway,' cried Jones in indignation.

'Nobody said he was a woman,' said a gruff voice, which I recognised for that of the bosun.

All this while there was no word of Blackwood or the doctor; and now the officer came to our side of the ship and asked, over the hurricane-deck rails, if the doctor were not yet come. We told him not.

'No?' he repeated with a breathing of anger; and we saw him hurry aft in person.

Ten minutes after the doctor made his appearance deliberately enough and examined our patient with the lantern. He made little of the case, had the man brought aft to the dispensary, dosed him, and sent him forward to his bunk. Two of his neighbours in the steerage had now come to our assistance, expressing loud sorrow that such 'a fine cheery body' should be sick; and these, claiming a sort of possession, took him entirely under their own care. The drug had probably relieved him, for he struggled no more, and was led along plaintive and patient, but protesting. His heart recoiled at the thought of the steerage. 'Oh, let me lie down upon the bieldy side,' he cried; 'Oh, dinna take me down!' And again: 'Oh, why did ever I come upon this miserable voyage?' And yet once more, with a gasp and a wailing prolongation of the fourth word: 'I had no *call* to come.' But there he was; and by the doctor's orders and the kind force of his two shipmates disappeared down the companion of Steerage No. 1 into the den allotted him.

At the foot of our own companion, just where I found Blackwood, Jones and the bosun were now engaged in talk. This last was a gruff, cruel-looking seaman, who must have passed near half a century upon the seas: square-headed, goat-bearded, with heavy blond eyebrows and an eye without radiance, but inflexibly steady and hard. I had not forgotten his rough speech; but I remembered also that he had helped us about the lantern; and now seeing him in conversation with Jones, and being choked with indignation, I proceeded to blow off my steam.

'Well,' said I, 'I make you my compliments upon your steward,' and furiously narrated what had happened.

'I've nothing to do with him,' replied the bosun. 'They're all alike. They wouldn't mind if they saw you all lying dead one upon the top of another.'

This was enough. A very little humanity went a long way with me after the experience of the evening. A sympathy grew up at once between the bosun and myself; and that night, and during the next few days, I learned to appreciate him better. He was a remarkable type, and not at all the kind of man you find in books. He had been at Sebastopol under English colours; and again in a States ship, 'after the *Alabama*, and praying God we shouldn't find her'. He was a high Tory and a high Englishman. No manufacturer could have held opinions more hostile to the working man and his strikes. 'The workmen,' he said, 'think nothing of their country. They think of nothing but themselves. They're damned greedy, selfish fellows.' He would not hear of the decadence of England. 'They say they send us beef from America,' he argued; 'but who pays for it? All the money in the world's in England.' The Royal Navy was the best of possible services, according to him. 'Anyway the officers are gentlemen,' said he; 'and you can't get hazed to death by a damned non-commissioned — as you can in the army.' Among nations, England was the first; then came France. He respected the French navy and liked the French people; and if he were forced to make a new choice in life, 'by God, he would try Frenchmen!' For all his looks and rough, cold manners, I observed that children were never frightened by him: they divined him at once to be a friend; and one night when he had chalked his hand and went about stealthily setting his mark on people's clothes, it was incongruous to hear this formidable old salt chuckling over his boyish monkey trick.

In the morning, my first thought was of the sick man. I was afraid I should not recognise him, so baffling had been the light of the lantern; and I found myself unable to decide if he were Scots, English or Irish. He had certainly employed north-country words and elisions; but the accent and the pronunciation seemed unfamiliar and incongruous in my ear.

To descend on an empty stomach into Steerage No. 1 was an adventure that required some nerve. The stench was atrocious; each respiration tasted in the throat like some horrible kind of cheese; and the squalid aspect of the place was aggravated by so many people worming themselves into their clothes in the twilight of the bunks. You may guess if I was pleased, not only for him, but for myself also, when I heard that the sick man was better and had gone on deck.

The morning was raw and foggy, though the sun suffused the fog with pink and amber; the fog-horn still blew, stertorous and inter-mittent; and to add to the discomfort, the seamen were just beginning to wash down the decks. But for a sick man this was heaven compared to the steerage. I found him standing on the hot-water pipe, just forward of the saloon deck-house. He was smaller than I had fancied, and plain-looking; but his face was distinguished by strange and fascinating eyes, limpid grey from a distance, but, when looked into, full of changing colours and grains of gold. His manners were mild and uncompromisingly plain; and I soon saw that, when once started, he delighted to talk. His accent and language had been formed in the most natural way, since he was born in Ireland, had lived a quarter of a century on the banks of the Tyne, and was married to a Scots wife. A fisherman in the season, he had fished the east coast from Fisherrow to Whitby. When the season was over, and the great boats, which required extra hands, were once drawn up on shore till the next spring, he worked as a labourer about chemical furnaces, or along the wharves unloading vessels. In this comparatively humble way of life he had gathered a competence, and could speak of his comfortable house, his hayfield and his garden. On this ship, where so many accomplished artisans were fleeing from starvation, he was present on a pleasure trip to visit a brother in New York.

Ere he started, he informed me, he had been warned against the steerage and the steerage fare, and recommended to bring with him a ham and tea and a spice loaf. But he laughed to scorn such counsels. 'I'm not afraid,' he had told his adviser; 'I'll get on for ten days. I've not been a fisherman for nothing.' For it is no light matter, as he reminded me, to be in an open boat, perhaps waist-deep with herrings, day breaking with a scowl, and for miles on every hand lee-shores, unbroken, iron-bound, surf-beat, with only here and there an anchorage where you dare not lie, or a harbour impossible to enter with the wind that blows. The life of a North Sea fisher is one long chapter of exposure and hard work and insufficient fare; and even if he makes land at some bleak fisher port, perhaps the season is bad or his boat has been unlucky and after fifty hours' unsleeping vigilance and toil, not a shop will give him credit for a loaf of bread. Yet the steerage of the emigrant ship had been too vile for the endurance of a man thus rudely trained. He had scarce eaten since he came on board, until the day before, when his appetite was tempted by some excellent pea-soup. We were all much of the same mind on board, and beginning with myself, had dined upon pea-soup not wisely but too well; only with him the excess had been punished, perhaps because he was weakened by former abstinence, and his first meal had resulted in a cramp. He had determined to live henceforth on biscuit; and when, two months later, he should return to England, to make the passage by saloon. The second cabin, after due enquiry, he scouted as another edition of the steerage.

He spoke apologetically of his emotion when ill. 'Ye see, I had no call to be here,' said he; 'and I thought it was by with me last night.

I've a good house at home, and plenty to nurse me, and I had no real call to leave them.' Speaking of the attentions he had received from his shipmates generally, 'they were all so kind,' he said, 'that there's none to mention.' And except in so far as I might share in this, he troubled me with no reference to my services.

But what affected me in the most lively manner was the wealth of this day-labourer, paying a two months' pleasure visit to the States, and preparing to return in the saloon, and the new testimony rendered by his story, not so much to the horrors of the steerage as to the habitual comfort of the working classes. One foggy, frosty December evening, I encountered on Liberton Hill, near Edinburgh, an Irish labourer trudging homeward from the fields. Our roads lay together, and it was natural that we should fall into talk. He was covered with mud; an inoffensive, ignorant creature, who thought the Atlantic Cable[83] was a secret contrivance of the masters the better to oppress labouring mankind; and I confess I was astonished to learn that he had nearly three hundred pounds in the bank. But this man had travelled over most of the world, and enjoyed wonderful opportunities on some American railroad, with two dollars a shift and double pay on Sunday and at night; whereas my fellow-passenger had never quitted Tyneside, and had made all that he possessed in that same accursed, down-falling England, whence skilled mechanics, engineers, millwrights and carpenters were fleeing as from the native country of starvation.

Fitly enough, we slid off on the subject of strikes and wages and hard times. Being from the Tyne, and a man who had gained and lost in his own pocket by these fluctuations, he had much to say, and held strong opinions on the subject. He spoke sharply of the masters, and, when I led him on, of the men also. The masters had been selfish and obstructive, the men selfish, silly and light-headed. He rehearsed to me the course of a meeting at which he had been present, and the somewhat long discourse which he had there pronounced, calling into question the wisdom and even the good faith of the Union delegates; and although he had escaped himself through flush times and starvation times with a handsomely provided purse, he had so little faith in either man or master, and so profound a terror for the unerring Nemesis of mercantile affairs, that he could think of no hope for our country outside of a sudden and complete political subversion. Down must go Lords and Church and Army; and capital, by some happy direction, must change hands from worse to better, or England stood condemned. Such principles, he said, were growing 'like a seed'.

From this mild, soft, domestic man, these words sounded unusually ominous and grave. I had heard enough revolutionary talk among my workmen fellow-passengers; but most of it was hot and turgid, and fell discredited from the lips of unsuccessful men. This man was calm; he had attained prosperity and ease; he disapproved the policy which had been pursued by labour in the past; and yet this was his panacea – to rend the old country from end to end, and from top to bottom, and in clamour and civil discord remodel it with the hand of violence.

The Stowaways

On the Sunday, among a party of men who were talking in our companion, Steerage Nos 2 and 3, we remarked a new figure. He wore tweed clothes, well enough made if not very fresh, and a plain smoking-cap. His face was pale, with pale eyes, and spiritedly enough designed; but though not yet thirty, a sort of blackguardly degeneration had already overtaken his features. The fine nose had grown fleshy towards the point, the pale eyes were sunk in fat. His hands were strong and elegant; his experience of life evidently varied; his speech full of pith and verve; his manners forward, but perfectly presentable. The lad who helped in the second cabin told me, in answer to a question, that he did not know who he was, but thought, 'by his way of speaking, and because he was so polite, that he was someone from the saloon.'

I was not so sure, for to me there was something equivocal in his air and bearing. He might have been, I thought, the son of some good family who had fallen early into dissipation and run from home. But, making every allowance, how admirable was his talk! I wish you could have heard him tell his own stories. They were so swingingly set forth, in such dramatic language, and illustrated here and there by such luminous bits of acting, that they could only lose in any reproduction. There were tales of the P&O Company, where he had been an officer; of the East Indies, where in former years he had lived lavishly; of the Royal Engineers, where he had served for a period; and of a dozen other sides of life, each introducing some vigorous thumb-nail portrait. He had the talk to himself that night, we were all so glad to listen. The best talkers usually address themselves to some particular society; there they are kings, elsewhere camp-followers, as a man may know Russian and yet be ignorant of Spanish; but this fellow had a frank, headlong power of style, and a broad, human choice of subject, that would have turned any circle in the world into a circle of hearers. He was a Homeric talker, plain, strong and cheerful; and the things and the people of which he spoke became readily and clearly present to the minds of those who heard him. This, with a certain added colouring of rhetoric and rodomontade, must have been the style of Burns, who equally charmed the ears of duchesses and hostlers.

Yet freely and personally as he spoke, many points remained obscure in his narration. The Engineers, for instance, was a service which he praised highly; it is true there would be trouble with the sergeants; but then the officers were gentlemen, and his own, in particular, one among ten thousand. It sounded so far exactly like an episode in the rakish, topsy-turvy life of such a one as I had imagined. But then there came incidents more doubtful, which showed an almost impudent greed after gratuities, and a truly impudent disregard for truth. And then there was the tale of his departure. He had wearied, it seems, of Woolwich, and one fine day, with a companion, slipped up to London for a spree. I have a suspicion that spree was meant to be a long one; but God disposes all things; and one morning, near Westminster Bridge, whom should he come across but the very sergeant who had recruited him at first! What followed? He himself indicated cavalierly that he had then resigned. Let us put it so. But these resignations are sometimes very trying.

At length, after having delighted us for hours, he took himself away from the companion; and I could ask Mackay who and what he was. 'That?' said Mackay. 'Why, that's one of the stowaways.'

'No man,' said the same authority, 'who has had anything to do with the sea, would ever think of paying for a passage.' I give the statement as Mackay's, without endorsement; yet I am tempted to believe that it contains a grain of truth; and if you add that the man shall be impudent and thievish, or else dead-broke, it may even pass for a fair representation of the facts. We gentlemen of England who live at home at ease have, I suspect, very insufficient ideas on the subject. All the world over, people are stowing away in coal-holes and dark corners, and when ships are once out to sea, appearing again, begrimed and bashful, upon deck. The career of these sea-tramps partakes largely of the adventurous. They may be poisoned by coal-gas, or die by starvation in their place of concealment; or when found they may be clapped at once and ignominiously into irons, thus to be carried to their promised land, the port of destination, and alas! brought back in the same way to that from which they started, and there delivered over to the magistrates and the seclusion of a county jail. Since I crossed the Atlantic, one miserable stowaway was found in a dying state among the fuel, uttered but a word or two, and departed for a farther country than America.

When the stowaway appears on deck, he has but one thing to pray for: that he be set to work, which is the price and sign of his forgiveness. After half an hour with a swab or a bucket, he feels himself as secure as if he had paid for his passage. It is not altogether a bad thing for the company, who get more or less efficient hands for nothing but a few plates of junk and duff; and every now and again find themselves better paid than by a whole family of cabin passengers. Not long ago, for instance, a packet was saved from nearly certain loss by the skill and courage of a stowaway engineer. As was no more than just, a handsome subscription rewarded him for his success: but even without such exceptional good fortune, as things stand in England and America, the stowaway will often make a good profit out of his adventure. Four engineers stowed away last summer on the same ship, the *Circassia*; and before two days after their arrival each of the four had found a comfortable berth. This was the most hopeful tale of emigration that I heard from first to last; and as you see, the luck was for stowaways.

My curiosity was much inflamed by what I heard; and the next morning, as I was making the round of the ship, I was delighted to find the ex-Royal Engineer engaged in washing down the white paint of a deck house. There was another fellow at work beside him, a lad not more than twenty, in the most miraculous tatters, his handsome face sown with grains of beauty and lighted up by expressive eyes. Four stowaways had been found aboard our ship before she left the Clyde, but these two had alone escaped the ignominy of being put ashore. Alick, my acquaintance of last night, was Scots by birth, and by trade a practical engineer; the other was from Devonshire, and had been to sea before the mast. Two people more unlike by training, character and habits it would be hard to imagine; yet here they were together, scrubbing paint.

Alick had held all sorts of good situations, and wasted many opportunities in life. I have heard him end a story with these words: 'That was in my golden days, when I used finger-glasses.' Situation after situation failed him; then followed the depression of trade, and for months he had hung round with other idlers, playing marbles all day in the West Park, and going home at night to tell his landlady how he had been seeking for a job. I believe this kind of existence was not unpleasant to Alick himself, and he might have long continued to enjoy idleness and a life on tick; but he had a comrade, let us call him Brown, who grew restive. This fellow was continually threatening to slip his cable for the States, and at last, one Wednesday, Glasgow was left widowed of her Brown. Some months afterwards, Alick met another old chum in Sauchiehall Street.

'By the by, Alick,' said he, 'I met a gentleman in New York who was asking for you.'

'Who was that?' asked Alick.

'The new second engineer on board the So-and-so,' was the reply.

'Well, and who is he?'

'Brown, to be sure.'

For Brown had been one of the fortunate quartette aboard the *Circassia*. If that was the way of it in the States, Alick thought it was high time to follow Brown's example. He spent his last day, as he put it, 'reviewing the yeomanry', and the next morning says he to his landlady, 'Mrs X—, I'll not take porridge today, please; I'll take some eggs.'

'Why, have you found a job?' she asked, delighted.

'Well, yes,' returned the perfidious Alick; 'I think I'll start today.'

And so, well lined with eggs, start he did, but for America. I am afraid that landlady has seen the last of him.

It was easy enough to get on board in the confusion that attends a vessel's departure; and in one of the dark corners of Steerage No. 1, flat in a bunk and with an empty stomach, Alick made the voyage from the Broomielaw to Greenock. That night, the ship's yeoman pulled him out by the heels and had him before the mate. Two other stowaways had already been found and sent ashore; but by this time darkness had fallen, they were out in the middle of the estuary, and the last steamer had left them till the morning.

'Take him to the forecastle and give him a meal,' said the mate, 'and see and pack him off the first thing tomorrow.'

In the forecastle he had supper, a good night's rest, and breakfast; and was sitting placidly with a pipe, fancying all was over and the game up for good with that ship, when one of the sailors grumbled out an oath at him, with a 'What are you doing there?' and 'Do you call that hiding, anyway?' There was need of no more; Alick was in another bunk before the day was older. Shortly before the passengers arrived, the ship was cursorily inspected. He heard the round come down the companion and look into one pen after another, until they came within two of the one in which he lay concealed. Into these last two they did not enter, but merely glanced from without; and Alick had no doubt that he was personally favoured in this escape. It was the character of the man to attribute nothing to luck and but little to kindness; whatever happened to him he had earned in his own right amply; favours came to him from his singular attraction and adroitness, and misfortunes he had always accepted with his eyes open. Half an hour after the searchers had departed, the steerage began to fill with legitimate passengers, and the worst of Alick's troubles was at an end. He was soon making himself popular, smoking other people's tobacco, and politely sharing their private stock delicacies, and when night came he retired to his bunk beside the others with composure.

Next day by afternoon, Lough Foyle being already far behind, and only the rough north-western hills of Ireland within view, Alick appeared on deck to court enquiry and decide his fate. As a matter of fact, he was known to several on board, and even intimate with one of the engineers; but it was plainly not the etiquette of such occasions for the authorities to avow their information. Everyone professed surprise and anger on his appearance, and he was led prisoner before the captain.

'What have you got to say for yourself?' enquired the captain.

'Not much,' said Alick; 'but when a man has been a long time out of a job, he will do things he would not under other circumstances.'

'Are you willing to work?'

Alick swore he was burning to be useful.

'And what can you do?' asked the captain.

He replied composedly that he was a brass-fitter by trade.

'I think you will be better at engineering?' suggested the officer, with a shrewd look.

'No, sir,' says Alick simply. ('There's few can beat me at a lie,' was his engaging commentary to me as he recounted the affair.)

'Have you been to sea?' again asked the captain.

'I've had a trip on a Clyde steamboat, sir, but no more,' replied the unabashed Alick.

'Well, we must try and find some work for you,' concluded the officer.

And hence we behold Alick, clear of the hot engine-room, lazily scraping paint and now and then taking a pull upon a sheet. 'You leave me alone,' was his deduction. 'When I get talking to a man, I can get round him.'

The other stowaway, whom I will call the Devonian – it was noticeable that neither of them told his name – had both been brought up and seen the world in a much smaller way. His father, a confectioner, died and was closely followed by his mother. His sisters had taken, I think, to dressmaking. He himself had returned from sea about a year ago and gone to live with his brother, who kept the George Hotel – 'it was not quite a real hotel,' added the candid fellow, 'and had a hired man to mind the horses.' At first the Devonian was very welcome; but as time went on his brother not unnaturally grew cool towards him, and he began to find himself one too many at the George Hotel. 'I don't think brothers care much for you,' he said, as a general reflection upon life. Hurt at this change, nearly penniless, and too proud to ask for more, he set off on foot and walked eighty miles to Weymouth, living on the journey as he could. He would have enlisted, but he was too small for the army and too old for the navy; and thought himself fortunate at last to find a berth on board a trading dandy. Somewhere in the Bristol Channel the dandy sprung a leak and went down; and though the crew were picked up and brought ashore by fishermen, they found themselves with nothing but the clothes upon their back. His next engagement was scarcely better starred; for the ship proved so leaky, and frightened them all so heartily during a short passage through the Irish Sea, that the entire crew deserted and remained behind upon the quays of Belfast.

Evil days were now coming thick on the Devonian. He could find no berth in Belfast, and had to work a passage to Glasgow on a steamer. She reached the Broomielaw on a Wednesday: the Devonian had a bellyful that morning, laying in breakfast manfully to provide against the future, and set off along the quays to seek employment. But he was now not only penniless, his clothes had begun to fall in tatters; he had begun to have the look of a street Arab; and captains will have nothing to say to a ragamuffin; for in that trade, as in all others, it is the coat that depicts the man. You may hand, reef and steer like an angel, but if you have a hole in your trousers, it is like a millstone round your neck. The Devonian lost heart at so many refusals. He had not the impudence to beg; although, as he said, 'When I had money of my own, I always gave it.' It was only on Saturday morning, after three whole days of starvation, that he asked a scone from a milkwoman, who added of her own accord a glass of milk. He had now made up his mind to stow away, not from any desire to see America, but merely to obtain the comfort of a place in the forecastle and a supply of familiar sea-fare. He lived by begging, always from milkwomen, and always scones and milk, and was not once refused. It was vile wet weather, and he could never have been dry. By night he walked the streets, and by day slept upon Glasgow Green, and heard, in the intervals of his dozing, the famous theologians of the spot clear up intricate points of doctrine and appraise the merits of the clergy. He had not much instruction; he could 'read bills on the street', but was 'main bad at writing'; yet these theologians seem to have impressed him with a genuine sense of amusement. Why he did not go to the Sailors' House I know not; I presume there is in Glasgow one of these institutions, which are by far the happiest and the wisest effort of contemporaneous charity; but I must stand to my author, as they say in old books, and relate the story as I heard it. In the meantime, he had tried four times to stow away in different vessels, and four times had been discovered and handed back to starvation. The fifth time was lucky; and you may judge if he were pleased to be aboard ship again, at his old work, and with duff twice a week. He was, said Alick, 'a devil for the duff'. Or if devil was not the word, it was one if anything stronger.

The difference in the conduct of the two was remarkable. The Devonian was as willing as any paid hand, swarmed aloft among the first, pulled his natural weight and firmly upon a rope, and found work for himself when there was none to show him. Alick, on the other hand, was not only a skulker in the brain, but took a humorous and fine gentlemanly view of the transaction. He would speak to me by the hour in ostentatious idleness; and only if the bosun or a mate came by, fell-to languidly for just the necessary time till they were out of sight. 'I'm not breaking my heart with it,' he remarked.

Once there was a hatch to be opened near where he was stationed; he watched the preparations for a second or so suspiciously, and then, 'Hello,' said he, 'here's some real work coming – I'm off,' and he was gone that moment. Again, calculating the six-guinea passage-money, and the probable duration of the passage, he remarked pleasantly that he was getting six shillings a day for this job, 'and it's pretty dear to the company at that'. 'They are making nothing by me,' was another of his observations; 'they're making something by that fellow.' And he pointed to the Devonian, who was just then busy to the eyes.

The more you saw of Alick, the more, it must be owned, you learned to despise him. His natural talents were of no use either to himself or others; for his character had degenerated like his face, and become pulpy and pretentious. Even his power of persuasion, which was certainly very surprising, stood in some danger of being lost or neutralised by over-confidence. He lied in an aggressive, brazen manner, like a pert criminal in the dock; and he was so vain of his own cleverness that he could not refrain from boasting, ten minutes after, of the very trick by which he had deceived you. 'Why, now I have more money than when I came on board,' he said one night, exhibiting a sixpence, 'and yet I stood myself a bottle of beer before I went to bed yesterday. And as for tobacco, I have fifteen sticks of it.' That was fairly successful indeed; yet a man of his superiority, and with a less obtrusive policy, might, who knows? have got the length of half a crown. A man who prides himself upon persuasion should learn the persuasive faculty of silence, above all as to his own misdeeds. It is only in the farce and for dramatic purposes that Scapin[84] enlarges on his peculiar talents to the world at large.

Scapin is perhaps a good name for this clever, unfortunate Alick; for at the bottom of all his misconduct there was a guiding sense of humour that moved you to forgive him. It was more than half a jest that he conducted his existence. 'Oh, man,' he said to me once with unusual emotion, like a man thinking of his mistress, 'I would give up anything for a lark.'

It was in relation to his fellow-stowaway that Alick showed the best, or perhaps I should say the only good, points of his nature. 'Mind you,' he said suddenly, changing his tone, 'mind you that's a good boy. He wouldn't tell you a lie. A lot of them think he is a scamp because his clothes are ragged, but he isn't; he's as good as gold.' To hear him, you become aware that Alick himself had a taste for virtue. He thought his own idleness and the other's industry equally becoming. He was no more anxious to ensure his own reputation as a liar than to uphold the truthfulness of his companion; and he seemed unaware of what was incongruous in his attitude, and was plainly sincere in both characters.

It was not surprising that he should take an interest in the Devonian, for the lad worshipped and served him in love and wonder. Busy as he was, he would find time to warn Alick of an approaching officer, or even to tell him that the coast was clear, and he might slip off and smoke a pipe in safety. 'Tom,' he once said to him, for that was the name which Alick ordered him to use, 'if you don't like going to the galley, I'll go for you. You ain't used to this kind of thing, you ain't. But I'm a sailor; and I can understand the feelings of any fellow, I can.' Again, he was hard up, and casting about for some tobacco, for he was not so liberally used in this respect as others perhaps less worthy, when Alick offered him the half of one of his fifteen sticks. I think, for my part, he might have increased the offer to a whole one, or perhaps a pair of them, and not lived to regret his liberality. But the Devonian refused. 'No,' he said, 'you're a stowaway like me; I won't take it from you, I'll take it from someone who's not down on his luck.'

It was notable in this generous lad that he was strongly under the influence of sex. If a woman passed near where he was working, his eyes lit up, his hand paused, and his mind wandered instantly to other thoughts. It was natural that he should exercise a fascination proportionally strong upon women. He begged, you will remember, from women only, and was never refused. Without wishing to explain away the charity of those who helped him, I cannot but fancy he may have owed a little to his handsome face, and to that quick, responsive nature, formed for love, which speaks eloquently through all disguises, and can stamp an impression in ten minutes' talk or an exchange of glances. He was the more dangerous in that he was far from bold, but seemed to woo in spite of himself, and with a soft and pleading eye. Ragged as he was, and many a scarecrow is in that respect more comfortably furnished, even on board he was not without some curious admirers.

There was a girl among the passengers, a tall, blonde, handsome, strapping Irishwoman, with a wild, accommodating eye, whom Alick had dubbed Tommy, with that transcendental appropriateness that defies analysis. One day the Devonian was lying for warmth in the upper stoke-hole, which stands open on the deck, when Irish Tommy came past, very neatly attired, as was her custom.

'Poor fellow,' she said, stopping, 'you haven't a vest.'

'No,' he said; 'I wish I 'ad.'

Then she stood and gazed on him in silence, until, in his embarrassment, for he knew not how to look under this scrutiny, he pulled out his pipe and began to fill it with tobacco.

'Do you want a match?' she asked. And before he had time to reply, she ran off and presently returned with more than one.

That was the beginning and the end, as far as our passage is concerned, of what I will make bold to call this love-affair. There are many relations which go on to marriage and last during a lifetime, in which less human feeling is engaged than in this scene of five minutes at the stoke-hole.

Rigidly speaking, this would end the chapter of the stowaways; but in a larger sense of the word I have yet more to add. Jones had discovered and pointed out to me a young woman who was remarkable among her fellows for a pleasing and interesting air. She was poorly clad, to the verge, if not over the line, of disrespectability, with a ragged old jacket and a bit of a sealskin cap no bigger than your fist; but her eyes, her whole expression, and her manner, even in ordinary moments, told of a true womanly nature, capable of love, anger and devotion. She had a look, too, of refinement, like one who might have been a better lady than most, had she been allowed the opportunity. When alone she seemed preoccupied and sad; but she was not often alone; there was usually by her side a heavy, dull, gross man in rough clothes, chary of speech and gesture – not from caution, but poverty of disposition; a man like a ditcher, unlovely and uninteresting, whom she petted and tended and waited on with her eyes as if he had been Amadis of Gaul.[85] It was strange to see this hulking fellow dog-sick, and this delicate, sad woman caring for him. He seemed, from first to last, insensible of her caresses and attentions, and she seemed unconscious of his insensibility. The Irish husband, who sang his wife to sleep, and this Scottish girl serving her Orson,[86] were the two bits of human nature that most appealed to me throughout the voyage.

On the Thursday before we arrived, the tickets were collected; and soon a rumour began to go round the vessel; and this girl, with her bit of sealskin cap, became the centre of whispering and pointed fingers. She also, it was said, was a stowaway of a sort; for she was on board with neither ticket nor money; and the man with whom she travelled was the father of a family, who had left wife and children to be hers. The ship's officers discouraged the story, which may therefore have been a story and no more; but it was believed in the steerage, and the poor girl had to encounter many curious eyes from that day forth.

Personal Experience and Review

Travel is of two kinds; and this voyage of mine across the ocean combined both. 'Out of my country and myself I go,'[87] sings the old poet: and I was not only travelling out of my country in latitude and longitude, but out of myself in diet, associates and consideration. Part of the interest and a great deal of the amusement flowed, at least to me, from this novel situation in the world.

I found that I had what they call fallen in life with absolute success and verisimilitude. I was taken for a steerage passenger; no one seemed surprised that I should be so; and there was nothing but the brass plate between decks to remind me that I had once been a gentleman. In a former book, describing a former journey, I expressed some wonder that I could be readily and naturally taken for a pedlar, and explained the accident by the difference of language and manners between England and France. I must now take a humbler view; for here I was among my own countrymen, somewhat roughly clad to be sure, but with every advantage of speech and manner; and I am bound to confess that I passed for nearly anything you please except an educated gentleman. The sailors called me 'mate', the officers addressed me as 'my man', my comrades accepted me without hesitation for a person of their own character and experience, but with some curious information. One, a mason himself, believed I was a mason; several, and among these at least one of the seaman, judged me to be a petty officer in the American navy; and I was so often set down for a practical engineer that at last I had not the heart to deny it. From all these guesses I drew one conclusion, which told against the insight of my companions. They might be close observers in their own way, and read the manners in the face; but it was plain that they did not extend their observation to the hands.

To the saloon passengers also I sustained my part without a hitch. It is true I came little in their way; but when we did encounter, there was no recognition in their eye, although I confess I sometimes courted it in silence. All these, my inferiors and equals, took me, like the transformed monarch in the story, for a mere common, human man. They gave me a hard, dead look, with the flesh about the eye kept unrelaxed.

With the women this surprised me less, as I had already experimented on the sex by going abroad through a suburban part of London simply attired in a sleeve-waistcoat. The result was curious. I then learned for the first time, and by the exhaustive process, how much attention ladies are accustomed to bestow on all male creatures of their own station; for, in my humble rig, each one who went by me caused me a certain shock of surprise and a sense of something wanting. In my normal circumstances, it appeared every young lady must have paid me some tribute of a glance; and though I had often not detected it when it was given, I was well aware of its absence when it was withheld. My height seemed to decrease with every woman who passed me, for she passed me like a dog. This is one of my grounds for supposing that what are called the upper classes may sometimes produce a disagreeable impression in what are called the lower; and I wish someone would continue my experiment, and find out exactly at what stage of toilette a man becomes invisible to the well-regulated female eye.

Here on shipboard the matter was put to a more complete test; for, even with the addition of speech and manner, I passed among the ladies for precisely the average man of the steerage. It was one afternoon that I saw this demonstrated. A very plainly dressed woman was taken ill on deck. I think I had the luck to be present at every sudden seizure during all the passage; and on this occasion found myself in the place of importance, supporting the sufferer. There was not only a large crowd immediately around us, but a considerable knot of saloon passengers leaning over our heads from the hurricane-deck. One of these, an elderly managing woman, hailed me with counsels. Of course I had to reply; and as the talk went on, I began to discover that the whole group took me for the husband. I looked upon my new wife, poor creature, with mingled feelings; and I must own she had not even the appearance of the poorest class of city servant-maids, but looked more like a country wench who should have been employed at a roadside inn. Now was the time for me to go and study the brass plate.

To such of the officers as knew about me – the doctor, the purser and the stewards – I appeared in the light of a broad joke. The fact that I spent the better part of my day in writing had gone abroad over the ship and tickled them all prodigiously. Whenever they met me they referred to my absurd occupation with familiarity and breadth of humorous intention. Their manner was well calculated to remind me of my fallen fortunes. You may be sincerely amused by the amateur literary efforts of a gentleman, but you scarce publish the feeling to his face. 'Well!' they would say: 'still writing?' And the smile would widen into a laugh. The purser came one day into the cabin, and, touched to the heart by my misguided industry, offered me some other kind of writing, 'for which,' he added pointedly, 'you will be paid.' This was nothing else than to copy out the list of passengers.

Another trick of mine which told against my reputation was my choice of roosting-place in an active draught upon the cabin floor. I was openly jeered and flouted for this eccentricity; and a considerable knot would sometimes gather at the door to see my last dispositions for the night. This was embarrassing, but I learned to support the trial with equanimity.

Indeed I may say that, upon the whole, my new position sat lightly and naturally upon my spirits. I accepted the consequences with readiness, and found them far from difficult to bear. The steerage conquered me; I conformed more and more to the type of the place, not only in manner but at heart, growing hostile to the officers and cabin passengers who looked down upon me, and day by day greedier for small delicacies. Such was the result, as I fancy, of a diet of bread and butter, soup and porridge. We think we have no sweet tooth as long as we are full to the brim of molasses; but a man must have sojourned in the workhouse before he boasts himself indifferent to dainties. Every evening, for instance, I was more and more pre-occupied about our doubtful fare at tea. If it was delicate my heart was much lightened; if it was but broken fish I was proportionally downcast. The offer of a little jelly from a fellow-passenger more provident than myself caused a marked elevation in my spirits. And I would have gone to the ship's end and back again for an oyster or a chipped fruit.

In other ways I was content with my position. It seemed no disgrace to be confounded with my company; for I may as well declare at once I found their manners as gentle and becoming as those of any other class. I do not mean that my friends could have sat down without embarrassment and laughable disaster at the table of a duke. That does not imply an inferiority of breeding, but a difference of usage. Thus I flatter myself that I conducted myself well among my fellow-passengers; yet my most ambitious hope is not to have avoided faults, but to have committed as few as possible. I know too well that my tact is not the same as their tact, and that my habit of a different society constituted, not only no qualification, but a positive disability to move easily and becomingly in this. When Jones complimented me – because I 'managed to behave very pleasantly' to my fellow-passengers, was how he put it – I could follow the thought in his mind, and knew his compliment to be such as we pay foreigners on their proficiency in English. I dare say this praise was given me immediately on the back of some unpardonable solecism, which had led him to review my conduct as a whole. We are all ready to laugh at the ploughman among lords; we should consider also the case of a lord among the ploughmen. I have seen a lawyer in the house of a Hebridean fisherman; and I know, but nothing will induce me to disclose, which of these two was the better gentleman. Some of our finest behaviour, though it looks well enough from the boxes, may seem even brutal to the gallery. We boast too often manners that are parochial rather than universal; that, like a country wine, will not bear transportation for a hundred miles, nor from the parlour to the kitchen. To be a gentleman is to be one all the world over, and in every relation and grade of society. It is a high calling, to which a man must first be born, and then devote himself for life. And, unhappily, the manners of a certain so-called upper grade have a kind of currency, and meet with a certain external acceptation throughout all the others, and this tends to keep us well satisfied with slight acquirements and the amateurish accomplishments of a clique. But manners, like art, should be human and central.

Some of my fellow-passengers, as I now moved among them in a relation of equality, seemed to me excellent gentlemen. They were not rough, nor hasty, nor disputatious; debated pleasantly, differed kindly; were helpful, gentle, patient and placid. The type of manners was plain, and even heavy; there was little to please the eye, but nothing to shock; and I thought gentleness lay more nearly at the spring of behaviour than in many more ornate and delicate societies. I say delicate, where I cannot say refined; a thing may be fine, like ironwork, without being delicate, like lace. There was here less delicacy; the skin supported more callously the natural surface of events, the mind received more bravely the crude facts of human existence; but I do not think that there was less effective refinement, less consideration for others, less polite suppression of self. I speak of the best among my fellow-passengers; for in the steerage, as well as in the saloon, there is a mixture. Those, then, with whom I found myself in sympathy, and of whom I may therefore hope to write with a greater measure of truth, were not only as good in their manners, but endowed with very much the same natural capacities, and about as wise in deduction, as the bankers and barristers of what is called society. One and all were too much interested in disconnected facts, and loved information for its own sake with too rash a devotion; but people in all classes display the same appetite as they gorge themselves daily with the miscellaneous gossip of the newspaper. Newspaper-reading, as far as I can make out, is often rather a sort of brown study than an act of culture. I have myself palmed off yesterday's issue on a friend, and seen him re-peruse it for a continuance of minutes with an air at once refreshed and solemn. Workmen, perhaps, pay more attention; but though they may be eager listeners, they have rarely seemed to me either willing or careful thinkers. Culture is not measured by the greatness of the field which is covered by our knowledge, but by the nicety with which we can perceive relations in that field, whether great or small. Workmen, certainly those who were on board with me, I found wanting in this quality or habit of the mind. They did not perceive relations, but leaped to a so-called cause, and thought the problem settled. Thus the cause of everything in England was the form of government, and the cure for all evils was, by consequence, a revolution. It is surprising how many of them said this, and that none should have had a definite thought in his head as he said it. Some hated the Church because they disagreed with it; some hated Lord Beaconsfield because of war and taxes; all hated the masters, possibly with reason. But these failings were not at the root of the matter; the true reasoning of their souls ran thus – I have not got on; I ought to have got on; if there was a revolution I should get on. How? They had no idea. Why? Because – because – well, look at America!

To be politically blind is no distinction; we are all so, if you come to that. At bottom, as it seems to me, there is but one question in modern home politics, though it appears in many shapes, and that is the question of money; and but one political remedy, that the people should grow wiser and better. My workmen fellow-passengers were as impatient and dull of hearing on the second of these points as any member of Parliament; but they had some glimmerings of the first. They would not hear of improvement on their part, but wished the world made over again in a crack, so that they might remain improvident and idle and debauched, and yet enjoy the comfort and respect that should accompany the opposite virtues; and it was in this expectation, as far as I could see, that many of them were now on their way to America. But on the point of money they saw clearly enough that inland politics, so far as they were concerned, were reducible to the question of annual income; a question which should long ago have been settled by a revolution, they did not know how, and which they were now about to settle for themselves, once more they knew not how, by crossing the Atlantic in a steamship of considerable tonnage.

And yet it has been amply shown them that the second or income question is in itself nothing, and may as well be left undecided, if there be no wisdom and virtue to profit by the change. It is not by a man's purse, but by his character that he is rich or poor. Barney will be poor, Alick will be poor, Mackay will be poor; let them go where they will, and wreck all the governments under heaven, they will be poor until they die.

Nothing is perhaps more notable in the average workman than his surprising idleness, and the candour with which he confesses to the failing. It has to me been always something of a relief to find the poor, as a general rule, so little oppressed with work. I can in consequence enjoy my own more fortunate beginning with a better grace. The other day I was living with a farmer in America, an old frontiersman, who had worked and fought, hunted and farmed, from his childhood up. He excused himself for his defective education on the ground that he had been overworked from first to last. Even now, he said, anxious as he was, he had never the time to take up a book. In consequence of this, I observed him closely; he was occupied for four or, at the extreme outside, for five hours out of the twenty-four, and then principally in walking; and the remainder of the day he passed in born idleness, either eating fruit or standing with his back against a door. I have known men do hard literary work all morning, and then undergo quite as much physical fatigue by way of relief as satisfied this powerful frontiersman for the day. He, at least, like all the educated class, did so much homage to industry as to persuade himself he was industrious. But the average mechanic recognises his idleness with effrontery; he has even, as I am told, organised it.

I give the story as it was told me, and it was told me for a fact. A man fell from a house top in the city of Aberdeen, and was brought into hospital with broken bones. He was asked what was his trade, and replied that he was a *tapper*. No one had ever heard of such a thing before; the officials were filled with curiosity; they besought an explanation. It appeared that when a party of slaters were engaged upon a roof, they would now and then be taken with a fancy for the public-house. Now a seamstress, for example, might slip away from her work and no one be the wiser; but if these fellows adjourned, the tapping of the mallets would cease, and thus the neighbourhood be advertised of their defection. Hence the career of the tapper. He has to do the tapping and keep up an industrious bustle on the house top during the absence of the slaters. When he taps for only one or two the thing is child's-play, but when he has to represent a whole troop, it is then that he earns his money in the sweat of his brow. Then must he bound from spot to spot, reduplicate, triplicate, sexduplicate his single personality, and swell and hasten his blows, until he produce a perfect illusion for the ear, and you would swear that a crowd of emulous masons were continuing merrily to roof the house. It must be a strange sight from an upper window.

I heard nothing on board of the tapper; but I was astonished at the stories told by my companions. Skulking, shirking, malingering, were all established tactics, it appeared. They could see no dishonesty where a man who is paid for an hour's work gives half an hour's consistent idling in its place. Thus the tapper would refuse to watch for the police during a burglary, and call himself a honest man. It is not sufficiently recognised that our race detests to work. If I thought that I should have to work every day of my life as hard as I am working now, I should be tempted to give up the struggle. And the workman early begins on his career of toil. He has never had his fill of holidays in the past, and his prospect of holidays in the future is both distant and uncertain. In the circumstances, it would require a high degree of virtue not to snatch alleviations for the moment.

There were many good talkers on the ship; and I believe good talking of a certain sort is a common accomplishment among working men. Where books are comparatively scarce, a greater amount of information will be given and received by word of mouth; and this tends to produce good talkers, and, what is no less needful for conversation, good listeners. They could all tell a story with effect. I am sometimes tempted to think that the less literary class show always better in narration; they have so much more patience with detail, are so much less hurried to reach the points, and preserve so much juster a proportion among the facts. At the same time their talk is dry; they pursue a topic ploddingly, have not an agile fancy, do not throw sudden lights from unexpected quarters, and when the talk is over they often leave the matter where it was. They mark time instead of marching. They think only to argue, not to reach new conclusions, and use their reason rather as a weapon of offence than as a tool for self-improvement. Hence the talk of some of the cleverest was unprofitable in result, because there was no give and take; they would grant you as little as possible for premise, and begin to dispute under an oath to conquer or to die.

But the talk of a workman is apt to be more interesting than that of a wealthy merchant, because the thoughts, hopes and fears of which the workman's life is built lie nearer to necessity and nature. They are more immediate to human life. An income calculated by the week is a far more human thing than one calculated by the year, and a small income, simply from its smallness, than a large one. I never wearied listening to the details of a workman's economy, because every item stood for some real pleasure. If he could afford pudding twice a week, you know that twice a week the man ate with genuine gusto and was physically happy; while if you learn that a rich man has seven courses a day, ten to one the half of them remain untasted, and the whole is but misspent money and a weariness to the flesh.

The difference between England and America to a working man was thus most humanly put to me by a fellow-passenger: 'In America,' said he, 'you get pies and puddings.' I do not hear enough, in economy books, of pies and pudding. A man lives in and for the delicacies, adornments and accidental attributes of life, such as pudding to eat and pleasant books and theatres to occupy his leisure. The bare terms of existence would be rejected with contempt by all. If a man feeds on bread and butter, soup and porridge, his appetite grows wolfish after dainties. And the workman dwells in a borderland, and is always within sight of those cheerless regions where life is more difficult to sustain than worth sustaining. Every detail of our existence, where it is worth while to cross the ocean after pie and pudding, is made alive and enthralling by the presence of genuine desire; but it is all one to me whether Croesus has a hundred or a thousand thousands in the bank. There is more adventure in the life of the working man who descends as a common soldier into the battle of life, than in that of the millionaire who sits apart in an office, like Von Moltke, and only directs the manoeuvres by telegraph. Give me to hear about the career of him who is in the thick of business; to whom one change of market means an empty belly, and another a copious and savoury meal. This is not the philosophical, but the human side of economics; it interests like a story; and the life of all who are thus situated partakes in a small way the charm of *Robinson Crusoe*; for every step is critical and human life is presented to you naked and verging to its lowest terms.

New York

As we drew near to New York I was at first amused, and then somewhat staggered, by the cautious and the grisly tales that went the round. You would have thought we were to land upon a cannibal island. You must speak to no one in the streets, as they would not leave you till you were rooked and beaten. You must enter a hotel with military precautions, for the least you had to apprehend was to awake next morning without money or baggage, or necessary raiment, a lone forked radish in a bed; and if the worst befell, you would instantly and mysteriously disappear from the ranks of mankind.

I have usually found such stories correspond to the least modicum of fact. Thus I was warned, I remember, against the roadside inns of the Cévennes, and that by a learned professor; and when I reached Pradelles the warning was explained – it was but the faraway rumour and reduplication of a single terrifying story already half a century old, and half forgotten in the theatre of the events. So I was tempted to make light of these reports against America. But we had on board with us a man whose evidence it would not do to put aside. He had come near these perils in the body; he had visited a robber inn. The public has an old and well-grounded favour for this class of incident, and shall be gratified to the best of my power.

My fellow-passenger, whom we shall call McNaughten, had come from New York to Boston with a comrade, seeking work. They were a pair of rattling blades; and, leaving their baggage at the station, passed the day in beer saloons, and with congenial spirits, until midnight struck. Then they applied themselves to find a lodging, and walked the streets till two, knocking at houses of entertainment and being refused admittance, or themselves declining the terms. By two the inspiration of their liquor had begun to wear off; they were weary and humble, and after a great circuit found themselves in the same street where they had begun their search, and in front of a French hotel where they had already sought accommodation. Seeing the house still open, they returned to the charge. A man in a white cap sat in an office by the door. He seemed to welcome them more warmly than when they had first presented themselves, and the charge for the night had somewhat unaccountably fallen from a dollar to a quarter. They thought him ill-looking, but paid their quarter apiece, and were shown upstairs to the top of the house. There, in a small room, the man in the white cap wished them pleasant slumbers.

It was furnished with a bed, a chair, and some conveniences. The door did not lock on the inside; and the only sign of adornment was a couple of framed pictures, one close above the head of the bed, and the other opposite the foot, and both curtained, as we may sometimes see valuable watercolours, or the portraits of the dead, or works of art more than usually skittish in the subject. It was perhaps in the hope of finding something of this last description that McNaughten's comrade pulled aside the curtain of the first. He was startlingly disappointed. There was no picture. The frame surrounded, and the curtain was designed to hide, an oblong aperture in the partition, through which they looked forth into the dark corridor. A person standing without could easily take a purse from under the pillow, or even strangle a sleeper as he lay abed. McNaughten and his comrade stared at each other like Vasco's seamen, 'with a wild surmise'; and then the latter, catching up the lamp, ran to the other frame and roughly raised the curtain. There he stood, petrified; and McNaughten, who had followed, grasped him by the wrist in terror. They could see into another room, larger in size than that which they occupied, where three men sat crouching and silent in the dark. For a second or so these five persons looked each other in the eyes, then the curtain was dropped, and McNaughten and his friend made but one bolt of it out of the room and downstairs. The man in the white cap said nothing as they passed him; and they were so pleased to be once more in the open night that they gave up all notion of a bed, and walked the streets of Boston till the morning.

No one seemed much cast down by these stories, but all enquired after the address of a respectable hotel; and I, for my part, put myself under the conduct of Mr Jones. Before noon of the second Sunday we sighted the low shores outside of New York harbour; the steerage passengers must remain on board to pass through Castle Garden[88] on the following morning; but we of the second cabin made our escape along with the lords of the saloon; and by six o'clock Jones and I issued into West Street, sitting on some straw in the bottom of an open baggage-wagon. It rained miraculously; and from that moment till on the following night I left New York, there was scarce a lull, and no cessation of the downpour. The roadways were flooded; a loud strident noise of falling water filled the air; the restaurants smelt heavily of wet people and wet clothing.

It took us but a few minutes, though it cost us a good deal of money, to be rattled along West Street to our destination: 'Reunion House, No. 10 West Street, one minute's walk from Castle Garden; convenient to Castle Garden, the Steamboat Landings, California Steamers and Liverpool Ships; Board and Lodging per day 1 dollar, single meals 25 cents, lodging per night 25 cents; private rooms for families; no charge for storage of baggage; satisfaction guaranteed to all persons; Michael Mitchell, Proprietor.' Reunion House was, I may go the length of saying, a humble hostelry. You entered through a long bar-room, thence passed into a little dining-room, and thence into a still smaller kitchen. The furniture was of the plainest; but the bar was hung in the American taste, with encouraging and hospitable mottoes.

Jones was well known; we were received warmly; and two minutes afterwards I had refused a drink from the proprietor, and was going on, in my plain European fashion, to refuse a cigar, when Mr Mitchell sternly interposed, and explained the situation. He was offering to treat me, it appeared; whenever an American barkeeper proposes anything, it must be borne in mind that he is offering to treat; and if I did not want a drink, I must at least take the cigar. I took it bashfully, feeling I had begun my American career on the wrong foot. I did not enjoy that cigar; but this may have been from a variety of reasons, even the best cigar often failing to please if you smoke three-quarters of it in a drenching rain.

For many years America was to me a sort of promised land: 'Westward the march of empire holds its way'; the race is for the moment to the young; what has been and what is we imperfectly and obscurely know; what is to be yet lies beyond the flight of our imaginations. Greece, Rome and Judaea are gone by for ever, leaving to generations the legacy of their accomplished work; China still endures, an old-inhabited house in the brand-new city of nations; England has already declined, since she has lost the States; and to these States, therefore, yet undeveloped, full of dark possibilities, and grown, like another Eve, from one rib out of the side of their own old land, the minds of young men in England turn naturally at a certain hopeful period of their age. It will be hard for an American to understand the spirit. But let him imagine a young man, who shall have grown up in an old and rigid circle, following bygone fashions and taught to distrust his own fresh instincts, and who now suddenly hears of a family of cousins, all about his own age, who keep house together by themselves and live far from restraint and tradition; let him imagine this, and he will have some imperfect notion of the sentiment with which spirited English youths turn to the thought of the American Republic. It seems to them as if, out West, the war of life was still conducted in the open air, and on free barbaric terms; as if it had not yet been narrowed into parlours, nor begun to be conducted, like some unjust and dreary arbitration, by compromise, costume, forms of procedure, and sad, senseless self-denial. Which of these two he prefers, a man with any youth still left in him will decide rightly for himself. He would rather be houseless than denied a pass-key; rather go without food than partake of stalled ox in stiff, respectable society; rather be shot out of hand than direct his life according to the dictates of the world.

He knows or thinks nothing of the Maine Laws, the Puritan sourness, the fierce, sordid appetite for dollars or the dreary existence of country towns. A few wild story-books which delighted his child-hood form the imaginative basis of his picture of America. In course of time, there is added to this a great crowd of stimulating details – vast cities that grow up as by enchantment; the birds, that have gone south in autumn, returning with the spring to find thousands camped upon their marshes, and the lamps burning far and near along populous streets; forests that disappear like snow; countries larger than Britain that are cleared and settled, one man running forth with his household gods before another, while the bear and the Indian are yet scarce aware of their approach; oil that gushes from the earth; gold that is washed or quarried in the brooks or glens of the Sierras; and all that bustle, courage, action and constant kaleidoscopic change that Walt Whitman[89] has seized and set forth in his vigorous, cheerful, and loquacious verses.

Here I was at last in America, and was soon out upon New York streets, spying for things foreign. The place had to me an air of Liverpool; but such was the rain that not Paradise itself would have looked inviting. We were a party of four, under two umbrellas: Jones and I and two Scots lads, recent immigrants, and not indisposed to welcome a compatriot. They had been six weeks in New York, and neither of them had yet found a single job or earned a single halfpenny. Up to the present they were exactly out of pocket by the amount of the fare.

The lads soon left us. Now I had sworn by all my gods to have such a dinner as would rouse the dead; there was scarce any expense at which I should have hesitated; the devil was in it, but Jones and I should dine like heathen emperors. I set to work, asking after a restaurant, and I chose the wealthiest and most gastronomical-looking passers-by to ask from. Yet, although I had told them I was willing to pay anything in reason, one and all sent me off to cheap, fixed-price houses, where I would not have eaten that night for the cost of twenty dinners. I do not know if this were characteristic of New York, or whether it was only Jones and I who looked un-dinerly and discouraged enterprising suggestions. But at length, by our own sagacity, we found a French restaurant, where there was a French waiter, some fair French cooking, some so-called French wine, and French coffee to conclude the whole. I never entered into the feelings of Jack on land so completely as when I tasted that coffee.

I suppose we had one of the 'private rooms for families' at Reunion House. It was very small, furnished with a bed, a chair and some clothes-pegs; and it derived all that was necessary for the life of the human animal through two borrowed lights, one looking into the passage and the second opening, without sash, into another apartment, where three men fitfully snored, or in intervals of wakefulness, drearily mumbled to each other all night long. It will be observed that this was almost exactly the disposition of the room in McNaughten's story. Jones had the bed; I pitched my camp upon the floor; he did not sleep until near morning, and I, for my part, never closed an eye.

At sunrise I heard a cannon fired; and shortly afterwards the men in the next room gave over snoring for good, and began to rustle over their toilettes. The sound of their voices as they talked was low and like that of people watching by the sick. Jones, who had at last begun to doze, tumbled and murmured, and every now and then opened unconscious eyes upon me where I lay. I found myself growing eerier and eerier, for I dare say I was a little fevered by my restless night, and hurried to dress and get downstairs.

You had to pass through the rain, which still fell thick and resonant, to reach a lavatory on the other side of the court. There were three basin-stands, and a few crumpled towels and pieces of wet soap, white and slippery like fish; nor should I forget a looking-glass and a pair of questionable combs. Another Scots lad was here, scrubbing his face with a good will. He had been three months in New York and had not yet found a single job nor earned a single halfpenny. Up to the present, he also was exactly out of pocket by the amount of the fare. I began to grow sick at heart for my fellow-emigrants.

Of my nightmare wanderings in New York I spare to tell. I had a thousand and one things to do, only the day to do them in, and a journey across the continent before me in the evening. It rained with patient fury; every now and then I had to get under cover for a while in order, so to speak, to give my mackintosh a rest; for under this continued drenching it began to grow damp on the inside. I went to banks, post-offices, railway-offices, restaurants, publishers, booksellers, money-changers, and wherever I went a pool would gather about my feet, and those who were careful of their floors would look on with an unfriendly eye. Wherever I went, too, the same traits struck me: the people were all surprisingly rude and surprisingly kind. The money-changer cross-questioned me like a French commissary, asking my age, my business, my average income and my destination, beating down my attempts at evasion, and receiving my answers in silence; and yet when all was over, he shook hands with me up to the elbows, and sent his lad nearly a quarter of a mile in the rain to get me books at a reduction. Again, in a very large publishing and bookselling establishment, a man, who seemed to be the manager, received me as I had certainly never before been received in any human shop, indicated squarely that he put no faith in my honesty, and refused to look up the names of books or give me the slightest help or information, on the ground, like the steward, that it was none of his business. I lost my temper at last, said I was a stranger in America and not learned in their etiquette; but I would assure him, if he went to any bookseller in England, of more handsome usage. The boast was perhaps exaggerated; but like many a long shot, it struck the gold. The manager passed at once from one extreme to the other; I may say that from that moment he loaded me with kindness; he gave me all sorts of good advice, wrote me down addresses, and came bareheaded into the rain to point me out a restaurant, where I might lunch, nor even then did he seem to think that he had done enough. These are (it is as well to be bold in statement) the manners of America. It is this same opposition that has most struck me in people of almost all classes and from east to west. By the time a man had about strung me up to be the death of him by his insulting behaviour, he himself would be just upon the point of melting into confidence and serviceable attentions. Yet I suspect, although I have met with the like in so many parts, that this must be the character of some particular state or group of states, for in America, and this again in all classes, you will find some of the softest-mannered gentlemen in the world.

I was so wet when I got back to Mitchell's towards the evening, that I had simply to divest myself of my shoes, socks and trousers, and leave them behind for the benefit of New York City. No fire could have dried them ere I had to start; and to pack them in their present condition was to spread ruin among my other possessions. With a heavy heart I said farewell to them as they lay a pulp in the middle of a pool upon the floor of Mitchell's kitchen. I wonder if they are dry by now. Mitchell hired a man to carry my baggage to the station, which was hard by, accompanied me thither himself, and recommended me to the particular attention of the officials. No one could have been kinder. Those who are out of pocket may go safely to Reunion House, where they will get decent meals and find an honest and obliging landlord. I owed him this word of thanks, before I enter fairly on the second and far less agreeable chapter of my emigrant experience.

Across the Plains

Leaves from the Notebook of an Emigrant between New York and San Francisco

Monday

It was, if I remember rightly, five o'clock when we were all signalled to be present at the Ferry Depot of the railroad. An emigrant ship had arrived at New York on the Saturday night, another on the Sunday morning, our own on Sunday afternoon, a fourth early on Monday; and as there is no emigrant train on Sunday a great part of the passengers from these four ships was concentrated on the train by which I was to travel. There was a babel of bewildered men, women and children. The wretched little booking-office, and the baggage-room, which was not much larger, were crowded thick with emigrants, and were heavy and rank with the atmosphere of dripping clothes. Open carts full of bedding stood by the half-hour in the rain. The officials loaded each other with recriminations. A bearded, mildewed little man, whom I take to have been an emigrant agent, was all over the place, his mouth full of brimstone, blustering and interfering. It was plain that the whole system, if system there was, had utterly broken down under the strain of so many passengers.

My own ticket was given me at once, and an oldish man, who preserved his head in the midst of this turmoil, got my baggage registered, and counselled me to stay quietly where I was till he should give me the word to move. I had taken along with me a small valise, a knapsack, which I carried on my shoulders, and in the bag of my railway rug the whole of Bancroft's *History of the United States*,[90] in six fat volumes. It was as much as I could carry with convenience even for short distances, but it ensured me plenty of clothing, and the valise was at that moment, and often after, useful for a stool. I am sure I sat for an hour in the baggage-room, and wretched enough it was; yet, when at last the word was passed to me and I picked up my bundles and got under way, it was only to exchange discomfort for downright misery and danger.

I followed the porters into a long shed reaching downhill from West Street to the river. It was dark, the wind blew clean through it from end to end; and here I found a great block of passengers and baggage, hundreds of one and tons of the other. I feel I shall have a difficulty to make myself believed; and certainly the scene must have been exceptional, for it was too dangerous for daily repetition. It was a tight jam; there was no fair way through the mingled mass of brute and living obstruction. Into the upper skirts of the crowd porters, infuriated by hurry and overwork, clove their way with shouts. I may say that we stood like sheep, and that the porters charged among us like so many maddened sheep-dogs; and I believe these men were no longer answerable for their acts. It mattered not what they were carrying, they drove straight into the press, and when they could get no farther, blindly discharged their barrowful. With my own hand, for instance, I saved the life of a child as it sat upon its mother's knee, she sitting on a box; and since I heard of no accident, I must suppose that there were many similar interpositions in the course of the evening. It will give some idea of the state of mind to which we were reduced if I tell you that neither the porter nor the mother of the child paid the least attention to my act. It was not till some time after that I understood what I had done myself, for to ward off heavy boxes seemed at the moment a natural incident of human life. Cold, wet, clamour, dead opposition to progress, such as one encounters in an evil dream, had utterly daunted the spirits. We had accepted this purgatory as a child accepts the conditions of the world. For my part, I shivered a little, and my back ached wearily; but I believe I had neither a hope nor a fear, and all the activities of my nature had become tributary to one massive sensation of discomfort.

At length, and after how long an interval I hesitate to guess, the crowd began to move, heavily straining through itself. About the same time some lamps were lighted, and threw a sudden flare over the shed. We were being filtered out into the river boat for Jersey City. You may imagine how slowly this filtering proceeded, through the dense, choking crush, everyone overladen with packages or children, and yet under the necessity of fishing out his ticket by the way; but it ended at length for me, and I found myself on deck under a flimsy awning and with a trifle of elbow-room to stretch and breathe in. This was on the starboard; for the bulk of the emigrants stuck hopelessly on the port side, by which we had entered. In vain the seamen shouted to them to move on, and threatened them with shipwreck. These poor people were under a spell of stupor, and did not stir a foot. It rained as heavily as ever, but the wind now came in sudden claps and capfuls, not without danger to a boat so badly ballasted as ours; and we crept over the river in the darkness, trailing one paddle in the water like a wounded duck, and passed ever and again by huge, illuminated steamers running many knots, and heralding their approach by strains of music. The contrast between these pleasure embarkations and our own grim vessel, with her list to port and her freight of wet and silent emigrants, was of that glaring description which we count too obvious for the purposes of art.

The landing at Jersey City was done in a stampede. I had a fixed sense of calamity, and to judge by conduct, the same persuasion was common to us all. A panic selfishness, like that produced by fear, presided over the disorder of our landing. People pushed, and elbowed, and ran, their families following how they could. Children fell, and were picked up to be rewarded by a blow. One child, who had lost her parents, screamed steadily and with increasing shrillness, as though verging towards a fit; an official kept her by him, but no one else seemed so much as to remark her distress; and I am ashamed to say that I ran among the rest. I was so weary that I had twice to make a halt and set down my bundles in the hundred yards or so between the pier and the railway station, so that I was quite wet by the time that I got under cover. There was no waiting-room, no refreshment room; the cars were locked; and for at least another hour, or so it seemed, we had to camp upon the draughty, gas-lit platform. I sat on my valise, too crushed to observe my neighbours; but as they were all cold, and wet, and weary, and driven stupidly crazy by the mismanagement to which we had been subjected, I believe they can have been no happier than myself. I bought half a dozen oranges from a boy, for oranges and nuts were the only refection to be had. As only two of them had even a pretence of juice, I threw the other four under the cars, and beheld, as in a dream, grown people and children groping on the track after my leavings.

At last we were admitted into the cars, utterly dejected, and far from dry. For my own part, I got out a clothes-brush, and brushed my trousers as hard as I could till I had dried them and warmed my blood into the bargain; but no one else, except my next neighbour to whom I lent the brush, appeared to take the least precaution. As they were, they composed themselves to sleep. I had seen the lights of

Philadelphia, and been twice ordered to change carriages and twice countermanded, before I allowed myself to follow their example.

Tuesday

When I awoke, it was already day; the train was standing idle; I was in the last carriage, and, seeing some others strolling to and fro about the lines, I opened the door and stepped forth, as from a caravan by the wayside. We were near no station, nor even, as far as I could see, within reach of any signal. A green, open, undulating country stretched away upon all sides. Locust trees and a single field of Indian corn gave it a foreign grace and interest; but the contours of the land were soft and English. It was not quite England, neither was it quite France; yet like enough either to seem natural in my eyes. And it was in the sky, and not upon the earth, that I was surprised to find a change. Explain it how you may, and for my part I cannot explain it at all, the sun rises with a different splendour in America and Europe. There is more clear gold and scarlet in our old country mornings; more purple, brown and smoky orange in those of the new. It may be from habit, but to me the coming of day is less fresh and inspiriting in the latter; it has a duskier glory, and more nearly resembles sunset; it seems to fit some subsequential, evening epoch of the world, as though America were in fact, and not merely in fancy, farther from the orient of Aurora and the springs of day. I thought so then, by the railroad side in Pennsylvania, and I have thought so a dozen times since in far distant parts of the continent. If it be an illusion it is one very deeply rooted, and in which my eyesight is accomplice.

Soon after a train whisked by, announcing and accompanying its passage by the swift beating of a sort of chapel bell upon the engine; and as it was for this we had been waiting, we were summoned by the cry of 'All aboard!' and went on again upon our way. The whole line, it appeared, was topsy-turvy; an accident at midnight having thrown all the traffic hours into arrear. We paid for this in the flesh, for we had no meals all that day. Fruit we could buy upon the cars; and now and then we had a few minutes at some station with a meagre show of rolls and sandwiches for sale; but we were so many and so ravenous that, though I tried at every opportunity, the coffee was always exhausted before I could elbow my way to the counter.

Our American sunrise had ushered in a noble summer's day. There was not a cloud; the sunshine was baking; yet in the woody river valleys among which we wound our way, the atmosphere preserved a sparkling freshness till late in the afternoon. It had an inland sweetness and variety to one newly from the sea; it smelt of woods, rivers and the delved earth. These, though in so far a country, were airs from home. I stood on the platform by the hour; and as I saw, one after another, pleasant villages, carts upon the highway and fishers by the stream, and heard cockcrows and cheery voices in the distance, and beheld the sun, no longer shining blankly on the plains of ocean but striking among shapely hills, his light dispersed and coloured by a thousand accidents of form and surface, I began to exult with myself upon this rise in life like a man who had come into a rich estate. And when I had asked the name of a river from the brakesman, and heard that it was called the Susquehanna, the beauty of the name seemed to be part and parcel of the beauty of the land.[91] As when Adam with divine fitness named the creatures, so this word Susquehanna was at once accepted by the fancy. That was the name, as no other could be, for that shining river and desirable valley.

None can care for literature in itself who do not take a special pleasure in the sound of names; and there is no part of the world where nomenclature is so rich, poetical, humorous and picturesque as the United States of America. All times, races and languages have brought their contribution. Pekin is in the same state with Euclid, with Bellefontaine and with Sandusky. Chelsea, with its London associations of red brick, Sloane Square and the King's Road, is own suburb to stately and primeval Memphis; there they have their seat, translated names of cities, where the Mississippi runs by Tennessee and Arkansas; and both, while I was crossing the continent, lay, watched by armed men, in the horror and isolation of a plague. Old, red Manhattan lies, like an Indian arrowhead under a steam factory, below anglified New York. The names of the states and territories themselves form a chorus of sweet and most romantic vocables: Delaware, Ohio, Indiana, Florida, Dakota, Iowa, Wyoming, Minnesota and the Carolinas; there are few poems with a nobler music for the ear: a songful, tuneful land; and if the new Homer shall arise from the Western continent, his verse will be enriched, his pages sing spontaneously, with the names of states and cities that would strike the fancy in a business circular.

Late in the evening we were landed in a waiting-room at Pittsburg. I had now under my charge a young and sprightly Dutch widow with her children; these I was to watch over providentially for a certain distance farther on the way; but as I found she was furnished with a basket of eatables, I left her in the waiting-room to seek a dinner for myself. I mention this meal, not only because it was the first of which I had partaken for about thirty hours, but because it was the means of my first introduction to a coloured gentleman. He did me the honour to wait upon me, after a fashion, while I was eating; and with every word, look and gesture marched me farther into the country of surprise. He was indeed strikingly unlike the negroes of Mrs Beecher Stowe [92] or the Christy Minstrels of my youth. Imagine a gentleman, certainly somewhat dark, but of a pleasant warm hue, speaking English with a slight and rather odd foreign accent, every inch a man of the world, and armed with manners so patronisingly superior that I am at a loss to name their parallel in England. A butler perhaps rides as high over the unbutlered, but then he sets you right with a reserve and a sort of sighing patience which one is often moved to admire. And again, the abstract butler never stoops to familiarity. But the coloured gentleman will pass you a wink at a time; he is familiar like an upper-form boy to a fag; he unbends to you like Prince Hal with Poins and Falstaff. He makes himself at home and welcome. Indeed, I may say, this waiter behaved himself to me throughout that supper much as, with us, a young, free and not very self-respecting master might behave to a good-looking chambermaid. I had come prepared to pity the poor negro, to put him at his ease, to prove in a thousand condescensions that I was no sharer in the prejudice of race; but I assure you I put my patronage away for another occasion, and had the grace to be pleased with that result.

Seeing he was a very honest fellow, I consulted him upon a point of etiquette: if one should offer to tip the American waiter? Certainly not, he told me. Never. It would not do. They considered themselves too highly to accept. They would even resent the offer. As for him and me, we had enjoyed a very pleasant conversation; he, in particular, had found much pleasure in my society; I was a stranger; this was exactly one of those rare conjunctures . . . Without being very clear seeing, I can still perceive the sun at noonday; and the coloured gentleman deftly pocketed a quarter.

Wednesday

A little after midnight I convoyed my widow and orphans on board the train; and morning found us far into Ohio. This had early been a favourite home of my imagination; I have played at being in Ohio by the week, and enjoyed some capital sport there with a dummy gun, my person being still unbreeched. My preference was founded on a work which appeared in Cassell's *Family Paper*, and was read aloud to me by my nurse. It narrated the doings of one Custaloga, an Indian brave, who, in the last chapter, very obligingly washed the paint off his face and became Sir Reginald Somebody-or-other; a trick I never forgave him. The idea of a man being an Indian brave, and then giving that up to be a baronet, was one which my mind rejected. It offended verisimilitude, like the pretended anxiety of Robinson Crusoe and others to escape from uninhabited islands.

But Ohio was not at all as I had pictured it. We were now on those great plains which stretch unbroken to the Rocky Mountains. The country was flat like Holland, but far from being dull. All through Ohio, Indiana, Illinois and Iowa, or for as much as I saw of them from the train and in my waking moments, it was rich and various, and breathed an elegance peculiar to itself. The tall corn pleased the eye; the trees were graceful in themselves, and framed the plain into long, aerial vistas; and the clean, bright, gardened townships spoke of country fare and pleasant summer evenings on the stoop. It was a sort of flat paradise; but, I am afraid, not unfrequented by the devil. That morning dawned with such a freezing chill as I have rarely felt; a chill that was not perhaps so measurable by instrument, as it struck home upon the heart and seemed to travel with the blood. Day came in with a shudder. White mists lay thinly over the surface of the plain, as we see them more often on a lake; and though the sun had soon dispersed and drunk them up, leaving an atmosphere of fever heat and crystal pureness from horizon to horizon, the mists had still been there, and we knew that this paradise was haunted by killing damps and foul malaria. The fences along the line bore but two descriptions of advertisement; one to recommend tobaccos, and the other to vaunt remedies against the ague. At the point of day, and while we were all in the grasp of that first chill, a native of the state, who had got in at some way station, pronounced it, with a doctoral air, 'a fever and ague morning'.

The Dutch widow was a person of some character. She had conceived at first sight a great aversion for the present writer, which she was at no pains to conceal. But being a woman of a practical spirit, she made no difficulty about accepting my attentions, and encouraged me to buy her children fruits and candies, to carry all her parcels, and even to sleep upon the floor that she might profit by my empty seat. Nay, she was such a rattle by nature, and so powerfully moved to autobiographical talk, that she was forced, for want of a better, to take me into confidence and tell me the story of her life. I heard about her late husband, who seemed to have made his chief

impression by taking her out pleasuring on Sundays. I could tell you
her prospects, her hopes, the amount of her fortune, the cost of her
housekeeping by the week, and a variety of particular matters that
are not usually disclosed except to friends. At one station, she shook
up her children to look at a man on the platform and say if he were
not like Mr Z—; while to me she explained how she had been
keeping company with this Mr Z—, how far matters had proceeded,
and how it was because of his desistance that she was now travelling
to the West. Then, when I was thus put in possession of the facts,
she asked my judgement on that type of manly beauty. I admired it
to her heart's content. She was not, I think, remarkably veracious in
talk, but broidered as fancy prompted, and built castles in the air out
of her past; yet she had that sort of candour to keep me, in spite of
all these confidences, steadily aware of her aversion. Her parting
words were ingeniously honest. 'I am sure,' said she, 'we all *ought* to
be very much obliged to you.' I cannot pretend that she put me at
my ease; but I had a certain respect for such a genuine dislike. A
poor nature would have slipped, in the course of these familiarities,
into a sort of worthless toleration for me.

We reached Chicago in the evening. I was turned out of the cars,
bundled into an omnibus, and driven off through the streets to the
station of a different railroad. Chicago seemed a great and gloomy
city. I remember having subscribed, let us say sixpence, towards its
restoration at the period of the fire;[93] and now when I beheld street
after street of ponderous houses and crowds of comfortable burghers,
I thought it would be a graceful act for the corporation to refund
that sixpence, or, at the least, to entertain me to a cheerful dinner.
But there was no word of restitution. I was that city's benefactor, yet
I was received in a third-class waiting-room, and the best dinner I
could get was a dish of ham and eggs at my own expense.

I can safely say, I have never been so dog-tired as that night in
Chicago. When it was time to start, I descended the platform like a
man in a dream. It was a long train, lighted from end to end; and car
after car, as I came up with it, was not only filled but overflowing.
My valise, my knapsack, my rug, with those six ponderous tomes of
Bancroft, weighed me double; I was hot, feverish, painfully a-thirst;
and there was a great darkness over me, an internal darkness, not to
be dispelled by gas. When at last I found an empty bench, I sank into
it like a bundle of rags, the world seemed to swim away into the
distance, and my consciousness dwindled within me to a mere pin's
head, like a taper on a foggy night.

When I came a little more to myself, I found that there had sat down beside me a very cheerful, rosy little German gentleman, somewhat gone in drink, who was talking away to me, nineteen to the dozen, as they say. I did my best to keep up the conversation; for it seemed to me dimly as if something depended upon that. I heard him relate, among many other things, that there were pickpockets on the train, who had already robbed a man of forty dollars and a return ticket; but though I caught the words, I do not think I properly understood the sense until next morning; and I believe I replied at the time that I was very glad to hear it. What else he talked about I have no guess; I remember a gabbling sound of words, his profuse gesticulation, and his smile, which was highly explanatory: but no more. And I suppose I must have shown my confusion very plainly; for, first, I saw him knit his brows at me like one who has conceived a doubt; next, he tried me in German, supposing perhaps that I was unfamiliar with the English tongue; and finally, in despair, he rose and left me. I felt chagrined; but my fatigue was too crushing for delay, and, stretching myself as far as that was possible upon the bench, I was received at once into a dreamless stupor.

The little German gentleman was only going a little way into the suburbs after a *diner fin*, and was bent on entertainment while the journey lasted. Having failed with me, he pitched next upon another emigrant, who had come through from Canada, and was not one jot less weary than myself. Nay, even in a natural state, as I found next morning when we scraped acquaintance, he was a heavy, uncommunicative man. After trying him on different topics, it appears that the little German gentleman flounced into a temper, swore an oath or two, and departed from that car in quest of livelier society. Poor little gentleman! I suppose he thought an emigrant should be a rollicking, free-hearted blade, with a flask of foreign brandy and a long, comical story to beguile the moments of digestion.

Thursday

I suppose there must be a cycle in the fatigue of travelling, for when I awoke next morning, I was entirely renewed in spirits and ate a hearty breakfast of porridge, with sweet milk, and coffee and hot cakes, at Burlington upon the Mississippi. Another long day's ride followed, with but one feature worthy of remark. At a place called Creston, a drunken man got in. He was aggressively friendly, but, according to English notions, not at all unpresentable upon a train. For one stage he eluded the notice of the officials; but just as we were beginning to move out of the next station, Cromwell by name, by came the conductor. There was a word or two of talk; and then the official had the man by the shoulders, twitched him from his seat, marched him through the car, and sent him flying on to the track. It was done in three motions, as exact as a piece of drill. The train was still moving slowly, although beginning to mend her pace, and the drunkard got his feet without a fall. He carried a red bundle, though not so red as his cheeks; and he shook this menacingly in the air with one hand, while the other stole behind him to the region of the kidneys. It was the first indication that I had come among revolvers, and I observed it with some emotion. The conductor stood on the steps with one hand on his hip, looking back at him; and perhaps this attitude imposed upon the creature, for he turned without further ado, and went off staggering along the track towards Cromwell followed by a peal of laughter from the cars. They were speaking English all about me, but I knew I was in a foreign land.

Twenty minutes before nine that night, we were deposited at the Pacific Transfer Station near Council Bluffs,[94] on the eastern bank of the Missouri River. Here we were to stay the night at a kind of caravanserai, set apart for emigrants. But I gave way to a thirst for luxury, separated myself from my companions, and marched with my effects into the Union Pacific Hotel. A white clerk and a coloured gentleman whom, in my plain European way, I should call the boots, were installed behind a counter like bank tellers. They took my name, assigned me a number, and proceeded to deal with my packages. And here came the tug of war. I wished to give up my packages into safe keeping; but I did not wish to go to bed. And this, it appeared, was impossible in an American hotel.

It was, of course, some inane misunderstanding, and sprang from my unfamiliarity with the language. For although two nations use the same words and read the same books, intercourse is not conducted by the dictionary. The business of life is not carried on by words, but in set phrases, each with a special and almost a slang signification. Some international obscurity prevailed between me and the coloured gentleman at Council Bluffs; so that what I was asking, which seemed very natural to me, appeared to him a monstrous exigency. He refused, and that with the plainness of the West. This American manner of conducting matters of business is, at first, highly unpalatable to the European. When we approach a man in the way of his calling, and for those services by which he earns his bread, we consider him for the time being our hired servant. But in the American opinion, two gentlemen meet and have a friendly talk with a view to exchanging favours if they shall agree to please. I know not which is the more convenient, nor even which is the more truly courteous. The English stiffness unfortunately tends to be continued after the particular transaction is at an end, and thus favours class separations. But on the other hand, these equalitarian plainnesses leave an open field for the insolence of Jack-in-office.

I was nettled by the coloured gentleman's refusal, and unbuttoned my wrath under the similitude of ironical submission. I knew nothing, I said, of the ways of American hotels; but I had no desire to give trouble. If there was nothing for it but to get to bed immediately, let him say the word, and though it was not my habit, I should cheerfully obey.

He burst into a shout of laughter. 'Ah!' said he, 'you do not know about America. They are fine people in America. Oh! you will like them very well. But you mustn't get mad. I know what you want. You come along with me.'

And issuing from behind the counter, and taking me by the arm like an old acquaintance, he led me to the bar of the hotel.

'There,' said he, pushing me from him by the shoulder, 'go and have a drink!'

The Emigrant Train

All this while I had been travelling by mixed trains, where I might meet with Dutch widows and little German gentry fresh from table. I had been but a latent emigrant; now I was to be branded once more, and put apart with my fellows. It was about two in the afternoon of Friday that I found myself in front of the Emigrant House, with more than a hundred others, to be sorted and boxed for the journey. A white-haired official, with a stick under one arm, and a list in the other hand, stood apart in front of us, and called name after name in the tone of a command. At each name you would see a family gather up its brats and bundles and run for the hindmost of the three cars that stood awaiting us, and I soon concluded that this was to be set apart for the women and children. The second or central car, it turned out, was devoted to men travelling alone, and the third to the Chinese. The official was easily moved to anger at the least delay; but the emigrants were both quick at answering their names, and speedy in getting themselves and their effects on board.

The families once housed, we men carried the second car without ceremony by simultaneous assault. I suppose the reader has some notion of an American railroad-car, that long, narrow wooden box, like a flat-roofed Noah's ark, with a stove and a convenience, one at either end, a passage down the middle, and transverse benches upon either hand. Those destined for emigrants on the Union Pacific are only remarkable for their extreme plainness, nothing but wood entering in any part into their constitution, and for the usual inefficacy of the lamps, which often went out and shed but a dying glimmer even while they burned. The benches are too short for anything but a young child. Where there is scarce elbow-room for two to sit, there will not be space enough for one to lie. Hence the company, or rather, as it appears from certain bills about the Transfer Station, the company's servants, have conceived a plan for the better accommodation of travellers. They prevail on every two to chum together. To each of the chums they sell a board and three square cushions stuffed with straw, and covered with thin cotton. The benches can be made to face each other in pairs, for the backs are reversible. On the approach of night the boards are laid from bench to bench, making a couch wide enough for two, and long enough for a man of the middle height; and the chums lie down side by side upon the cushions with the head to the conductor's van and the feet to the engine. When the train is full, of course this plan is impossible, for there must not be more than one to every bench, neither can it be carried out unless the chums agree. It was to bring about this last condition that our white-haired official now bestirred himself. He made a most active master of ceremonies, introducing likely couples, and even guaranteeing the amiability and honesty of each. The greater the number of happy couples the better for his pocket, for it was he who sold the raw material of the beds. His price for one board and three straw cushions began with two dollars and a half; but before the train left, and, I am sorry to say, long after I had purchased mine, it had fallen to one dollar and a half.

The match-maker had a difficulty with me; perhaps, like some ladies, I showed myself too eager for union at any price; but certainly the first who was picked out to be my bedfellow, declined the honour without thanks. He was an old, heavy, slow-spoken man, I think from Yankeeland, looked me all over with great timidity, and then began to excuse himself in broken phrases. He didn't know the young man, he said. The young man might be very honest, but how was he to know that? There was another young man whom he had met already in the train; he guessed he was honest, and would prefer to chum with him upon the whole. All this without any sort of excuse, as though I had been inanimate or absent. I began to tremble lest everyone should refuse my company, and I be left rejected. But the next in turn was a tall, strapping, long-limbed, small-headed, curly-haired Pennsylvania Dutchman, with a soldierly smartness in his manner. To be exact, he had acquired it in the navy. But that was all one; he had at least been trained to desperate resolves, so he accepted the match, and the white-haired swindler pronounced the connubial benediction, and pocketed his fees.

The rest of the afternoon was spent in making up the train. I am afraid to say how many baggage-wagons followed the engine, certainly a score; then came the Chinese, then we, then the families, and the rear was brought up by the conductor in what, if I have it rightly, is called his caboose. The class to which I belonged was of course far the largest, and we ran over, so to speak, to both sides; so that there were some Caucasians among the Chinamen, and some bachelors among the families. But our own car was pure from admixture, save for one little boy of eight or nine who had the whooping-cough. At last, about six, the long train crawled out of the Transfer Station and across the wide Missouri River to Omaha, westward bound.

It was a troubled uncomfortable evening in the cars. There was thunder in the air, which helped to keep us restless. A man played many airs upon the cornet, and none of them were much attended to, until he came to 'Home, sweet home'. It was truly strange to note how the talk ceased at that, and the faces began to lengthen. I have no idea whether musically this air is to be considered good or bad; but it belongs to that class of art which may be best described as a brutal assault upon the feelings. Pathos must be relieved by dignity of treatment. If you wallow naked in the pathetic, like the author of 'Home, sweet home', you make your hearers weep in an unmanly fashion; and even while yet they are moved, they despise themselves and hate the occasion of their weakness. It did not come to tears that night, for the experiment was interrupted. An elderly, hard-looking man, with a goatee beard and about as much appearance of sentiment an you would expect from a retired slaver, turned with a start and bade the performer stop that 'damned thing'. 'I've heard about enough of that,' he added; 'give us something about the good country we're going to.' A murmur of adhesion ran round the car; the performer took the instrument from his lips, laughed and nodded, and then struck into a dancing measure; and, like a new Timotheus, stilled immediately the emotion he had raised.

The day faded; the lamps were lit; a party of wild young men, who got off next evening at North Platte, stood together on the stern platform, singing 'The Sweet By and By' with very tuneful voices; the chums began to put up their beds; and it seemed as if the business of the day were at an end. But it was not so; for, the train stopping at some station, the cars were instantly thronged with the natives, wives and fathers, young men and maidens, some of them in little more than night gear, some with stable lanterns, and all offering beds for sale. Their charge began with twenty-five cents a cushion, but fell, before the train went on again, to fifteen, with the bed-board gratis, or less than one-fifth of what I had paid for mine at the Transfer. This is my contribution to the economy of future emigrants.

A great personage on an American train is the newsboy. He sells books (such books!), papers, fruit, lollipops and cigars; and on emigrant journeys, soap, towels, tin washing dishes, tin coffee pitchers, coffee, tea, sugar and tinned eatables, mostly hash or beans and bacon. Early next morning the newsboy went around the cars, and chumming on a more extended principle became the order of the hour. It requires but a co-partnery of two to manage beds; but washing and eating can be carried on most economically by a syndicate of three. I myself entered a little after sunrise into articles of agreement, and became one of the firm of Pennsylvania, Shakespeare and Dubuque. Shakespeare was my own nickname on the cars; Pennsylvania that of my bedfellow; and Dubuque, the name of a place in the state of Iowa, that of an amiable young fellow going West to cure an asthma, and retarding his recovery by incessantly chewing or smoking, and sometimes chewing and smoking together. I have never seen tobacco so sillily abused. Shakespeare bought a tin washing-dish, Dubuque a towel and Pennsylvania a brick of soap. The partners used these instruments, one after another, according to the order of their first awaking; and when the firm had finished there was no want of borrowers. Each filled the tin dish at the water filter opposite the stove, and retired with the whole stock in trade to the platform of the car. There he knelt down, supporting himself by a shoulder against the woodwork or one elbow crooked about the railing, and made a shift to wash his face and neck and hands; a cold, an insufficient, and, if the train is moving rapidly, a somewhat dangerous toilet.

On a similar division of expense, the firm of Pennsylvania, Shakespeare and Dubuque supplied themselves with coffee, sugar and necessary vessels; and their operations are a type of what went on through all the cars. Before the sun was up the stove would be brightly burning; at the first station the natives would come on board with milk and eggs and coffee cakes; and soon from end to end the car would be filled with little parties breakfasting upon the bed-boards. It was the pleasantest hour of the day.

There were meals to be had, however, by the wayside: a breakfast in the morning, a dinner somewhere between eleven and two, and supper from five to eight or nine at night. We had rarely less than twenty minutes for each; and if we had not spent many another twenty minutes waiting for some express upon a side track among miles of desert, we might have taken an hour to each repast and arrived at San Francisco up to time. For haste is not the foible of an emigrant train. It gets through on sufferance, running the gauntlet among its more considerable brethren; should there be a block, it is unhesitatingly sacrificed; and they cannot, in consequence, predict the length of the passage within a day or so. Civility is the main comfort that you miss. Equality, though conceived very largely in America, does not extend so low down as to an emigrant. Thus in all other trains, a warning cry of 'All aboard!' recalls the passengers to take their seats; but as soon as I was alone with emigrants, and from the Transfer all the way to San Francisco, I found this ceremony was pretermitted; the train stole from the station without note of warning, and you had to keep an eye upon it even while you ate. The annoyance is considerable, and the disrespect both wanton and petty.

Many conductors, again, will hold no communication with an emigrant. I asked a conductor one day at what time the train would stop for dinner; as he made no answer I repeated the question, with a like result; a third time I returned to the charge, and then Jack-in-office looked me coolly in the face for several seconds and turned ostentatiously away. I believe he was half ashamed of his brutality; for when another person made the same enquiry, although he still refused the information, he condescended to answer, and even to justify his reticence in a voice loud enough for me to hear. It was, he said, his principle not to tell people where they were to dine; for one answer led to many other questions, as what o'clock it was? or, how soon should we be there? and he could not afford to be eternally worried.

As you are thus cut off from the superior authorities, a great deal of your comfort depends on the character of the newsboy. He has it in his power indefinitely to better and brighten the emigrant's lot. The newsboy with whom we started from the Transfer was a dark, bullying, contemptuous, insolent scoundrel, who treated us like dogs. Indeed, in his case, matters came nearly to a fight. It happened thus: he was going his rounds through the cars with some commodities for sale, and coming to a party who were at Seven-up or Cascino (our two games), upon a bed-board, slung down a cigar-box in the middle of the cards, knocking one man's hand to the floor. It was the last straw. In a moment the whole party were upon their feet, the cigars were upset, and he was ordered to 'get out of that directly, or he would get more than he reckoned for'. The fellow grumbled and muttered, but ended by making off, and was less openly insulting in the future. On the other hand, the lad who rode with us in this capacity from Ogden to Sacramento made himself the friend of all, and helped us with information, attention, assistance, and a kind countenance. He told us where and when we should have our meals, and how long the train would stop; kept seats at table for those who were delayed, and watched that we should neither be left behind nor yet unnecessarily hurried. You, who live at home at ease, can hardly realise the greatness of this service, even had it stood alone. When I think of that lad coming and going, train after train, with his bright face and civil words, I see how easily a good man may become the benefactor of his kind. Perhaps he is discontented with himself, perhaps troubled with ambitions; why, if he but knew it, he is a hero of the old Greek stamp; and while he thinks he is only earning a profit of a few cents, and that perhaps exorbitant, he is doing a man's work, and bettering the world.

I must tell here an experience of mine with another newsboy. I tell it because it gives so good an example of that uncivil kindness of the American, which is perhaps their most bewildering character to one newly landed. It was immediately after I had left the emigrant train; and I am told I looked like a man at death's door, so much had this long journey shaken me. I sat at the end of a car, and the catch being broken, and myself feverish and sick, I had to hold the door open with my foot for the sake of air. In this attitude my leg debarred the newsboy from his box of merchandise. I made haste to let him pass when I observed that he was coming; but I was busy with a book, and so once or twice he came upon me unawares. On these occasions he most rudely struck my foot aside; and though I myself apologised, as if to show him the way, he answered me never a word. I chafed furiously, and I fear the next time it would have come to words. But suddenly I felt a touch upon my shoulder, and a large juicy pear was put into my hand. It was the newsboy, who had observed that I was looking ill, and so made me this present out of a tender heart. For the rest of the journey I was petted like a sick child; he lent me newspapers, thus depriving himself of his legitimate profit on their sale, and came repeatedly to sit by me and cheer me up.

The Plains of Nebraska[95]

It had thundered on the Friday night, but the sun rose on Saturday without a cloud. We were at sea – there is no other adequate expression – on the plains of Nebraska. I made my observatory on the top of a fruit-wagon, and sat by the hour upon that perch to spy about me, and to spy in vain for something new. It was a world almost without a feature; an empty sky, an empty earth; front and back, the line of railway stretched from horizon to horizon, like a cue across a billiard-board; on either hand, the green plain ran till it touched the skirts of heaven. Along the track innumerable wild sunflowers, no bigger than a crown-piece, bloomed in a continuous flower-bed; grazing beasts were seen upon the prairie at all degrees of distance and diminution; and now and again we might perceive a few dots beside the railroad which grew more and more distinct as we drew nearer till they turned into wooden cabins, and then dwindled and dwindled in our wake until they melted into their surroundings, and we were once more alone upon the billiard-board. The train toiled over this infinity like a snail; and being the one thing moving, it was wonderful what huge proportions it began to assume in our regard. It seemed miles in length, and either end of it within but a step of the horizon. Even my own body or my own head seemed a great thing in that emptiness. I note the feeling the more readily as it is the contrary of what I have read of in the experience of others. Day and night, above the roar of the train, our ears were kept busy with the incessant chirp of grasshoppers – a noise like the winding up of countless clocks and watches, which began after a while to seem proper to that land.

To one hurrying through by steam there was a certain exhilaration in this spacious vacancy, this greatness of the air, this discovery of the whole arch of heaven, this straight, unbroken, prison-line of the horizon. Yet one could not but reflect upon the weariness of those who passed by there in old days, at the foot's pace of oxen, painfully urging their teams, and with no landmark but that unattainable evening sun for which they steered, and which daily fled them by an equal stride. They had nothing, it would seem, to overtake; nothing by which to reckon their advance; no sight for repose or for encouragement; but stage after stage, only the dead green waste underfoot, and the mocking, fugitive horizon. But the eye, as I have been told, found differences even here; and at the worst the emigrant came, by perseverance, to the end of his toil. It is the settlers, after all, at whom we have a right to marvel. Our consciousness, by which we live, is itself but the creature of variety. Upon what food does it subsist in such a land? What livelihood can repay a human creature for a life spent in this huge sameness? He is cut off from books, from news, from company, from all that can relieve existence but the prosecution of his affairs. A sky full of stars is the most varied spectacle that he can hope. He may walk five miles and see nothing; ten, and it is as though he had not moved; twenty, and still he is in the midst of the same great level, and has approached no nearer to the one object within view, the flat horizon which keeps pace with his advance. We are full at home of the question of agreeable wallpapers, and wise people are of opinion that the temper may be quieted by sedative surroundings. But what is to be said of the Nebraskan settler? His is a wallpaper with a vengeance – one quarter of the universe laid bare in all its gauntness.

His eye must embrace at every glance the whole seeming concave of the visible world; it quails before so vast an outlook, it is tortured by distance; yet there is no rest or shelter till the man runs into his cabin, and can repose his sight upon things near at hand. Hence, I am told, a sickness of the vision peculiar to these empty plains.

Yet perhaps with sunflowers and cicadae, summer and winter, cattle, wife and family, the settler may create a full and various existence. One person at least I saw upon the plains who seemed in every way superior to her lot. This was a woman who boarded us at a way station, selling milk. She was largely formed; her features were more than comely; she had that great rarity – a fine complexion which became her; and her eyes were kind, dark and steady. She sold milk with patriarchal grace. There was not a line in her countenance, not a note in her soft and sleepy voice, but spoke of an entire contentment with her life. It would have been fatuous arrogance to pity such a woman. Yet the place where she lived was to me almost ghastly. Less than a dozen wooden houses, all of a shape and all nearly of a size, stood planted along the railway lines. Each stood apart in its own lot. Each opened direct off the billiard-board, as if it were a billiard-board indeed, and these only models that had been set down upon it ready made. Her own, into which I looked, was clean but very empty, and showed nothing homelike but the burning fire. This extreme newness, above all in so naked and flat a country, gives a strong impression of artificiality. With none of the litter and discoloration of human life; with the paths unworn, and the houses still sweating from the axe, such a settlement as this seems purely scenic. The mind is loth to accept it for a piece of reality; and it seems incredible that life can go on with so few properties, or the great child, man, find entertainment in so bare a playroom.

And truly it is as yet an incomplete society in some points; or at least it contained, as I passed through, one person incompletely civilised. At North Platte, where we supped that evening, one man asked another to pass the milk-jug. This other was well dressed and of what we should call a respectable appearance: a darkish man, high spoken, eating as though he had some usage of society; but he turned upon the first speaker with extraordinary vehemence of tone: 'There's a waiter here!' he cried.

'I only asked you to pass the milk,' explained the first.

Here is the retort verbatim: 'Pass! Hell! I'm not paid for that business; the waiter's paid for it. You should use civility at table, and, by God, I'll show you how!'

The other man very wisely made no answer, and the bully went on with his supper as though nothing had occurred. It pleases me to think that someday soon he will meet with one of his own kidney; and that perhaps both may fall.

The Desert of Wyoming

To cross such a plain is to grow homesick for the mountains. I longed for the Black Hills of Wyoming, which I knew we were soon to enter, like an ice-bound whaler for the spring. Alas! and it was a worse country than the other. All Sunday and Monday we travelled through these sad mountains, or over the main ridge of the Rockies, which is a fair match to them for misery of aspect. Hour after hour it was the same unhomely and unkindly world about our onward path; tumbled boulders, cliffs that drearily imitate the shape of monuments and fortifications – how drearily, how tamely, none can tell who has not seen them; not a tree, not a patch of sward, not one shapely or commanding mountain form; sage-brush, eternal sage-brush; over all, the same weariful and gloomy colouring, greys warming into brown, greys darkening towards black; and for sole sign of life, here and there a few fleeing antelopes; here and there, but at incredible intervals, a creek running in a canyon. The plains have a grandeur of their own; but here there is nothing but a contorted smallness. Except for the air, which was light and stimulating, there was not one good circumstance in that God-forsaken land.

I had been suffering in my health a good deal all the way; and at last, whether I was exhausted by my complaint or poisoned in some wayside eating-house, the evening we left Laramie, I fell sick outright.[96] That was a night which I shall not readily forget. The lamps did not go out; each made a faint shining in its own neighbourhood, and the shadows were confounded together in the long, hollow box of the car. The sleepers lay in uneasy attitudes; here two chums alongside, flat upon their backs like dead folk; there a man sprawling on the floor, with his face upon his arm; there another half seated with his head and shoulders on the bench. The most passive were continually and roughly shaken by the movement of the train; others stirred, turned, or stretched out their arms like children; it was surprising how many groaned and murmured in their sleep; and as I passed to and fro, stepping across the prostrate, and caught now a snore, now a gasp, now a half-formed word, it gave me a measure of the worthlessness of rest in that unresting vehicle. Although it was chill, I was obliged to open my window, for the degradation of the air soon became intolerable to one who was awake and using the full supply of life. Outside, in a glimmering night, I saw the black, amorphous hills shoot by unweariedly into our wake. They that long for morning have never longed for it more earnestly than I.

And yet when day came, it was to shine upon the same broken and unsightly quarter of the world. Mile upon mile, and not a tree, a bird or a river. Only down the long, sterile canyons, the train shot hooting and awoke the resting echo. That train was the one piece of life in all the deadly land; it was the one actor, the one spectacle fit to be observed in this paralysis of man and nature. And when I think how the railroad has been pushed through this unwatered wilderness and haunt of savage tribes, and now will bear an emigrant for some twelve pounds from the Atlantic to the Golden Gates; how at each stage of the construction, roaring, impromptu cities, full of gold and lust and death, sprang up and then died away again, and are now but wayside stations in the desert; how in these uncouth places pig-tailed Chinese pirates[97] worked side by side with border ruffians and broken men from Europe, talking together in a mixed dialect, mostly oaths, gambling, drinking, quarrelling and murdering like wolves; how the plumed hereditary lord[98] of all America heard, in this last fastness, the scream of the 'bad medicine wagon' charioting his foes; and then when I go on to remember that all this epical turmoil was conducted by gentlemen in frock coats, and with a view to nothing more extraordinary than a fortune and a subsequent visit to Paris, it seems to me, I own, as if this railway were the one typical achievement of the age in which we live, as if it brought together into one plot all the ends of the world and all the degrees of social rank, and offered to some great writer the busiest, the most extended, and the most varied subject for an enduring literary work. If it be romance, if it be contrast, if it be heroism that we require, what was Troy town to this? But, alas! it is not these things that are necessary – it is only Homer.

Here also we are grateful to the train, as to some god who conducts us swiftly through these shades and by so many hidden perils. Thirst, hunger, the sleight and ferocity of Indians are all no more feared, so lightly do we skim these horrible lands; as the gull, who wings safely through the hurricane and past the shark. Yet we should not be forgetful of these hardships of the past; and to keep the balance true, since I have complained of the trifling discomforts of my journey, perhaps more than was enough, let me add an original document. It was not written by Homer, but by a boy of eleven, long since dead, and is dated only twenty years ago. I shall punctuate, to make things clearer, but not change the spelling.

My dear Sister Mary – I am afraid you will go nearly crazy when you read my letter. If Jerry [the writer's eldest brother] has not written to you before now, you will be surprised to heare that we are in California, and that poor Thomas [another brother, of fifteen] is dead. We started from — in July, with plenly of provisions and too yoke oxen. We went along very well till we got within six or seven hundred miles of California, when the Indians attacked us. We found places where they had killed the emigrants. We had one passenger with us, too guns, and one revolver; so we ran all the lead We had into bullets (and) hung the guns up in the wagon so that we could get at them in a minit. It was about two o'clock in the afternoon; droave the cattel a little way; when a prairie chicken alited a little way from the wagon.

Jerry took out one of the guns to shoot it, and told Tom drive the oxen. Tom and I drove the oxen, and Jerry and the passenger went on. Then, after a little, I left Tom and caught up with Jerry and the other man. Jerry stopped for Tom to come up; me and the man went on and sit down by a little stream. In a few minutes, we heard some noise; then three shots (they all struck poor Tom, I suppose); then they gave the war hoop, and as many as twenty of the redskins came down upon us. The three that shot Tom was hid by the side of the road in the bushes.

I thought that Tom and Jerry were shot; so I told the other man that Tom and Jerry were dead, and that we had better try to escape, if possible. I had no shoes on; having a sore foot, I thought I would not put them on. The man and me run down the road, but We was soon stopt by an Indian on a pony. We then turend the other way, and run up the side of the Mountain, and hid behind some cedar trees, and stayed there till dark. The Indians hunted all over after us, and verry close to us, so close that we could here there tomyhawks Jingle. At dark the man and me started on, I stubing my toes against sticks and stones. We traveld on all night; and next morning, just as it was getting grey, we saw something in the shape of a man. It layed Down in the grass. We went up to it, and it was Jerry. He thought we ware Indians. You can imagine how glad he was to see me. He thought we was all dead but him, and we thought him and Tom was dead. He had the gun that he took out of the wagon to shoot the prairie Chicken; all he had was the load that was in it.

We traveld on till, about eight o'clock, We caught up with one wagon with too men with it. We had traveld with them before one day; we stopt and they Drove on; we knew that they was ahead of us, unless they had been killed to. My feet was so sore when we caught up with them that I had to ride; I could not step. We traveld on for too days, when the men that owned the cattle said they would [could] not drive them another inch. We unyoked the oxen; we had about seventy pounds of flour; we took it out and divided it into four packs. Each of the men took about 18 pounds apiece and a blanket. I carried a little bacon, dried meat, and little quilt; I had in all about twelve pounds. We had one pint of flour a day for our alloyance. Sometimes we made soup of it; sometimes we [made] pancakes; and sometimes mixed it up with cold water and eat it that way. We traveld twelve or fourteen days. The time came at last when we should have to reach some place or starve. We saw fresh horse and cattle tracks. The morning come, we scraped all the flour out of the sack, mixed it up, and baked it into bread, and made some soup, and eat everything we had. We traveld on all day without anything to eat, and that evening we Caught up with a sheep train of eight wagons. We traveld with them till we arrived at the settlements; and know I am safe in California, and got to good home, and going to school.

Jerry is working in —. It is a good country. You can get from 50 to 60 and 75 Dollars for cooking. Tell me all about the affairs in the States, and how all the folks get along.

And so ends this artless narrative. The little man was at school again, God bless him, while his brother lay scalped upon the deserts.

Fellow Passengers

At Ogden[99] we changed cars from the Union Pacific to the Central Pacific line of railroad. The change was doubly welcome; for, first, we had better cars on the new line; and, second, those in which we had been cooped for more than ninety hours had begun to stink abominably. Several yards away, as we returned, let us say from dinner, our nostrils were assailed by rancid air. I have stood on a platform while the whole train was shunting; and as the dwelling-cars drew near, there would come a whiff of pure menagerie, only a little sourer, as from men instead of monkeys. I think we are human only in virtue of open windows. Without fresh air, you only require a bad heart, and a remarkable command of the Queen's English, to become such another as Dean Swift:[100] a kind of leering, human goat, leaping and wagging your scut on mountains of offence. I do my best to keep my head the other way, and look for the human rather than the bestial in this Yahoo-like business of the emigrant train. But one thing I must say, the car of the Chinese was notably the least offensive.

The cars on the Central Pacific were nearly twice as high, and so proportionally airier; they were freshly varnished, which gave us all a sense of cleanliness an though we had bathed; the seats drew out and joined in the centre, so that there was no more need for bed boards; and there was an upper tier of berths which could be closed by day and opened at night.

I had by this time some opportunity of seeing the people whom I was among. They were in rather marked contrast to the emigrants I had met on board ship while crossing the Atlantic. They were mostly lumpish fellows, silent and noisy, a common combination; somewhat sad, I should say, with an extraordinary poor taste in humour, and little interest in their fellow-creatures beyond that of a cheap and merely external curiosity. If they heard a man's name and business, they seemed to think they had the heart of that mystery; but they were as eager to know that much as they were indifferent to the rest. Some of them were on nettles till they learned your name was Dickson and you were a journeyman baker; but beyond that, whether you were Catholic or Mormon, dull or clever, fierce or friendly, was all one to them. Others who were not so stupid, gossiped a little, and, I am bound to say, unkindly. A favourite witticism was for some lout to raise the alarm of 'All aboard!' while the rest of us were dining, thus contributing his mite to the general discomfort. Such a one was always much applauded for his high spirits. When I was ill coming through Wyoming, I was astonished – fresh from the eager humanity on board ship – to meet with little but laughter. One of the young men even amused himself by incommoding me, as was then very easy; and that not from ill-nature, but mere clodlike incapacity to think, for he expected me to join the laugh. I did so, but it was phantom merriment. Later on, a man from Kansas had three violent epileptic fits, and though, of course, there were not wanting some to help him, it was rather superstitious terror than sympathy that his case evoked among his fellow-passengers. 'Oh, I hope he's not going to die!' cried a woman; 'it would be terrible to have a dead body!' And there was a very general movement to leave the man behind at the next station. This, by good fortune, the conductor negatived.

There was a good deal of story-telling in some quarters; in others, little but silence. In this society, more than any other that ever I was in, it was the narrator alone who seemed to enjoy the narrative. It was rarely that anyone listened for the listening. If he lent an ear to another man's story, it was because he was in immediate want of a hearer for one of his own. Food and the progress of the train were the subjects most generally treated; many joined to discuss these who otherwise would hold their tongues. One small knot had no better occupation than to worm out of me my name; and the more they tried, the more obstinately fixed I grew to baffle them. They assailed me with artful questions and insidious offers of correspondence in the future; but I was perpetually on my guard, and parried their assaults with inward laughter. I am sure Dubuque would have given me ten dollars for the secret. He owed me far more, had he understood life, for thus preserving him a lively interest throughout the journey. I met one of my fellow-passengers months after, driving a street tramway car in San Francisco; and, as the joke was now out of season, told him my name without subterfuge. You never saw a man more chapfallen. But had my name been Demogorgon,[101] after so prolonged a mystery he had still been disappointed.

There were no emigrants direct from Europe – save one German family and a knot of Cornish miners who kept grimly by themselves, one reading the New Testament all day long through steel spectacles, the rest discussing privately the secrets of their old-world, mysterious race. Lady Hester Stanhope believed she could make something great of the Cornish; for my part, I can make nothing of them at all. A division of races, older and more original than that of Babel, keeps this close, esoteric family apart from neighbouring Englishmen. Not even a Red Indian seems more foreign in my eyes. This is one of the lessons of travel – that some of the strangest races dwell next door to you at home.

The rest were all American born, but they came from almost every quarter of that Continent. All the states of the North had sent out a fugitive to cross the plains with me. From Virginia, from Pennsylvania, from New York, from far western Iowa and Kansas, from Maine that borders on the Canadas, and from the Canadas themselves – some one or two were fleeing in quest of a better land and better wages. The talk in the train, like the talk I heard on the steamer, ran upon hard times, short commons, and hope that moves ever Westward. I thought of my shipful from Great Britain with a feeling of despair. They had come three thousand miles, and yet not far enough. Hard times bowed them out of the Clyde, and stood to welcome them at Sandy Hook. Where were they to go? Pennsylvania, Maine, Iowa, Kansas? These were not places for immigration, but for emigration, it appeared; not one of them, but I knew a man who had lifted up his heel and left it for an ungrateful country. And it was still Westward that they ran. Hunger, you would have thought, came out of the east like the sun, and the evening was made of edible gold. And, meantime, in the car in front of me, were there not half a hundred emigrants from the opposite quarter? Hungry Europe and hungry China, each pouring from their gates in search of provender, had here come face to face. The two waves had met; East and West had alike failed; the whole round world had been prospected and condemned; there was no El Dorado anywhere; and till one could emigrate to the moon, it seemed as well to stay patiently at home. Nor was there wanting another sign, at once more picturesque and more disheartening; for, as we continued to steam westward towards the land of gold, we were continually passing other emigrant trains upon the journey east; and these were as crowded as our own. Had all these return voyagers made a fortune in the mines? Were they all bound for Paris, and to be in Rome by Easter? It would seem not, for, whenever we met them, the passengers ran on the platform and cried to us through the windows, in a kind of wailing chorus, to 'come back'. On the plains of Nebraska, in the mountains of Wyoming, it was still the same cry, and dismal to my heart, 'Come back!' That was what we heard by the way 'about the good country we were going to'. And at that very hour the Sand-lot of San Francisco was crowded with the unemployed, and the echo from the other side of Market Street was repeating the rant of demagogues.

If, in truth, it were only for the sake of wages that men emigrate, how many thousands would regret the bargain! But wages, indeed, are only one consideration out of many; for we are a race of gypsies, and love change and travel for themselves.

Despised Races

Of all stupid ill-feelings, the sentiment of my fellow Caucasians towards our companions in the Chinese car was the most stupid and the worst. They seemed never to have looked at them, listened to them or thought of them, but hated them *a priori*. The Mongols were their enemies in that cruel and treacherous battlefield of money. They could work better and cheaper in half a hundred industries, and hence there was no calumny too idle for the Caucasians to repeat, and even to believe. They declared them hideous vermin, and affected a kind of choking in the throat when they beheld them. Now, as a matter of fact, the young Chinese man is so like a large class of European women, that on raising my head and suddenly catching sight of one at a considerable distance, I have for an instant been deceived by the resemblance. I do not say it is the most attractive class of our women, but for all that many a man's wife is less pleasantly favoured. Again, my emigrants declared that the Chinese were dirty. I cannot say they were clean, for that was impossible upon the journey; but in their efforts after cleanliness they put the rest of us to shame. We all pigged and stewed in one infamy, wet our hands and faces for half a minute daily on the platform, and were unashamed. But the Chinese never lost an opportunity, and you would see them washing their feet – an act not dreamed of among ourselves – and going as far as decency permitted to wash their whole bodies. I may remark by the way that the dirtier people are in their persons the more delicate is their sense of modesty. A clean man strips in a crowded boathouse; but he who is unwashed slinks in and out of bed without uncovering an inch of skin. Lastly, these very foul and malodorous Caucasians entertained the surprising illusion that it was the Chinese wagon, and that alone, which stank. I have said already that it was the exception, and notably the freshest of the three.

These judgements are typical of the feeling in all Western America. The Chinese are considered stupid, because they are imperfectly acquainted with English. They are held to be base, because their dexterity and frugality enable them to underbid the lazy, luxurious Caucasian. They are said to be thieves; I am sure they have no monopoly of that. They are called cruel; the Anglo-Saxon and the cheerful Irishman may each reflect before he bears the accusation. I am told, again, that they are of the race of river pirates, and belong to the most despised and dangerous class in the Celestial Empire. But if this be so, what remarkable pirates have we here! and what must be the virtues, the industry, the education and the intelligence of their superiors at home!

Awhile ago it was the Irish, now it is the Chinese that must go. Such is the cry. It seems, after all, that no country is bound to submit to immigration any more than to invasion; each is war to the knife, and resistance to either but legitimate defence. Yet we may regret the free tradition of the republic, which loved to depict herself with open arms, welcoming all unfortunates. And certainly, as a man who believes that he loves freedom, I may be excused some bitterness when I find her sacred name misused in the contention. It was but the other day that I heard a vulgar fellow in the Sand-lot, the popular tribune of San Francisco, roaring for arms and butchery. 'At the call of Abraham Lincoln,' said the orator, 'ye rose in the name of freedom to set free the negroes; can ye not rise and liberate yourselves from a few dirty Mongolians?'

For my own part, I could not look but with wonder and respect on the Chinese. Their forefathers watched the stars before mine had begun to keep pigs. Gunpowder and printing, which the other day we imitated, and a school of manners which we never had the delicacy so much as to desire to imitate, were theirs in a long-past antiquity. They walk the earth with us, but it seems they must be of different clay. They hear the clock strike the same hour, yet surely of a different epoch. They travel by steam conveyance, yet with such a baggage of old Asiatic thoughts and superstitions as might check the locomotive in its course. Whatever is thought within the circuit of the Great Wall; what the wry-eyed, spectacled schoolmaster teaches in the hamlets round Pekin; religions so old that our language looks a halfling boy alongside; philosophy so wise that our best philosophers find things therein to wonder at: all this travelled alongside of me for thousands of miles over plain and mountain. Heaven knows if we had one common thought or fancy all that way, or whether our eyes, which yet were formed upon the same design, beheld the same world out of the railway windows. And when either of us turned his thoughts to home and childhood, what a strange dissimilarity must there not have been in these pictures of the mind – when I beheld that old, grey, castled city,[102] high throned above the Firth, with the flag of Britain flying, and the redcoat sentry pacing over all; and the man in the next car to me would conjure up some junks and a pagoda and a fort of porcelain, and call it, with the same affection, home.

Another race shared among my fellow-passengers in the disfavour of the Chinese; and that, it is hardly necessary to say, was the noble red man of old story – over whose own hereditary continent we had been steaming all these days. I saw no wild or independent Indian; indeed, I hear that such avoid the neighbourhood of the train; but now and again at way stations, a husband and wife and a few children, disgracefully dressed out with the sweepings of civilisation, came forth and stared upon the emigrants. The silent stoicism of their conduct, and the pathetic degradation of their appearance, would have touched any thinking creature, but my fellow-passengers danced and jested round them with a truly Cockney baseness. I was ashamed for the thing we call civilisation. We should carry upon our consciences so much, at least, of our forefathers' misconduct as we continue to profit by ourselves.

If oppression drives a wise man mad, what should be raging in the hearts of these poor tribes, who have been driven back and back, step after step, their promised reservations torn from them one after another as the States extended westward, until at length they are shut up into these hideous mountain deserts of the centre – and even there find themselves invaded, insulted and hunted out by ruffianly diggers? The eviction of the Cherokees[103] (to name but an instance), the extortion of Indian agents, the outrages of the wicked, the ill-faith of all, nay, down to the ridicule of such poor beings as were here with me upon the train, make up a chapter of injustice and indignity such as a man must be in some ways base if his heart will suffer him to pardon or forget. These old, well-founded, historical hatreds have a savour of nobility for the independent. That the Jew should not love the Christian, nor the Irishman love the English, nor the Indian brave tolerate the thought of the American, is not disgraceful to the nature of man; rather, indeed, honourable, since it depends on wrongs ancient like the race, and not personal to him who cherishes the indignation.

To the Golden Gates

A little corner of Utah is soon traversed, and leaves no particular impressions on the mind. By an early hour on Wednesday morning we stopped to breakfast at Toano, a little station on a bleak, high-lying plateau in Nevada. The man who kept the station eating-house was a Scot, and learning that I was the same, he grew very friendly, and gave me some advice on the country I was now entering. 'You see,' said he, 'I tell you this, because I come from your country.' Hail, brither Scots!

His most important hint was on the moneys of this part of the world. There is something in the simplicity of a decimal coinage which is revolting to the human mind; thus the French, in small affairs, reckon strictly by halfpence; and you have to solve, by a spasm of mental arithmetic, such posers as thirty-two, forty-five, or even a hundred halfpence. In the Pacific States they have made a bolder push for complexity, and settle their affairs by a coin that no longer exists – the *bit*, or old Mexican real. The supposed value of the bit is twelve and a half cents, eight to the dollar. When it comes to two bits, the quarter-dollar stands for the required amount. But how about an odd bit? The nearest coin to it is a dime, which is, short by a fifth. That, then, is called a *short* bit. If you have one, you lay it triumphantly down, and save two and a half cents. But if you have not, and lay down a quarter, the barkeeper or shopman calmly tenders you a dime by way of change; and thus you have paid what is called a *long bit*, and lost two and a half cents, or even, by comparison with a short bit, five cents. In country places all over the Pacific coast, nothing lower than a bit is ever asked or taken, which vastly increases the cost of life; as even for a glass of beer you must pay fivepence or sevenpence-halfpenny, as the case may be. You would say that this system of mutual robbery was as broad as it was long; but I have discovered a plan to make it broader, with which I here endow the public. It is brief and simple – radiantly simple. There is one place where five cents are recognised, and that is the post-office. A quarter is only worth two bits, a short and a long. Whenever you have a quarter, go to the post-office and buy five cents' worth of postage-stamps; you will receive in change two dimes, that is, two short bits. The purchasing power of your money is undiminished. You can go and have your two glasses of beer all the same; and you have made yourself a present of five cents' worth of postage-stamps into the bargain. Benjamin Franklin would have patted me on the head for this discovery.

From Toano we travelled all day through deserts of alkali and sand, horrible to man, and bare sage-brush country that seemed little kindlier, and came by suppertime to Elko. As we were standing, after our manner, outside the station, I saw two men whip suddenly from underneath the cars, and take to their heels across country. They were tramps, it appeared, who had been riding on the beams since eleven of the night before; and several of my fellow-passengers had already seen and conversed with them while we broke our fast at Toano. These land stowaways[104] play a great part over here in America, and I should have liked dearly to become acquainted with them.

At Elko an odd circumstance befell me. I was coming out from supper, when I was stopped by a small, stout, ruddy man, followed by two others taller and ruddier than himself.

'Excuse me, sir,' he said, 'but do you happen to be going on?'

I said I was, whereupon he said he hoped to persuade me to desist from that intention. He had a situation to offer me, and if we could come to terms, why, good and well. 'You see,' he continued, 'I'm running a theatre here, and we're a little short in the orchestra. You're a musician, I guess?'

I assured him that, beyond a rudimentary acquaintance with 'Auld Lang Syne' and 'The Wearing of the Green', I had no pretension whatever to that style. He seemed much put out of countenance; and one of his taller companions asked him, on the nail, for five dollars.

'You see, sir,' added the latter to me, 'he bet you were a musician; I bet you weren't. No offence, I hope?'

'None whatever,' I said, and the two withdrew to the bar, where I presume the debt was liquidated.

This little adventure woke bright hopes in my fellow-travellers, who thought they had now come to a country where situations went a-begging. But I am not so sure that the offer was in good faith. Indeed, I am more than half persuaded it was but a feeler to decide the bet.

Of all the next day I will tell you nothing, for the best of all reasons, that I remember no more than that we continued through desolate and desert scenes, fiery hot and deadly weary. But some time after I had fallen asleep that night, I was awakened by one of my companions. It was in vain that I resisted. A fire of enthusiasm and whisky burned in his eyes; and he declared we were in a new country, and I must come forth upon the platform and see with my own eyes.

The train was then, in its patient way, standing halted in a by-track. It was a clear, moonlit night; but the valley was too narrow to admit the moonshine direct, and only a diffused glimmer whitened the tall rocks and relieved the blackness of the pines. A hoarse clamour filled the air; it was the continuous plunge of a cascade somewhere near at hand among the mountains. The air struck chill, but tasted good and vigorous in the nostrils – a fine, dry, old mountain atmosphere. I was dead sleepy, but I returned to roost with a grateful mountain feeling at my heart.

When I awoke next morning, I was puzzled for a while to know if it were day or night, for the illumination was unusual. I sat up at last, and found we were grading slowly downward through a long snow shed; and suddenly we shot into the open; and before we were swallowed into the next length of wooden tunnel, I had one glimpse of a huge pine-forested ravine upon my left, a foaming river, and a sky already coloured with the fires of dawn. I am usually very calm over the displays of nature; but you will scarce believe how my heart leaped at this. It was like meeting one's wife. I had come home again – home from unsightly deserts to the green and habitable corners of the earth. Every spire of pine along the hilltop, every trouty pool along that mountain river, was more dear to me than a blood relation. Few people have praised God more happily than I did. And thenceforward, down by Blue Canyon, Alta, Dutch Flat, and all the old mining camps, through a sea of mountain forests, dropping thousands of feet towards the far sea-level as we went, not I only, but all the passengers on board, threw off their sense of dirt and heat and weariness, and bawled like schoolboys, and thronged with shining eyes upon the platform and became new creatures within and without. The sun no longer oppressed us with heat, it only shone laughingly along the mountainside, until we were fain to laugh ourselves for glee. At every turn we could see farther into the land and our own happy futures. At every town the cocks were tossing their clear notes into the golden air, and crowing for the new day and the new country. For this was indeed our destination; this was 'the good country' we had been going to so long.

By afternoon we were at Sacramento,[105] the city of gardens in a plain of corn; and the next day before the dawn we were lying to upon the Oakland side of San Francisco Bay. The day was breaking as we crossed the ferry; the fog was rising over the citied hills of San Francisco; the bay was perfect – not a ripple, scarce a stain, upon its blue expanse; everything was waiting, breathless, for the sun. A spot of cloudy gold lit first upon the head of Tamalpais,[106] and then widened downward on its shapely shoulder; the air seemed to awaken, and began to sparkle; and suddenly

> The tall hills Titan discovered

and the city of San Francisco, and the bay of gold and corn, were lit from end to end with summer daylight.

The Old and New Pacific Capitals

Monterey

The Woods and the Pacific

The Bay of Monterey has been compared by no less a person than General Sherman[107] to a bent fishing-hook; and the comparison, if less important than the march through Georgia, still shows the eye of a soldier for topography. Santa Cruz sits exposed at the shank; the mouth of the Salinas River is at the middle of the bend; and Monterey itself is cosily ensconced beside the barb. Thus the ancient capital of California[108] faces across the bay, while the Pacific Ocean, though hidden by low hills and forests, bombards her left flank and rear with never-dying surf. In front of the town, the long line of sea-beach trends north and north-west, and then westward to enclose the bay. The waves which lap so quietly about the jetties of Monterey grow louder and larger in the distance; you can see the breakers leaping high and white by day; at night, the outline of the shore is traced in transparent silver by the moonlight and the flying foam; and from all round, even in quiet weather, the low, distant, thrilling roar of the Pacific hangs over the coast and the adjacent country like smoke above a battle.

These long beaches are enticing to the idle man. It would be hard to find a walk more solitary and at the same time more exciting to the mind. Crowds of ducks and seagulls hover over the sea. Sand-pipers trot in and out by troops after the retiring waves, trilling together in a chorus of infinitesimal song. Strange sea-tangles, new to the European eye, the bones of whales, or sometimes a whole whale's carcass, white with carrion-gulls and poisoning the wind, lie scattered here and there along the sands. The waves come in slowly, vast and green, curve their translucent necks, and burst with a surprising uproar, that runs, waxing and waning, up and down the long keyboard of the beach. The foam of these great ruins mounts in an instant to the ridge of the sand glacis, swiftly fleets back again, and is met and buried by the next breaker. The interest is perpetually fresh. On no other coast that I know shall you enjoy, in calm, sunny weather, such a spectacle of ocean's greatness, such beauty of changing colour, or such degrees of thunder in the sound. The very air is more than usually salt by this Homeric deep.[109]

Inshore, a tract of sandhills borders on the beach. Here and there a lagoon, more or less brackish, attracts the birds and hunters. A rough, spotty undergrowth partially conceals the sand. The crouching, hardy live oaks flourish singly or in thickets – the kind of wood for murderers to crawl among – and here and there the skirts of the forest extend downward from the hills with a floor of turf and long aisles of pine trees hung with Spaniard's Beard. Through this quaint desert the railway cars drew near to Monterey from the junction at Salinas City – though it and so many other things are now for ever altered – and it was from here that you had the first view of the old township lying in the sands, its white windmills bickering in the chill, perpetual wind, and the first fogs of the evening drawing drearily around it from the sea.

The one common note of all this country is the haunting presence of the ocean. A great faint sound of breakers follows you high up into the inland canyons; the roar of water dwells in the clean, empty rooms of Monterey as in a shell upon the chimney; go where you will, you have but to pause and listen to hear the voice of the Pacific. You pass out of the town to the south-west, and mount the hill among pine woods. Glade, thicket and grove surround you. You follow winding sandy tracks that lead nowhither. You see a deer; a multitude of quail arises. But the sound of the sea still follows you as you advance, like that of wind among the trees, only harsher and stranger to the ear; and when at length you gain the summit, out breaks on every hand and with freshened vigour, that same unending, distant, whispering rumble of the ocean; for now you are on the top of Monterey peninsula, and the noise no longer only mounts to you from behind, along the beach towards Santa Cruz, but from your right also, round by Chinatown and Pinos lighthouse, and from down before you to the mouth of the Carmello River. The whole woodland is begirt with thundering surges. The silence that immediately surrounds you where you stand is not so much broken as it is haunted by this distant, circling rumour. It sets your senses upon edge; you strain your attention; you are clearly and unusually conscious of small sounds near at hand; you walk listening like an Indian hunter; and that voice of the Pacific is a sort of disquieting company to you in your walk.

When once I was in these woods I found it difficult to turn homeward. All woods lure a rambler onward; but in those of Monterey it was the surf that particularly invited me to prolong my walks. I would push straight for the shore where I thought it to be nearest. Indeed, there was scarce a direction that would not, sooner or later, have brought me forth on the Pacific. The emptiness of the woods gave me a sense of freedom and discovery in these excursions. I never in all my visits met but one man. He was a Mexican, very dark of hue, but smiling and fat, and he carried an axe, though his true business at that moment was to seek for straying cattle. I asked him what o'clock it was, but he seemed neither to know nor care; and when he in his turn asked me for news of his cattle, I showed myself equally indifferent. We stood and smiled upon each other for a few seconds, and then turned without a word and took our several ways across the forest.

One day – I shall never forget it – I had taken a trail that was new to me. After a while the woods began to open, the sea to sound nearer at hand. I came upon a road, and, to my surprise, a stile. A step or two farther, and, without leaving the woods, I found myself among trim houses. I walked through street after street, parallel and at right angles, paved with sward and dotted with trees, but still undeniable streets, and each with its name posted at the corner, as in a real town. Facing down the main thoroughfare – 'Central Avenue', as it was ticketed – I saw an open-air temple, with benches and sounding-board, as though for an orchestra. The houses were all tightly shuttered; there was no smoke, no sound but of the waves, no moving thing. I have never been in any place that seemed so dreamlike. Pompeii is all in a bustle with visitors, and its antiquity and strangeness deceive the imagination; but this town had plainly not been built above a year or two, and perhaps had been deserted overnight. Indeed, it was not so much like a deserted town as like a scene upon the stage by daylight, and with no one on the boards. The barking of a dog led me at last to the only house still occupied, where a Scots pastor and his wife pass the winter alone in this empty theatre. The place was 'The Pacific Camp Grounds, the Christian Seaside Resort'. Thither, in the warm season, crowds come to enjoy a life of teetotalism, religion and flirtation, which I am willing to think blameless and agreeable. The neighbourhood at least is well selected. The Pacific booms in front. Westward is Point Pinos, with the lighthouse in a wilderness of sand, where you will find the lightkeeper playing the piano, making models and bows and arrows, studying dawn and sunrise in amateur oil-painting, and with a dozen other elegant pursuits and interests to surprise his brave, old-country rivals. To the east, and still nearer, you will come upon a space of open down, a hamlet, a haven among rocks, a world of surge and screaming sea-gulls. Such scenes are very similar in different climates; they appear homely to the eyes of all; to me this was like a dozen spots in Scotland. And yet the boats that ride in the haven are of strange outlandish design; and, if you walk into the hamlet, you will behold costumes and faces and hear a tongue that are unfamiliar to the memory. The joss-stick burns, the opium-pipe is smoked, the floors are strewn with slips of coloured paper – prayers, you would say, that had somehow missed their destination – and a man guiding his upright pencil from right to left across the sheet, writes home the news of Monterey to the Celestial Empire.[110]

The woods and the Pacific rule between them the climate of this seaboard region. On the streets of Monterey, when the air does not smell salt from the one, it will be blowing perfumed from the resinous treetops of the other. For days together a hot, dry air will overhang the town, close as from an oven, yet healthful and aromatic in the nostrils. The cause is not far to seek, for the woods are afire, and the hot wind is blowing from the hills. These fires are one of the great dangers of California. I have seen from Monterey as many as three at the same time, by day a cloud of smoke, by night a red coal of conflagration in the distance. A little thing will start them, and, if the wind be favourable, they gallop over miles of country faster than a horse. The inhabitants must turn out and work like demons, for it is not only the pleasant groves that are destroyed; the climate and the soil are equally at stake, and these fires prevent the rains of the next winter and dry up perennial fountains. California has been a land of promise in its time, like Palestine; but if the woods continue so swiftly to perish, it may become, like Palestine, a land of desolation.

To visit the woods while they are languidly burning is a strange piece of experience. The fire passes through the underbrush at a run. Every here and there a tree flares up instantaneously from root to summit, scattering tufts of flame, and is quenched, it seems, as quickly. But this last is only in semblance. For after this first squib-like conflagration of the dry moss and twigs, there remains behind a deep-rooted and consuming fire in the very entrails of the tree. The resin of the pitch-pine[111] is principally condensed at the base of the bole and in the spreading roots. Thus, after the light, showy, skirmishing flames, which are only as the match to the explosion, have already scampered down the wind into the distance, the true harm is but beginning for this giant of the woods. You may approach the tree from one side, and see it, scorched indeed from top to bottom, but apparently survivor of the peril. Make the circuit, and there, on the other side of the column, is a clear mass of living coal, spreading like an ulcer; while underground, to their most extended fibre, the roots are being eaten out by fire, and the smoke is rising through the fissures to the surface. A little while and, without a nod of warning, the huge pine tree snaps off short across the ground and falls prostrate with a crash. Meanwhile the fire continues its silent business; the roots are reduced to a fine ash; and long afterwards, if you pass by, you will find the earth pierced with radiating galleries, and preserving the design of all these subterranean spurs, as though it were the mould for a new tree instead of the print of an old one. These pitch-pines of Monterey are, with the single exception of the Monterey cypress, the most fantastic of forest trees. No words can give an idea of the contortion of their growth; they might figure without change in a circle of the nether hell as Dante pictured it; and at the rate at which trees grow, and at which forest fires spring up and gallop through the hills of California, we may look forward to a time when there will not be one of them left standing in that land of their nativity. At least they have not so much to fear from the axe, but perish by what may be called a natural although a violent death; while it is man in his short-sighted greed that robs the country of the nobler redwood. Yet a little while and perhaps all the hills of seaboard California may be as bald as Tamalpais.

I have an interest of my own in these forest fires, for I came so near to lynching on one occasion, that a braver man might have retained a thrill from the experience. I wished to be certain whether it was the moss,[112] that quaint funereal ornament of Californian forests, which blazed up so rapidly when the flame first touched the tree. I suppose I must have been under the influence of Satan, for instead of plucking off a piece for my experiment, what should I do but walk up to a great pine tree in a portion of the wood which had escaped so much as scorching, strike a match, and apply the flame gingerly to one of the tassels. The tree went off simply like a rocket; in three seconds it was a roaring pillar of fire. Close by I could hear the shouts of those who were at work combating the original conflagration. I could see the wagon that had brought them tied to a live oak in a piece of open; I could even catch the flash of an axe as it swung up through the underwood into the sunlight. Had anyone observed the result of my experiment my neck was literally not worth a pinch of snuff; after a few minutes of passionate expostulation I should have been run up to a convenient bough.

> To die for faction is a common evil;
> But to be hanged for nonsense is the devil.[113]

I have run repeatedly, but never as I ran that day. At night I went out of town, and there was my own particular fire, quite distinct from the other, and burning as I thought with even greater vigour.

But it is the Pacific that exercises the most direct and obvious power upon the climate. At sunset, for months together, vast, wet, melancholy fogs arise and come shoreward from the ocean. From the hilltop above Monterey the scene is often noble, although it is always sad. The upper air is still bright with sunlight; a glow still rests upon the Gabelano Peak; but the fogs are in possession of the lower levels; they crawl in scarves among the sandhills; they float, a little higher, in clouds of a gigantic size and often of a wild configuration; to the south, where they have struck the seaward shoulder of the mountains of Santa Lucia, they double back and spire up skyward like smoke. Where their shadow touches, colour dies out of the world. The air grows chill and deadly as they advance. The trade-wind freshens, the trees begin to sigh, and all the windmills in Monterey are whirling and creaking and filling their cisterns with the brackish water of the sands. It takes but a little while till the invasion is complete. The sea, in its lighter order, has submerged the earth. Monterey is curtained in for the night in thick, wet, salt and frigid clouds, so to remain till day returns and before the sun's rays they slowly disperse and retreat in broken squadrons to the bosom of the sea. And yet often when the fog is thickest and most chill, a few steps out of the town and up the slope, the night will be dry and warm and full of inland perfume.

Mexicans, Americans and Indians

The history of Monterey has yet to be written. Founded by Catholic missionaries, a place of wise beneficence to Indians, a place of arms, a Mexican capital continually wrested by one faction from another, an American capital when the first House of Representatives held its deliberations, and then falling lower and lower from the capital of the state to the capital of a county, and from that again, by the loss of its charter and town lands, to a mere bankrupt village, its rise and decline is typical of that of all Mexican institutions and even Mexican families in California.

Nothing is stranger in that strange state than the rapidity with which the soil has changed hands. The Mexicans, you may say, are all poor and landless, like their former capital; and yet both it and they hold themselves apart and preserve their ancient customs and something of their ancient air.

The town, when I was there, was a place of two or three streets, economically paved with sea-sand, and two or three lanes, which were watercourses in the rainy season, and were, at all times, rent up by fissures four or five feet deep. There were no street lights. Short sections of wooden sidewalk only added to the dangers of the night, for they were often high above the level of the roadway and no one could tell where they would be likely to begin or end. The houses were, for the most part, built of unbaked adobe brick, many of them old for so new a country, some of very elegant proportions, with low, spacious, shapely rooms, and walls so thick that the heat of summer never dried them to the heart. At the approach of the rainy season a deathly chill and a graveyard smell began to hang about the lower floors; and diseases of the chest are common and fatal among house-keeping people of either sex.

There was no activity but in and around the saloons, where people sat almost all day long playing cards. The smallest excursion was made on horseback. You would scarcely ever see the main street without a horse or two tied to posts, and making a fine figure with their Mexican housings. It struck me oddly to come across some of the *Cornhill* illustrations to Mr Blackmore's *Erema*, and see all the characters astride on English saddles. As a matter of fact, an English saddle is a rarity even in San Francisco, and, you may say, a thing unknown in all the rest of California. In a place so exclusively Mexican as Monterey, you saw not only Mexican saddles but true vaquero riding[114] – men always at the hand-gallop up hill and down dale, and round the sharpest corner, urging their horses with cries and gesticulations and cruel rotatory spurs, checking them dead with a touch, or wheeling them right-about-face in a square yard. The type of face and character of bearing are surprisingly un-American. The first ranged from something like the pure Spanish, to something, in its sad fixity, not unlike the pure Indian, although I do not suppose there was one pure blood of either race in all the country. As for the second, it was a matter of perpetual surprise to find in that world of absolutely mannerless Americans, a people full of deportment, solemnly courteous, and doing all things with grace and decorum. In dress they ran to colour and bright sashes. Not even the most Americanised could always resist the temptation to stick a red rose into his hatband. Not even the most Americanised would descend to wear the vile dress-hat of civilisation. Spanish was the language of the streets. It was difficult to get along without a word or two of that language for an occasion. The only communications in which the population joined were with a view to amusement. A weekly public ball took place with great etiquette, in addition to the numerous fandangoes in private houses. There was a really fair amateur brass band. Night after night serenaders would be going about the street, sometimes in a company and with several instruments and voices together, sometimes severally, each guitar before a different window. It was a strange thing to lie awake in nineteenth-century America, and hear one of these old, heartbreaking Spanish love-songs mount into the night air, perhaps in a deep baritone, perhaps in that high-pitched, pathetic, womanish alto which is so common among Mexican men, and which strikes on the unaccustomed ear as something not entirely human but altogether sad.

The town, then, was essentially and wholly Mexican; and yet almost all the land in the neighbourhood was held by Americans, and it was from the same class, numerically so small, that the principal officials were selected. This Mexican and that Mexican would describe to you his old family estates, not one rood of which remained to him. You would ask him how that came about, and elicit some tangled story back-foremost, from which you gathered that the Americans had been greedy like designing men, and the Mexicans greedy like children, but no other certain fact. Their merits and their faults contributed alike to the ruin of the former landholders. It is true they were improvident, and easily dazzled with the sight of ready money; but they were gentlefolk besides, and that in a way which curiously unfitted them to combat Yankee craft. Suppose they have a paper to sign, they would think it a reflection on the other party to examine the terms with any great minuteness; nay, suppose them to observe some doubtful clause, it is ten to one they would refuse from delicacy to object to it. I know I am speaking within the mark, for I have seen such a case occur, and the Mexican, in spite of the advice of his lawyer, has signed the imperfect paper like a lamb. To have spoken in the matter, he said, above all to have let the other party guess that he had seen a lawyer, would have 'been like doubting his word'. The scruple sounds oddly to one of ourselves, who have been brought up to understand all business as a competition in fraud, and honesty itself to be a virtue which regards the carrying out, but not the creation, of agreements. This single unworldly trait will account for much of that revolution of which we are speaking. The Mexicans have the name of being great swindlers, but certainly the accusation cuts both ways. In a contest of this sort, the entire booty would scarcely have passed into the hands of the more scrupulous race.

Physically the Americans have triumphed; but it is not entirely seen how far they have themselves been morally conquered. This is, of course, but a part of a part of an extraordinary problem now in the course of being solved in the various states of the American Union. I am reminded of an anecdote. Some years ago, at a great sale of wine, all the odd lots were purchased by a grocer in a small way in the old town of Edinburgh. The agent had the curiosity to visit him some time after and enquire what possible use he could have for such material. He was shown, by way of answer, a huge vat where all the liquors from humble Gladstone to imperial Tokay, were fermenting together. 'And what,' he asked, 'do you propose to call this?' 'I'm not very sure,' replied the grocer, 'but I think it's going to turn out port.' In the older eastern states, I think we may say that this hotch-potch of races is going to turn out English, or thereabout. But the problem is indefinitely varied in other zones. The elements are differently mingled in the south, in what we may call the territorial belt, and in the group of states on the Pacific coast. Above all, in these last, we may look to see some monstrous hybrid – whether good or evil, who shall forecast? – but certainly original and all their own. In my little restaurant at Monterey, we have sat down to table, day after day, a Frenchman, two Portuguese, an Italian, a Mexican and a Scotsman; we had for common visitors an American from Illinois, a nearly pure-blood Indian woman and a naturalised Chinese; and from time to time a Switzer and a German came down from country ranches for the night. No wonder that the Pacific coast is a foreign land to visitors from the eastern states, for each race contributes something of its own. Even the despised Chinese have taught the youth of California, none indeed of their virtues, but the debasing use of opium. And chief among these influences is that of the Mexicans.

The Mexicans although in the state are out of it. They still preserve a sort of international independence, and keep their affairs snug to themselves. Only four or five years ago Vasquez the bandit, his troops being dispersed and the hunt too hot for him in other parts of California, returned to his native Monterey, and was seen publicly in her streets and saloons, fearing no man. The year that I was there there occurred two reputed murders. As the Montereyans are exceptionally vile speakers of each other and of everyone behind his back, it is not possible for me to judge how much truth there may have been in these reports; but in the one case everyone believed, and in the other some suspected, that there had been foul play; and nobody dreamed for an instant of taking the authorities into their counsel. Now this is, of course, characteristic enough of the Mexicans; but it is a noteworthy feature that all the Americans in Monterey acquiesced without a word in this inaction. Even when I spoke to them upon the subject, they seemed not to understand my surprise; they had forgotten the traditions of their own race and upbringing and become, in a word, wholly Mexicanised.

Again, the Mexicans, having no ready money to speak of, rely almost entirely in their business transactions upon each other's worthless paper. Pedro the penniless pays you with an IOU from the equally penniless Miguel. It is a sort of local currency by courtesy. Credit in these parts has passed into a superstition. I have seen a strong, violent man struggling for months to recover a debt, and getting nothing but an exchange of waste paper. The very store-keepers are averse to asking for cash payments, and are more surprised than pleased when they are offered. They fear there must be something under it, and that you mean to withdraw your custom from them. I have seen the enterprising chemist and stationer begging me with fervour to let my account run on, although I had my purse open in my hand; and partly from the commonness of the case, partly from some remains of that generous old Mexican tradition which made all men welcome to their tables, a person may be notoriously both unwilling and unable to pay, and still find credit for the necessaries of life in the stores of Monterey. Now this villainous habit of living upon 'tick' has grown into Californian nature. I do not mean that the American and European storekeepers of Monterey are as lax as Mexicans; I mean that American farmers in many parts of the state expect unlimited credit, and profit by it in the meanwhile, without a thought for consequences. Jew storekeepers have already learned the advantage to be gained from this; they lead on the farmer into irretrievable indebtedness, and keep him ever after as their bond-slave hopelessly grinding in the mill. So the whirligig of time brings in its revenges, and except that the Jew knows better than to foreclose, you may see Americans bound in the same chains with which they themselves had formerly bound the Mexicans. It seems as if certain sorts of follies, like certain sorts of grain, were natural to the soil rather than to the race that holds and tills it for the moment.

In the meantime, however, the Americans rule in Monterey County. The new county seat, Salinas City, in the bald, corn-bearing plain under the Gabelano Peak, is a town of a purely American character. The land is held, for the most part, in those enormous tracts which are another legacy of Mexican days, and form the present chief danger and disgrace of California; and the holders are mostly of American or British birth. We have here in England no idea of the troubles and inconveniences which flow from the existence of these large landholders – land-thieves, land-sharks or land-grabbers they are more commonly and plainly called. Thus the townlands of Monterey are all in the hands of a single man. How they came there is an obscure, vexatious question, and, rightly or wrongly, the man is hated with a great hatred. His life has been repeatedly in danger. Not very long ago, I was told, the stage was stopped and examined three evenings in succession by disguised horsemen thirsting for his blood. A certain house on the Salinas road, they say, he always passes in his buggy at full speed, for the squatter sent him warning long ago. But a year since he was publicly pointed out for death by no less a man than Mr Dennis Kearney.[115] Kearney is a man too well known in California, but a word of explanation is required for English readers. Originally an Irish drayman, he rose, by his command of bad language, to almost dictatorial authority in the state; throned it there for six months or so, his mouth full of oaths, gallowses and conflagrations; was first snuffed out last winter by Mr Coleman, backed by his San Francisco Vigilantes and three Gatling guns; completed his own ruin by throwing in his lot with the grotesque Greenbacker Party; and had at last to be rescued by his old enemies, the police, out of the hands of his rebellious followers. It was while he was at the top of his fortune that Kearney visited Monterey with his battle-cry against Chinese labour, the railroad monopolists and the land-thieves; and his one articulate counsel to the Montereyans was to 'hang David Jacks'. Had the town been American, in my private opinion, this would have been done years ago. Land is a subject on which there is no jesting in the West, and I have seen my friend the lawyer drive out of Monterey to adjust a competition of titles with the face of a captain going into battle and his Smith-and-Wesson convenient to his hand.

On the ranch of another of these landholders you may find our old friend the Truck system[116] in full operation. Men live there, year in year out, to cut timber for a nominal wage, which is all consumed in supplies. The longer they remain in this desirable service the deeper they will fall in debt – a burlesque injustice in a new country, where labour should be precious, and one of those typical instances which explains the prevailing discontent and the success of the demagogue Kearney.

In a comparison between what was and what is in California, the praisers of times past will fix upon the Indians of Carmel. The valley drained by the river so named is a true Californian valley, bare, dotted with chaparral, overlooked by quaint, unfinished hills. The Carmel runs by many pleasant farms, a clear and shallow river, loved by wading kine; and at last, as it is falling towards a quicksand and the great Pacific, passes a ruined mission on a hill. From the mission church the eye embraces a great field of ocean, and the ear is filled with a continuous sound of distant breakers on the shore. But the day of the Jesuit has gone by, the day of the Yankee has succeeded, and there is no one left to care for the converted savage. The church is roofless and ruinous, sea-breezes and sea-fogs, and the alternation of the rain and sunshine, daily widening the breaches and casting the crockets from the wall. As an antiquity in this new land, a quaint specimen of missionary architecture, and a memorial of good deeds, it had a triple claim to preservation from all thinking people; but neglect and abuse have been its portion. There is no sign of American interference, save where a headboard has been torn from a grave to be a mark for pistol-bullets. So it is with the Indians for whom it was erected. Their lands, I was told, are being yearly encroached upon by the neighbouring American proprietor, and with that exception no man troubles his head for the Indians of Carmel. Only one day in the year, the day before our Guy Fawkes, the padre drives over the hill from Monterey; the little sacristy, which is the only covered portion of the church, is filled with seats and decorated for the service; the Indians troop together, their bright dresses contrasting with their dark and melancholy faces; and there, among a crowd of somewhat unsympathetic holiday-makers, you may hear God served with perhaps more touching circumstances than in any other temple under heaven. An Indian, stone-blind and about eighty years of age, conducts the singing; other Indians compose the choir; yet they have the Gregorian music at their finger-ends, and pronounce the Latin so correctly that I could follow the meaning as they sang. The pronunciation was odd and nasal, the singing hurried and staccato. 'In saecula saeculo-ho-horum,' they went, with a vigorous aspirate to every additional syllable. I have never seen faces more vividly lit up with joy than the faces of these Indian singers. It was to them not only the worship of God, nor an act by which they recalled and commemorated better days, but was besides an exercise of culture, where all they knew of art and letters was united and expressed. And it made a man's heart sorry for the good fathers of yore who had taught them to dig and to reap, to read and to sing, who had given them European mass-books, which they will still preserve and study in their cottages, and who had now passed away from all authority and influence in that land – to be succeeded by greedy land-thieves and sacrilegious pistol-shots. So ugly a thing may our Anglo-Saxon Protestantism appear beside the doings of the Society of Jesus.

But revolution in this world succeeds to revolution. All that I say in this paper is in a paulo-past tense.[117] The Monterey of last year exists no longer. A huge hotel has sprung up in the desert by the railway. Three sets of diners sit down successively to table. Invaluable toilettes figure along the beach and between the live oaks; and Monterey is advertised in the newspapers, and posted in the waiting-rooms at railway stations, as a resort for wealth and fashion. Alas for the little town! it is not strong enough to resist the influence of the flaunting caravanserai, and the poor, quaint, penniless native gentlemen of Monterey must perish, like a lower race, before the millionaire vulgarians of the Big Bonanza.[118]

San Francisco

The Pacific Coast of the United States, as you may see by the map, and still better in that admirable book *Two Years before the Mast* by Dana,[119] is one of the most exposed and shelterless on earth. The trade-wind blows fresh: the huge Pacific swell booms along degree after degree of an unbroken line of coast. South of the joint firth of the Columbia and Williamette there flows in no considerable river; south of Puget Sound there is no protected inlet of the ocean. Along the whole seaboard of California there are but two unexceptional anchorages – the bight of the Bay of Monterey, and the inland sea that takes its name from San Francisco.

Whether or not it was here that Drake put in, in 1597, we cannot tell. There is no other place so suitable; and yet the narrative of Francis Pretty scarcely seems to suit the features of the scene. Viewed from seaward, the Golden Gates should give no very English impression to justify the name of a New Albion. On the west, the deep lies open; nothing near but the still vexed Farallones.[120] The coast is rough and barren. Tamalpais,[121] a mountain of a memorable figure, springing direct from the sea level, over-plumbs the narrow entrance from the north. On the south, the loud music of the Pacific sounds along beaches and cliffs, and among broken reefs, the sporting-place of the sea-lion. Dismal, shifting sandhills, wrinkled by the wind, appear behind. Perhaps, too, in the days of Drake, Tamalpais would be clothed to its peak with the majestic redwoods.

Within the memory of persons not yet old, a mariner might have steered into these narrows – not yet the Golden Gates – opened out the surface of the bay – here girt with hills, there lying broad to the horizon – and beheld a scene as empty of the presence, as pure from the handiwork, of man, as in the days of our old sea-commander. A Spanish mission, fort and church took the place of those 'houses of the people of the country' which were seen by Pretty 'close to the waterside'. All else would be unchanged. Now, a generation later, a great city covers the sandhills on the west, a growing town lies along the muddy shallows of the east; steamboats pant continually between them from before sunrise till the small hours of the morning; lines of great sea-going ships lie ranged at anchor; colours fly upon the islands; and from all around the hum of corporate life, of beaten bells, and steam, and running carriages, goes cheerily abroad in the sunshine. Choose a place on one of the huge throbbing ferry-boats, and, when you are midway between the city and the suburb, look around. The air is fresh and salt as if you were at sea. On the one hand is Oakland, gleaming white among its gardens. On the other, to seaward, hill after hill is crowded and crowned with the palaces of San Francisco; its long streets lie in regular bars of darkness, east and west, across the sparkling picture; a forest of masts bristles like bulrushes about its feet; nothing remains of the days of Drake but the faithful trade-wind scattering the smoke, the fogs that will begin to muster about sundown, and the fine bulk of Tamalpais looking down on San Francisco, like Arthur's Seat on Edinburgh.

Thus, in the course of a generation only, this city and its suburb have arisen. Men are alive by the score who have hunted all over the foundations in a dreary waste. I have dined, near the 'punctual centre' of San Francisco, with a gentleman (then newly married) who told me of his former pleasures, wading with his fowling-piece in sand and scrub, on the site of the house where we were dining. In this busy, moving generation, we have all known cities to cover our boyish playgrounds, we have all started for a country walk and stumbled on a new suburb; but I wonder what enchantment of *The Arabian Nights* can equal this evocation of a roaring city, in a few years of a man's life, from the marshes and the blowing sand. Such swiftness[122] of increase, as with an overgrown youth, suggests a corresponding swiftness of destruction. The sandy peninsula of San Francisco, mirroring itself on one side in the bay, beaten on the other by the surge of the Pacific, and shaken to the heart by frequent earth-quakes, seems in itself no very durable foundation. According to Indian tales, perhaps older than the name of California, it once rose out of the sea in a moment, and sometime or other shall, in a moment, sink again. No Indian, they say, cares to linger on that doubtful land. 'The earth hath bubbles as the water has, and this is one of them.' Here, indeed, all is new, nature as well as towns. The very hills of California have an unfinished look; the rains and streams have not yet carved them to their perfect shape. The forests spring like mushrooms from the unexhausted soil; and they are mown down yearly by the forest fires. We are in early geological epochs, change-ful and insecure, and we feel, as with a sculptor's model, that the author may yet grow weary of and shatter the rough sketch.

Fancy apart, San Francisco is a city beleaguered with alarms. The lower parts, along the bay side, sit on piles; old wrecks decaying, fish dwelling unsunned, beneath the populous houses; and a trifling subsidence might drown the business quarters in an hour. Earthquakes are not only common, they are sometimes threatening in their violence; the fear of them grows yearly on a resident; lie begins with indifference, ends in sheer panic; and no one feels safe in any but a wooden house. Hence it comes that, in that rainless clime, the whole city is built of timber – a woodyard of unusual extent and complication; that fires spring up readily, and served by the unwearying trade-wind, swiftly spread; that all over the city there are fire-signal boxes; that the sound of the bell, telling the number of the threatened ward, is soon familiar to the ear; and that nowhere else in the world is the art of the fireman carried to so nice a point.[123]

Next, perhaps, in order of strangeness to the rapidity of its appearance, is the mingling of the races that combine to people it. The town is essentially not Anglo-Saxon; still more essentially not American. The Yankee and the Englishman find themselves alike in a strange country. There are none of these touches – not of nature, and I dare scarcely say of art – by which the Anglo-Saxon feels himself at home in so great a diversity of lands. Here, on the contrary, are airs of Marseilles and of Pekin. The shops along the streets are like the consulates of different nations.[124] The passers-by vary in feature like the slides of a magic-lantern. For we are here in that city of gold to which adventurers congregated out of all the winds of heaven; we are in a land that till the other day was ruled and peopled by the countrymen of Cortes; and the sea that laves the piers of San Francisco is the ocean of the East and of the isles of summer. There goes the Mexican unmistakable; there the blue-clad Chinaman with his white slippers; there the soft-spoken, brown Kanaka, or perhaps a waif from faraway Malay. You hear French, German, Italian, Spanish and English indifferently. You taste the food of all nations in the various restaurants; passing from a French *prix-fixe* where everyone is French, to a roaring German ordinary where everyone is German; ending, perhaps, in a cool and silent Chinese tea-house. For every man, for every race and nation, that city is a foreign city; humming with foreign tongues and customs; and yet each and all have made themselves at home. The Germans have a German theatre and innumerable beer-gardens. The French Fall of the Bastille is celebrated with squibs and banners, and marching patriots, as noisily as the American Fourth of July. The Italians have their dear domestic quarter, with Italian caricatures in the windows, Chianti and polenta in the taverns. The Chinese are settled as in China. The goods they offer for sale are as foreign as the lettering on the sign-board of the shop: dried fish from the China seas; pale cakes and sweetmeats – the like, perhaps, once eaten by Badroubadour;[125] nuts of unfriendly shape; ambiguous, outlandish vegetables, misshapen, lean or bulbous – telling of a country where the trees are not as our trees, and the very back-garden is a cabinet of curiosities. The joss-house is hard by, heavy with incense, packed with quaint carvings and the paraphernalia of a foreign ceremonial. All these you behold, crowded together in the narrower arteries of the city, cool, sunless, a little mouldy, with the unfamiliar faces at your elbow and the high, musical sing-song of that alien language in your ears. Yet the houses are of Occidental build; the lines of a hundred telegraphs pass, thick as a ship's rigging, overhead, a kite hanging among them, perhaps, or perhaps two, one European, one Chinese, in shape and colour; mercantile Jack, the Italian fisher, the Dutch merchant, the Mexican vaquero, go hustling by; at the sunny end of the street, a thoroughfare roars with European traffic; and meanwhile, high and clear, out breaks perhaps the San Francisco fire-alarm, and people pause to count the strokes, and in the stations of the double fire-service you know that the electric bells are ringing, the traps opening and clapping to, and the engine, manned and harnessed, being whisked into the street, before the sound of the alarm has ceased to vibrate on your ear. Of all romantic places for a boy to loiter in, that Chinese quarter is the most romantic. There on a half-holiday, three doors from home, he may visit an actual foreign land, foreign in people, language, things and customs. The very barber of *The Arabian Nights* shall be at work before him, shaving heads; he shall see Aladdin playing on the streets; who knows but among those nameless vegetables the fruit of the nose tree itself[126] may be exposed for sale? And the interest is heightened with a chill of horror. Below, you hear, the cellars are alive with mystery; opium dens, where the smokers lie one above another, shelf above shelf, close-packed and grovelling in deadly stupor; the seats of unknown vices and cruelties, the prisons of unacknowledged slaves and the secret lazarettos of disease.

With all this mass of nationalities, crime is common. There are rough quarters where it is dangerous of nights; cellars of public entertainment which the wary pleasure-seeker chooses to avoid. Concealed weapons are unlawful, but the law is continually broken. One editor was shot dead while I was there; another walked the streets accompanied by a bravo, his guardian angel. I have been quietly eating a dish of oysters in a restaurant, where, not more than ten minutes after I had left, shots were exchanged and took effect; and one night, about ten o'clock, I saw a man standing watchfully at a street corner with a long Smith-and-Wesson glittering in the hand behind his back. Somebody had done something he should not, and was being looked for with a vengeance. It is odd, too, that the seat of the last vigilance committee I know of – a medieval *Vehmgericht*[127] – was none other than the Palace Hotel, the world's greatest caravan-serai, served by lifts and lit by electricity; where, in the great glazed court, a band nightly discourses music from a grove of palms. So do extremes meet in this city of contrasts: extremes of wealth and poverty, apathy and excitement, the conveniences of civilisation and the red justice of Judge Lynch.[128]

The streets lie straight up and down the hills, and straight across at right angles, these in sun, those in shadow, a trenchant pattern of gloom and glare; and what with the crisp illumination, the sea air singing in your ears, the chill and glitter, the changing aspects both of things and people, the fresh sights at every corner of your walk – sights of the bay, of Tamalpais, of steep descending streets, of the outspread city – whiffs of alien speech, sailors singing on shipboard, Chinese coolies toiling on the shore, crowds brawling all day in the street before the Stock Exchange – one brief impression follows and obliterates another, and the city leaves upon the mind no general and stable picture, but a profusion of airy and incongruous images, of the sea and shore, the east and west, the summer and the winter.

In the better parts of the most interesting city there is apt to be a touch of the commonplace. It is in the slums and suburbs that the city dilettante finds his game. And there is nothing more characteristic and original than the outlying quarters of San Francisco. The Chinese district is the most famous; but it is far from the only truffle in the pie. There is many another dingy corner, many a young antiquity, many a *terrain vague* with that stamp of quaintness that the city lover seeks and dwells on; and the indefinite prolongation of its streets, up hill and down dale, makes San Francisco a place apart. The same street in its career visits and unites so many different classes of society, here echoing with drays, there lying decorously silent between the mansions of Bonanza millionaires, to founder at last among the drifting sands beside Lone Mountain cemetery, or die out among the sheds and lumber of the north. Thus you may be struck with a spot, set it down for the most romantic of the city, and, glancing at the name-plate, find it is in the same street that you yourself inhabit in another quarter of the town.

The great net of straight thoroughfares lying at right angles, east and west and north and south, over the shoulders of Nob Hill, the hill of palaces, must certainly be counted the best part of San Francisco. It is there that the millionaires are gathered together, vying with each other in display. From thence, looking down over the business wards of the city, we can descry a building with a little belfry, and that is the Stock Exchange, the heart of San Francisco: a great pump we might call it, continually pumping up the savings of the lower quarters into the pockets of the millionaires upon the hill. But these same thoroughfares that enjoy for a while so elegant a destiny have their lines prolonged into more unpleasant places. Some meet their fate in the sands; some must take a cruise in the ill-famed China quarters; some run into the sea; some perish unwept among pigsties and rubbish-heaps.

Nob Hill comes, of right, in the place of honour; but the two other hills of San Francisco are more entertaining to explore. On both there are a world of old wooden houses snoozing together all forgotten. Some are of the quaintest design, others only romantic by neglect and age. Some have been almost undermined by new thoroughfares, and sit high up on the margin of the sandy cutting, only to be reached by stairs. Some are curiously painted, and I have seen one at least with ancient carvings panelled in its wall. Surely they are not of Californian building, but far voyagers from round the stormy Horn, like those who sent for them and dwelt in them at first. Brought to be the favourites of the wealthy, they have sunk in these poor, forgotten districts, where, like old town toasts, they keep each other silently in countenance. Telegraph Hill and Rincon Hill, these are the two dozing quarters that I recommend to the city dilettante. There stand these forgotten houses, enjoying the unbroken sun and quiet. There, if there were such an author, would the San Francisco Fortuné de Boisgobey[129] pitch the first chapter of his mystery. But the first is the quainter of the two, and commands, moreover, a noble view. As it stands at the turn of the bay, its skirts are all waterside, and round from North Reach to the Bay Front you can follow doubtful paths from one quaint corner to another. Everywhere the same tumbledown decay and sloppy progress, new things yet unmade, old things tottering to their fall; everywhere the same out-at-elbows, many-nationed loungers at dim, irregular grog-shops; everywhere the same sea air and isleted sea-prospect; and, for a last and more romantic note, you have on the one hand Tamalpais standing high in the blue air, and on the other the tail of that long alignment of three-masted, full-rigged, deep-sea ships that make a forest of spars along the eastern front of San Francisco. In no other port is such a navy congregated. For the coast trade is so trifling, and the ocean trade from round the Horn so large, that the smaller ships are swallowed up, and can do nothing to confuse the majestic order of these merchant princes. In an age when the ship-of-the-line is already a thing of the past, and we can never again hope to go coasting in a cock-boat between the 'wooden walls' of a squadron at anchor, there is perhaps no place on earth where the power and beauty of sea architecture can be so perfectly enjoyed as in this bay.

The Silverado Squatters

The scene of this little book is on a high mountain. There are, indeed, many higher; there are many of a nobler outline. It is no place of pilgrimage for the summary globe-trotter; but to one who lives upon its sides, Mount St Helena soon becomes a centre of interest. It is the Mont Blanc of one section of the Californian Coast Range, none of its near neighbours rising to one-half its altitude. It looks down on much green, intricate country. It feeds in the spring-time many splashing brooks. From its summit you must have an excellent lesson of geography:[130] seeing, to the south, San Francisco Bay, with Tamalpais on the one hand and Monte Diablo on the other; to the west and thirty miles away, the open ocean; eastward, across the cornlands and thick tule swamps of Sacramento Valley, to where the Central Pacific railroad begins to climb the sides of the Sierras; and northward, for what I know, the white head of Shasta[131] looking down on Oregon. Three counties, Napa County, Lake County and Sonoma County, march across its cliffy shoulders. Its naked peak stands nearly four thousand five hundred feet above the sea; its sides are fringed with forest; and the soil, where it is bare, glows warm with cinnabar.[132]

Life in its shadow goes rustically forward. Bucks and bears and rattlesnakes and former mining operations are the staple of men's talk. Agriculture has only begun to mount above the valley. And though in a few years from now the whole district may be smiling with farms, passing trains shaking the mountain to the heart, many-windowed hotels lighting up the night like factories and a prosperous city occupying the site of sleepy Calistoga; yet in the meantime, around the foot of that mountain the silence of nature reigns in a great measure unbroken, and the people of hill and valley go sauntering about their business as in the days before the flood.

To reach Mount St Helena from San Francisco, the traveller has twice to cross the bay:[133] once by the busy Oakland Ferry, and again, after an hour or so of the railway, from Vallejo junction to Vallejo.

Thence he takes rail once more to mount the long green strath of Napa Valley.[134]

In all the contractions and expansions of that inland sea, the Bay of San Francisco, there can be few drearier scenes than the Vallejo Ferry. Bald shores and a low, bald islet enclose the sea; through the narrows the tide bubbles, muddy like a river. When we made the passage (bound, although yet we knew it not, for Silverado) the steamer jumped, and the black buoys were dancing in the jabble; the ocean breeze blew killing chill; and, although the upper sky was still unflecked with vapour, the sea fogs were pouring in from seaward, over the hilltops of Marin County, in one great, shapeless, silver cloud.

South Vallejo is typical of many Californian towns. It was a blunder; the site has proved untenable; and, although it is still such a young place by the scale of Europe, it has already begun to be deserted for its neighbour and namesake, North Vallejo. A long pier, a number of drinking saloons, a hotel of a great size, marshy pools where the frogs keep up their croaking and, even at high noon, the entire absence of any human face or voice – these are the marks of South Vallejo. Yet there was a tall building beside the pier, labelled the Star Flour Mills, and sea-going, full-rigged ships lay close along shore, waiting for their cargo. Soon these would be plunging round the Horn, soon the flour from the Star Flour Mills would be landed on the wharves of Liverpool. For that, too, is one of England's outposts; thither, to this gaunt mill, across the Atlantic and Pacific deeps and round about the icy Horn, this crowd of great, three-masted, deep-sea ships comes, bringing nothing, and returns with bread.

The Frisby House, for that was the name of the hotel, was a place of fallen fortunes, like the town. It was now given up to labourers, and partly ruinous. At dinner there was the ordinary display of what is called in the West a *two-bit house*: the tablecloth checked red and white, the plague of flies, the wire hencoops over the dishes, the great variety and invariable vileness of the food and the rough coatless men devouring it in silence. In our bedroom, the stove would not burn, though it would smoke; and while one window would not open, the other would not shut. There was a view on a bit of empty road, a few dark houses, a donkey wandering with its shadow on a slope, and a blink of sea, with a tall ship lying anchored in the moonlight. All about that dreary inn frogs sang their ungainly chorus.

Early the next morning we mounted the hill along a wooden footway, bridging one marish spot after another. Here and there, as we ascended, we passed a house embowered in white roses. More of the bay became apparent, and soon the blue peak of Tamalpais rose above the green level of the island opposite. It told us we were still but a little way from the city of the Golden Gates, already, at that hour, beginning to awake among the sandhills. It called to us over the waters as with the voice of a bird. Its stately head, blue as a sapphire on the paler azure of the sky, spoke to us of wider outlooks and the bright Pacific. For Tamalpais stands sentry, like a lighthouse, over the Golden Gates, between the bay and the open ocean, and looks down indifferently on both. Even as we saw and hailed it from Vallejo, seamen, far out at sea, were scanning it with shaded eyes; and, as if to answer to the thought, one of the great ships below began silently to clothe herself with white sails, homeward bound for England.

For some way beyond Vallejo the railway led us through bald green pastures. On the west the rough highlands of Marin shut off the ocean; in the midst, in long, straggling, gleaming arms, the bay died out among the grass; there were few trees and few enclosures; the sun shone wide over open uplands, the displumed hills stood clear against the sky. But by and by these hills began to draw nearer on either hand, and first thicket and then wood began to clothe their sides; and soon we were away from all signs of the sea's neighbourhood, mounting an inland, irrigated valley. A great variety of oaks stood, now severally, now in a becoming grove, among the fields and vineyards. The towns were compact, in about equal proportions, of bright, new wooden houses and great and growing forest trees; and the chapel bell on the engine sounded most festally that sunny Sunday, as we drew up at one green town after another, with the townsfolk trooping in their Sunday's best to see the strangers, with the sun sparkling on the clean houses, and great domes of foliage humming overhead in the breeze.

This pleasant Napa Valley is, at its north end, blockaded by our mountain. There, at Calistoga, the railroad ceases, and the traveller who intends faring farther, to the Geysers or to the springs in Lake County, must cross the spurs of the mountain by stage. Thus, Mount St Helena is not only a summit, but a frontier; and, up to the time of writing, it has stayed the progress of the iron horse.

In the Valley

CHAPTER I

Calistoga

It is difficult for a European to imagine Calistoga, the whole place is so new, and of such an accidental pattern; the very name, I hear, was invented at a supper-party by the man who found the springs.

The railroad and the highway come up the valley about parallel to one another. The street of Calistoga joins the perpendicular to both – a wide street, with bright, clean, low houses, here and there a verandah over the sidewalk, here and there a horse-post, here and there lounging townsfolk. Other streets are marked out, and most likely named; for these towns in the New World begin with a firm resolve to grow larger, Washington and Broadway, and then First and Second, and so forth, being boldly plotted out as soon as the community indulges in a plan. But, in the meanwhile, all the life and most of the houses of Calistoga are concentrated upon that street between the railway station and the road. I never heard it called by any name, but I will hazard a guess that it is either Washington or Broadway. Here are the blacksmith's, the chemist's, the general merchant's, and Kong Sam Kee, the Chinese laundryman's; here, probably, is the office of the local paper (for the place has a paper – they all have papers); and here certainly is one of the hotels, Cheese-borough's, whence the daring Foss, a man dear to legend, starts his horses for the Geysers.

It must be remembered that we are here in a land of stage-drivers and highwaymen: a land, in that sense, like England a hundred years ago. The highway robber – road-agent, he is quaintly called – is still busy in these parts. The fame of Vasquez is still young. Only a few years go, the Lakeport stage was robbed a mile or two from Calistoga. In 1879, the dentist of Mendocino City, fifty miles away upon the coast, suddenly threw off the garments of his trade, like Grindoff, in *The Miller and his Men*, and flamed forth in his second dress as a captain of banditti. A great robbery was followed by a long chase, a chase of days if not of weeks, among the intricate hill-country; and the chase was followed by much desultory fighting, in which several – and the dentist, I believe, amongst the number – bit the dust. The grass was springing for the first time, nourished upon their blood, when I arrived in Calistoga. I am reminded of another highwayman of that same year. 'He had been unwell,' so ran his humorous defence, 'and the doctor told him to take something, so he took the express-box.'

The cultus of the stagecoachman always flourishes highest where there are thieves on the road, and where the guard travels armed, and the stage is not only a link between country and city, and the vehicle of news, but has a faint warfaring aroma, like a man who should be brother to a soldier. California boasts her famous stage-drivers, and among the famous Foss is not forgotten.[135] Along the unfenced, abominable mountain roads, he launches his team with small regard to human life or the doctrine of probabilities. Flinching travellers, who behold themselves coasting eternity at every corner, look with natural admiration at their driver's huge, impassive, fleshy countenance. He has the very face for the driver in Sam Weller's anecdote, who upset the election party at the required point. Wonderful tales are current of his readiness and skill. One in particular, of how one of his horses fell at a ticklish passage of the road, and how Foss let slip the reins, and, driving over the fallen animal, arrived at the next stage with only three. This I relate as I heard it, without guarantee.

I only saw Foss once, though, strange as it may sound, I have twice talked with him. He lives out of Calistoga, at a ranch called Fossville. One evening, after he was long gone home, I dropped into Cheese-borough's, and was asked if I should like to speak with Mr Foss. Supposing that the interview was impossible, and that I was merely called upon to subscribe the general sentiment, I boldly answered 'Yes.' Next moment, I had one instrument at my ear, another at my mouth and found myself, with nothing in the world to say, conversing with a man several miles off among desolate hills. Foss rapidly and somewhat plaintively brought the conversation to an end; and he returned to his night's grog at Fossville, while I strolled forth again on Calistoga high street. But it was an odd thing that here, on what we are accustomed to consider the very skirts of civilisation, I should have used the telephone for the first time in my civilised career. So it goes in these young countries: telephones, and telegraphs, and news-papers, and advertisements running far ahead among the Indians and the grizzly bears.

Alone, on the other side of the railway, stands the Springs Hotel, with its attendant cottages. The floor of the valley is extremely level to the very roots of the hills; only here and there a hillock, crowned with pines, rises like the barrow of some chieftain famed in war; and right against one of these hillocks is the Springs Hotel – is or was, for since I was there the place has been destroyed by fire and has risen again from its ashes. A lawn runs about the house, and the lawn is in its turn surrounded by a system of little five-roomed cottages, each with a verandah and a weedy palm before the door. Some of the cottages are let to residents, and these are wreathed in flowers. The rest are occupied by ordinary visitors to the hotel; and a very pleasant way this is, by which you have a little country cottage of your own, without domestic burthens, and by the day or week.

The whole neighbourhood of Mount St Helena is full of sulphur and of boiling springs. The Geysers are famous; they were the great health resort of the Indians before the coming of the whites. Lake County is dotted with spas; Hot Springs and White Sulphur Springs are the names of two stations on the Napa Valley railroad; and Calistoga itself seems to repose on a mere film above a boiling, subterranean lake.[136] At one end of the hotel enclosure are the springs from which it takes its name, hot enough to scald a child seriously while I was there. At the other end, the tenant of a cottage sank a well, and there also the water came up boiling. It keeps this end of the valley as warm as toast. I have gone across to the hotel a little after five in the morning, when a sea fog from the Pacific was hanging thick and grey, and dark and dirty overhead, and found the thermometer had been up before me, and had already climbed among the nineties; and in the stress of the day it was sometimes too hot to move about.

But in spite of this heat from above and below, doing one on both sides, Calistoga was a pleasant place to dwell in; beautifully green, for it was then that favoured moment in the Californian year when the rains are over and the dusty summer has not yet set in; often visited by fresh airs, now from the mountain, now across Sonoma from the sea; very quiet, very idle, very silent but for the breezes and the cattle bells afield. And there was something satisfactory in the sight of that great mountain that enclosed us to the north: whether it stood, robed in sunshine, quaking to its topmost pinnacle with the heat and brightness of the day; or whether it set itself to weaving vapours, wisp after wisp growing, trembling, fleeting and fading in the blue.

The tangled, woody, and almost trackless foothills that enclose the valley, shutting it off from Sonoma on the west and from Yolo on the east – rough as they were in outline, dug out by winter streams, crowned by cliffy bluffs and nodding pine trees – were dwarfed into satellites by the bulk and bearing of Mount St Helena. She over-towered them by two-thirds of her own stature. She excelled them by the boldness of her profile. Her great bald summit, clear of trees and pasture, a cairn of quartz and cinnabar, rejected kinship with the dark and shaggy wilderness of lesser hilltops.

CHAPTER 2

The Petrified Forest

We drove off from the Springs Hotel about three in the afternoon. The sun warmed me to the heart. A broad, cool wind streamed pauselessly down the valley, laden with perfume. Up at the top stood Mount St Helena, a bulk of mountain, bare atop, with tree-fringed spurs, and radiating warmth. Once we saw it framed in a grove of tall and exquisitely graceful white oaks, in line and colour a finished composition. We passed a cow stretched by the roadside, her bell slowly beating time to the movement of her ruminating jaws, her big red face crawled over by half a dozen flies, a monument of content.

A little farther, and we struck to the left up a mountain road, and for two hours threaded one valley after another, green, tangled, full of noble timber, giving us every now and again a sight of Mount St Helena and the blue hilly distance, and crossed by many streams, through which we splashed to the carriage-step. To the right or the left, there was scarce any trace of man but the road we followed; I think we passed but one ranchero's house in the whole distance, and that was closed and smokeless. But we had the society of these bright streams – dazzlingly clear, as is their wont, splashing from the wheels in diamonds, and striking a lively coolness through the sunshine. And what with the innumerable variety of greens, the masses of foliage tossing in the breeze, the glimpses of distance, the descents into seemingly impenetrable thickets, the continual dodging of the road which made haste to plunge again into the covert, we had a fine sense of woods, and springtime, and the open air.

Our driver gave me a lecture by the way on Californian trees – a thing I was much in need of, having fallen among painters who know the name of nothing, and Mexicans who know the name of nothing in English. He taught me the madrona, the manzanita, the buck-eye, the maple; he showed me the crested mountain quail; he showed me where some young redwoods were already spiring heavenwards from the ruins of the old; for in this district all had already perished: redwoods and redskins, the two noblest indigenous living things, alike condemned.

At length, in a lonely dell, we came on a huge wooden gate with a sign upon it like an inn: 'The Petrified Forest. Proprietor: C. Evans', ran the legend.[137] Within, on a knoll of sward, was the house of the proprietor, and another smaller house hard by to serve as a museum, where photographs and petrifactions were retailed. It was a pure little isle of touristry among these solitary hills.

The proprietor was a brave old white-faced Swede. He had wandered this way, heaven knows how, and taken up his acres – I forget how many years ago – all alone, bent double with sciatica, and with six bits in his pocket and an axe upon his shoulder. Long, useless years of seafaring had thus discharged him at the end, penniless and sick. Without doubt he had tried his luck at the diggings, and got no good from that; without doubt he had loved the bottle, and lived the life of Jack ashore. But at the end of these adventures, here he came; and, the place hitting his fancy, down he sat to make a new life of it, far from crimps and the salt sea. And the very sight of his ranch had done him good. It was 'the handsomest spot in the Californy mountains'. 'Isn't it handsome, now?' he said. Every penny he makes goes into that ranch to make it handsomer. Then the climate, with the sea-breeze every afternoon in the hottest summer weather, had gradually cured the sciatica; and his sister and niece were now domesticated with him for company – or, rather, the niece came only once in the two days, teaching music the meanwhile in the valley. And then, for a last piece of luck, 'the handsomest spot in the Californy mountains' had produced a petrified forest, which Mr Evans now shows at the modest figure of half a dollar a head, or two-thirds of his capital when he first came there with an axe and a sciatica.

This tardy favourite of fortune – hobbling a little, I think, as if in memory of the sciatica, but with not a trace that I can remember of the sea – thoroughly ruralised from head to foot, proceeded to escort us up the hill behind his house.

'Who first found the forest?' asked my wife.

'The first? I was that man,' said he. 'I was cleaning up the pasture for my beasts, when I found *this*' – kicking a great redwood seven feet in diameter, that lay there on its side, hollow heart, clinging lumps of bark, all changed into grey stone, with veins of quartz between what had been the layers of the wood.

'Were you surprised?'

'Surprised? No! What would I be surprised about? What did I know about petrifactions – following the sea? Petrifaction! There was no such word in my language! I knew about putrifaction, though! I thought it was a stone; so would you, if you was cleaning up pasture.'

And now he had a theory of his own, which I did not quite grasp, except that the trees had not 'grewed' there. But he mentioned, with evident pride, that he differed from all the scientific people who had visited the spot; and he flung about such words as 'tufa' and 'silica' with careless freedom.

When I mentioned I was from Scotland, 'My old country,' he said; 'my old country' – with a smiling look and a tone of real affection in his voice. I was mightily surprised, for he was obviously Scandinavian, and begged him to explain. It seemed he had learned his English and done nearly all his sailing in Scotch ships. 'Out of Glasgow,' said he, 'or Greenock; but that's all the same – they all hail from Glasgow.' And he was so pleased with me for being a Scotsman, and his adopted compatriot, that he made me a present of a very beautiful piece of petrifaction – I believe the most beautiful and portable he had.

Here was a man, at least, who was a Swede, a Scot and an American, acknowledging some kind allegiance to three lands. Mr Wallace's Scoto-Circassian will not fail to come before the reader. I have myself met and spoken with a Fifeshire German, whose combination of abominable accents struck me dumb. But, indeed, I think we all belong to many countries. And perhaps this habit of much travel, and the engendering of scattered friendships, may prepare the euthanasia of ancient nations.

And the forest itself? Well, on a tangled, briery hillside – for the pasture would bear a little further cleaning up, to my eyes – there lie scattered thickly various lengths of petrified trunk, such as the one already mentioned. It is very curious, of course, and ancient enough, if that were all. Doubtless, the heart of the geologist beats quicker at the sight; but, for my part, I was mightily unmoved. Sightseeing is the art of disappointment.[138]

> There's nothing under heaven so blue,
> That's fairly worth the travelling to.[139]

But, fortunately, Heaven rewards us with many agreeable prospects and adventures by the way; and sometimes, when we go out to see a petrified forest, prepares a far more delightful curiosity, in the form of Mr Evans, whom may all prosperity attend throughout a long and green old age.

CHAPTER 3

Napa Wine

I was interested in Californian wine. Indeed, I am interested in all wines, and have been all my life, from the raisin wine that a school-fellow kept secreted in his play-box up to my last discovery, those notable Valtellines that once shone upon the board of Caesar.

Some of us, kind old Pagans, watch with dread the shadows falling on the age: how the unconquerable worm[140] invades the sunny terraces of France, and Bordeaux is no more, and the Rhone a mere Arabia Petraea.[141] Château Neuf is dead, and I have never tasted it; Hermitage – a hermitage indeed from all life's sorrows – lies expiring by the river. And in the place of these imperial elixirs, beautiful to every sense, gem-hued, flower-scented, dream-compellers – behold upon the quays at Cette the chemicals arrayed; behold the analyst at Marseilles, raising hands in obsecration, attesting god Lyaeus, and the vats staved in, and the dishonest wines poured forth among the sea. It is not Pan only; Bacchus, too, is dead.

If wine is to withdraw its most poetic countenance, the sun of the white dinner-cloth, a deity to be invoked by two or three, all fervent, hushing their talk, degusting tenderly and storing reminiscences – for a bottle of good wine, like a good act, shines ever in the retrospect – if wine is to desert us, go thy ways, old Jack! Now we begin to have compunctions, and look back at the brave bottles squandered upon dinner-parties, where the guests drank grossly, discussing politics the while, and even the schoolboy 'took his whack', like liquorice water. And at the same time, we look timidly forward, with a spark of hope, to where the new lands, already weary of producing gold, begin to green with vineyards. A nice point in human history falls to be decided by Californian and Australian wines.

Wine in California is still in the experimental stage; and when you taste a vintage, grave economical questions are involved. The beginning of vine-planting is like the beginning of mining for precious metals: the wine-grower also 'prospects'. One corner of land after another is tried with one kind of grape after another. This is a failure; that is better; a third best. So, bit by bit, they grope about for their Clos Vougeot and Lafite. Those lodes and pockets of earth, more precious than the precious ores, that yield inimitable fragrance and soft fire; those virtuous Bonanzas, where the soil has sublimated under sun and stars to something finer, and the wine is bottled poetry: these still lie undiscovered; chaparral conceals, thicket embowers them; the miner chips the rock and wanders farther, and the grizzly muses undisturbed. But there they bide their hour, awaiting their Columbus; and nature nurses and prepares them. The smack of Californian earth shall linger on the palate of your grandson.

Meanwhile the wine is merely a good wine; the best that I have tasted better than a Beaujolais, and not unlike. But the trade is poor; it lives from hand to mouth, putting its all into experiments, and forced to sell its vintages. To find one properly matured, and bearing its own name, is to be fortune's favourite.

Bearing its own name, I say, and dwell upon the innuendo.

'You want to know why California wine is not drunk in the States?' a San Francisco wine merchant said to me, after he had shown me through his premises. 'Well, here's the reason.'

And opening a large cupboard, fitted with many little drawers, he proceeded to shower me all over with a great variety of gorgeously tinted labels, blue, red or yellow, stamped with crown or coronet, and hailing from such a profusion of *clos* and *châteaux*, that a single department could scarce have furnished forth the names. But it was strange that all looked unfamiliar.

'Chateau X—?' said I. 'I never heard of that.'

'I dare say not,' said he. 'I had been reading one of X—'s novels.'

They were all castles in Spain! But that sure enough is the reason why California wine is not drunk in the States.

Napa Valley has been long a seat of the wine-growing industry. It did not here begin, as it does too often, in the low valley lands along the river, but took at once to the rough foothills, where alone it can expect to prosper. A basking inclination, and stones, to be a reservoir of the day's heat, seem necessary to the soil for wine; the grossness of the earth must be evaporated, its marrow daily melted and refined for ages; until at length these clods that break below our footing, and to the eye appear but common earth, are truly and to the perceiving mind, a masterpiece of nature. The dust of Richebourg, which the

wind carries away, what an apotheosis of the dust! Not man himself
can seem a stranger child of that brown, friable powder, than the
blood and sun in that old flask behind the faggots.

A Californian vineyard, one of man's outposts in the wilderness, has
features of its own. There is nothing here to remind you of the Rhine
or Rhône, of the low Côte d'Or, or the infamous and scabby deserts of
Champagne; but all is green, solitary, covert. We visited two of them,
Mr Schram's and Mr McEckron's, sharing the same glen.

Some way down the valley below Calistoga, we turned sharply to
the south and plunged into the thick of the wood. A rude trail rapidly
mounting; a little stream tinkling by on the one hand, big enough
perhaps after the rains, but already yielding up its life; overhead and
on all sides a bower of green and tangled thicket, still fragrant and
still flower-bespangled by the early season, where thimble-berry
played the part of our English hawthorn, and the buckeyes were
putting forth their twisted horns of blossom: through all this, we
struggled toughly upwards, canted to and fro by the roughness of the
trail, and continually switched across the face by sprays of leaf or
blossom. The last is no great inconvenience at home; but here in
California it is a matter of some moment. For in all woods and by
every wayside there prospers an abominable shrub or weed called
poison-oak, whose very neighbourhood is venomous to some, and
whose actual touch is avoided by the most impervious.

The two houses, with their vineyards, stood each in a green niche
of its own in this steep and narrow forest dell. Though they were so
near, there was already a good difference in level; and Mr McEckron's
head must be a long way under the feet of Mr Schram. No more had
been cleared than was necessary for cultivation; close around each
oasis ran the tangled wood; the glen enfolds them; there they lie
basking in sun and silence, concealed from all but the clouds and the
mountain birds.

Mr McEckron's is a bachelor establishment; a little bit of a wooden
house, a small cellar hard by in the hillside, and a patch of vines
planted and tended single-handed by himself. He had but recently
begun; his vines were young, his business young also; but I thought
he had the look of the man who succeeds. He hailed from Greenock:
he remembered his father putting him inside Mons Meg, and that
touched me home; and we exchanged a word or two of Scotch,
which pleased me more than you would fancy.

Mr Schram's, on the other hand, is the oldest vineyard in the
valley, eighteen years old, I think; yet he began a penniless barber,

and even after he had broken ground up here with his black malvoisies, continued for long to tramp the valley with his razor. Now, his place is the picture of prosperity: stuffed birds in the verandah, cellars far dug into the hillside, and resting on pillars like a bandit's cave – all trimness, varnish, flowers and sunshine, among the tangled wild-wood. Stout, smiling Mrs Schram, who has been to Europe and apparently all about the States for pleasure, entertained Fanny in the verandah, while I was tasting wines in the cellar. To Mr Schram this was a solemn office; his serious gusto warmed my heart; prosperity had not yet wholly banished a certain neophite and girlish trepidation, and he followed every sip and read my face with proud anxiety. I tasted all. I tasted every variety and shade of Schramberger: red and white Schramberger, Burgundy Schramberger, Schramberger Hock, Schramberger Golden Chasselas, the latter with a notable bouquet, and I fear to think how many more. Much of it goes to London – most, I think; and Mr Schram has a great notion of the English taste.

In this wild spot, I did not feel the sacredness of ancient cultivation. It was still raw, it was no Marathon, and no Johannisberg; yet the stirring sunlight, and the growing vines, and the vats and bottles in the cavern, made a pleasant music for the mind. Here, also, earth's cream was being skimmed and garnered; and the London customers can taste, such as it is, the tang of the earth in this green valley. So local, so quintessential is a wine, that it seems the very birds in the verandah might communicate a flavour, and that romantic cellar influence the bottle next to be uncorked in Pimlico, and the smile of jolly Mr Schram might mantle in the glass.

But these are but experiments. All things in this new land are moving farther on: the wine-vats and the miner's blasting tools but picket for a night, like Bedouin pavilions; and tomorrow, to fresh woods! This stir of change and these perpetual echoes of the moving footfall, haunt the land. Men move eternally, still chasing Fortune; and, fortune found, still wander. As we drove back to Calistoga, the road lay empty of mere passengers, but its green side was dotted with the camps of travelling families: one cumbered with a great wagonful of household stuff, settlers going to occupy a ranch they had taken up in Mendocino, or perhaps Tehama County; another, a party in dust coats, men and women, whom we found camped in a grove on the roadside, all on pleasure bent, with a Chinaman to cook for them, and who waved their hands to us as we drove by.

CHAPTER 4

The Scot Abroad

A few pages back, I wrote that a man belonged, in these days, to a variety of countries; but the old land is still the true love, the others are but pleasant infidelities. Scotland is indefinable; it has no unity except upon the map. Two languages, many dialects, innumerable forms of piety, and countless local patriotisms and prejudices, part us among ourselves more widely than the extreme east and west of that great continent of America. When I am at home, I feel a man from Glasgow to be something like a rival, a man from Barra to be more than half a foreigner. Yet let us meet in some far country, and, whether we hail from the braes of Manor or the braes of Mar, some ready-made affection joins us on the instant. It is not race. Look at us. One is Norse, one Celtic, and another Saxon. It is not community of tongue. We have it not among ourselves; and we have it almost to perfection, with English, or Irish, or American. It is no tie of faith, for we detest each other's errors. And yet somewhere, deep down in the heart of each one of us, something yearns for the old land, and the old kindly people.

Of all mysteries of the human heart, this is perhaps the most inscrutable. There is no special loveliness in that grey country, with its rainy, sea-beat archipelago; its fields of dark mountains; its unsightly places, black with coal; its treeless, sour, unfriendly looking cornlands; its quaint, grey, castled city, where the bells clash of a Sunday, and the wind squalls, and the salt showers fly and beat. I do not even know if I desire to live there; but let me hear, in some far land, a kindred voice sing out, 'Oh, why left I my hame?' and it seems at once as if no beauty under the kind heavens, and no society of the wise and good, can repay me for my absence from my country. And though I think I would rather die elsewhere, yet in my heart of hearts I long to be buried among good Scots clods. I will say it fairly, it grows on me with every year: there are no stars so lovely as Edinburgh street-lamps. When I forget thee, Auld Reekie,[142] may my right hand forget its cunning!

The happiest lot on earth is to be born a Scotchman. You must pay for it in many ways, as for all other advantages on earth. You have to learn the paraphrases[143] and the shorter catechism;[144] you generally take to drink; your youth, as far as I can find out, is a time of louder war against society, of more outcry and tears and turmoil, than if you had been born, for instance, in England. But somehow life is warmer and closer; the hearth burns more redly; the lights of home shine softer on the rainy street; the very names, endeared in verse and music, cling nearer round our hearts. An Englishman may meet an Englishman tomorrow, upon Chimborazo,[145] and neither of them care; but when the Scotch wine-grower told me of Mons Meg, it was like magic.

> From the dim shieling on the misty island
>   Mountains divide us, and a world of seas;
> Yet still our hearts are true, our hearts are Highland,
>   And we, in dreams, behold the Hebrides.[146]

And, Highland and Lowland, all our hearts are Scotch.

Only a few days after I had seen McEckron, a message reached me in my cottage. It was a Scotchman who had come down a long way from the hills to market. He had heard there was a countryman in Calistoga, and came round to the hotel to see him. We said a few words to each other; we had not much to say – should never have seen each other had we stayed at home, separated alike in space and in society; and then we shook hands, and he went his way again to his ranch among the hills, and that was all.

Another Scotchman there was, a resident, who for the more love of the common country, douce, serious, religious man, drove me all about the valley, and took as much interest in me as if I had been his son: more, perhaps; for the son has faults too keenly felt, while the abstract countryman is perfect – like a whiff of peats.

And there was yet another. Upon him I came suddenly, as he was calmly entering my cottage, his mind quite evidently bent on plunder: a man of about fifty, filthy, ragged, roguish, with a chimney-pot hat and a tail coat, and a pursing of his mouth that might have been envied by an elder of the kirk. He had just such a face as I have seen a dozen times behind the plate.

'Hello, sir!' I cried. 'Where are you going?'

He turned round without a quiver.

'You're a Scotchman, sir?' he said gravely. 'So am I; I come from Aberdeen. This is my card,' presenting me with a piece of pasteboard which he had raked out of some gutter in the period of the rains. 'I was just examining this palm,' he continued, indicating the misbegotten plant before our door, 'which is the largest specimen I have yet observed in Califoarnia.'

There were four or five larger within sight. But where was the use of argument? He produced a tape-line, made me help him to measure the tree at the level of the ground, and entered the figures in a large and filthy pocketbook, all with the gravity of Solomon. He then thanked me profusely, remarking that such little services were due between countrymen; shook hands with me, 'for auld lang syne', as he said; and took himself solemnly away, radiating dirt and humbug as he went.

A month or two after this encounter of mine, there came a Scot to Sacramento – perhaps from Aberdeen. Anyway, there never was anyone more Scotch in this wide world. He could sing and dance – and drink, I presume; and he played the pipes with vigour and success. All the Scotch in Sacramento became infatuated with him, and spent their spare time and money driving him about in an open cab, between drinks, while he blew himself scarlet at the pipes. This is a very sad story. After he had borrowed money from everyone, he and his pipes suddenly disappeared from Sacramento, and when I last heard, the police were looking for him.

I cannot say how this story amused me, when I felt myself so thoroughly ripe on both sides to be duped in the same way.

It is at least a curious thing, to conclude that the races which wander widest, Jews and Scotch, should be the most clannish in the world. But perhaps these two are cause and effect: 'For ye were strangers in the land of Egypt.'[147]

With the Children of Israel

CHAPTER I

To Introduce Mr Kelmar

One thing in this new country very particularly strikes a stranger, and that is the number of antiquities. Already there have been many cycles of population succeeding each other, and passing away and leaving behind them relics. These, standing on into changed times, strike the imagination as forcibly as any pyramid or feudal tower. The towns, like the vineyards, are experimentally founded: they grow great and prosper by passing occasions; and when the lode comes to an end, and the miners move elsewhere, the town remains behind them, like Palmyra[148] in the desert. I suppose there are, in no country in the world, so many deserted towns as here in California.

The whole neighbourhood of Mount St Helena, now so quiet and sylvan, was once alive with mining camps and villages. Here there would be two thousand souls under canvas; there one thousand or fifteen hundred ensconced, as if for ever, in a town of comfortable houses. But the luck had failed, the mines petered out; and the army of miners had departed, and left this quarter of the world to the rattlesnakes and deer and grizzlies, and to the slower but steadier advance of husbandry.

It was with an eye on one of these deserted places, Pine Flat, on the Geysers road, that we had come first to Calistoga. There is something singularly enticing in the idea of going, rent-free, into a ready-made house. And to the British merchant, sitting at home at ease, it may appear that, with such a roof over your head and a spring of clear water hard by, the whole problem of the squatter's existence would be solved. Food, however, has yet to be considered. I will go as far as most people on tinned meats; some of the brightest moments of my life were passed over tinned mulligatawney in the cabin of a sixteen-ton schooner, storm-stayed in Portree Bay; but after suitable experiments, I pronounce authoritatively that man cannot live by tins alone. Fresh meat must be had on an occasion. It is true that the great Foss, driving by along the Geysers road, wooden-faced, but glorified with legend, might have been induced to bring us meat, but the great Foss could hardly bring us milk. To take a cow would have involved taking a field of grass and a milkmaid; after which it would have been hardly worth while to pause, and we might have added to our colony a flock of sheep and an experienced butcher.

It is really very disheartening how we depend on other people in this life. *Mihi est propositum*, as you may see by the motto, *id quod regibus*;[149] and behold it cannot be carried out, unless I find a neighbour rolling in cattle.

Now, my principal adviser in this matter was one whom I will call Kelmar.[150] That was not what he called himself, but as soon as I set eyes on him, I knew it was or ought to be his name; I am sure it will be his name among the angels. Kelmar was the store-keeper, a Russian Jew, good-natured, in a very thriving way of business, and, on equal terms, one of the most serviceable of men. He also had something of the expression of a Scotch country elder, who, by some peculiarity, should chance to be a Hebrew. He had a projecting under lip, with which he continually smiled, or rather smirked. Mrs Kelmar was a singularly kind woman; and the oldest son had quite a dark and romantic bearing, and might be heard on summer evenings playing sentimental airs on the violin.

I had no idea, at the time I made his acquaintance, what an important person Kelmar was. But the Jew store-keepers of California, profiting at once by the needs and habits of the people, have made themselves in too many cases the tyrants of the rural population. Credit is offered, is pressed on the new customer, and when once he is beyond his depth, the tune changes, and he is from thenceforth a white slave. I believe, even from the little I saw, that Kelmar, if he choose to put on the screw, could send half the settlers packing in a radius of seven or eight miles round Calistoga. These are continually paying him, but are never suffered to get out of debt. He palms dull goods upon them, for they dare not refuse to buy; he goes and dines with them when he is on an outing, and no man is loudlier welcomed; he is their family friend, the director of their business, and, to a degree elsewhere unknown in modern days, their king.

For some reason, Kelmar always shook his head at the mention of Pine Flat, and for some days I thought he disapproved of the whole scheme and was proportionately sad. One fine morning, however, he met me, wreathed in smiles. He had found the very place for me – Silverado, another old mining town, right up the mountain. Rufe Hanson, the hunter, could take care of us – fine people the Hansons;

we should be close to the Toll House, where the Lakeport stage called daily; it was the best place for my health, besides. Rufe had been consumptive, and was now quite a strong man, ain't it? In short, the place and all its accompaniments seemed made for us on purpose.

He took me to his back door, whence, as from every point of Calistoga, Mount St Helena could be seen towering in the air. There, in the nick, just where the eastern foothills joined the mountain, and she herself began to rise above the zone of forest – there was Silverado. The name had already pleased me; the high station pleased me still more. I began to enquire with some eagerness. It was but a little while ago that Silverado was a great place. The mine – a silver mine, of course – had promised great things. There was quite a lively population, with several hotels and boarding-houses; and Kelmar himself had opened a branch store, and done extremely well – 'Ain't it?' he said, appealing to his wife. And she said, 'Yes; extremely well.' Now there was no one living in the town but Rufe the hunter; and once more I heard Rufe's praises by the yard, and this time sung in chorus.

I could not help perceiving at the time that there was something underneath; that no unmixed desire to have us comfortably settled had inspired the Kelmars with this flow of words. But I was impatient to be gone, to be about my kingly project; and when we were offered seats in Kelmar's wagon, I accepted on the spot. The plan of their next Sunday's outing took them, by good fortune, over the border into Lake County. They would carry us so far, drop us at the Toll House, present us to the Hansons, and call for us again on Monday morning early.

CHAPTER 2

First Impressions of Silverado[151]

We were to leave by six precisely; that was solemnly pledged on both sides; and a messenger came to us the last thing at night, to remind us of the hour. But it was eight before we got clear of Calistoga: Kelmar, Mrs Kelmar, a friend of theirs whom we named Abramina, her little daughter, my wife, myself, and, stowed away behind us, a cluster of ship's coffee-kettles. These last were highly ornamental in the sheen of their bright tin, but I could invent no reason for their presence. Our carriageful reckoned up, as near as we could get at it, some three hundred years to the six of us. Four of the six, besides, were Hebrews. But I never, in all my life, was conscious of so strong an atmosphere of holiday. No word was spoken but of pleasure; and even when we drove in silence, nods and smiles went round the party like refreshments.

The sun shone out of a cloudless sky. Close at the zenith rode the belated moon, still clearly visible, and, along one margin, even bright. The wind blew a gale from the north; the trees roared; the corn and the deep grass in the valley fled in whitening surges; the dust towered into the air along the road and dispersed like the smoke of battle. It was clear in our teeth from the first, and for all the windings of the road it managed to keep clear in our teeth until the end.

For some two miles we rattled through the valley, skirting the eastern foothills; then we struck off to the right, through haughland, and presently, crossing a dry watercourse, entered the toll road, or, to be more local, entered on 'the grade'. The road mounts the near shoulder of Mount St Helena, bound northward into Lake County. In one place it skirts along the edge of a narrow and deep canyon, filled with trees, and I was glad, indeed, not to be driven at this point by the dashing Foss. Kelmar, with his unvarying smile, jogging to the motion of the trap, drove for all the world like a good, plain, country clergyman at home; and I profess I blessed him unawares for his timidity.

Vineyards and deep meadows, islanded and framed with thicket, gave place more and more as we ascended to woods of oak and madrona, dotted with enormous pines. It was these pines, as they shot above the lower wood, that produced that pencilling of single trees I had so often remarked from the valley. Thence, looking up and from however far, each fir stands separate against the sky no bigger than an eyelash; and all together lend a quaint, fringed aspect to the hills. The oak is no baby; even the madrona, upon these spurs of Mount St Helena, comes to a fine bulk and ranks with forest trees – but the pines look down upon the rest for underwood. As Mount St Helena among her foothills, so these dark giants out-top their fellow-vegetables. Alas! if they had left the redwoods, the pines, in turn, would have been dwarfed. But the redwoods, fallen from their high estate, are serving as family bedsteads, or yet more humbly as field fences, along all Napa Valley.

A rough smack of resin was in the air, and a crystal mountain purity. It came pouring over these green slopes by the oceanful. The woods sang aloud, and gave largely of their healthful breath. Gladness seemed to inhabit these upper zones, and we had left indifference behind us in the valley. 'I to the hills lift mine eyes!' There are days in a life when thus to climb out of the lowlands seems like scaling heaven.

As we continued to ascend, the wind fell upon us with increasing strength. It was a wonder how the two stout horses managed to pull us up that steep incline and still face the athletic opposition of the wind, or how their great eyes were able to endure the dust. Ten minutes after we went by, a tree fell, blocking the road; and even before us leaves were thickly strewn, and boughs had fallen, large enough to make the passage difficult. But now we were hard by the summit. The road crosses the ridge, just in the nick that Kelmar showed me from below, and then, without pause, plunges down a deep, thickly wooded glen on the farther side. At the highest point a trail strikes up the main hill to the leftward; and that leads to Silverado. A hundred yards beyond, and in a kind of elbow of the glen, stands the Toll House Hotel. We came up the one side, were caught upon the summit by the whole weight of the wind as it poured over into Napa Valley, and a minute after had drawn up in shelter, but all buffeted and breathless, at the Toll House door.

A water-tank, and stables, and a grey house of two storeys, with gable ends and a verandah, are jammed hard against the hillside, just where a stream has cut for itself a narrow canyon, filled with pines. The pines go right up overhead; a little more and the stream might have played, like a fire-hose, on the Toll House roof. In front the ground drops as sharply as it rises behind. There is just room for the road and a sort of promontory of croquet ground, and then you can lean over the edge and look deep below you through the wood. I said croquet *ground*, not *green*; for the surface was of brown, beaten earth. The toll-bar itself was the only other note of originality: a long beam, turning on a post, and kept slightly horizontal by a counter-weight of stones. Regularly about sundown this rude barrier was swung, like a derrick, across the road and made fast, I think, to a tree upon the farther side.

On our arrival there followed a gay scene in the bar. I was presented to Mr Corwin, the landlord; to Mr Jennings, the engineer, who lives there for his health; to Mr Hoddy, a most pleasant little gentleman, once a member of the Ohio legislature, again the editor of a local paper, and now, with undiminished dignity, keeping the Toll House bar. I had a number of drinks and cigars bestowed on me, and enjoyed a famous opportunity of seeing Kelmar in his glory, friendly, radiant, smiling, steadily edging one of the ship's kettles on the reluctant Corwin.

Corwin, plainly aghast, resisted gallantly, and for that bout victory crowned his arms.

At last we set forth for Silverado on foot. Kelmar and his jolly Jew girls were full of the sentiment of Sunday outings, breathed geniality and vagueness, and suffered a little vile boy from the hotel to lead them here and there about the woods. For three people all so old, so bulky in body, and belonging to a race so venerable, they could not but surprise us by their extreme and almost imbecile youthfulness of spirit. They were only going to stay ten minutes at the Toll House; had they not twenty long miles of road before them on the other side? Stay to dinner? Not they! Put up the horses? Never. Let us attach them to the verandah by a wisp of straw rope, such as would not have held a person's hat on that blustering day. And with all these protestations of hurry, they proved irresponsible like children. Kelmar himself, shrewd old Russian Jew, with a smirk that seemed just to have concluded a bargain to its satisfaction, entrusted himself and us devoutly to that boy. Yet the boy was patently fallacious; and for that matter a most unsympathetic urchin, raised apparently on gingerbread. He was bent on his own pleasure, nothing else; and Kelmar followed him to his ruin, with the same shrewd smirk. If the boy said there was 'a hole there in the hill' – a hole, pure and simple, neither more nor less – Kelmar and his Jew girls would follow him a hundred yards to look complacently down that hole. For two hours we looked for houses; and for two hours they followed us, smelling trees, picking flowers, foisting false botany on the unwary. Had we taken five, with that vile lad to head them off on idle divagations, for five they would have smiled and stumbled through the woods.

However, we came forth at length, and as by accident, upon a lawn, sparse planted like an orchard, but with forest instead of fruit trees. That was the site of Silverado mining town. A piece of ground was levelled up, where Kelmar's store had been; and facing that we saw Rufe Hanson's house, still bearing on its front the legend Silverado Hotel. Not another sign of habitation. Silverado town had all been carted from the scene; one of the houses was now the schoolhouse far down the road; one was gone here, one there, but all were gone away.

It was now a sylvan solitude, and the silence was unbroken but by the great, vague voice of the wind. Some days before our visit, a grizzly bear had been sporting round the Hansons' chicken-house.

Mrs Hanson was at home alone, we found. Rufe had been out after a 'bar', had risen late, and was now gone, it did not clearly appear whither. Perhaps he had had wind of Kelmar's coming, and was now ensconced among the underwood, or watching us from the shoulder of the mountain. We, hearing there were no houses to be had, were for immediately giving up all hopes of Silverado. But this, somehow, was not to Kelmar's fancy. He first proposed that we should 'camp someveres around, ain't it?' waving his hand cheerily as though to weave a spell; and when that was firmly rejected, he decided that we must take up house with the Hansons. Mrs Hanson had been, from the first, flustered, subdued and a little pale; but from this proposition she recoiled with haggard indignation. So did we, who would have preferred, in a manner of speaking, death. But Kelmar was not to be put by. He edged Mrs Hanson into a corner, where for a long time he threatened her with his forefinger, like a character in Dickens; and the poor woman, driven to her entrenchments, at last remembered with a shriek that there were still some houses at the tunnel.

Thither we went; the Jews, who should already have been miles into Lake County, still cheerily accompanying us. For about a furlong we followed a good road alone, the hillside through the forest, until suddenly that road widened out and came abruptly to an end. A canyon, woody below, red, rocky and naked overhead, was here walled across by a dump of rolling stones, dangerously steep, and from twenty to thirty feet in height. A rusty iron chute on wooden legs came flying, like a monstrous gargoyle, across the parapet. It was down this that they poured the precious ore; and below here the carts stood to wait their lading and carry it mill-ward down the mountain.

The whole canyon was so entirely blocked, as if by some rude guerrilla fortification, that we could only mount by lengths of wooden ladder, fixed in the hillside. These led us round the farther corner of the dump; and when they were at an end, we still persevered over loose rubble and wading deep in poison oak, till we struck a triangular platform, filling up the whole glen, and shut in on either hand by bold projections of the mountain. Only in front the place was open like the proscenium of a theatre, and we looked forth into a great realm of air, and down upon treetops and hilltops, and far and near on wild and varied country. The place still stood as on the day it was deserted: a line of iron rails with a bifurcation; a truck in working order; a world of lumber, old wood, old iron; a blacksmith's forge on one side, half buried in the leaves of dwarf madronas; and on the other, an old brown wooden house.

Fanny and I dashed at the house. It consisted of three rooms, and was so plastered against the hill that one room was right atop of another, that the upper floor was more than twice as large as the lower, and that all three apartments must be entered from a different side and level. Not a window-sash remained.

The door of the lower room was smashed, and one panel hung in splinters. We entered that, and found a fair amount of rubbish: sand and gravel that had been sifted in there by the mountain winds; straw, sticks, and stones; a table, a barrel; a plate-rack on the wall; two home-made bootjacks, signs of miners and their boots; and a pair of papers pinned on the boarding, headed respectively 'Funnel No. 1' and 'Funnel No. 2', but with the tails torn away. The window, sashless of course, was choked with the green and sweetly smelling foliage of a bay; and through a chink in the floor, a spray of poison oak had shot up and was handsomely prospering in the interior. It was my first care to cut away that poison oak, Fanny standing by at a respectful distance. That was our first improvement by which we took possession.

The room immediately above could only be entered by a plank propped against the threshold, along which the intruder must foot it gingerly, clutching for support to sprays of poison oak, the proper product of the country. Herein was, on either hand, a triple tier of beds, where miners had once lain; and the other gable was pierced by a sashless window and a doorless doorway opening on the air of heaven, five feet above the ground. As for the third room, which entered squarely from the ground level, but higher up the hill and farther up the canyon, it contained only rubbish and the uprights for another triple tier of beds.

The whole building was overhung by a bold, lion-like, red rock. Poison oak, sweet bay trees, calcanthus, brush and chaparral grew freely but sparsely all about it. In front, in the strong sunshine, the platform lay over-strewn with busy litter, as though the labours of the mine might begin again tomorrow in the morning.

Following back into the canyon, among the mass of rotting plant and through the flowering bushes, we came to a great crazy staging, with a wry windless on the top; and clambering up, we could look into an open shaft, leading edgeways down into the bowels of the mountain, trickling with water, and lit by some stray sun-gleams, whence I know not. In that quiet place the still, faraway tinkle of the water-drops was loudly audible. Close by, another shaft led edgeways up into the super-incumbent shoulder of the hill. It lay partly open; and sixty or a hundred feet above our head, we could see the strata propped apart by solid wooden wedges, and a pine, half undermined, precariously nodding on the verge. Here also a rugged, horizontal tunnel ran straight into the unsunned bowels of the rock. This secure angle in the mountain's flank was, even on this wild day, as still as my lady's chamber. But in the tunnel a cold, wet draught tempestuously blew. Nor have I ever known that place otherwise than cold and windy.

Such was our first prospect of Juan Silverado. I own I had looked for something different: a clique of neighbourly houses on a village green, we shall say, all empty to be sure, but swept and varnished; a trout stream brawling by; great elms or chestnuts, humming with bees and nested in by song-birds; and the mountains standing round about, as at Jerusalem. Here, mountain and house and the old tools of industry were all alike rusty and down-falling. The hill was here wedged up, and there poured forth its bowels in a spout of broken mineral; man with his picks and powder, and nature with her own great blasting tools of sun and rain, labouring together at the ruin of that proud mountain. The view up the canyon was a glimpse of devastation: dry red minerals sliding together, here and there a crag, here and there dwarf thicket clinging in the general glissade, and over all a broken outline trenching on the blue of heaven. Downwards indeed, from our rock eyrie, we beheld the greener side of nature; and the bearing of the pines and the sweet smell of bays and nutmegs commended themselves gratefully to our senses. One way and another, now the die was cast. Silverado be it!

After we had got back to the Toll House, the Jews were not long of striking forward. But I observed that one of the Hanson lads came down, before their departure, and returned with a ship's kettle. Happy Hansons! Nor was it until after Kelmar was gone, if I remember rightly, that Rufe put in an appearance to arrange the details of our installation.

The latter part of the day, Fanny and I sat in the verandah of the Toll House, utterly stunned by the uproar of the wind among the trees on the other side of the valley. Sometimes, we would have it it was like a sea, but it was not various enough for that; and again, we thought it like the roar of a cataract, but it was too changeful for the cataract; and then we would decide, speaking in sleepy voices, that it could be compared with nothing but itself. My mind was entirely preoccupied by the noise. I hearkened to it by the hour, gapingly hearkened, and let my cigarette go out. Sometimes the wind would make a sally nearer hand, and send a shrill, whistling crash among the foliage on our side of the glen; and sometimes a back-draught would strike into the elbow where we sat, and cast the gravel and torn leaves into our faces. But for the most part, this great, streaming gale passed unweariedly by us into Napa Valley, not two hundred yards away, visible by the tossing boughs, stunningly audible, and yet not moving a hair upon our heads. So it blew all night long while I was writing up my journal, and after we were in bed, under a cloudless, starset heaven; and so it was blowing still next morning when we rose.

It was a laughable thought to us, what had become of our cheerful, wandering Hebrews. We could not suppose they had reached a destination. The meanest boy could lead them miles out of their way to see a gopher-hole. Boys, we felt to be their special danger; none others were of that exact pitch of cheerful irrelevancy to exercise a kindred sway upon their minds: but before the attractions of a boy their most settled resolutions would be wax. We thought we could follow in fancy these three aged Hebrew truants wandering in and out on hilltop and in thicket, a demon boy trotting far ahead, their will-o'-the-wisp conductor; and at last, about midnight, the wind still roaring in the darkness, we had a vision of all three on their knees upon a mountain-top around a glowworm.

CHAPTER 3

The Return

Next morning we were up by half-past five, according to agreement, and it was ten by the clock before our Jew boys returned to pick us up. Kelmar, Mrs Kelmar and Abramina, all smiling from ear to ear, and full of tales of the hospitality they had found on the other side. It had not gone unrewarded; for I observed with interest that the ship's kettles, all but one, had been 'placed'. Three Lake County families, at least, endowed for life with a ship's kettle. Come, this was no misspent Sunday. The absence of the kettles told its own story: our Jews said nothing about them; but, on the other hand, they said many kind and comely things about the people they had met. The two women, in particular, had been charmed out of themselves by the sight of a young girl surrounded by her admirers; all evening, it appeared, they had been triumphing together in the girl's innocent successes, and to this natural and unselfish joy they gave expression in language that was beautiful by its simplicity and truth.

Take them for all in all, few people have done my heart more good; they seemed so thoroughly entitled to happiness, and to enjoy it in so large a measure and so free from afterthought; almost they persuaded me to be a Jew. There was, indeed, a chink of money in their talk. They particularly commanded people who were well to do. '*He* don't care – ain't it?' was their highest word of commendation to an individual fate; and here I seem to grasp the root of their philosophy – it was to be free from care, to be free to make these Sunday wanderings, that they so eagerly pursued after wealth; and all this carefulness was to be careless. The fine, good humour of all three seemed to declare they had attained their end. Yet there was the other side to it; and the recipients of kettles perhaps cared greatly.

No sooner had they returned, than the scene of yesterday began again. The horses were not even tied with a straw rope this time – it was not worth while; and Kelmar disappeared into the bar, leaving them under a tree on the other side of the road. I had to devote myself. I stood under the shadow of that tree for, I suppose, hard upon an hour, and had not the heart to be angry. Once someone remembered me, and brought me out half a tumblerful of the playful, innocuous American cocktail. I drank it, and lo! veins of living fire ran down my leg; and then a focus of conflagration remained seated in my stomach, not unpleasantly, for a quarter of an hour. I love these sweet, fiery pangs, but I will not court them. The bulk of the time I spent in repeating as much French poetry as I could remember to the horses, who seemed to enjoy it hugely. And now it went –

> O ma vieille Font-georges
> Où volent les rouges-gorges:

and again, to a more trampling measure –

> Et tout tremble, Irun, Coïmbre,
> Santander, Almodovar,
> Sitôt qu'on entend le timbre
> Des cymbales de Bivar.[152]

The redbreasts and the brooks of Europe, in that dry and songless land; brave old names and wars, strong cities, cymbals, and bright armour, in that nook of the mountain, sacred only to the Indian and the bear! This is still the strangest thing in all man's travelling, that he should carry about with him incongruous memories. There is no foreign land; it is the traveller only that is foreign, and now and again, by a flash of recollection, lights up the contrasts of the earth.[153]

But while I was thus wandering in my fancy, great feats had been transacted in the bar. Corwin the bold had fallen, Kelmar was again crowned with laurels, and the last of the ship's kettles had changed hands. If I had ever doubted the purity of Kelmar's motives, if I had ever suspected him of a single eye to business in his eternal dallyings, now at least, when the last kettle was disposed of, my suspicions must have been allayed. I dare not guess how much more time was wasted; nor how often we drove off, merely to drive back again and renew interrupted conversations about nothing, before the Toll House was fairly left behind. Alas! and not a mile down the grade there stands a ranch in a sunny vineyard, and here we must all dismount again and enter.

Only the old lady was at home, Mrs Guele, a brown old Swiss dame, the picture of honesty; and with her we drank a bottle of wine and had an age-long conversation, which would have been highly delightful if Fanny and I had not been faint with hunger. The ladies each narrated the story of her marriage, our two Hebrews with the prettiest combination of sentiment and financial bathos. Abramina, specially, endeared herself with every word. She was as simple, natural and engaging as a kid that should have been brought up to the business of a money-changer. One touch was so resplendently Hebraic that I cannot pass it over. When her 'old man' wrote home for her from America, her old man's family would not entrust her with the money for the passage till she had bound herself by an oath – on her knees, I think she said – not to employ it otherwise. This had tickled Abramina hugely, but I think it tickled me fully more.

Mrs Guele told of her home-sickness up here in the long winters; of her honest, country-woman troubles and alarms upon the journey; how in the bank at Frankfort she had feared lest the banker, after having taken her cheque, should deny all knowledge of it – a fear I have myself every time I go to a bank; and how crossing the Lüneburger Heath, an old lady, witnessing her trouble and finding whither she was bound, had given her 'the blessing of a person eighty years old, which would be sure to bring her safely to the States. And the first thing I did,' added Mrs Guele, 'was to fall downstairs.'

At length we got out of the house, and some of us into the trap, when – judgement of heaven! – here came Mr Guele from his vineyard. So another quarter of an hour went by; till at length, at our earnest pleading, we set forth again in earnest, Fanny and I white-faced and silent, but the Jews still smiling. The heart fails me. There was yet another stoppage! And we drove at last into Calistoga past two in the afternoon, Fanny and I having breakfasted at six in the morning, eight mortal hours before. We were a pallid couple; but still the Jews were smiling.

So ended our excursion with the village usurers; and, now that it was done, we had no more idea of the nature of the business, nor of the part we had been playing in it, than the child unborn. That all the people we had met were the slaves of Kelmar, though in various degrees of servitude; that we ourselves had been sent up the mountain in the interests of none but Kelmar; that the money we laid out, dollar by dollar, cent by cent, and through the hands of various intermediaries, should all hop ultimately into Kelmar's till – these were facts that we only grew to recognise in the course of time and by the accumulation of evidence. At length all doubt was quieted, when one of the kettle-holders confessed. Stopping his trap in the moonlight, a little way out of Calistoga, he told me, in so many words, that he dare not show his face there with an empty pocket. 'You see, I don't mind if it was only five dollars, Mr Stevens,' he said, 'but I must give Mr Kelmar *something*.'

Even now, when the whole tyranny is plain to me, I cannot find it in my heart to be as angry as perhaps I should be with the Hebrew tyrant. The whole game of business is beggar my neighbour; and though perhaps that game looks uglier when played at such close quarters and on so small a scale, it is none the more intrinsically inhumane for that. The village usurer is not so sad a feature of humanity and human progress as the millionaire manufacturer, fattening on the toil and loss of thousands, and yet declaiming from the platform against the greed and dishonesty of landlords. If it were fair for Cobden to buy up land from owners whom he thought unconscious of its proper value, it was fair enough for my Russian Jew to give credit to his farmers. Kelmar, if he was unconscious of the beam in his own eye, was at least silent in the matter of his brother's mote.

The Act of Squatting

There were four of us squatters – myself and my wife, the King and Queen of Silverado; Sam,[154] the Crown Prince; and Chuchu, the Grand Duke. Chuchu, a setter crossed with spaniel, was the most unsuited for a rough life. He had been nurtured tenderly in the society of ladies; his heart was large and soft; he regarded the sofa-cushion as a bedrock necessary of existence. Though about the size of a sheep, he loved to sit in ladies' laps; he never said a bad word in all his blameless days; and if he had seen a flute, I am sure he could have played upon it by nature. It may seem hard to say it of a dog, but Chuchu was a tame cat.

The King and Queen, the Grand Duke, and a basket of cold provender for immediate use, set forth from Calistoga in a double buggy; the Crown Prince, on horseback, led the way like an outrider. Bags and boxes and a second-hand stove were to follow close upon our heels by Hanson's team.

It was a beautiful still day; the sky was one field of azure. Not a leaf moved, not a speck appeared in heaven. Only from the summit of the mountain one little snowy wisp of cloud after another kept detaching itself, like smoke from a volcano, and blowing southward in some high stream of air: Mount St Helena still at her interminable task, making the weather, like a Lapland witch.

By noon we had come in sight of the mill: a great brown building, halfway up the hill, big as a factory, two storeys high, and with tanks and ladders along the roof; which, as a pendicle of Silverado mine, we held to be an outlying province of our own. Thither, then, we went, crossing the valley by a grassy trail; and there lunched out of the basket, sitting in a kind of portico, and wondering, while we ate, at this great bulk of useless building. Through a chink we could look far down into the interior, and see sunbeams floating in the dust and striking on tier after tier of silent, rusty machinery. It cost six thousand dollars, twelve hundred English sovereigns; and now, here it stands deserted, like the temple of a forgotten religion, the busy millers toiling somewhere else. All the time we were there, mill and mill town showed no sign of life; that part of the mountainside, which is very open and green, was tenanted by no living creature but ourselves and the insects; and nothing stirred but the cloud manufactory upon the mountain summit. It was odd to compare this with the former days, when the engine was in fall blast, the mill palpitating to its strokes, and the carts came rattling down from Silverado, charged with ore.

By two we had been landed at the mine, the buggy was gone again, and we were left to our own reflections and the basket of cold provender, until Hanson should arrive. Hot as it was by the sun, there was something chill in such a homecoming, in that world of wreck and rust, splinter and rolling gravel, where for so many years no fire had smoked.

Silverado platform filled the whole width of the canyon. Above, as I have said, this was a wild, red, stony gully in the mountains; but below it was a wooded dingle. And through this, I was told, there had gone a path between the mine and the Toll House – our natural north-west passage to civilisation. I found and followed it, clearing my way as I went through fallen branches and dead trees. It went straight down that steep canyon, till it brought you out abruptly over the roofs of the hotel. There was nowhere any break in the descent. It almost seemed as if, were you to drop a stone down the old iron chute at our platform, it would never rest until it hopped upon the Toll House shingles. Signs were not wanting of the ancient greatness of Silverado. The footpath was well marked, and had been well trodden in the old days by thirsty miners. And far down, buried in foliage, deep out of sight of Silverado, I came on a last outpost of the mine – a mound of gravel, some wreck of wooden aqueduct, and the mouth of a tunnel, like a treasure grotto in a fairy story. A stream of water, fed by the invisible leakage from our shaft, and dyed red with cinnabar or iron, ran trippingly forth out of the bowels of the cave; and, looking far under the arch, I could see something like an iron lantern fastened on the rocky wall. It was a promising spot for the imagination. No boy could have left it unexplored.

The stream thenceforward stole along the bottom of the dingle, and made, for that dry land, a pleasant warbling in the leaves. Once, I suppose, it ran splashing down the whole length of the canyon, but now its head waters had been tapped by the shaft at Silverado, and for a great part of its course it wandered sunless among the joints of the mountain. No wonder that it should better its pace when it sees, far before it, daylight whitening in the arch, or that it should come trotting forth into the sunlight with a song.

The two stages had gone by when I got down, and the Toll House stood, dozing in sun and dust and silence, like a place enchanted. My mission was after hay for bedding, and that I was readily promised.

But when I mentioned that we were waiting for Rufe, the people shook their heads. Rufe was not a regular man anyway, it seemed; and if he got playing poker – Well, poker was too many for Rufe. I had not yet heard them bracketed together; but it seemed a natural conjunction, and commended itself swiftly to my fears; and as soon as I returned to Silverado and had told my story, we practically gave Hanson up, and set ourselves to do what we could find do-able in our desert-island state.[155]

The lower room had been the assayer's office. The floor was thick with debris – part human, from the former occupants; part natural, sifted in by mountain winds. In a sea of red dust there swam or floated sticks, boards, hay, straw, stones and paper; ancient newspapers, above all – for the newspaper, especially when torn, soon becomes an antiquity – and bills of the Silverado boarding-house, some dated Silverado, some Calistoga Mine. Here is one, verbatim; and if anyone can calculate the scale of charges, he has my envious admiration.

Calistoga Mine, May 3rd, 1875

John Stanley
To S. Chapman, Cr.

To board from	April 1st to April 30th	$25.75
	May 1st to 3rd	$2.00
		$27.75

Where is John Stanley mining now? Where is S. Chapman, within whose hospitable walls we were to lodge? The date was but five years old, but in that time the world had changed for Silverado; like Palmyra[156] in the desert, it had outlived its people and its purpose; we camped, like Layard,[157] amid ruins, and these names spoke to us of prehistoric time. A boot-jack, a pair of boots, a dog-hutch and these bills of Mr Chapman's were the only speaking relics that we disinterred from all that vast Silverado rubbish-heap; but what would I not have given to unearth a letter, a pocketbook, a diary, only a ledger, or a roll of names, to take me back, in a more personal manner, to the past?[158] It pleases me, besides, to fancy that Stanley or Chapman, or one of their companions, may light upon this chronicle, and be struck by the name, and read some news of their anterior home, coming, as it were, out of a subsequent epoch of history in that quarter of the world.

As we were tumbling the mingled rubbish on the floor, kicking it with our feet, and groping for these written evidences of the past,

Sam, with a somewhat whitened face, produced a paper bag. 'What's this?' said he. It contained a granulated powder, something the colour of Gregory's Mixture, but rosier; and as there were several of the bags, and each more or less broken, the powder was spread widely on the floor. Had any of us ever seen giant powder? No, nobody had; and instantly there grew up in my mind a shadowy belief, verging with every moment nearer to certitude, that I had somewhere heard somebody describe it as just such a powder as the one around us. I have learnt since that it is a substance not unlike tallow, and is made up in rolls for all the world like tallow candles.

Fanny, to add to our happiness, told us a story of a gentleman who had camped one night, like ourselves, by a deserted mine. He was a handy, thrifty fellow, and looked right and left for plunder, but all he could lay his hands on was a can of oil. After dark he had to see to the horses with a lantern; and not to miss an opportunity, filled up his lamp from the oil can. Thus equipped, he set forth into the forest. A little while after, his friends heard a loud explosion; the mountain echoes bellowed, and then all was still. On examination, the can proved to contain oil, with the trifling addition of nitroglycerine; but no research disclosed a trace of either man or lantern.

It was a pretty sight, after this anecdote, to see us sweeping out the giant powder. It seemed never to be far enough away. And, after all, it was only some rock pounded for assay.

So much for the lower room. We scraped some of the rougher dirt off the floor, and left it. That was our sitting-room and kitchen, though there was nothing to sit upon but the table, and no provision for a fire except a hole in the roof of the room above, which had once contained the chimney of a stove.

To that upper room we now proceeded. There were the eighteen bunks in a double tier, nine on either hand, where from eighteen to thirty-six miners had once snored together all night long, John Stanley, perhaps, snoring loudest. There was the roof, with a hole in it through which the sun now shot an arrow. There was the floor, in much the same state as the one below, though, perhaps, there was more hay, and certainly there was the added ingredient of broken glass, the man who stole the window-frames having apparently made a miscarriage with this one. Without a broom, without hay or bedding, we could but look about us with a beginning of despair. The one bright arrow of day, in that gaunt and shattered barrack, made the rest look dirtier and darker, and the sight drove us at last into the open.

Here, also, the handiwork of man lay ruined: but the plants were all alive and thriving; the view below was fresh with the colours of nature; and we had exchanged a dim, human garret for a corner, even although it were untidy, of the blue hall of heaven. Not a bird, not a beast, not a reptile. There was no noise in that part of the world, save when we passed beside the staging, and heard the water musically falling in the shaft.

We wandered to and fro. We searched among that drift of lumberwood and iron, nails and rails, and sleepers and the wheels of tracks. We gazed up the cleft into the bosom of the mountain. We sat by the margin of the dump and saw, far below us, the green treetops standing still in the clear air. Beautiful perfumes, breaths of bay, resin and nutmeg, came to us more often and grew sweeter and sharper as the afternoon declined. But still there was no word of Hanson.

I set to with pick and shovel, and deepened the pool behind the shaft, till we were sure of sufficient water for the morning; and by the time I had finished, the sun had begun to go down behind the mountain shoulder, the platform was plunged in quiet shadow, and a chill descended from the sky. Night began early in our cleft. Before us, over the margin of the dump, we could see the sun still striking aslant into the wooded nick below and on the battlemented, pine-bescattered ridges on the farther side.

There was no stove, of course, and no hearth in our lodging, so we betook ourselves to the blacksmith's forge across the platform. If the platform be taken as a stage, and the out-curving margin of the dump to represent the line of the footlights, then our house would be the first wing on the actor's left, and this blacksmith's forge, although no match for it in size, the foremost on the right. It was a low, brown cottage, planted close against the hill, and overhung by the foliage and peeling boughs of a madrona thicket. Within, it was full of dead leaves and mountain dust, and rubbish from the mine. But we soon had a good fire brightly blazing, and sat close about it on impromptu seats. Chuchu, the slave of sofa-cushions, whimpered for a softer bed; but the rest of us were greatly revived and comforted by that good creature, fire, which gives us warmth and light and companionable sounds, and colours up the emptiest building with better than frescoes. For a while it was even pleasant in the forge, with the blaze in the midst, and a look over our shoulders on the woods and mountains where the day was dying like a dolphin.

It was between seven and eight before Hanson arrived, with a wagonful of our effects and two of his wife's relatives to lend him a hand. The elder showed surprising strength. He would pick up a huge packing-case, full of books of all things, swing it on his shoulder, and away up the two crazy ladders and the breakneck spout of rolling mineral, familiarly termed a path, that led from the cart-track to our house. Even for a man unburthened, the ascent was toilsome and precarious; but Irvine scaled it with a light foot, carrying box after box, as the hero whisks the stage child up the practicable footway beside the waterfall of the fifth act. With so strong a helper, the business was speedily transacted. Soon the assayer's office was thronged with our belongings, piled higgledy-piggledy, and upside down, about the floor. There were our boxes, indeed, but my wife had left her keys in Calistoga. There was the stove, but, alas! our carriers had forgot the chimney, and lost one of the plates along the road. The Silverado problem was scarce solved.

Rufe himself was grave and good-natured over his share of blame; he even, if I remember right, expressed regret. But his crew, to my astonishment and anger, grinned from ear to ear, and laughed aloud at our distress. They thought it 'real funny' about the stovepipe they had forgotten; 'real funny' that they should have lost a plate. As for hay, the whole party refused to bring us any till they should have supped. See how late they were! Never had there been such a job as coming up that grade! Nor often, I suspect, such a game of poker as that before they started. But about nine, as a particular favour, we should have some hay.

So they took their departure, leaving me still staring, and we resigned ourselves to wait for their return. The fire in the forge had been suffered to go out, and we were one and all too weary to kindle another. We dined, or, not to take that word in vain, we ate after a fashion, in the nightmare disorder of the assayer's office, perched among boxes. A single candle lighted us. It could scarce be called a housewarming; for there was, of course, no fire, and with the two open doors and the open window gaping on the night, like breaches in a fortress, it began to grow rapidly chill. Talk ceased; nobody moved but the unhappy Chuchu, still in quest of sofa-cushions, who tumbled complainingly among the trunks. It required a certain happiness of disposition to look forward hopefully from so dismal a beginning, across the brief hours of night, to the warm shining of tomorrow's sun.

But the hay arrived at last, and we turned, with our last spark of courage, to the bedroom. We had improved the entrance, but it was still a kind of rope-walking; and it would have been droll to see us mounting, one after another, by candlelight, under the open stars.

The western door – that which looked up the canyon, and through which we entered by our bridge of flying plank – was still entire, a handsome, panelled door, the most finished piece of carpentry in Silverado. And the two lowest bunks next to this we roughly filled with hay for that night's use. Through the opposite, or eastern-looking gable, with its open door and window, a faint, diffused starshine came into the room like mist; and when we were once in bed, we lay, awaiting sleep, in a haunted, incomplete obscurity. At first the silence of the night was utter. Then a high wind began in the distance among the treetops, and for hours continued to grow higher. It seemed to me much such a wind as we had found on our visit; yet here in our open chamber we were fanned only by gentle and refreshing draughts, so deep was the canyon, so close was our house planted under the overhanging rock.[159]

The Hunter's Family

There is quite a large race or class of people in America for whom we scarcely seem to have a parallel in England. Of pure white blood, they are unknown or unrecognisable in towns; inhabit the fringes of settlements and the deep, quiet places of the country; are rebellious to all labour, and pettily thievish, like the English gypsies; are rustically ignorant, but with a touch of wood-lore and the dexterity of the savage. Whence they came is a moot point. At the time of the war, they poured north in crowds to escape the conscription; lived during summer on fruits, wild animals and petty theft; and at the approach of winter, when these supplies failed, built great fires in the forest, and there died stoically by starvation. They are widely scattered, however, and easily recognised. Loutish, but not ill-looking, they will sit all day, swinging their legs on a field fence, the mind seemingly as devoid of all reflection as a Suffolk peasant's, careless of politics, for the most part incapable of reading, but with a rebellious vanity and a strong sense of independence. Hunting is their most congenial business, or, if the occasion offers, a little amateur detection. In tracking a criminal, following a particular horse along a beaten highway, and drawing inductions from a hair or a footprint, one of those somnolent, grinning Hodges will suddenly display activity of body and finesse of mind. By their names ye may know them, the women figuring as Loveina, Larsenia, Serena, Leanna, Orreana; the men answering to Alvin, Alva or Orion, pronounced Orrion, with the accent on the first. Whether they are indeed a race, or whether this is the form of degeneracy common to all back-woodsmen, they are at least known by a generic byword as Poor Whites or Low-downers.

I will not say that the Hanson family was Poor White, because the name savours of offence; but I may go as far as this – they were, in many points, not unsimilar to the people usually so-called. Rufe himself combined two of the qualifications, for he was both a hunter and an amateur detective. It was he who pursued Russel and Dollar, the robbers of the Lake Port stage, and captured them the very morning after the exploit, while they were still sleeping in a hayfield. Russel, a drunken Scotch carpenter, was even an acquaintance of his own, and he expressed much grave commiseration for his fate. In all that he said and did, Rufe was grave. I never saw him hurried. When he spoke, he took out his pipe with ceremonial deliberation, looked east and west, and then, in quiet tones and few words, stated his business or told his story. His gait was to match; it would never have surprised you if, at any step, he had turned round and walked away again, so warily and slowly, and with so much seeming hesitation did he go about. He lay long in bed in the morning – rarely, indeed, rose before noon; he loved all games, from poker to clerical croquet; and in the Toll House croquet ground I have seen him toiling at the latter with the devotion of a curate. He took an interest in education, was an active member of the local school-board, and when I was there, he had recently lost the schoolhouse key. His wagon was broken, but it never seemed to occur to him to mend it. Like all truly idle people, he had an artistic eye. He chose the print stuff for his wife's dresses, and counselled her in the making of a patchwork quilt, always, as she thought, wrongly, but to the more educated eye, always with bizarre and admirable taste – the taste of an Indian. With all this, he was a perfect, unoffending gentleman in word and act. Take his clay pipe from him, and he was fit for any society but that of fools. Quiet as he was, there burned a deep, permanent excitement in his dark blue eyes; and when this grave man smiled, it was like sunshine in a shady place.

Mrs Hanson (née, if you please, Lovelands) was more commonplace than her lord. She was a comely woman, too, plump, fair-coloured, with wonderful white teeth; and in her print dresses (chosen by Rufe) and with a large sun bonnet shading her valued complexion, made, I assure you, a very agreeable figure. But she was on the surface, what there was of her, outspoken and loud-spoken. Her noisy laughter had none of the charm of one of Hanson's rare, slow-spreading smiles; there was no reticence, no mystery, no manner about the woman: she was a first-class dairymaid, but her husband was an unknown quantity between the savage and the nobleman. She was often in and out with us, merry, and healthy, and fair; he came far seldomer – only, indeed, when there was business, or now and again, to pay a visit of ceremony, brushed up for the occasion, with his wife on his arm and a clean clay pipe in his teeth. These visits, in our forest state, had quite the air of an event, and turned our red canyon into a salon.

Such was the pair who ruled in the old Silverado Hotel, among the windy trees, on the mountain shoulder overlooking the whole length of Napa Valley, as the man aloft looks down on the ship's deck. There they kept house, with sundry horses and fowls, and a family of sons, Daniel Webster and, I think, George Washington among the number. Nor did they want for visitors. An old gentleman, of singular stolidity, and called Breedlove – I think he had crossed the plains in the same caravan with Rufe – housed with them for awhile during our stay; and they had besides a permanent lodger, in the form of Mrs Hanson's brother, Irvine Lovelands. I spell Irvine by guess, for I could get no information on the subject; just as I could never find out, in spite of many enquiries, whether or not Rufe was a contraction for Rufus. They were all cheerfully at sea about their names in that generation. And this is surely the more notable where the names are all so strange, and even the family names appear to have been coined. At one time, at least, the ancestors of all these Alvins and Alvas, Loveinas, Lovelands, and Breedloves, must have taken serious council and found a certain poetry in these denominations; that must have been, then, their form of literature. But still times change; and their next descendants, the George Washingtons and Daniel Websters, will at least be clear upon the point. And anyway, and however his name should be spelt, this Irvine Lovelands was the most unmitigated Caliban[160] I ever knew.

Our very first morning at Silverado, when we were full of business, patching up doors and windows, making beds and seats, and getting our rough lodging into shape, Irvine and his sister made their appearance together: she for neighbourliness and general curiosity; he because he was working for me, to my sorrow, cutting firewood at I forget how much a day. The way that he set about cutting wood was characteristic. We were at that moment patching up and unpacking in the kitchen. Down he sat on one side, and down sat his sister on the other. Both were chewing pine-tree gum, and he, to my annoyance, accompanied that simple pleasure with profuse expectoration. She rattled away, talking up hill and down dale, laughing, tossing her head, showing her brilliant teeth. He looked on in silence, now spitting heavily on the floor, now putting his head back and uttering a loud, discordant, joyless laugh. He had a tangle of shock hair, the colour of wool; his mouth was a grin; although as strong as a horse, he looked neither heavy nor yet adroit, only leggy, coltish and in the road. But it was plain he was in high spirits, thoroughly enjoying his visit; and he laughed frankly whenever we failed to accomplish what we were about. This was scarcely helpful: it was even, to amateur carpenters, embarrassing; but it lasted until we knocked off work and began to get dinner. Then Mrs Hanson remembered she should have been gone an hour ago; and the pair retired, and the lady's laughter died away among the nutmegs down the path. That was Irvine's first day's work in my employment – the devil take him!

The next morning he returned and, as he was this time alone, he bestowed his conversation upon us with great liberality. He prided himself on his intelligence; asked us if we knew the school-ma'am. *He* didn't think much of her, anyway. He had tried her, he had. He had put a question to her. If a tree a hundred feet high were to fall a foot a day, how long would it take to fall right down? She had not been able to solve the problem. 'She don't know nothing,' he opined. He told us how a friend of his kept a school with a revolver, and chuckled mightily over that; his friend could teach school, he could. All the time he kept chewing gum and spitting. He would stand a while looking down; and then he would toss back his shock of hair, and laugh hoarsely, and spit, and bring forward a new subject. A man, he told us, who bore a grudge against him, had poisoned his dog. 'That was a low thing for a man to do now, wasn't it? It wasn't like a man, that, nohow. But I got even with him: I pisoned *his* dog.' His clumsy utterance, his rude embarrassed manner, set a fresh value on the stupidity of his remarks. I do not think I ever appreciated the meaning of two words until I knew Irvine – the verb *loaf*, and the noun *oaf*; between them, they complete his portrait. He could lounge, and wriggle, and rub himself against the wall, and grin, and be more in everybody's way than any other two people that I ever set my eyes on. Nothing that he did became him; and yet you were conscious that he was one of your own race, that his mind was cumbrously at work, revolving the problem of existence like a quid of gum, and in his own cloudy manner enjoying life, and passing judgement on his fellows. Above all things, he was delighted with himself. You would not have thought it, from his uneasy manners and troubled, struggling utterance; but he loved himself to the marrow, and was happy and proud like a peacock on a rail.

His self-esteem was, indeed, the one joint in his harness. He could be got to work, and even kept at work, by flattery. As long as my wife stood over him, crying out how strong he was, so long exactly he would stick to the matter in hand; and the moment she turned her back, or ceased to praise him, he would stop. His physical strength was wonderful; and to have a woman stand by and admire his achievements, warmed his heart like sunshine. Yet he was as cowardly as he was powerful, and felt no shame in owning to the weakness. Something was once wanted from the crazy platform over the shaft, and he at once refused to venture there – 'did not like,' as he said, 'foolen' round them kind o' places', and let my wife go instead of him, looking on with a grin. Vanity, where it rules, is usually more heroic: but Irvine steadily approved himself, and expected others to approve him; rather looked down upon my wife, and decidedly expected her to look up to him, on the strength of his superior prudence.

Yet the strangest part of the whole matter was perhaps this, that Irvine was as beautiful as a statue. His features were, in themselves, perfect; it was only his cloudy, uncouth and coarse expression that disfigured them. So much strength residing in so spare a frame was proof sufficient of the accuracy of his shape. He must have been built somewhat after the pattern of Jack Sheppard;[161] but the famous house-breaker, we may be certain, was no lout. It was by the extraordinary powers of his mind no less than by the vigour of his body that he broke his strong prison with such imperfect implements, turning the very obstacles to service. Irvine, in the same case, would have sat down and spat, and grumbled curses. He had the soul of a fat sheep, but, regarded as an artist's model, the exterior of a Greek god. It was a cruel thought to persons less favoured in their birth, that this creature, endowed – to use the language of theatres – with extra-ordinary 'means', should so manage to misemploy them that he looked ugly and almost deformed. It was only by an effort of abstraction, and after many days, that you discovered what he was.

By playing on the oaf's conceit, and standing closely over him, we got a path made round the corner of the dump to our door, so that we could come and go with decent ease; and he even enjoyed the work, for there were boulders to be plucked up bodily, bushes to be uprooted and other occasions for athletic display: but cutting wood was a different matter. Anybody could cut wood; and, besides, my wife was tired of supervising him, and had other things to attend to. And, in short, days went by, and Irvine came daily, and talked and lounged and spat; but the firewood remained intact as sleepers on the platform or growing trees upon the mountainside. Irvine, as a woodcutter, we could tolerate; but Irvine as a friend of the family, at so much a day, was too bald an imposition, and at length, on the afternoon of the fourth or fifth day of our connection, I explained to him, as clearly as I could, the light in which I had grown to regard his presence. I pointed out to him that I could not continue to give him a salary for spitting on the floor; and this expression, which came after a good many others, at last penetrated his obdurate wits. He rose at once, and said if that was the way he was going to be spoke to, he reckoned he would quit. And, no one interposing, he departed.

So far, so good. But we had no firewood. The next afternoon, I strolled down to Rufe's and consulted him on the subject. It was a very droll interview, in the large, bare north room of the Silverado Hotel, Mrs Hanson's patchwork on a frame, and Rufe, and his wife, and I, and the oaf himself, all more or less embarrassed. Rufe announced there was nobody in the neighbourhood but Irvine who could do a day's work for anybody. Irvine, thereupon, refused to have any more to do with my service; he 'wouldn't work no more for a man as had spoke to him's I had done'. I found myself on the point of the last humiliation – driven to beseech the creature whom I had just dismissed with insult: but I took the high hand in despair, said there must be no talk of Irvine coming back unless matters were to be differently managed; that I would rather chop firewood for myself than be fooled; and, in short, the Hansons being eager for the lad's hire, I so imposed upon them with merely affected resolution, that they ended by begging me to re-employ him again, on a solemn promise that he should be more industrious. The promise, I am bound to say, was kept. We soon had a fine pile of firewood at our door; and if Caliban gave me the cold shoulder and spared me his conversation, I thought none the worse of him for that, nor did I find my days much longer for the deprivation.

The leading spirit of the family was, I am inclined to fancy, Mrs Hanson. Her social brilliancy somewhat dazzled the others, and she had more of the small change of sense. It was she who faced Kelmar, for instance; and perhaps, if she had been alone, Kelmar would have had no rule within her doors. Rufe, to be sure, had a fine, sober, open-air attitude of mind, seeing the world without exaggeration – perhaps, we may even say, without enough; for he lacked, along with the others, that commercial idealism which puts so high a value on time and money. Sanity itself is a kind of convention. Perhaps Rufe was wrong; but, looking on life plainly, he was unable to perceive that croquet or poker were in any way less important than, for instance, mending his wagon. Even his own profession, hunting, was dear to him mainly as a sort of play; even that he would have neglected, had it not appealed to his imagination. His hunting-suit, for instance, had cost I should be afraid to say how many bucks – the currency in which he paid his way: it was all befringed, after the Indian fashion, and it was dear to his heart. The pictorial side of his daily business was never forgotten. He was even anxious to stand for his picture in those buckskin hunting clothes; and I remember how he once warmed almost into enthusiasm, his dark blue eyes growing perceptibly larger, as he planned the composition in which he should appear, 'with the horns of some real big bucks, and dogs, and a camp on a crick' (meaning creek or stream).

There was no trace in Irvine of this woodland poetry. He did not care for hunting, nor yet for buckskin suits. He had never observed scenery. The world, as it appeared to him, was almost obliterated by his own great grinning figure in the foreground: Caliban Malvolio.[162] And it seems to me as if, in the persons of these brothers-in-law, we had the two sides of rusticity fairly well represented: the hunter living really in nature; the clodhopper living merely out of society: the one bent up in every corporal agent to capacity in one pursuit, doing at least one thing keenly and thoughtfully, and thoroughly alive to all that touches it; the other in the inert and bestial state, walking in a faint dream, and taking so dim an impression of the myriad sides of life that he is truly conscious of nothing but himself. It is only in the fastnesses of nature, forests, mountains and the back of man's beyond, that a creature endowed with five senses can grow up into the perfection of this crass and earthy vanity. In towns or the busier countrysides, he is roughly reminded of other men's existence; and if he learns no more, he learns at least to fear contempt. But Irvine had come scatheless through life, conscious only of himself, of his great strength and intelligence; and, in the silence of the universe, to which he did not listen, dwelling with delight on the sound of his own thoughts.

The Sea Fogs

A change in the colour of the light usually called me in the morning. By a certain hour, the long, vertical chinks in our western gable, where the boards had shrunk and separated, flashed suddenly into my eyes as stripes of dazzling blue, at once so dark and splendid that I used to marvel how the qualities could be combined. At an earlier hour, the heavens in that quarter were still quietly coloured, but the shoulder of the mountain which shuts in the canyon already glowed with sunlight in a wonderful compound of gold and rose and green; and this too would kindle, although more mildly and with rainbow tints, the fissures of our crazy gable. If I were sleeping heavily, it was the bold blue that struck me awake; if more lightly, then I would come to myself in that earlier and fairer fight.

One Sunday morning, about five, the first brightness called me. I rose and turned to the east, not for my devotions, but for air. The night had been very still. The little private gale that blew every evening in our canyon, for ten minutes or perhaps a quarter of an hour, had swiftly blown itself out; in the hours that followed not a sigh of wind had shaken the treetops; and our barrack, for all its breaches, was less fresh that morning than of wont. But I had no sooner reached the window than I forgot all else at the sight that met my eyes, and I made but two bounds into my clothes and down the crazy plank to the platform.

The sun was still concealed below the opposite hilltops, though it was shining already, not twenty feet above my head, on our own mountain slope. But the scene, beyond a few near features, was entirely changed. Napa valley was gone; gone were all the lower slopes and woody foothills of the range; and in their place, not a thousand feet below me, rolled a great level ocean. It was as though I had gone to bed the night before, safe in a nook of inland mountains, and had awakened in a bay upon the coast. I had seen these inundations from below; at Calistoga I had risen and gone abroad in the early morning, coughing and sneezing, under fathoms on fathoms of grey sea vapour, like a cloudy sky – a dull sight for the artist, and a painful experience for the invalid. But to sit aloft oneself in the pure air and under the unclouded dome of heaven, and thus look down on the submergence of the valley, was strangely different and even delightful to the eyes. Far away were hilltops like little islands. Nearer, a smoky surf beat about the foot of precipices and poured into all the coves of these rough mountains. The colour of that fog ocean was a thing never to be forgotten. For an instant, among the Hebrides[163] and just about sundown, I have seen something like it on the sea itself. But the white was not so opaline; nor was there, what surprisingly increased the effect, that breathless, crystal stillness over all. Even in its gentlest moods the salt sea travails, moaning among the weeds or lisping on the sand; but that vast fog ocean lay in a trance of silence, nor did the sweet air of the morning tremble with a sound.

As I continued to sit upon the dump, I began to observe that this sea was not so level as at first sight it appeared to be. Away in the extreme south, a little hill of fog arose against the sky above the general surface, and as it had already caught the sun, it shone on the horizon like the topsails of some giant ship. There were huge waves, stationary, as it seemed, like waves in a frozen sea; and yet, as I looked again, I was not sure but they were moving after all, with a slow and august advance. And while I was yet doubting, a promontory of the hills some four or five miles away, conspicuous by a bouquet of tall pines, was in a single instant overtaken and swallowed up. It reappeared in a little, with its pines, but this time as an islet, and only to be swallowed up once more and then for good. This set me looking nearer, and I saw that in every cove along the line of mountains the fog was being piled in higher and higher, as though by some wind that was inaudible to me. I could trace its progress, one pine tree first growing hazy and then disappearing after another; although sometimes there was none of this fore-running haze, but the whole opaque white ocean gave a start and swallowed a piece of mountain at a gulp. It was to flee these poisonous fogs that I had left the seaboard, and climbed so high among the mountains. And now, behold, here came the fog to besiege me in my chosen altitudes, and yet came so beautifully that my first thought was of welcome.

The sun had now gotten much higher, and through all the gaps of the hills it cast long bars of gold across that white ocean. An eagle, or some other very great bird of the mountain, came wheeling over the nearer pine-tops, and hung, poised and something sideways, as if to look abroad on that unwonted desolation, spying, perhaps with terror, for the eyries of her comrades. Then, with a long cry, she disappeared again towards Lake County and the clearer air. At length it seemed to me as if the flood were beginning to subside. The old landmarks, by whose disappearance I had measured its advance, here a crag, there a brave pine tree, now began, in the inverse order, to make their reappearance into daylight. I judged all danger of the fog was over. This was not Noah's flood; it was but a morning spring, and would now drift out seaward whence it came. So, mightily relieved, and a good deal exhilarated by the sight, I went into the house to light the fire.

I suppose it was nearly seven when I once more mounted the platform to look abroad. The fog ocean had swelled up enormously since last I saw it; and a few hundred feet below me, in the deep gap where the Toll House stands and the road runs through into Lake County, it had already topped the slope, and was pouring over and down the other side like driving smoke. The wind had climbed along with it; and though I was still in calm air, I could see the trees tossing below me, and their long, strident sighing mounted to me where I stood.

Half an hour later, the fog had surmounted all the ridge on the opposite side of the gap, though a shoulder of the mountain still warded it out of our canyon. Napa Valley and its bounding hills were now utterly blotted out. The fog, sunny white in the sunshine, was pouring over into Lake County in a huge, ragged cataract, tossing treetops appearing and disappearing in the spray. The air struck with a little chill, and set me coughing. It smelt strong of the fog, like the smell of a washing-house, but with a shrewd tang of the sea salt.

Had it not been for two things – the sheltering spur which answered as a dyke, and the great valley on the other side which rapidly engulfed whatever mounted – our own little platform in the canyon must have been already buried a hundred feet in salt and poisonous air. As it was, the interest of the scene entirely occupied our minds. We were set just out of the wind, and but just above the fog; we could listen to the voice of the one as to music on the stage; we could plunge our eyes down into the other, as into some flowing stream from over the parapet of a bridge; thus we looked on upon a strange, impetuous, silent, shifting exhibition of the powers of nature, and saw the familiar landscape changing from moment to moment like figures in a dream.

The imagination loves to trifle with what is not. Had this been indeed the deluge, I should have felt more strongly, but the emotion would have been similar in kind. I played with the idea, as the child flees in delighted terror from the creations of his fancy. The look of the thing helped me. And when at last I began to flee up the mountain, it was indeed partly to escape from the raw air that kept me coughing, but it was also part in play.

As I ascended the mountainside, I came once more to overlook the upper surface of the fog; but it wore a different appearance from what I had beheld at daybreak. For, first, the sun now fell on it from high overhead, and its surface shone and undulated like a great nor'land moor country, sheeted with untrodden morning snow. And next the new level must have been a thousand or fifteen hundred feet higher than the old, so that only five or six points of all the broken country below me, still stood out. Napa Valley was now one with Sonoma on the west. On the hither side, only a thin scattered fringe of bluffs was unsubmerged; and through all the gaps the fog was pouring over, like an ocean, into the blue clear sunny country on the east. There it was soon lost; for it fell instantly into the bottom of the valleys, following the watershed; and the hilltops in that quarter were still clear cut upon the eastern sky.

Through the Toll House gap and over the near ridges on the other side, the deluge was immense. A spray of thin vapour was thrown high above it, rising and falling, and blown into fantastic shapes. The speed of its course was like a mountain torrent. Here and there a few treetops were discovered and then whelmed again; and for one second, the bough of a dead pine beckoned out of the spray like the arm of a drowning man. But still the imagination was dissatisfied, still the ear waited for something more. Had this indeed been water (as it seemed so to the eye), with what a plunge of reverberating thunder would it have rolled upon its course, disembowelling mountains and deracinating pines! And yet water it was, and sea-water at that – true Pacific billows, only somewhat rarefied, rolling in mid-air among the hilltops.

I climbed still higher, among the red rattling gravel and dwarf underwood of Mount St Helena, until I could look right down upon Silverado, and admire the favoured nook in which it lay. The sunny plain of fog was several hundred feet higher; behind the protecting spur a gigantic accumulation of cottony vapour threatened, with every second, to blow over and submerge our homestead; but the vortex setting past the Toll House was too strong; and there lay our little platform, in the arms of the deluge, but still enjoying its unbroken sunshine. About eleven, however, thin spray came flying over the friendly buttress, and I began to think the fog had hunted out its Jonah after all. But it was the last effort. The wind veered while we were at dinner, and began to blow squally from the mountain summit; and by half-past one, all that world of sea-fogs was utterly routed and flying here and there into the south in little rags of cloud.

And instead of a lone sea-beach, we found ourselves once more inhabiting a high mountainside, with the clear green country far below us, and the light smoke of Calistoga blowing in the air.

This was the great Russian campaign[164] for that season. Now and then, in the early morning, a little white lakelet of fog would be seen far down in Napa Valley; but the heights were not again assailed, nor was the surrounding world again shut off from Silverado.

The Toll House

The Toll House – standing alone by the wayside under nodding pines, with its streamlet and water-tank; its backwoods, toll-bar and well trodden croquet ground; the ostler standing by the stable door, chewing a straw; a glimpse of the Chinese cook in the back parts; and Mr Hoddy in the bar, gravely alert and serviceable, and equally anxious to lend or borrow books – dozed all day in the dusty sunshine, more than half asleep. There were no neighbours, except the Hansons up the hill. The traffic on the road was infinitesimal; only, at rare intervals, a couple in a wagon, or a dusty farmer on a springboard, toiling over 'the grade' to that metropolitan hamlet, Calistoga; and, at the fixed hours, the passage of the stages.

The nearest building was the schoolhouse, down the road; and the school-ma'am boarded at the Toll House, walking thence in the morning to the little brown shanty, where she taught the young ones of the district, and returning thither pretty weary in the afternoon. She had chosen this outlying situation, I understood, for her health. Mr Corwin was consumptive; so was Rufe; so was Mr Jennings, the engineer. In short, the place was a kind of small Davos:[165] consumptive folk consorting on a hilltop in the most unbroken idleness. Jennings never did anything that I could see, except now and then to fish, and generally to sit about in the bar and the verandah, waiting for something to happen. Corwin and Rufe did as little as possible; and if the school-ma'am, poor lady, had to work pretty hard all morning, she subsided when it was over into much the same dazed beatitude as all the rest.

Her special corner was the parlour – a very genteel room, with Bible prints, a crayon portrait of Mrs Corwin in the height of fashion, a few years ago, another of her son (Mr Corwin was not represented), a mirror, and a selection of dried grasses. A large book was laid religiously on the table – *From Palace to Hovel*,[166] I believe, its name – full of the raciest experiences in England. The author had mingled freely with all classes, the nobility particularly meeting him with open arms; and I must say that traveller had ill requited his reception. His book, in short, was a capital instance of the Penny Messalina school of literature; and there arose from it, in that cool parlour, in that silent, wayside, mountain inn, a rank atmosphere of gold and blood and 'Jenkins', and the 'Mysteries of London', and sickening, inverted snobbery, fit to knock you down. The mention of this book reminds me of another and far racier picture of our island life. The latter parts of *Rocambole* [167] are surely too sparingly consulted in the country which they celebrate. No man's education can be said to be complete, nor can he pronounce the world yet emptied of enjoyment, till he has made the acquaintance of the 'Reverend Patterson, director of the Evangelical Society'. To follow the evolutions of that reverend gentleman, who goes through scenes in which even Mr Duffield would hesitate to place a bishop, is to rise to new ideas. But, alas! there was no Patterson about the Toll House. Only, alongside of *From Palace to Hovel*, a sixpenny 'Ouida' [168] figured. So literature, you see, was not unrepresented.

The school-ma'am had friends to stay with her, other school-ma'ams enjoying their holidays, quite a bevy of damsels. They seemed never to go out, or not beyond the verandah, but sat close in the little parlour, quietly talking or listening to the wind among the trees. Sleep dwelt in the Toll House, like a fixture: summer sleep, shallow, soft and dreamless. A cuckoo-clock, a great rarity in such a place, hooted at intervals about the echoing house; and Mr Jennings would open his eyes for a moment in the bar, and turn the leaf of a newspaper, and the resting school-ma'ams in the parlour would be recalled to the consciousness of their inaction. Busy Mrs Corwin and her busy Chinaman might be heard indeed, in the penetralia, [169] pounding dough or rattling dishes; or perhaps Rufe had called up some of the sleepers for a game of croquet, and the hollow strokes of the mallet sounded far away among the woods; but with these exceptions, it was sleep and sunshine and dust, and the wind in the pine trees, all day long.

A little before stage time, that castle of indolence awoke. The ostler threw his straw away and set to his preparations. Mr Jennings rubbed his eyes; happy Mr Jennings, the something he had been waiting for all day about to happen at last! The boarders gathered in the verandah, silently giving ear, and gazing down the road with shaded eyes. And as yet there was no sign for the senses, not a sound, not a tremor of the mountain road. The birds, to whom the secret of the hooting cuckoo is unknown, must have set down to instinct this premonitory bustle.

And then the first of the two stages swooped upon the Toll House with a roar and in a cloud of dust; and the shock had not yet time to subside, before the second was abreast of it. Huge concerns they were, well horsed and loaded, the men in their shirt-sleeves, the women swathed in veils, the long whip cracking like a pistol; and as they charged upon that slumbering hostelry, each shepherding a dust storm, the dead place blossomed into life and talk and clatter. This the Toll House? – with its city throng, its jostling shoulders, its infinity of instant business in the bar? The mind would not receive it! The heartfelt bustle of that hour is hardly credible; the thrill of the great shower of letters from the post-bag, the childish hope and interest with which one gazed in all these strangers' eyes. They paused there but to pass: the blue-clad China boy, the San Francisco magnate, the mystery in the dust coat, the secret memoirs in tweed, the ogling, well-shod lady with her troop of girls; they did but flash and go; they were hull-down for us behind life's ocean, and we but hailed their topsails on the line. Yet, out of our great solitude of four-and-twenty mountain hours, we thrilled to their momentary presence; gauged and divined them, loved and hated; and stood light-headed in that storm of human electricity. Yes, like Piccadilly Circus, this is also one of life's crossing-places.[170] Here I beheld one man, already famous or infamous, a centre of pistol-shots: and another who, if not yet known to rumour, will fill a column of the Sunday paper when he comes to hang – a burly, thick-set, powerful Chinese desperado, six long bristles upon either lip; redolent of whiskey, playing cards and pistols; swaggering in the bar with the lowest assumption of the lowest European manners; rapping out blackguard English oaths in his canorous Oriental voice; and combining in one person the depravities of two races and two civilisations. For all his lust and vigour, he seemed to look cold upon me from the valley of the shadow of the gallows. He imagined a vain thing; and while he drained his cocktail, Holbein's Death[171] was at his elbow. Once, too, I fell in talk with another of these flitting strangers – like the rest, in his shirt-sleeves and all begrimed with dust – and the next minute we were discussing Paris and London, theatres and wines. To him, journeying from one human place to another, this was a trifle; but to me! No, Mr Lillie, I have not forgotten it.

And presently the city-tide was at its flood and began to ebb. Life runs in Piccadilly Circus, say, from nine to one, and then, there also, ebbs into the small hours of the echoing policeman and the lamps and stars. But the Toll House is far upstream, and near its rural springs; the bubble of the tide but touches it. Before you had yet grasped your pleasure, the horses were put to, the loud whips volleyed, and the tide was gone. North and south had the two stages vanished, the towering dust subsided in the woods; but there was still an interval

before the flush had fallen on your cheeks, before the ear became
once more contented with the silence, or the seven sleepers of the
Toll House dozed back to their accustomed corners. Yet a little, and
the ostler would swing round the great barrier across the road; and
in the golden evening, that dreamy inn begin to trim its lamps and
spread the board for supper.

As I recall the place – the green dell below; the spires of pine; the
sun-warm, scented air; that grey, gabled inn, with its faint stirrings
of life amid the slumber of the mountains – I slowly awake to a sense
of admiration, gratitude and almost love. A fine place, after all, for a
wasted life to doze away in – the cuckoo clock hooting of its far
home country; the croquet mallets, eloquent of English lawns; the
stages daily bringing news of the turbulent world away below there;
and perhaps once in the summer, a salt fog pouring overhead with its
tale of the Pacific.[172]

A Starry Drive

In our rule at Silverado, there was a melancholy interregnum.[173] The Queen and the Crown Prince with one accord fell sick; and, as I was sick to begin with, our lone position on Mount St Helena was no longer tenable, and we had to hurry back to Calistoga and a cottage on the green. By that time we had begun to realise the difficulties of our position. We had found what an amount of labour it cost to support life in our red canyon; and it was the dearest desire of our hearts to get a China boy to go along with us when we returned. We could have given him a whole house to himself, self-contained, as they say in the advertisements; and on the money question we were prepared to go far. Kong Sam Kee, the Calistoga washerman, was entrusted with the affair; and from day to day it languished on, with protestations on our part and mellifluous excuses on the part of Kong Sam Kee.

At length, about half-past eight of our last evening, with the wagon ready harnessed to convey us up the grade, the washerman, with a somewhat sneering air, produced the boy. He was a handsome, gentlemanly lad, attired in rich dark blue, and shod with snowy white; but, alas! he had heard rumours of Silverado. He knew it for a lone place on the mountainside, with no friendly wash-house near by, where he might smoke a pipe of opium o' nights with other China boys, and lose his little earnings at the game of tan; and he first backed out for more money; and then, when that demand was satisfied, refused to come point-blank. He was wedded to his wash-houses; he had no taste for the rural life; and we must go to our mountain servantless. It must have been near half an hour before we reached that conclusion, standing in the midst of Calistoga high street under the stars, and the China boy and Kong Sam Kee singing their pigeon English in the sweetest voices and with the most musical inflections.

We were not, however, to return alone; for we brought with us Joe Strong,[174] the painter, a most good-natured comrade and a capital hand at an omelette. I do not know in which capacity he was most valued – as a cook or a companion; and he did excellently well in both.

The Kong Sam Kee negotiation had delayed us unduly; it must have been half-past nine before we left Calistoga, and night came fully ere we struck the bottom of the grade. I have never seen such a night. It seemed to throw calumny in the teeth of all the painters that ever dabbled in starlight. The sky itself was of a ruddy, powerful, nameless, changing colour, dark and glossy like a serpent's back. The stars, by innumerable millions, stuck boldly forth like lamps. The milky way was bright, like a moonlit cloud; half heaven seemed milky way. The greater luminaries shone each more clearly than a winter's moon. Their light was dyed in every sort of colour – red, like fire; blue, like steel; green, like the tracks of sunset; and so sharply did each stand forth in its own lustre that there was no appearance of that flat, star-spangled arch we know so well in pictures, but all the hollow of heaven was one chaos of contesting luminaries – a hurly-burly of stars. Against this the hills and rugged treetops stood out redly dark.

As we continued to advance, the lesser lights and milky ways first grew pale, and then vanished; the countless hosts of heaven dwindled in number by successive millions; those that still shone had tempered their exceeding brightness and fallen back into their customary wistful distance; and the sky declined from its first bewildering splendour into the appearance of a common night. Slowly this change proceeded, and still there was no sign of any cause. Then a whiteness like mist was thrown over the spurs of the mountain. Yet a while, and, as we turned a corner, a great leap of silver light and net of forest shadows fell across the road and upon our wondering wagonful; and, swimming low among the trees, we beheld a strange, misshapen, waning moon, half-tilted on her back.

'Where are ye when the moon appears?' so the old poet sang, half-taunting, to the stars, bent upon a courtly purpose.

'As the sunlight round the dim earth's midnight tower
                                     of shadow pours,
        Streaming past the dim, wide portals,
        Viewless to the eyes of mortals,
    Till it floods the moon's pale islet or the morning's
                                     golden shores.'

So sings Mr Trowbridge, with a noble inspiration. And so had the sunlight flooded that pale islet of the moon, and her lit face put out, one after another, that galaxy of stars. The wonder of the drive was over; but, by some nice conjunction of clearness in the air and fit shadow in the valley where we travelled, we had seen for a little while that brave display of the midnight heavens. It was gone, but it had been; nor shall I ever again behold the stars with the same mind. He who has seen the sea commoved with a great hurricane, thinks of it very differently from him who has seen it only in a calm. And the difference between a calm and a hurricane is not greatly more striking than that between the ordinary face of night and the splendour that shone upon us in that drive. Two in our wagon knew night as she shines upon the tropics, but even that bore no comparison. The nameless colour of the sky, the hues of the star-fire, and the incredible projection of the stars themselves, starting from their orbits, so that the eye seemed to distinguish their positions in the hollow of space – these were things that we had never seen before and shall never see again.

Meanwhile, in this altered night, we proceeded on our way among the scents and silence of the forest, reached the top of the grade, wound up by Hanson's, and came at last to a stand under the flying gargoyle of the chute. Sam, who had been lying back, fast asleep, with the moon on his face, got down, with the remark that it was pleasant 'to be home'. The wagon turned and drove away, the noise gently dying in the woods, and we clambered up the rough path, Caliban's great feat of engineering, and came home to Silverado.

The moon shone in at the eastern doors and windows, and over the lumber on the platform. The one tall pine beside the ledge was steeped in silver. Away up the canyon, a wild cat welcomed us with three discordant squalls. But once we had lit a candle, and begun to review our improvements, homely in either sense, and count our stores, it was wonderful what a feeling of possession and permanence grew up in the hearts of the lords of Silverado. A bed had still to be made up for Strong, and the morning's water to be fetched, with clinking pail; and as we set about these household duties, and showed off our wealth and conveniences before the stranger, and had a glass of wine, I think, in honour of our return, and trooped at length one after another up the flying bridge of plank and lay down to sleep in our shattered, moon-pierced barrack, we were among the happiest sovereigns in the world, and certainly ruled over the most contented people. Yet, in our absence, the palace had been sacked. Wild cats, so the Hansons said, had broken in and carried off a side of bacon, a hatchet and two knives.

Episodes in the Story of a Mine

No one could live at Silverado and not be curious about the story of the mine. We were surrounded by so many evidences of expense and toil, we lived so entirely in the wreck of that great enterprise, like mites in the ruins of a cheese, that the idea of the old din and bustle haunted our repose. Our own house, the forge, the dump, the chutes, the rails, the windlass, the mass of broken plant; the two tunnels, one far below in the green dell, the other on the platform where we kept our wine; the deep shaft, with the sun-glints and the water-drops; above all, the ledge, that great gaping slice out of the mountain shoulder, propped apart by wooden wedges, on whose immediate margin, high above our heads, the one tall pine precariously nodded – these stood for its greatness; while, the dog-hutch, boot-jacks, old boots, old tavern bills, and the very beds that we inherited from bygone miners, put in human touches and realised for us the story of the past.

I have sat on an old sleeper, under the thick madronas near the forge, with just a look over the dump on the green world below, and seen the sun lying broad among the wreck, and heard the silence broken only by the tinkling water in the shaft, or a stir of the royal family about the battered palace, and my mind has gone back to the epoch of the Stanleys and the Chapmans, with a grand *tutti* of pick and drill, hammer and anvil, echoing about the canyon; the assayer hard at it in our dining-room; the carts below on the road, and their cargo of red mineral bounding and thundering down the iron chute. And now all gone – all fallen away into this sunny silence and desertion: a family of squatters dining in the assayer's office, making their beds in the big sleeping room erstwhile so crowded, keeping their wine in the tunnel that once rang with picks.

But Silverado itself, although now fallen in its turn into decay, was once but a mushroom, and had succeeded to other mines and other flitting cities. Twenty years ago, away down the glen on the Lake County side there was a place, Jonestown by name, with two thousand inhabitants dwelling under canvas, and one roofed house for the sale of whiskey. Round on the western side of Mount St Helena, there was at the same date, a second large encampment, its name, if it ever had one, lost for me. Both of these have perished, leaving not a stick and scarce a memory behind them. Tide after tide of hopeful miners have thus flowed and ebbed about the mountain, coming and going, now by lone prospectors, now with a rush. Last in order of time came Silverado, reared the big mill, in the valley, founded the town which is now represented, monumentally, by Hanson's, pierced all these slaps and shafts and tunnels, and in turn declined and died away.

> Our noisy years seem moments in the being
> Of the eternal silence.[175]

As to the success of Silverado in its time of being, two reports were current. According to the first, six hundred thousand dollars were taken out of that great upright seam that still hung open above us on crazy wedges. Then the ledge pinched out, and there followed, in quest of the remainder, a great drifting and tunnelling in all directions, and a great consequent effusion of dollars, until, all parties being sick of the expense, the mine was deserted, and the town decamped. According to the second version, told me with much secrecy of manner, the whole affair, mine, mill and town, were parts of one majestic swindle. There had never come any silver out of any portion of the mine; there was no silver to come. At midnight trains of packhorses might have been observed winding by devious tracks about the shoulder of the mountain. They came from far away, from Amador or Placer, laden with silver in 'old cigar boxes'. They discharged their load at Silverado, in the hour of sleep; and before the morning they were gone again with their mysterious drivers to their unknown source. In this way, twenty thousand pounds' worth of silver was smuggled in under cover of night, in these old cigar boxes; mixed with Silverado mineral; carted down to the mill; crushed, amalgamated and refined, and despatched to the city as the proper product of the mine. Stock-jobbing,[176] if it can cover such expenses, must be a profitable business in San Francisco.

I give these two versions as I got them. But I place little reliance on either, my belief in history having been greatly shaken. For it chanced that I had come to dwell in Silverado at a critical hour; great events in its history were about to happen – did happen, as I am led to believe; nay, and it will be seen that I played a part in that revolution myself. And yet from first to last I never had a glimmer of an idea what was going on; and even now, after full reflection, profess myself at sea. That there was some obscure intrigue of the cigar-box order, and that I, in the character of a wooden puppet, set pen to paper in the interest of somebody – so much, and no more, is certain.

Silverado, then under my immediate sway, belonged to one whom I will call a Mr Ronalds. I only knew him through the extraordinarily distorting medium of local gossip – now as a momentous jobber; now as a dupe to point an adage; and again, and much more probably, as an ordinary Christian gentleman like you or me, who had opened a mine and worked it for a while with better and worse fortune. So, through a defective window-pane, you may see the passer-by shoot up into a hunchbacked giant or dwindle into a potbellied dwarf.

To Ronalds, at least, the mine belonged; but the notice by which he held it would run out upon the 30th of June – or rather, as I suppose, it had run out already, and the month of grace would expire upon that day, after which any American citizen might post a notice of his own, and make Silverado his. This, with a sort of quiet slyness, Rufe told me at an early period of our acquaintance. There was no silver, of course; the mine 'wasn't worth nothing, Mr Stevens', but there was a deal of old iron and wood around, and to gain possession of this old wood and iron, and get a right to the water, Rufe proposed, if I had no objections, to 'jump the claim'.

Of course, I had no objection. But I was filled with wonder. If all he wanted was the wood and iron, what, in the name of fortune, was to prevent him taking them? 'His right there was none to dispute.' He might lay hands on all tomorrow, as the wild cats had laid hands upon our knives and hatchet. Besides, was this mass of heavy mining plant worth transportation? If it was, why had not the rightful owners carted it away? If it was, would they not preserve their title to these movables, even after they had lost their title to the mine? And if it were not, what the better was Rufe? Nothing would grow at Silverado; there was even no wood to cut; beyond a sense of property, there was nothing to be gained. Lastly, was it at all credible that Ronalds would forget what Rufe remembered? The days of grace were not yet over: any fine morning he might appear, paper in hand, and enter for another year on his inheritance. However, it was none of my business; all seemed legal; Rufe or Ronalds, all was one to me.

On the morning of the 27th, Mrs Hanson appeared with the milk as usual, in her sun bonnet. The time would be out on Tuesday, she reminded us, and bade me be in readiness to play my part, though I had no idea what it was to be. And suppose Ronalds came? we asked. She received the idea with derision, laughing aloud with all her fine teeth. He could not find the mine to save his life, it appeared, without Rufe to guide him. Last year, when he came, they heard him 'up and down the road a hollerin' and a raisin' Cain'. And at last he had to come to the Hansons in despair, and bid Rufe, 'Jump into your pants and shoes, and show me where this old mine is, anyway!' Seeing that Ronalds had laid out so much money in the spot, and that a beaten road led right up to the bottom of the dump, I thought this a remarkable example. The sense of locality must be singularly in abeyance in the case of Ronalds.

That same evening, supper comfortably over, Joe Strong busy at work on a drawing of the dump and the opposite hills, we were all out on the platform together, sitting there, under the tented heavens, with the same sense of privacy as if we had been cabined in a parlour, when the sound of brisk footsteps came mounting up the path. We pricked our ears at this, for the tread seemed lighter and firmer than was usual with our country neighbours. And presently, sure enough, two town gentlemen, with cigars and kid gloves, came debauching past the house. They looked in that place like a blasphemy.

'Good-evening,' they said. For none of us had stirred; we all sat stiff with wonder.

'Good-evening,' I returned; and then, to put them at their ease, 'A stiff climb,' I added.

'Yes,' replied the leader; 'but we have to thank you for this path.'

I did not like the man's tone. None of us liked it. He did not seem embarrassed by the meeting, but threw us his remarks like favours, and strode magisterially by us towards the shaft and tunnel.

Presently we heard his voice raised to his companion. 'We drifted every sort of way, but couldn't strike the ledge.' Then again: 'It pinched out here.' And once more: 'Every minor that ever worked upon it says there's bound to be a ledge somewhere.'

These were the snatches of his talk that reached us, and they had a damning significance. We, the lords of Silverado, had come face to face with our superior. It is the worst of all quaint and of all cheap ways of life that they bring us at last to the pinch of some humiliation. I liked well enough to be a squatter when there was none but Hanson by; before Ronalds, I will own, I somewhat quailed. I hastened to do him fealty, said I gathered he was the Squattee, and apologised. He threatened me with ejection, in a manner grimly pleasant – more pleasant to him, I fancy, than to me; and then he passed off into praises of the former state of Silverado. 'It was the busiest little mining town you ever saw': a population of between a thousand and fifteen hundred souls, the engine in full blast, the mill newly erected; nothing going but champagne, and hope the order of the day. Ninety thousand dollars came out; a hundred and forty thousand were put in, making a net loss of fifty thousand. The last days, I gathered, the days of John Stanley, were not so bright; the champagne had ceased to flow, the population was already moving elsewhere, and Silverado had begun to wither in the branch before it was cut at the root. The last shot that was fired knocked over the stove chimney, and made that hole in the roof of our barrack, through which the sun was wont to visit slug-a-beds towards afternoon. A noisy, last shot, to inaugurate the days of silence.

Throughout this interview, my conscience was a good deal exercised; and I was moved to throw myself on my knees and own the intended treachery. But then I had Hanson to consider. I was in much the same position as Old Rowley,[177] that royal humorist, whom 'the rogue had taken into his confidence'. And again, here was Ronalds on the spot. He must know the day of the month as well as Hanson and I. If a broad hint were necessary, he had the broadest in the world. For a large board had been nailed by the Crown Prince on the very front of our house, between the door and window, painted in cinnabar – the pigment of the country – with doggerel rhymes and contumelious pictures, and announcing, in terms unnecessarily figurative, that the trick was already played, the claim already jumped, and the author of the placard the legitimate successor of Mr Ronalds. But no, nothing could save that man; *quem deus vult perdere, prius dementat.*[178] As he came so he went, and left his rights depending.

Late at night, by Silverado reckoning, and after we were all abed, Mrs Hanson returned to give us the newest of her news. It was like a scene in a ship's steerage: all of us abed in our different tiers, the single candle struggling with the darkness, and this plump, handsome woman, seated on an upturned valise beside the bunks, talking and showing her fine teeth, and laughing till the rafters rang. Any ship, to be sure, with a hundredth part as many holes in it as our barrack, must long ago have gone to her last port. Up to that time I had always imagined Mrs Hanson's loquacity to be mere incontinence, that she said what was uppermost for the pleasure of speaking, and laughed and laughed again as a kind of musical accompaniment. But I now found there was an art in it, I found it less communicative than silence itself. I wished to know why Ronalds had come; how he had found his way without Rufe; and why, being on the spot, he had not refreshed his title. She talked interminably on, but her replies were never answers. She fled under a cloud of words; and when I had made sure that she was purposely eluding me, I dropped the subject in my turn, and let her rattle where she would.

She had come to tell us that, instead of waiting for Tuesday, the claim was to be jumped on the morrow. How? If the time were not out, it was impossible. Why? If Ronalds had come and gone, and done nothing, there was the less cause for hurry. But again I could reach no satisfaction. The claim was to be jumped next morning, that was all that she would condescend upon.

And yet it was not jumped the next morning, nor yet the next, and a whole week had come and gone before we heard more of this exploit. That day week, however, a day of great heat, Hanson, with a little roll of paper in his hand, and the eternal pipe alight; Breedlove, his large, dull friend, to act, I suppose, as witness; Mrs Hanson, in her Sunday best; and all the children, from the oldest to the youngest, arrived in a procession, tailing one behind another up the path. Caliban was absent, but he had been chary of his friendly visits since the row; and with that exception, the whole family was gathered together as for a marriage or a christening. Strong was sitting at work, in the shade of the dwarf madronas near the forge; and they planted themselves about him in a circle, one on a stone, another on the wagon rails, a third on a piece of plank. Gradually the children stole away up the canyon to where there was another chute, somewhat smaller than the one across the dump; and down this chute, for the rest of the afternoon, they poured one avalanche of stones after another, waking the echoes of the glen. Meantime, we elders sat together on the platform, Hanson and his friend smoking in silence like Indian sachems, Mrs Hanson rattling on as usual with an adroit volubility, saying nothing, but keeping the party at their ease like a courtly hostess.

Not a word occurred about the business of the day. Once, twice and thrice I tried to slide the subject in, but was discouraged by the stoic apathy of Rufe, and beaten down before the pouring verbiage of his wife. There is nothing of the Indian brave about me, and I began to grill with impatience. At last, like a highway robber, I cornered Hanson, and bade him stand and deliver his business. Thereupon he gravely rose, as though to hint that this was not a proper place, nor the subject one suitable for squaws, and I, following his example, led him up the plank into our barrack. There he bestowed himself on a box, and unrolled his papers with fastidious deliberation. There were two sheets of notepaper, and an old mining notice, dated May 30th, 1879, part print, part manuscript, and the latter much obliterated by the rains. It was by this identical piece of paper that the mine had been held last year. For thirteen months it had endured the weather and the change of seasons on a cairn behind the shoulder of the canyon; and it was now my business, spreading it before me on the table, and sitting on a valise, to copy its terms, with some necessary changes, twice over on the two sheets of notepaper. One was then to be placed on the same cairn – a 'mound of rocks' the notice put it; and the other to be lodged for registration.

Rufe watched me, silently smoking, till I came to the place for the locator's name at the end of the first copy; and when I proposed that he should sign, I thought I saw a scare in his eye. 'I don't think that'll be necessary,' he said slowly; 'just you write it down.' Perhaps this mighty hunter, who was the most active member of the local school-board, could not write. There would be nothing strange in that. The constable of Calistoga is, and has been for years, a bedridden man, and, if I remember rightly, blind. He had more need of the emoluments than another, it was explained; and it was easy for him to 'depytise', with a strong accent on the last. So friendly and so free are popular institutions.

When I had done my scrivening, Hanson strolled out, and addressed Breedlove, 'Will you step up here a bit?' and after they had disappeared a little while into the chaparral and madrona thicket, they came back again, minus a notice, and the deed was done. The claim was jumped; a tract of mountainside, fifteen hundred feet long by six hundred wide, with all the earth's precious bowels, had passed from Ronalds to Hanson, and, in the passage, changed its name from the 'Mammoth' to the 'Calistoga'. I had tried to get Rufe to call it after his wife, after himself, and after Garfield, the Republican presidential candidate of the hour – since then elected, and, alas! dead – but all was in vain. The claim had once been called the Calistoga before, and he seemed to feel safety in returning to that.

And so the history of that mine became once more plunged in darkness, lit only by some monster pyrotechnical displays of gossip. And perhaps the most curious feature of the whole matter is this: that we should have dwelt in this quiet corner of the mountains, with not a dozen neighbours, and yet struggled all the while, like desperate swimmers, in this sea of falsities and contradictions. Wherever a man is, there will be a lie.

Toils and Pleasures

I must try to convey some notion of our life, of how the days passed and what pleasure we took in them, of what there was to do and how we set about doing it, in our mountain hermitage.[179] The house, after we had repaired the worst of the damages, and filled in some of the doors and windows with white cotton cloth, became a healthy and a pleasant dwelling-place, always airy and dry, and haunted by the outdoor perfumes of the glen. Within, it had the look of habitation, the human look. You had only to go into the third room, which we did not use, and see its stones, its sifting earth, its tumbled litter; and then return to our lodging, with the beds made, the plates on the rack, the pail of bright water behind the door, the stove crackling in a corner, and perhaps the table roughly laid against a meal – and man's order, the little clean spots that he creates to dwell in, were at once contrasted with the rich passivity of nature. And yet our house was everywhere so wrecked and shattered, the air came and went so freely, the sun found so many portholes, the golden outdoor glow shone in so many open chinks, that we enjoyed, at the same time, some of the comforts of a roof and much of the gaiety and brightness of *al fresco* life. A single shower of rain, to be sure, and we should have been drowned out like mice. But ours was a Californian summer, and an earthquake was a far likelier accident than a shower of rain.

Trustful in this fine weather, we kept the house for kitchen and bedroom, and used the platform as our summer parlour. The sense of privacy, as I have said already, was complete. We could look over the dump on miles of forest and rough hilltop; our eyes commanded some of Napa Valley, where the train ran, and the little country townships sat so close together along the line of the rail. But here there was no man to intrude. None but the Hansons were our visitors. Even they came but at long intervals, or twice daily, at a stated hour, with milk. So our days, as they were never interrupted, drew out to the greater length; hour melted insensibly into hour; the household duties, though they were many, and some of them laborious, dwindled into mere islets of business in a sea of sunny daytime; and it appears to me, looking back, as though the far greater part of our life at Silverado had been passed, propped upon an elbow, or seated on a plank, listening to the silence that there is among the hills.

My work, it is true, was over early in the morning. I rose before anyone else, lit the stove, put on the water to boil, and strolled forth upon the platform to wait till it was ready. Silverado would then be still in shadow, the sun shining on the mountain higher up. A clean smell of trees, a smell of the earth at morning, hung in the air. Regularly, every day, there was a single bird, not singing, but awkwardly chirruping among the green madronas, and the sound was cheerful, natural and stirring. It did not hold the attention, nor interrupt the thread of meditation, like a blackbird or a nightingale; it was mere woodland prattle, of which the mind was conscious like a perfume. The freshness of these morning seasons remained with me far on into the day.

As soon as the kettle boiled, I made porridge and coffee; and that, beyond the literal drawing of water, and the preparation of kindling, which it would be hyperbolical to call the hewing of wood, ended my domestic duties for the day. Thenceforth my wife laboured single-handed in the palace, and I lay or wandered on the platform at my own sweet will. The little corner near the forge, where we found a refuge under the madronas from the unsparing early sun, is indeed connected in my mind with some nightmare encounters over Euclid, and the Latin Grammar. These were known as Sam's lessons. He was supposed to be the victim and the sufferer; but here there must have been some misconception, for whereas I generally retired to bed after one of these engagements, he was no sooner set free than he dashed up to the Chinaman's house, where he had installed a printing press, that great element of civilisation, and the sound of his labours would be faintly audible about the canyon half the day.

To walk at all was a laborious business; the foot sank and slid, the boots were cut to pieces among sharp, uneven, rolling stones. When we crossed the platform in any direction, it was usual to lay a course, following as much as possible the line of wagon rails. Thus, if water were to be drawn, the water-carrier left the house along some tilting planks that we had laid down, and not laid down very well. These carried him to that great high-road, the railway; and the railway served him as far as to the head of the shaft. But from thence to the spring and back again he made the best of his unaided way, staggering among the stones, and wading in the low growth of the calycanthus, where the rattlesnakes lay hissing at his passage. Yet I liked to draw water. It was pleasant to dip the grey metal pail into the clean, colourless, cool water; pleasant to carry it back, with the water lipping at the edge, and a broken sunbeam quivering in the midst.

But the extreme roughness of the walking confined us in common practice to the platform, and indeed to those parts of it that were most easily accessible along the line of rails. The rails came straight forward from the shaft, here and there overgrown with little green bushes, but still entire, and still carrying a truck, which it was Sam's delight to trundle to and fro by the hour with various ladings. About midway down the platform, the railroad trended to the right, leaving our house and coasting along the far side within a few yards of the madronas and the forge, and not far from the latter, ended in a sort of platform on the edge of the dump. There, in old days, the trucks were tipped, and their load sent thundering down the chute. There, besides, was the only spot where we could approach the margin of the dump. Anywhere else, you took your life in your right hand when you came within a yard and a half to peer over. For at any moment the dump might begin to slide and carry you down and bury you below its ruins. Indeed, the neighbourhood of an old mine is a place beset with dangers. For as still as Silverado was, at any moment the report of rotten wood might tell us that the platform had fallen into the shaft; the dump might begin to pour into the road below; or a wedge slip in the great upright seam, and hundreds of tons of mountain bury the scene of our encampment.

I have already compared the dump to a rampart, built certainly by some rude people, and for prehistoric wars. It was likewise a frontier. All below was green and woodland, the tall pines soaring one above another, each with a firm outline and full spread of bough. All above was arid, rocky and bald. The great spout of broken mineral, that had dammed the canyon up, was a creature of man's handiwork, its material dug out with a pick and powder, and spread by the service of the tracks. But nature herself, in that upper district, seemed to have had an eye to nothing besides mining; and even the natural hillside was all sliding gravel and precarious boulder. Close at the margin of the well leaves would decay to skeletons and mummies, which at length some stronger gust would carry clear of the canyon and scatter in the subjacent woods. Even moisture and decaying vegetable matter could not, with all nature's alchemy, concoct enough soil to nourish a few poor grasses. It is the same, they say, in the neighbourhood of all silver mines, the nature of that precious rock being stubborn with quartz and poisonous with cinnabar. Both were plenty in our Silverado. The stones sparkled white in the sunshine with quartz; they were all stained red with cinnabar. Here, doubtless, came the Indians of yore to paint their faces for the warpath; and cinnabar, if

I remember rightly, was one of the few articles of Indian commerce. Now, Sam had it in his undisturbed possession, to pound down and slake and paint his rude designs with. But to me it had always a fine flavour of poetry, compounded out of Indian story and Hawthornden's allusion:

> Desire, alas! I desire a Zeuxis new,
> From Indies borrowing gold, from Eastern skies
> Most bright cinoper . . . [180]

Yet this is but half the picture; our Silverado platform has another side to it. Though there was no soil, and scarce a blade of grass, yet out of these tumbled gravel-heaps and broken boulders, a flower garden bloomed as at home in a conservatory. Calycanthus crept, like a hardy weed, all over our rough parlour, choking the railway, and pushing forth its rusty, aromatic cones from between two blocks of shattered mineral. Azaleas made a big snow-bed just above the well. The shoulder of the hill waved white with Mediterranean heath. In the crannies of the ledge and about the spurs of the tall pine, a red flowering stone-plant hung in clusters. Even the low, thorny chaparral was thick with pea-like blossom.[181] Close at the foot of our path nutmegs prospered, delightful to the sight and smell. At sunrise, and again late at night, the scent of the sweet bay trees filled the canyon, and the down-blowing night wind must have borne it hundreds of feet into the outer air.

All this vegetation, to be sure, was stunted. The madrona was here no bigger than the manzanita; the bay was but a stripling shrub; the very pines, with four or five exceptions in all our upper canyon, were not so tall as myself, or but a little taller, and the most of them came lower than my waist. For a prosperous forest tree, we must look below, where the glen was crowded with green spires. But for flowers and ravishing perfume, we had none to envy: our heap of road-metal was thick with bloom, like a hawthorn in the front of June; our red, baking angle in the mountain, a laboratory of poignant scents. It was an endless wonder to my mind, as I dreamed about the platform, following the progress of the shadows, where the madrona with its leaves, the azalea and calycanthus with their blossoms, could find moisture to support such thick, wet, waxy growths, or the bay tree collect the ingredients of its perfume. But there they all grew together, healthy, happy and happy-making, as though rooted in a fathom of black soil.

Nor was it only vegetable life that prospered. We had, indeed, few birds, and none that had much of a voice or anything worthy to be called a song. My morning comrade had a thin chirp, unmusical and monotonous, but friendly and pleasant to hear. He had but one rival: a fellow with an ostentatious cry of near an octave descending, not one note of which properly followed another. This is the only bird I ever knew with a wrong ear; but there was something enthralling about his performance. You listened and listened, thinking each time he must surely get it right; but no, it was always wrong, and always wrong the same way. Yet he seemed proud of his song, delivered it with execution and a manner of his own, and was charming to his mate. A very incorrect, incessant human whistler[182] had thus a chance of knowing how his own music pleased the world. Two great birds – eagles, we thought – dwelt at the top of the canyon, among the crags that were printed on the sky. Now and again, but very rarely, they wheeled high over our heads in silence, or with a distant, dying scream; and then, with a fresh impulse, winged fleetly forward, dipped over a hilltop, and were gone. They seemed solemn and ancient things, sailing the blue air: perhaps coeval with the mountain where they haunted, perhaps emigrants from Rome, where the glad legions may have shouted to behold them on the morn of battle.[183]

But if birds were rare, the place abounded with rattlesnakes – the rattlesnake's nest, it might have been named. Wherever we brushed among the bushes, our passage woke their angry buzz. One dwelt habitually in the wood-pile, and sometimes, when we came for firewood, thrust up his small head between two logs, and hissed at the intrusion. The rattle has a legendary credit; it is said to be awe-inspiring, and, once heard, to stamp itself for ever in the memory. But the sound is not at all alarming; the hum of many insects, and the buzz of the wasp convince the ear of danger quite as readily. As a matter of fact, we lived for weeks in Silverado, coming and going, with rattles sprung on every side, and it never occurred to us to be afraid. I used to take sunbaths and do calisthenics in a certain pleasant nook among azalea and calycanthus, the rattles whizzing on every side like spinning-wheels, and the combined hiss or buzz rising louder and angrier at any sudden movement; but I was never in the least impressed, nor ever attacked. It was only towards the end of our stay that a man down at Calistoga, who was expatiating on the terrifying nature of the sound, gave me at last a very good imitation; and it burst on me at once that we dwelt in the very metropolis of deadly snakes, and that the rattle was simply the commonest noise in Silverado. Immediately on our return, we attacked the Hansons on the subject. They had formerly assured us that our canyon was favoured, like Ireland, with an entire immunity from poisonous reptiles; but, with the perfect inconsequence of the natural man, they were no sooner found out than they went off at score in the contrary direction, and we were told that in no part of the world did rattlesnakes attain to such a monstrous bigness as among the warm, flower-dotted rocks of Silverado. This is a contribution rather to the natural history of the Hansons, than to that of snakes.

One person, however, better served by his instinct, had known the rattle from the first; and that was Chuchu, the dog. No rational creature has ever led an existence more poisoned by terror than that dog's at Silverado. Every whizz of the rattle made him bound. His eyes rolled; he trembled; he would be often wet with sweat. One of our great mysteries was his terror of the mountain. A little away above our nook, the azaleas and almost all the vegetation ceased. Dwarf pines not big enough to be Christmas trees, grew thinly among loose stone and gravel scaurs. Here and there a big boulder sat quiescent on a knoll, having paused there till the next rain in his long slide down the mountain. There was here no ambuscade for the snakes, you could see clearly where you trod; and yet the higher I went, the more abject and appealing became Chuchu's terror. He was an excellent master of that composite language in which dogs communicate with men, and he would assure me, on his honour, that there was some peril on the mountain; appeal to me, by all that I held holy, to turn back; and at length, finding all was in vain, and that I still persisted, ignorantly foolhardy, he would suddenly whip round and make a beeline down the slope for Silverado, the gravel showering after him. What was he afraid of? There were admittedly brown bears and California lions on the mountain; and a grizzly visited Rufe's poultry yard not long before, to the unspeakable alarm of Caliban, who dashed out to chastise the intruder, and found himself, by moonlight, face to face with such a tartar. Something at least there must have been: some hairy, dangerous brute lodged permanently among the rocks a little to the north-west of Silverado, spending his summer thereabout, with wife and family.

And there was, or there had been, another animal. Once, under the broad daylight, on that open stony hillside, where the baby pines were growing, scarcely tall enough to be a badge for a MacGregor's bonnet,[184] I came suddenly upon his innocent body, lying mummified by the dry air and sun: a pigmy kangaroo. I am ingloriously ignorant of these subjects; had never heard of such a beast; thought myself face to face with some incomparable sport of nature; and began to cherish hopes of immortality in science. Rarely have I been conscious of a stranger thrill than when I raised that singular creature from the stones, dry as a board, his innocent heart long quiet, and all warm with sunshine. His long hind legs were stiff, his tiny forepaws clutched upon his breast, as if to leap; his poor life cut short upon that mountain by some unknown accident. But the kangaroo rat, it proved, was no such unknown animal; and my discovery was nothing.

Crickets were not wanting. I thought I could make out exactly four of them, each with a corner of his own, who used to make night musical at Silverado. In the matter of voice, they far excelled the birds, and their ringing whistle sounded from rock to rock, calling and replying the same thing, as in a meaningless opera. Thus, children in full health and spirits shout together, to the dismay of neighbours; and their idle, happy, deafening vociferations rise and fall, like the song of the crickets. I used to sit at night on the platform, and wonder why these creatures were so happy; and what was wrong with man that he also did not wind up his days with an hour or two of shouting; but I suspect that all long-lived animals are solemn. The dogs alone are hardly used by nature; and it seems a manifest injustice for poor Chuchu to die in his teens, after a life so shadowed and troubled, continually shaken with alarm, and the tear of elegant sentiment permanently in his eye.

There was another neighbour of ours at Silverado, small but very active, a destructive fellow. This was a black, ugly fly – a bore, the Hansons called him – who lived by hundreds in the boarding of our house. He entered by a round hole, more neatly pierced than a man could do it with a gimlet, and he seems to have spent his life in cutting out the interior of the plank, but whether as a dwelling or a store-house, I could never find. When I used to lie in bed in the morning for a rest – we had no easy-chairs in Silverado – I would hear, hour after hour, the sharp cutting sound of his labours, and from time to time a dainty shower of sawdust would fall upon the blankets. There lives no more industrious creature than a bore.

And now that I have named to the reader all our animals and insects without exception – only I find I have forgotten the flies – he will be able to appreciate the singular privacy and silence of our days. It was not only man who was excluded: animals, the song of birds, the lowing of cattle, the bleating of sheep, clouds even, and the variations of the weather, were here also wanting; and as, day after day, the sky was one dome of blue, and the pines below us stood motionless in the still air, so the hours themselves were marked out from each other only by the series of our own affairs, and the sun's great period as he ranged westward through the heavens. The two birds cackled a while in the early morning; all day the water tinkled in the shaft, the bores ground sawdust in the planking of our crazy palace – infinitesimal sounds; and it was only with the return of night that any change would fall on our surroundings, or the four crickets begin to flute together in the dark.

Indeed, it would be hard to exaggerate the pleasure that we took in the approach of evening. Our day was not very long, but it was very tiring. To trip along unsteady planks or wade among shifting stones, to go to and fro for water, to clamber down the glen to the Toll House after meat and letters, to cook, to make fires and beds, were all exhausting to the body. Life out of doors, besides, under the fierce eye of day, draws largely on the animal spirits. There are certain hours in the afternoon when a man, unless he is in strong health or enjoys a vacant mind, would rather creep into a cool corner of a house and sit upon the chairs of civilisation. About that time, the sharp stones, the planks, the upturned boxes of Silverado, began to grow irksome to my body; I set out on that hopeless, never-ending quest for a more comfortable posture; I would be fevered and weary of the staring sun; and just then he would begin courteously to withdraw his countenance, the shadows lengthened, the aromatic airs awoke, and an indescribable but happy change announced the coming of the night.

The hours of evening, when we were once curtained in the friendly dark, sped lightly. Even as with the crickets, night brought to us a certain spirit of rejoicing. It was good to taste the air; good to mark the dawning of the stars, as they increased their glittering company; good, too, to gather stones, and send them crashing down the chute, a wave of light. It seemed, in some way, the reward and the fulfilment of the day. So it is when men dwell in the open air; it is one of the simple pleasures that we lose by living cribbed and covered in a house, that, though the coming of the day is still the most inspiriting, yet day's departure, also, and the return of night, refresh, renew and quiet us; and in the pastures of the dusk we stand, like cattle, exulting in the absence of the load.

Our nights were never cold, and they were always still, but for one remarkable exception. Regularly, about nine o'clock, a warm wind sprang up, and blew for ten minutes, or maybe a quarter of an hour, right down the canyon, fanning it well out, airing it as a mother airs the night nursery before the children sleep. As far as I could judge, in the clear darkness of the night, this wind was purely local: perhaps dependant on the configuration of the glen. At least, it was very welcome to the hot and weary squatters; and if we were not abed already, the springing up of this Lilliputian valley-wind would often be our signal to retire.

I was the last to go to bed, as I was still the first to rise. Many a night I have strolled about the platform, taking a bath of darkness before I slept. The rest would be in bed, and even from the forge I could hear them talking together from bunk to bunk. A single candle in the neck of a pint bottle was their only illumination; and yet the old cracked house seemed literally bursting with the light. It shone keen as a knife through all the vertical chinks; it struck upward through the broken shingles; and through the eastern door and window, it fell in a great splash upon the thicket and the overhanging rock. You would have said a conflagration, or at the least a roaring forge; and behold, it was but a candle. Or perhaps it was yet more strange to see the procession moving bedwards round the corner of the house, and up the plank that brought us to the bedroom door; under the immense spread of the starry heavens, down in a crevice of the giant mountain these few human shapes, with their unshielded taper, made so disproportionate a figure in the eye and mind. But the more he is alone with nature, the greater man and his doings bulk in the consideration of his fellow-men. Miles and miles away upon the opposite hilltops, if there were any hunter belated or any traveller who had lost his way, he must have stood, and watched and wondered, from the time the candle issued from the door of the assayer's office till it had mounted the plank and disappeared again into the miners' dormitory.

The Silverado Diary

Vallejo and the Singing Cobbler

May 22nd, 1880 [185]

When we arrived at Vallejo junction, I stood aside. This was a piece of policy. Fanny and I, being the least capable of persons, fell back on innocent device to get us unharmed through life.[186] When a woman was to be dealt with, I looked as sick as I could, and worked upon her pity. When it was a man that had to be softened, I stood aside and Fanny appealed to their gallantry in the character of a lone woman. She had thus corrupted the heart of the baggage master at San Francisco, to make some special provision for Chuchu: and now, although all trouble was at an end, we were too good artists to spoil the conclusion. I still kept myself aloof, and the baggage master did not blush for his favouritism.

South Vallejo was soon reached, and we set off shoreward along the pier, I with the bundles, Fanny with the dog.

A hostelry (Frisby House) on such a scale pleased my English notions, and I was for a hopeful view. But Fanny would not permit me to be hopeful; and as we drew nearer I began to see that she was in the right. The house stood in marshes, on every side there was stagnant water; something, flood or earthquake, had dislocated the whole structure at one joint, so that it hung two ways, with a great crack widest at the roof and narrowing down till it was hid by the verandah. On all sides there were saloons, risen from the marsh like bulrushes. A strange dearth of human beings completed the melancholy, though there were full-rigged ships lying close in along the shore, and a glimpse of North Vallejo, very white and spick and span, in the distance. Who was to drink in these saloons? Who was there to lodge in that vast ruin that they called the Frisby House?

We entered the bar, and the barkeeper led us upstairs to a room, all fallen away towards the outside, like a piece of over-cliff, and furnished with a few drawing-room chairs huddled into one corner and a table in the middle. Here we sat a long while, saddening with the moments; till there appeared a brisk, chatty, lame old lady, hobbling on a cane, who gave us a very pleasant welcome and showed us at length to our room. The stove would not burn though it could smoke a bit; the supper, to which we presently descended, was, I am told, all that can be expected of the American country inn. Fanny had predicted, plate by plate, and down even to the dessert, the entire bill of fare, which seemed to me a strange feat; but was perhaps simpler than it looked. A number of men in shirt sleeves ate of that supper greedily; I may say that Fanny did the same, and it was a sore thought to her that night that she had filled herself with viands so ungrateful to the eye and palate. Hunger may triumph, but a woman preserves a kind of self-respect; or regains it rather, once the appetite is quieted; and blushes for such gross indulgence. Man only blushes sometimes; but I trespass here . . .

A lad had taken our baggage checks and was to bring our baggage; but it appears, alas! he had but recently joined himself to some description of the Lodge and was still newfangled over this advance in manhood. He forgot all about our baggage, and was off to the Lodge to spend a social evening. Those to whom I appealed, shook their heads, said it should not have been, but yet found the incident pleasantly characteristic of youth and could not refuse it the tribute of a smile. I was old and spiteful; I resented this view of the matter and retired to pour forth my dudgeon to Fanny. She, with that remarkable force of character which (occasionally) I so much admire in her, became at once a petrifaction. I breathed death on all the Frisbians; but it was only she who meant it. So when the landlady appeared, a poor, sick creature, to offer her apologies and the loan of night clothes, the night clothes but not the apologies were accepted by my better half. 'That is not the way to manage an hotel,' said Fanny. Whereupon the landlady, though a freeborn American, actually made a sort of curtsey, and sniffed herself from the room in a very appalling temper. Fanny, upon my representations, became so much softened that nothing would please her but to follow the landlady and apologise. It is these sudden excesses upon either hand that lead a married man to suppose himself very judicial in temper. I conceived that Fanny was right upon the facts: therefore, no apology; that she had been wrong in manner, therefore, some sop to the landlady's feeling. But this, acting upon our theory of the continued opposition of sexes, should be administered by me. I found the landlady already sorely repentant of her ill-temper, drew her a touching little picture of my illness, which increased her penitence, and returned laden with flannel underclothing. A man to work a woman. In the meantime Fanny ferreted out a male understrapper, and got him to dispose of Chuchu for the night. A woman to work upon a man.

May 23rd

We were wakened in the morning by a strong voice singing out in a declamatory manner but without words. The singer seemed to know a prodigious number of airs for he changed from one to another all the time we were dressing. When we got downstairs, it was just six. The saloons were already open, hungrily awaiting custom in a place that seemed deserted. Nothing was awake but these drinking shops – the Gem saloon, the Frisby saloon and others – and the voice of the singer declaiming air after air with a sort of pointless vigour. We mounted the hill on a wooden footway, highly necessary in that place of marshes. Here and there, as we mounted, we passed a house embowered in white roses; more of the bay became apparent, and soon after the tall blue peak of Tamalpais arose above the green level of the island opposite: it told us we were still but a little way from the city of the Golden Gate, and added one note of beauty to the scene. For another, one of the seagoing ships began to clothe herself with white sails; she had her cargo complete from the Star Mills, and was now bound for England with flour. Right at the top we met the chill wind from a new quarter. South Vallejo died out into cattle pastures upon three sides of us, with desperate abruptness. There was no sign of breakfast; the houses were asleep: there was no one abroad but the cattle and horses and ourselves. Just then a boy came by with a milk can. Him we followed, and just about the same time a number of girls in summer dresses, each with a little book in her hand, began to appear and dot the grassy streets on their way to early mass or some other religious exercise. From one of these we learned where milk was to be had, and found a peaceful Irishman milking a cow upon the sidewalk. His wife brought us out a bowl of new milk, which we drank leaning against the rail of the garden, and the woman standing by and looking on with kindly looks. Finally identifying us for the helpless, lost-sheep couple that we truly were, she offered us coffee, took us into her poor little house and regaled us with coffee and bread and butter, to the speechless astonishment of a little, brawny, big-fisted girl child, who stared unwinkingly on Fanny from first to last, now drawing near, now backing away, but not from terror, merely, as it seemed to change the point of view. The kind Irish woman would hear of no payment either for the coffee or the milk, but she suffered me to make a present to the children to buy candy with. I have often wondered whether the destination of such gifts may not be changed; it were an innocent fraud.

When we got back to the neighbourhood of the Frisby House, the strong, tottering voice of the singer was still the only living sound. His spirits seemed to have brightened as the morning advanced; for now he launched himself into florid arias, with many a run and tremolo; perhaps it was from the age, I might almost say the antiquity, of his voice, but there seemed a dash of something false in the high spirits of the performance; a sad heart perhaps in this morning chanticleer. We learned he was once an opera singer, and now occupied a little shop in that yellow ruin of a Frisby House, where he cobbled old clothes at a dollar the job. Every morning, at the same unseasonable hour, he was to be heard a-chanticleering with that old voice over his repairs; what time the frogs left off, he struck up; so that neighbourhood of marshes and saloons was never long without music of a sort. It seems that someone had hurried down that morning to warn him there were strangers whom he might disturb, and he had promised cheerily 'to *try* to sing a little lower'. I liked that word; and I was still more pleased to think that, if he tried, he had failed so signally. There was a certain pressure at headquarters; music in his old blood that must, each morning, be evacuated; he could try to sing lower, but perhaps might not be able, was not able as the event proved, so strong and full was the inspiration. 'A spirit bade me sing.' I had not time to visit him; and perhaps it was as well; for I have my fancy picture undefaced. He is the one bright thing in South Vallejo, sitting there by the seaside, with his head full of operas, not forgetful of the faery footlights or the short-skirted ladies of the scene.

Everyone who is happy desires to sing, whether or not they be able. The power has nothing to do with it; it has nothing to do with a musical ear; it is the cry of joy, as a scream is the cry of pain. No one can go above a certain height into the mountains by himself, but what he will sing; no one can go alone in a railway carriage or walk rapidly alone upon a road, through any beautiful scenery, but what he will sing as to the manner born. I think we are all born poets and singers at heart; though the verses of some of us, and the songs of others, are better reserved strictly for ourselves and God. A man

who had been blind for about half a century was restored to sight by
one of those modern miracles we call operations. 'Glory be to God,
I can see,' he cried, leaping from the chair; and thenceforward all
that day he sang – Oh, but he sang, as the French say – with
unmitigated voice and out of a jolly and godly spirit, sang forenoon,
afternoon, evening, and so on and on and into the night, until the
doctor had to quiet him with a surreptitious opiate.

The driver was a spectacled Swede, extremely intelligent, and
speaking English like a very good book indeed. I had my attention
first directed to this fact by his description of a certain leaf, which, he
said, was 'fluted or rather corrugated'. The choice of words surprised
me; but all was of a piece; he could say whatever he wanted as good
as print; yet, he told me, he made but heavy weather of it, when it
came to Swedish.

I am a Scotsman, touch me and you will find the thistle; I am a
Briton and live and move and have my being in the greatness of our
national achievements; but am I to forget the long hospitality of that
beautiful and kind country, France? Or has not America done me
favours to confound my gratitude? Nay, they are all my relatives; I
love them all dearly: and should they fall out among themselves
(which God in his mercy forbid), I believe I should be driven mad
with their conflicting claims upon my heart.[187]

Wines on the Lees

Young Mr Johnson, his young wife, and Fanny and I set forth in a trap to visit the wine cellars of Mr Schram; you go down the valley a little way, among green meadows, and white oaks standing handsomely apart, and past comfortable houses with verandahs, and bald-looking, incomplete houses without verandahs standing in damp thickets. At one point the road lies along the bed of a stream, lined on either hand with sweet-smelling willows. At another it passes a great and rich establishment, with an enormous overshot water-wheel as tall as the trees that grow beside it, and fed by a little airy water-trough coming wandering towards it through the wood upon preposterous stilts. The hills are around us all the way and Mount St Helena at our backs, a great aerial bulk of mountain, buttressed on all sides by cliffy ridges. The chief character of the landscape I note is from the sparse tall trees along the mountain edges. However far you may be, each fir stands separate against the sky, no bigger than an eyelash, and all together lend a quaint, fringed aspect to the hill.

We went into his cellar and tasted his wines, red wines, respectively one and two years old; the younger seemed to me the more promising; but the quality of each was very pleasant, with a little *goût du terrain*[188] that reminds one of a burgundy.

. . . he talks of his debts too openly to have many or these at all serious; and Mrs Schram has been to Europe and apparently all about the States for pleasure. Her one trouble, worthy woman, is a question of clothing. Mr Schram wishes her to wear corsets; God help us, in this hot weather; she has to wear them when she goes to pay a visit, hence pays no visits, hence, as she says, 'people hate her'; Fanny and she condoled over this for quite a while in the verandah, while I was tasting wines in the cellar . . .

It is a good thing to have an unfeigned interest in wine, for it endears a man to wine-growers; but it is perhaps better for his popularity than his stomach. One way and another, I tasted eighteen different liqueurs yesterday, and my feelings today incline towards the temperance extreme. Somehow, I don't see why, there seem to be more than eighteen different flavours confounded in my mouth. But then, you know, natural liqueurs do you no harm. Mr Schram sends a good deal of his wine to London, and has, in consequence, a high opinion of the English taste. So have I, for a more personal reason. So there we had a point of agreement. But I had to withhold the last compliment from him, and I will continue to withhold, till I can taste some Californian wine grown old in bottle. But they all say they cannot afford to keep it, which I think a penny-wise proceeding.

On the way from Schram's to St Helena, Mr Johnson told us of his various qualifications. He learned the hotel business from a child, and beginning, so to speak, before the mast, he can cook, he can wait, he can run 'the house'; he holds the highest certificate as bookkeeper and accountant; he is a carpenter and showed us a barn on the hill, that he had built with his own hands; he is a farmer on a pretty huge scale; incidentally to that business, he has become an accomplished ostler; he has been a telegraph operator; he has built a section of telegraph lines in Oregon; and he has been local reporter on a newspaper. With all this, only twenty-eight years old, and a most agreeably intelligent and gentlemanly man. Nor should I omit that he is good-looking. This sort of Admirable Crichton is the just boast of America.

At St Helena, we went to Beringer Bros, a great wine house, with huge cellarage in the Hill, and thousands on thousands on thousands of gallons lying ready for the market on maturing.

A spasm of introductions, hand-shakings and liquors round in the bar. Since I have been in America, I have kept trotting to and fro with a kindled eye, my hand out and the cry of 'Who's next?' upon my lips. It is all the more strange to me as I had begun to forswear that ceremony ere I left Europe: thinking it, upon the whole, too considerable a familiarity to be squandered upon strangers. But here, you must shake hands with everybody, and twice rather than once. A man cannot black your boots unless in the character of a friend; and the ceremony of installation is to grip him passionately by the hand. Native Americans may pretermit that solemnity but not the pilgrim; he is ever slipping into a gulf of discredit, and saves himself by leaping frantically at the hand of every comer.

It was incongruous, and yet delightful, to see our ancient Abramina, first cousin to Chaos and old Night, skip over bank and brae after the cheapest of wild flowers, wallow on her old stomach making daisy chains, or load herself to the neck with ponderous specimens of stone. Again and again she regretted the absence of her 'old man'; it seemed he had a rural nature; on such an excursion, it appeared, not a tree, not a bird, would escape his approving observation; so I too regretted his absence for I thought he would have completed the party. So long as he might now and then draw up and descant upon the scenery, to get his wind again, it was identically the same to that Ebrew Jew whether we ever arrived anywhere or not.

Mrs Hanson said it would be a capital place to keep our milk and butter in. Wine, too, thought I. And anyway, I found in the very mouth of it a pick and a long shovel, which might be of use to us in the first trouble of path-making; so the tunnel was not there for nothing A little way back from there, a little clear, cold water lay in a pool at the foot of a choked-up wooden trough; and some feet higher up, hard by another house where Chinamen had slept in the days of the prosperity of Silverado, we were shown the upper end of the trough, and the same bright water welling from its spring.

The old lady who looked as good as she wasna bonny . . . The name Guele is pronounced 'guile', American pronunciation; just as Stevenson degenerates at once and for ever into Stevens. They want a new edition of *Webster*; judging from the treatment of my own name, I cannot see why the *American Dictionary* should be so pompously designated 'Unabridged': abridgment seems all the game. But the adventures of my name are various and fearful. There are few feats of which I am more proud than my capacity to pronounce it in true Britannic fashion, with but a single vowel, yet all the consonants preserved as thus: Stev'ns'n. But it is a feat in its own way to understand it. The ears as well as the mouth are exercised with us. An illiterate Frenchman makes 'Steam' of it quite invariably; a lettered Frenchman, who has seen the spelling, gives up all attempt to emulate my dexterity and pronounces Ste–veng–song like a man.

Abramina and Fanny were now as thick as thieves: it is not to be wondered at; there was something really beautiful in this old girl's gamesome, natural, Jew soul; and as the others were somewhat inclined to cut her garrulity short, she could not fail to appreciate so dutiful a listener as my wife. She promised us a visit, as soon as her 'old man' should arrive from the city. Someday, she said, 'you will see a man – 240 pounds – shust bounding up the hill'; I hope we shall, and his jolly old wife – 250 pounds – just bounding after him.

Take it at the best: the great patterns wrought with purple islands and with gleaming sea; the fairy birch woods; the loud jewel-coloured rivers, boiling in brown vats where the sun strikes in gold and amber; or the wide pastoral outlooks where grey rocks and sheep are scattered on the purple hills.

The Gueles have a delightful, light natural wine; made from the Mission, that is, the old California grape brought here from Spain by the churchmen; and I never knew them to make a palatable wine but here. We had speedily arranged to supply ourselves from thence.

Installation

It was a beautiful still day; the sky was one vast of blue; only from the summit of the mountain, one little snowy wisp of cloud after another kept detaching itself, like the smoke from a volcano, and blowing southward in some high stream of air.

Beyond putting the wine into the tunnel, there was nothing to be done but smoke until our effects should arrive. I found the path to the Toll House to get hay for the beds.

Rufe had told me that morning in Silverado, how he and his dogs had been after a brown bear all the day before, and up to midnight; and it occurred to me that after such a disappointment, poker might have more than its ordinary charms. The more you thought of Rufe, silent, slim and tanned, with his strange eyes, his habit of lying in bed till getting on for noon, and his general combination of the savage and the nobleman, the more it seemed as if gaming in general, and poker in particular, must be his most congenial occupation. At the Toll House, there was some dearth of hay; but they would manage to give us a little.

But how without a broom to cleanse this sty? How without hay or bedding to make preparations for the night? There was nothing to be done here but improve the entrance. I cut down the bushes which obstructed it; and Lloyd and I piled up stones until the plank lay at a less formidable incline.

Thence we betook ourselves to the spring. The water wells out first between two boulders, where it lies in a clear and perfectly still pool just a stone's throw from the upper house, the place of banishment of the Chinese in the old days of Silverado. There it returns to the earth to reappear again some fifty feet lower down on the level of our platform. Once the two pools had been connected by an iron pipe; but that was now stopped up and was as comfortless as a lightning conductor.

And one comfort leading on the mind to the consideration of another, we soon began to be in want of dinner. The bread, however, had given out, and I must go down to the Toil House for some more. Fanny has about as much locality as a toothpick; Lloyd rather less, and besides they had the whooping cough at the Toll House, so to him that was forbidden ground. Now I must tell you that Lloyd, being still young, carries a watch and attaches some importance to its preservation. Hence, as he had broken the chain riding up, it had been handed over to my care to put in a safe pocket. I had forgotten to restore it, and now, on my way to the Toll House, it occurred to me for my ruin that I had this watch in my possession. It was long since I had carried a watch: while I had one I never valued it, but as something handy to pawn should one run short of money; so I never studied its habits with that loving fidelity they talk so much of nowadays; and what little I ever knew I had long ago forgotten. I confess I was startled to find the thing still ticking; I thought that rough walk must certainly have stopped its impertinent career; but no, there it was, in the neighbourhood of seven o'clock and obviously with a mind to continue. Thus pleasantly surprised I returned it as I supposed to my pocket.

But the fire in the forge had been suffered to go out; and there was not energy enough left in the party to kindle another. Fatigue settled on us like a nightmare; I was a mere breathing wreck, the offal of myself. We could sit up no longer. Hay or no hay, we must go to bed, and then came the question what o'clock it was. I put my hand into the safe pocket; the pocket was as safe as ever, only there was no watch. Lloyd's face became a picture. The mind acts with great rapidity at such moments. I saw myself face to face with another excursion down the canyon, not to speak of coming up again, and a hunt by lantern light for an object about two inches and a half in circumference. Fanny lit the lantern; it was a weird affair: a great bubble of glass, a foot in height, rudely protected by a single hoop of wire, and designed to swing from the hand by a long loop of the same material; it begged to be broken; it had no prism for concentrating the light. I have no patience for the man who invented that lantern. Thus equipped, I set forth upon my exploration. The reader can imagine for himself what a pleasant business it was, bent double over the steep track and looking right and left among the dead leaves and general detritus; but he would never imagine, what is the *truth*, that at last, near the bottom, and after I had already sighted a glimmering window in the Toll House below my feet, I actually found the watch lying on its face in the middle of the footpath, a little round of yellow gold upon the leaves. It was on the return voyage, with a mind hugely relieved though with an aching body and wet brow, that I first had leisure to admire the striking features of this walk. Deep as was the glen, the lantern cast my shadow still higher. The fork of my body was lost against the star-set heavens; only my legs, huge unconnected columns of darkness, coursed along the slighter darkness of the opposing bank. By a strange consequence of my motion, they seemed not to accompany my progress, but to flee continually past me into my wake. The diffused starshine, and the broken, tossing glow of the lantern, variegated the foliage into a myriad faint lights and shadows; nothing was dense, nothing was solid, but these enormous stalking columns that seemed to flee and yet follow my advance. And now and again when one of the taller treetops climbed clear out of the glen and stood high against the faint heavens, my colossal shadow reached it even there, and cast a thin but awful night upon its upmost spear-points. In the meantime, down in the bottom, here was I plodding forward, a pigmy lantern-bearer, yet the original of this far-spreading and uncanny darkness. I could not have believed that a man with a bit of a lamp could so dreadfully haunt himself with spectres.

I had scarce arrived ere the hay followed me; and the bedroom was soon prepared. The western door, that which looked up the canyon and through which we entered by our flying bridge of plank, was still entire, a handsome panelled door, the most finished piece of carpentry in Silverado. And the two lowest bunks next to this were prepared for tonight's use. This was to keep us out of the draught; for the opposite or eastern-looking gable was pierced by two yawning apertures: a window without a sash and a doorway without a door, which opened into space some six feet above ground. From there you had a view of the low mountain tops running away before and below us, here in bold crags, there spired with pine, and in the extreme south one little corner of Napa Valley. The lowest bunk was for Lloyd, Fanny and I climbed into the other, and, broken with fatigue, we prepared ourselves for slumber.

So I lay listening, wakened first by an uneasiness, then by pain, then by a pang so sharp as almost to justify an exclamation; until at last I discovered that I had too far presumed upon my strength, and was to pay the price in the shape of a cramp in the stomach. I am glad to have had one cramp; earnestly as I pray against a second. They say it gives a man the nearest idea he is ever likely to have of the pains of childbirth; and the experience has greatly increased my respect for that institution. I remember standing a moment at the door and seeing dawn begin and the sky preparing for the sun across the wild hilltops; and then I remember trying to get back into bed, and my wife having to haul me in by main force; and lastly I remember having some laudanum administered, the sweetest cup that ever touched my lips, and the cramps diminishing and sleep coming over me gradually from the feet upward as it seemed, and opening to me at last that dear asylum from a tortured consciousness.

Thursday, June 10th

I returned to myself in a dream of peace. The sun shone in broadly through the eastern door and window; each chink in the eastern gable was a stripe of dazzling blue; a bird chirped with a thin chirp, unmusical, but yet pleasant, like all things that tell of the morning and of the woods. There are some pains that come and go, and all you can say is, they are gone; there are others that leave behind them an indescribable active sensation of relief; so that it seems almost worth while to have endured them. Now whether it was altogether the cramp, or whether the laudanum had something to do with it, I cannot say; but I awoke that morning in a seventh heaven of languor and satisfaction. Lloyd was despatched to Hanson's for the milk, for we had nearly used up our overnight's supply; we had soon a good fire in the forge; and had some porridge and coffee ready and some bacon fried for breakfast.

After I had eaten, I lay down at the door of the forge and for near upon two hours, I suppose, I hardly moved or thought. Unless you would call that a thought: to have a steady knowledge that you had had a cramp the night before and now were thoroughly shot of it. When I mustered my limbs together and got across to the house, I found there had been great doings in the assayer's office. The broken door and the frameless window were all nailed up with white calico, which kept out the wind and let in the kindly daylight; and there was Fanny on her knees hammering up a door of the same material for the gaping eastern doorway. I was soon despatched to hunt leather for hinges, and in the dog's hutch beside the forge, I found a pair of old boots – possibly Mr Stanley's.* I cannot think that miner had been fairly dealt with by his bootmaker, or perhaps I should blame the long weathering in the Silverado dog-hutch, for a day or two after all the hinges parted, and the door blew in upon the stove and upset a frying-pan of onions.

* All that is known of the said Mr Stanley is that a bill for his board was found by R. L. S. in the hut which he and his wife and stepson took possession of (see p. 224).

Sea fogs in my right as a sick man, I loathed and hated them;
I knew when I woke in the morning, by my difficult breath and
trembling knees, when there had been a fog the night before.

Some Toll House gossip. Twenty years ago when Mr Corwin
(landlord of the Toll House Hotel) first visited these parts, there
was a city of tents in the valley on the Lake County side: Jonestown
by name with 2,000 inhabitants at least, and one roofed house for
the sale of whiskey; on the western side of Mount St Helena there
was another large encampment, whose name he did not tell me,
perhaps it had none; there was, he thought, scarce a rock on the
whole mountain but what had been chipped at that time by the
prospector's hammer. All this bustle had apparently died away and
left no visible trace, before Silverado was so much as thought upon;
and now Silverado in its turn has become a thing of the past. All that
was got from our mine, it seems, was taken from that great upright
seam that still remains gaping open above our platform, leaving a
few crazy wedges. It seems there was a great deal made, certainly
$100,000; but when the corner was exhausted they spent a great
deal of money sinking the shaft and digging out the various tunnels,
but the remainder of the ledge was never found. In the house by the
roadside and opposite the mill, which still bears 'Saloon' upon the
gable, there lives one 'Old Wash', a drunken . . .

[Illness intervenes and the Diary shows abrupt termination here but
begins again in ink after the return of the party.]

There had come during our absence a change over the aspect of our
canyon. It had become more flowery: azalea, calycanthus, chaparral,
each in its own way was adorning our little stony platform; the
azaleas a bit above the spring two solid clumps of white and flesh-
coloured flowers.

Sunday of all days of the week, we were destined to do our location
business. It was a day of great heat, and considerable consequent
idleness; I remember all morning but one incident, when two great
birds flew up the canyon and disappeared into the rocks that there
touch the sky. Eagles, a mountain hawk, or what not, it was strange
how our interest depended on the name, for the eagle is so nobly
named, and figures in so many brave stories and legends, that no
other bird can be compared with it. Again late at night we heard
from up the canyon three strange squalls or screams; like, but somewhat different from, those I had attributed to a wild cat, on our first

arrival. In our usually silent canyon, they made a great effect. One thought it was an eagle; one of our eagles; for Joe could already make out the eagles' nest; another was sure it was a California lion; a third was once more in favour of the wildcat theory; and one of the Hanson boys, to whom the cry was imitated, and that scandalously ill, at once pronounced it was that of a fox. I leave the reader there. That night, also, the unwearied ringing whistle of a cricket rang for near an hour on end from the rocks above the ledge.

And like the light in darkness, so was this clumsy human speech, and the call of the cricket in the healing silence. After I was in bed and the candle out, looking right upward through the hole of the old stove chimney, I saw a single star looking right down into my eyes. It was faint, unspeakably distant, and so unspeakably small. Its smallness haunted me like a monstrosity; and I was fain to shut my eyes and keep it out.

Reynolds and his cigars and kid gloves were matters of the past, like Mr Stanley.

The more one stays here, the more one is struck by the arid character of the earth's face. There is nothing here but rock and stone and gravel.

Given such an aspect of the earth, we should expect the lizards, which swarmed thick on every side, and the rattlesnakes, which grew here, as they told us, to unusual bigness, but we should never expect the amount or the nature of the vegetation.

But all that grows here, but the eternal poison-oak, is beautiful, healthy, scented and rich in bloom.

It seems strange that the flies should at once have learned there was a house for them; and set up their tabernacles with us; and yet the wild cats and foxes came so little in our way.

Wednesday, June 30th

Hanson, his companion, Breedlove, and Mrs H— came up to be drawn. You would wonder to see how matter-of-factly the pair sat for their likenesses; there were no words about the matter; indeed I have rarely known people so sparing of talk as Hanson and Breedlove. Hanson, hearing that Joe was coming back, warmed into a little moment of enthusiasm, his kind dark blue eyes going perceptibly larger as he described a picture Joe must do of him, 'with the horns of some real big bucks and dogs, and a camp on a crick'. Perhaps they had all been drawn before. Caliban Loveland had been repeatedly painted, he boasted to my wife; that was one of Caliban's vanities; his physical strength being the other. Hanson told us at length the tale of how he had taken the stage robbers. One was Russel, a Scotsman, who had lived long in this part of the country and had built many houses at Pine Flat; he was an intelligent man and much thought of in the neighbourhood; but he had taken to drink; and the other, Dollar, who was a stranger, over-persuaded –

NOTES

Walking Tours

1 (p. 1) *Hazlitt*   William Hazlitt (1778–1830), prolific essayist, critic and journalist

Travels with a Donkey

2 (p. 8) *John Bunyan*   John Bunyan (1628–88), whose *The Pilgrim's Progress* (1678) describes a pilgrim's journey toward salvation

3 (p. 11) *A Mountain Town in France*   This unpublished essay only saw print in 1896–97, after Stevenson's death. Always intended as part of *Travels with a Donkey*, it has since been inserted therein as its prelude.

4 (p. 11) *Le Monastier*   The full name of the town is Le Monastier-sur-Gazeille.

5 (p. 11) *wolves sometimes pursue*   This may be a reminiscence of the medieval poet François Villon (1431–*c.*1463), who invokes wolves in the winter snows. Stevenson wrote a short story about him, 'A Lodging for the Night'(1877).

6 (p. 15) *patois*   French dialect speech, often linked to local patriotism

7 (p. 16) *Sir Toby Belch*   a dissolute character in Shakespeare's *Twelfth Night*

8 (p. 17) *Marquis de Villemer*   *Le Marquis de Villemer* (1860), romance partly set in the Cévennes; written by the best-selling female novelist George Sand (Amandine-Aurore Lucille Dupin, 1804–76), known for her love affair with the tubercular composer Frédéric Chopin (1810–49)

9 (p. 18) *qui s'amusait à faire ça*   'who did it to amuse himself'

10 (p. 18) *Ardèche*   the Ardèche region lies lower down and to the east of the Cévennes highlands

11 (p. 19) *Job*   this jokey epigraph is from the Book of Job, 39:5. All Stevenson's biblical references are to the Authorised King James Version (1611).

12 (p. 22) *like Christian*   Christian is the hero of the spiritual travel-narrative *The Pilgrim's Progress from This World to That Which is to Come: Delivered under the Similitude of a Dream* (1678) by John Bunyan (1628–88).

13 (p. 23) *as an ox goeth to the slaughter*   Proverbs 7:22

14 (p. 24) *Et vous marchez comme ça!*   'And this is how you're walking!'

15 (p. 25) *the Loire*   At over a thousand kilometres, the Loire is the longest river in France; it rises in the Cévennes and flows north and then west to the Atlantic.

16 (p. 29) *hedge-inn*   cheap wayside hostelry

17 (p. 32) *Allier*   meandering river which rises in the Cévennes and flows for over four hundred kilometres before entering the Loire

18 (p. 32) *wild Gévaudan*   former province, now the *département* of the Lozère, notorious for the man-eating monster which ran rampant there in 1764–7

19 (p. 33) *D'où'st-ce que vous venez ?*   'Where've you come from?'

20 (p. 34) *Pilgrim's Progress*   See Note 12 above.

21 (p. 34) *my journal*   Stevenson kept a travel-diary in a blue-lined notebook, the suprisingly polished first draft of *Travels*. It was published as *The Cévennes Journal* in 1978.

22 (p. 35) *Herbert Spencer*   Herbert Spencer (1820–1903), English philosopher and social theorist, best known for popularising the notion of 'the survival of the fittest'

23 (p. 36) *not Fouzilhic, but Fouzilhac*   These two villages, nowadays Fouzillic and Fouzillac, lie only a few hundred metres apart at a height of 1180 metres.

24 (p. 37) *C'est que, voyez-vous, il fait noir*   'The thing is, you see, it's dark.'

25 (p. 38) *Filia barbara pater barbarior*   Stevenson invents a Latin tag : 'Barbarous daughter, even more barbarous father.'

26 (p. 40) *Peyrat*   Napoléon Peyrat (1809–81), French historian, whose *Histoire des Pasteurs du Désert* (2 vols, 1842) narrates the Camisard insurrection. Stevenson's knowledge of the rebellion was derived from this book, and from later research in Edinburgh.

27 (p. 40) *Ulysses, left on Ithaca*   In Homer's epic the *Odyssey*, the Greek hero Ulysses (Odysseus) spends ten years struggling to get home to Ithaca to rejoin his wife Penelope. Stevenson seems to have confused Ithaca with the island of Ogygia, where Ulysses is delayed for seven years by the seductive enchantress Calypso.

28 (p. 45) *Matthew Arnold*   quotation from 'Stanzas from the Grande
Chartreuse', a poem by Matthew Arnold (1822–88) about his visit to
the Carthusian monastery near Grenoble, where monks observed
an unbroken silence

29 (p. 45) *Mende*   Capital of the Lozère *département*, the picturesque
city of Mende lies on the Lot river, west from Chasseradès.

30 (p. 45) *Heard* YE *that whistle?*   Stevenson is remembering 'Proud
were ye, mountains . . . ', an anti-railway poem by the wilderness-
loving William Wordsworth (1770–1850).

31 (p. 46) *As rude as God made them*   Stevenson's enthusiasm for the
untouched landscape marks him out as a forerunner of today's Green
movement.

32 (p. 46) *Our Lady of the Snows*   Notre-Dame des Neiges, a Catholic
monastery of the Cistercian (Trappist) Order

33 (p. 46) *Marco Sadeler*   Marcus Christopher Sadeler (1614–60),
Flemish engraver

34 (p. 47) *a literary man, who drew landscapes*   Stevenson's baggage also
included a sketchbook of landscapes and portraits, done in pencil
and tinted with a pink wash. This document is now in the Beinecke
Rare Book and Manuscript Library of Yale University; eight of the
drawings are reproduced in *The Cévennes Journal* (1978).

35 (p. 49) *Imitation   On the Imitation of Christ*, devotional book by the
Catholic monk Thomas à Kempis (*c.* 1380–1471)

36 (p. 49) *Cotton Mather*   Cotton Mather (1663–1728), zealous Puritan
minister in New England, asssociated with the Salem witchcraft
trials

37 (p. 49) *Le temps libre*   'One's free time is devoted to examining
one's conscience, confessing, making good resolutions'

38 (p. 50) *Waverley Novels*   best-selling cycle of historical novels by
Sir Walter Scott (1771–1832), one of Stevenson's favourite authors

39 (p. 50) *Odes et Ballades*   1828 poetry collection by Victor Hugo
(1802–85)

40 (p. 52) *compline and Salve Regina*   Cistercian last prayers of the day,
and solemn hymn to the Virgin, preceding the Grand Silence of
night-time

41 (p. 53) *Elizabeth Seton*   Elizabeth Seton (1774–1821), devout
American Catholic who founded the American Sisters of Charity;
author of *Memoir, Letters and Journal* (1869)

42 (p. 54) *Giroflé! Girofla!*   'Giroflé! Girofla!', popular French song of
love and war, originally from a comic opera by Charles Lecocq
(1832–1918)

43 (p. 54) *Gambetta*   Léon Gambetta (1838–82), French Republican politician who advocated moderation following the upheavals of the Franco-Prussian War and the Paris Commune

44 (p. 55) *Et vous prétendez mourir dans cette espèce de croyance?*   'And do you intend to die in that sort of belief?'

45 (p. 58) *God's green caravanserai*   This spoof epigraph is by Stevenson himself.

46 (p. 58) *Hé, bourgeois; il est cinq heures!*   'Hey, fine gentleman; it's five o'clock!' (i.e. 'Rise and shine, lazybones!')

47 (p. 59) *Chassezac*   The tiny Chassezac stream flows eastwards into the Ardèche, which then joins the Rhône on its southward route to the Mediterranean.

48 (p. 60) *upright stones*   These may have been prehistoric standing stones (*bondons*), which abound in the Lozère region.

49 (p. 60) *nor nymph nor faunus haunted*   slight misquotation from *Paradise Lost* by John Milton (1608–74), evoking the fragrant nuptial bed of Adam and Eve

50 (p. 61) *Montaigne*   quotation from 'On Experience' by Michel de Montaigne (1533–92), French stoic thinker renowned for his *Essays*, who also kept a *Travel Journal* during his Italian journey of 1580–1

51 (p. 64) *W. P. Bannatayne*   The epigraph is Stevenson's, Bannatyne being a pseudonym.

52 (p. 65) *like stout Cortez*   These lines from 'On First Looking into Chapman's Homer', a sonnet by John Keats (1795–1821), refer to Hernán Cortés, an early Spanish *conquistador* in Mexico.

53 (p. 65) *Pic de Finiels*   the highest peak of the Mont Lozère chain, 1,699 metres high

54 (p. 68) *patet dea*   'she shows herself a goddess', a Latin tag misremembered from Virgil (70–19BC). The correct text in the *Aeneid* (book I, line 405) is 'et vera incessu patuit dea' – 'and by her gait she showed herself a goddess'.

55 (p. 69) *these southern Covenanters*   Stevenson draws a parallel between the Cévennes Camisards and the Scottish Covenanters. The violent history of the latter was well known to him through Sir Walter Scott's novel *Old Mortality* (1816).

56 (p. 72) *a garden full of shelter and of fountains*   Séguier's declaration is loosely based on a biblical passage: see The Song of Solomon 4:12.

57 (p. 72) *Killiekrankie*   The narrow, densely wooded Pass of Killiecrankie in Perthshire was the scene of a famous battle in 1689, when Jacobite Highlanders loyal to King James routed Government troops supporting William of Orange.

58 (p. 73) *like herded elephants*   quotation from Keats's poem *Endymion*, where it is clustered clouds that are said to resemble elephants

59 (p. 74) *Antony Watteau*   Jean Antoine Watteau (1684–1721), French painter of idealised forest scenes full of flirtatious picnickers

60 (p. 76) *the first and the last beggar*   Stevenson's essay 'Beggars' appeared in 1888.

61 (p. 76) *Connaissez-vous le Seigneur?*   'Do you know the Lord?'

62 (p. 76) *an English pastor*   John Nelson Darby (1800–82), Christian evangelist who broke away from the establishment churches to found the Plymouth Brethren, otherwise known as Darbyists or Darbyites

63 (p. 77) *Plymouth Brother*   member of the Plymouth Brethren, also associated with the pietist Moravian Brethren of Bohemia

64 (p. 79) *Florac*   Stevenson makes an unexplained and rather long westward detour to visit Florac, at the confluence of the Mimente and the Tarn.

65 (p. 79) *Prophet Peden*   Alexander Peden (1626–86), Covenanter and charismatic open-air preacher

66 (p. 81) *à la belle étoile*   'under the beauteous stars', i.e. in the open air

67 (p. 85) *Bruce and Wallace*   Robert the Bruce (1274–1329) and William Wallace (1272–1305), Scottish national heroes

68 (p. 86) *Cependant, coucher dehors!*   'All the same, sleeping out of doors!'

69 (p. 87) *Rip van Winkle*   eponymous hero of a tale by Washington Irving (1783–1859), who sleeps through the American Revolution and awakes in an entirely new era

70 (p. 87) *Pippa*   the heroine of *Pippa Passes*, a dramatic poem by Robert Browning (1812–89). She sings as she walks along, thereby influencing others to act for the good.

71 (p. 88) *Volnay*   a prestigious red Burgundy wine from Volnay, made from the Pinot Noir grape

72 (p. 88) *our two shadows*   There may be an allusion here to two other incongruous wayfarers, Cervantes' Don Quixote and Sancho Panza.

73 (p. 91) *phylloxera*   tiny, sap-sucking aphid, the cause of a devastating blight in French vineyards in the late nineteenth century

74 (p. 93) *And, oh,/ The difference to me!*   lines from the poem 'She dwelt among the untrodden ways' by William Wordsworth (1770–1850), referring to the effect on her aspirant lover of the death of the self-effacing Lucy

75 (p. 93) *Farewell, and if for ever –* 'Fare thee well! and if for ever, / Still for ever, fare thee well', lines by Lord Byron (1788–1824)

The Amateur Emigrant

76 (p. 95) *Broomielaw*   famous waterfront in Glasgow, whence paddle-steamers carried passengers downstream

77 (p. 95) *Greenock*   town on the south bank of the River Clyde, anchorage for ocean-going vessels

78 (p. 95) *our ocean steamer*   The SS *Devonia* had one funnel and three masts, and could travel at 13 knots. There was accommodation for 200 in 1st class; 100 in 2nd class; and 800 in 3rd class (Steerage).

79 (p. 101) *borne down by the flying*   quotation from *Marmion* (1808), epic poem about the Scottish defeat at the battle of Flodden Field by Sir Walter Scott (1771–1832)

80 (p. 111) *Callot*   Jacques Callot (*c.*1592–1635), French printmaker, specialising in scenes of warfare and of low life

81 (p. 115) *Coelum non animam*   'Coelum non animam mutant qui trans mare currunt': 'those who traverse the seas change their skies but not their souls', aphorism of the Roman poet Horace (Quintus Horatius Flaccus, 65–8BC)

82 (p. 116) *Hoppus's Measurer*   a ready reckoner designed for the timber and allied trades

83 (p. 125) *Atlantic Cable*   the transatlantic telegraph cable, laid in 1866

84 (p. 133) *Scapin*   the scheming valet in the comedy *Les Fourberies de Scapin (Scapin's Schemings*, 1671) by Molière (1622–73)

85 (p. 135) *Amadis of Gaul*   hero of the medieval romance *Amadis de Gaul* (1508), a novel of knights errant and damsels in distress which Miguel de Cervantes (1547–1616) parodied in his *Don Quixote* (1605 & 1615)

86 (p. 136) *Orson*   a wild man of the woods, hero of the anonymous medieval romance *Valentine and Orson*

87 (p. 136) *Out of . . . myself I go*   phrase quoted by William Hazlitt in his essay 'On Going a Journey' (1822), which Stevenson greatly admired

88 (p. 145) *Castle Garden*   Castle Garden (now Castle Clinton National Monument) at the lower end of Manhattan, functioned as the immigration station during 1855–90.

89 (p. 147) *Whitman*   Walt Whitman (1819–92), American poet and advocate of a 'loafing' life-style; author of *Leaves of Grass* (1855)

Across the Plains

90 (p. 151) *Bancroft's History*   *History of the United States of America, from the Discovery of the American Continent* (numerous editions 1854–78) by George Bancroft (1800–91), educator, historian and statesman

91 (p. 155) *beauty of the land*   The mellifluous name of the Susquehanna River derives from that of the Susquehannock, an Indian tribe living in what is now Pennsylvania and Maryland.

92 (p. 156) *Mrs Beecher Stowe*   Harriet Beecher Stowe (1811–96), author of the best-selling anti-slavery novel *Uncle Tom's Cabin* (1852)

93 (p. 158) *period of the fire*   reference to the Great Chicago Fire of 1871, a momentous disaster in American history

94 (p. 160) *Council Bluffs*   Town in Iowa, on the Nebraska border; major rail junction, westwards of which ran the transcontinental railroad, built in the 1860s by the Union Pacific and the Central Pacific companies; this linked up with the Eastern rail network to connect the two extremities of the United States. Stevenson's long and tortuous trajectory involves changes between rail companies and therefore changes of train (not all trains were 'Emigrant trains').

95 (p. 167) *plains of Nebraska*   The Great Plains of Nebraska were notoriously arid, being flat stretches of sand-dunes and treeless prairie.

96 (p. 170) *I fell sick outright*   Stevenson makes a rare allusion to his poor health, which must have been sorely tested on this journey.

97 (p. 170) *Chinese pirates*   Stevenson's reference is hardly gentlemanly, though he makes up for it in the later chapter 'Despised Races'. It may be noted that the Western railroad was completed largely thanks to Chinese labour.

98 (p. 170) *the plumed hereditary lord*   apparent reference to the Native American peoples, whose lands were summarily appropriated to hasten the passage of the railroad

99 (p. 173) *Ogden*   Ogden, Utah, is close to the Great Salt Lake, and to the 'Golden Spike' location where the two western stretches of the transcontinental railroad joined in 1869.

100 (p. 173) *Dean Swift*   Jonathan Swift (1667–1745), author of the satirical *Gulliver's Travels* (1726), in which appear the filthy creatures known as the Yahoos

101 (p. 174) *Demogorgon*   a terrifying demon of ancient myth

102 (p. 178) *that old, grey, castled city*   Edinburgh, Stevenson's beloved
     home town

103 (p. 178) *the Cherokees*   major Native American tribal group, driven
     from its ancestral lands by white settlers. Stevenson's sympathy for
     'the noble red man' echoes his concern for the oppressed
     Covenanters and Camisards.

104 (p. 180) *land stowaways*   It's typical that Stevenson should feel
     drawn to the nomadic fraternity of the American hobo, famed for
     riding illegally on freight trains.

105 (p. 181) *Sacramento*   Sacramento took over from Monterey in 1854
     as the state capital of California. Having played a central part during
     the Gold Rush of 1849–55, it became a terminus of the Pony
     Express and then of the transcontinental railroad. Stevenson is in
     too much of a hurry to get to the coast to bother to comment on its
     historical significance.

106 (p. 182) *Tamalpais*   Mount Tamalpais is a lofty peak situated on
     the Marin Peninsula north of the Golden Gate channel. Stevenson
     repeatedly evokes its grandeur, particularly in the first chapter of
     The Silverado Squatters.

The Old and New Pacific Capitals

107 (p. 183) *General Sherman*   William Tecumseh Sherman (1820–
     91), highly successful, ruthless general in the Union Army during
     the American Civil War (1861–5). He later conducted military
     purges of the Native American tribes in the West to ensure the
     rapid completion of the transcontinental railroad.

108 (p. 183) *the ancient capital of California*   Monterey was capital of
     California, under Spanish, then Mexican control, from 1777 to
     1849. It became part of the United States after the American-
     Mexican War.

109 (p. 184) *Homeric deep*   Stevenson has a special fondness for Homer's
     Odyssey, with its well-known tag 'the wine-dark sea', i.e. the Aegean,
     across which his hero Ulysses voyages home to Ithaca.

110 (p. 186) *Celestial Empire*   i.e. China. Stevenson repeatedly evinces
     a fascination with the Chinese.

111 (p. 186) *pitch-pines*   The pitch-pine is medium-sized and resprouts
     readily after a forest fire.

112 (p. 187) *moss*   Spanish moss, a fruticose lichen that dangles from
     tree-branches

113 (p. 188) *for nonsense is the devil*   adage quoted from the satirical
     poem *Absalom and Achitophel* (1682) by the poet and critic John
     Dryden (1631–1700)

114 (p. 189) *true vaquero riding*   dashing Mexican style of riding

115 (p. 193) *Dennis Kearney*   Dennis Kearney (1847–1907), a racist agitator, notorious for his campaign against Chinese immigrants

116 (p. 194) *Truck system*   wage system in which employees are paid in limited commodities in lieu of cash

117 (p. 195) *in a paulo-past tense*   having taken place but recently

118 (p. 195) *Big Bonanza*   A bonanza is a 'lucky strike', when a rich vein of precious metal is found, or when an unexpected windfall occurs.

119 (p. 196) *Dana*   Richard Henry Dana, Jr (1815–82), lawyer and abolitionist. His memoir *Two Years before the Mast* (1840) draws on his experiences in the merchant navy and asserts solidarity with oppressed mariners.

120 (p. 196) *Farallones*   the rocky Farallon Islands, lying off the San Francisco coast

121 (p. 196) *Tamalpais*   See Note 106 above. Stevenson is never happier than when a foreign landscape reminds him of his native land. Arthur's Seat is an extinct volcano that looms over Edinburgh.

122 (p. 197) *such swiftness of increase*   Following the population boom of the Gold Rush in the 1850s, San Francisco became the largest city on the Pacific Coast, though never a formal capital of the region.

123 (p. 198) *so nice a point*   These remarks about earthquakes and fires are prescient, for in 1906 San Francisco was devastated by a major earthquake followed by a rampaging fire.

124 (p. 198) *consulates of different nations*   Stevenson repeatedly revels in the vision of a jostling multicultural society.

125 (p. 199) *Badroubadour*   Princess Badr-al-Budur, the Sultan's lovely daughter, whom Aladdin marries in the *Arabian Nights* tale

126 (p. 199) *the nose-tree itself*   'The Nose-Tree', one of the Grimm Brothers' fairytales

127 (p. 200) *Vehmgericht*   a much-feared secret tribunal in medieval Germany

128 (p. 200) *Judge Lynch*   Charles Lynch (1736–96) presided over an illegal court which condemned British Loyalists during the Revolutionary War. His abuse of power led to the application of his name to mob killing or 'lynching', typically of blacks by white supremacists, mainly in the American South.

129 (p. 201) *Fortuné de Boisgobey*   pseudonym of French writer Fortuné Hippolyte Auguste Castille (1821–91), author of popular crime fiction

The Silverado Squatters

130 (p. 203) *lesson of geography* The author provides an immaculate summary of the geographical and geological characteristics of a specific place, thereby executing a stock gambit of the practised travel writer. Yet already an inspirational note is struck: Silverado is being promoted as a site conducive to sublime experience.

131 (p. 203) *Shasta* Mount Shasta, a majestic volcanic peak in Northern California, over 14,000 feet high. Since it stands some 200 miles to the north, it is most unlikely to be visible from Mount St Helena.

132 (p. 203) *warm with cinnabar* a soft, orange-red granular stone, crushed for use as a pigment or an ingredient of mercury

133 (p. 203) *twice to cross the bay* Crossing San Francisco Bay by ferryboat remained necessary until the completion of the Golden Gate Bridge in 1937. This chapter's detailing of an itinerary is often consistent with the style of the tourist guidebook. We may feel that, on the whole, getting to Silverado involves no great physical effort; so that the honeymoon journey resembles less a taxing safari and more an excursion, an outing, a not-too-daring jaunt.

134 (p. 204) *Napa Valley* valley in Napa County, which Stevenson visited before its reputation had developed as a world-class wine-growing region

135 (p. 207) *Foss is not forgotten* Clark Foss (1819–95), famed stage-coach driver in the Napa Valley

136 (p. 208) *subterranean lake* The Calistoga Springs, with their attendant Springs Hotel, had opened in 1862 as a tourist attraction, seeking to emulate the Saratoga Springs spa in New York State.

137 (p. 210) *ran the legend* Discovered in 1857, the Petrified Forest was acquired in 1871 by Charles Petersen Evans, who turned it into a tourist site (still open to visitors today, with pious reminders of Stevenson's visit). Wood becomes 'petrified' when minerals gradually replace its cells.

138 (p. 211) *disappointment* The aphorism is one of Stevenson's sharpest paradoxes.

139 (p. 211) *worth the travelling to* presumably Stevenson's own doggerel

140 (p. 212) *the unconquerable worm* i.e. phylloxera. See Note 73 above.

141 (p. 212) *Arabia Petraea* ancient middle-eastern province of the Roman Empire

142 (p. 216) *Auld Reekie* Scots vernacular for 'Old Smoky', an affectionate nickname for Edinburgh

143 (p. 216) *Paraphrases* pithy renderings of biblical passages

144 (p. 216) *the shorter catechism* doctrinal material, based on a question-and-answer format, which young Presbyterians are expected to learn by heart

145 (p. 217) *Chimborazo* dormant volcano in Ecuador

146 (p. 217) *behold the Hebrides* patriotic lines from the 'Canadian Boat Song', which originated among Scottish settlers in Canada

147 (p. 218) *in the land of Egypt* quotation from God's commandment speech to Moses: see Exodus 22: 21. The selfsame phrase occurs in Deuteronomy 10:19, in an exhortation to 'love the stranger'.

148 (p. 219) *Palmyra* ancient ruined Aramaic city in what is now the Syrian desert; another instance of the author's fondness for drawing analogies between far-flung places

149 (p. 220) *Mihi est propositum idem quod regibus* 'the same is offered to me as to kings', a half-remembered Latin tag

150 (p. 220) *Kelmar* The storekeeper's real name was Morris Friedberg.

151 (p. 221) *Silverado* A vein of silver was discovered on the flank of Mount St Helena in 1872, and mining began at a spot dubbed Silverado. A small town of ardent prospectors was thrown up. Extraction of silver and gold ore peaked in 1874; mercury was also mined and used for refining gold. But by 1882 the lodes had run out; the mine was abandoned, and all shacks dismantled, leaving only the ruined mill and boarding house.

152 (p. 229) *Des cymbales de Bivar* The quotations are from (1) Théodore de Banville's poem 'À la Font-Georges', from *Les Stalactites* (1846), which celebrates an arrival in an idyllic place ; and (2) Victor Hugo's poem 'Le Romancero du Cid', from *La Légende des siècles* (1859), which lionises the Spanish military hero El Cid.

153 (p. 230) *contrasts of the earth* Stevenson's cultured reminiscences, incongruous in the context of a wild Californian mountainside, none the less illuminate a curious fact of travel in strange lands: namely, that the uprooted wanderer occasionally feels perfectly at home in the alien setting.

154 (p. 232) *Sam* i.e. Samuel Lloyd Osbourne, Fanny's son; normally called Lloyd

155 (p. 234) *our desert-island state* A fan of Daniel Defoe's *Robinson Crusoe* (1719), Stevenson often indulges in the fantasy of being a castaway.

156 (p. 234) *Palmyra*   See Note 148 above.

157 (p. 234) *Layard*   Austen Henry Layard (1817–94), archaeologist
and diplomat, known for his excavations at the ancient Assyrian
city of Nimrud in 1845–51

158 (p. 234) *to the past*   Stevenson is hankering for written evidence to
help establish a link with the past; but, unlike in the Cévennes,
there is no written document to enliven his imagination in this
deserted place.

159 (p. 238) *overhanging rock*   The 'inland castaway' is at pains to
underline the precariousness and austerity of his makeshift
honeymoon quarters, as if to revive the image of the ascetic camper
sketched in *Travels with a Donkey*.

160 (p. 241) *Caliban*   the uncouth savage in Shakespeare's *The Tempest*
(*c.*1610), sometimes seen as a representation of the repellent Other
faced by Western colonialism

161 (p. 243) *Jack Sheppard*   Jack Sheppard (1702–24), notorious
London burglar, who escaped four times from prison and ended up
being hanged at Tyburn

162 (p. 245) *Malvolio*   the bossy and conceited steward in Shakespeare's
Twelfth Night (*c.*1601)

163 (p. 247) *the Hebrides*   the large island group off Scotland's west
coast, among the least hospitable locations in the British Isles and
hence attractive to someone with a passion for wildness

164 (p. 250) *Russian campaign*   allusion to Napoleon Bonaparte's epic
winter march upon Moscow (1812), when the landscapes were
smothered in snow

165 (p. 251) *Davos*   mountain village in eastern Switzerland; an
expensive health-spa recommended to consumptives like Stevenson

166 (p. 251) *From Palace to Hovel*   more accurately *Palace and Hovel, or
Phases of London Life* (1878) by the American writer Daniel Joseph
Kirwan

167 (p. 252) *Rocambole*   The dashing criminal hero of a cycle of
adventure novels by the French writer Pierre Alexis Ponson du
Terrail (1829–71). The sinister Reverend Patterson was one of
Rocambole's enemies.

168 (p. 252) *sixpenny 'Ouida'*   Ouida was the pseudonym of Marie
Louise de la Ramée (1839–1908), author of *risqué* historical
romances and stories for children, and hostess of a London salon.
Stevenson has his tongue in his cheek when he implies that the
cheap paperback is a literary classic.

169 (p. 252) *penetralia*   the innermost sanctum of a holy building

170 (p. 253) *one of life's crossing-places*   The sedentary Stevenson enjoys visualising the remote Toll House as a turbulent transit-point for breathless globetrotters. His comparison to a well-known inter-section in London is a joke, but betrays a recurrent impulse to tie the unfamiliar to the known.

171 (p. 253) *Holbein's Death*   Hans Holbein the Younger (*c.*1498–1543), German painter and printmaker, produced *The Dance of Death* (1538), a set of engravings which introduce the skeletal figure of Death into everyday situations.

172 (p. 254) *tale of the Pacific*   The Toll House site is poeticised by the author as a kind of ubiquitous utopia, conducive to magical moods and atmospheres.

173 (p. 255) *interregnum*   The allusion is to a brief sojourn down the mountain when Fanny and Lloyd suffered a mild attack of diphtheria. All three rested up in a cottage in Calistoga, then returned to Silverado, accompanied by Fanny's daughter and her husband.

174 (p. 255) *Joe Strong*   Joseph Dwight Jr Strong (1852–99) was the American husband of Fanny's daughter Belle (Isobel); a landscape artist who later painted scenes of Hawaii and Samoa, he produced the woodcut frontispiece to the first edition of *The Silverado Squatters* (1883).

175 (p. 259) *the eternal silence*   lines from 'Ode: Intimations of Immortality from Recollections of Early Childhood' by William Wordsworth (1770–1850)

176 (p. 259) *Stock-jobbing*   trading in securities with the intention of grabbing early profits

177 (p. 262) *Old Rowley*   Late in life, Charles II (1630–85) earned the nicknames 'Old Rowley' and 'the Merrie Monarch'. The reference here is to an earlier episode when, after the defeat of his Scottish forces by Cromwell's army at the Battle of Worcester in 1651, the disguised king escaped to France: while shoeing his horse, he had a close shave at a blacksmith's, managing to parry the man's curiosity by feigning anti-royalist sympathies.

178 (p. 262) *prius dementat*   Latin saying: 'when a god wants to destroy someone, he first drives him mad'

179 (p. 265) *our mountain hermitage*   This chapter contains a remarkably detailed inventory of the environment at Silverado, testimony to the author's alertness to geological and climatic phenomena, along with birdsong and the activities of rattlesnakes, crickets and the bore-fly.

180 (p. 268) *most bright cinoper*   Lines from a love sonnet by William Drummond of Hawthornden (1585–1649) (which coincidentally contains the words 'silver springs' and 'cinnabar'). Zeuxis was a painter of renown in Ancient Greece.

181 (p. 268) *with pea-like blossom*   chaparral pea, a shrub with vibrant magenta blossoms

182 (p. 269) *incessant human whistler*   Presumably Stevenson was himself this tuneless human warbler; while the confident yet erratic song he evokes might be that of the western meadowlark.

183 (p. 269) *the morn of battle*   The eagle was the emblem of the Roman armies and figured on the standard that led them into battle.

184 (p. 270) *a MacGregor's bonnet*   The Clan MacGregor costume includes a bonnet upon which is pinned a badge bearing the motif of the Scots pine.

The Silverado Diary

185 (p. 275) *May 22nd, 1880*   These short extracts from the original manuscript of the diary kept at Silverado were appended to *The Silverado Squatters* in 1912. The full diary remains unpublished.

186 (p. 275) *unharmed through life*   The first pages of the diary reveal something of the invalid's strategy for confronting difficult situations, as well as generally hinting at the nature of his relationship to his new wife. That he lets her wheedle favours from authority figures is a rare confession, as indeed is the diarist's straightforward naming of her. (In the printed text of *Squatters*, we have to wait for twenty-odd pages before he refers to her as Fanny.)

187 (p. 279) *claims upon my heart*   another instance of the author's fervent wish to be a true cosmopolitan, loyal to several nations

188 (p. 280) *goût du terrain*   earthy taste